DICKENS AND THE ARTISTS

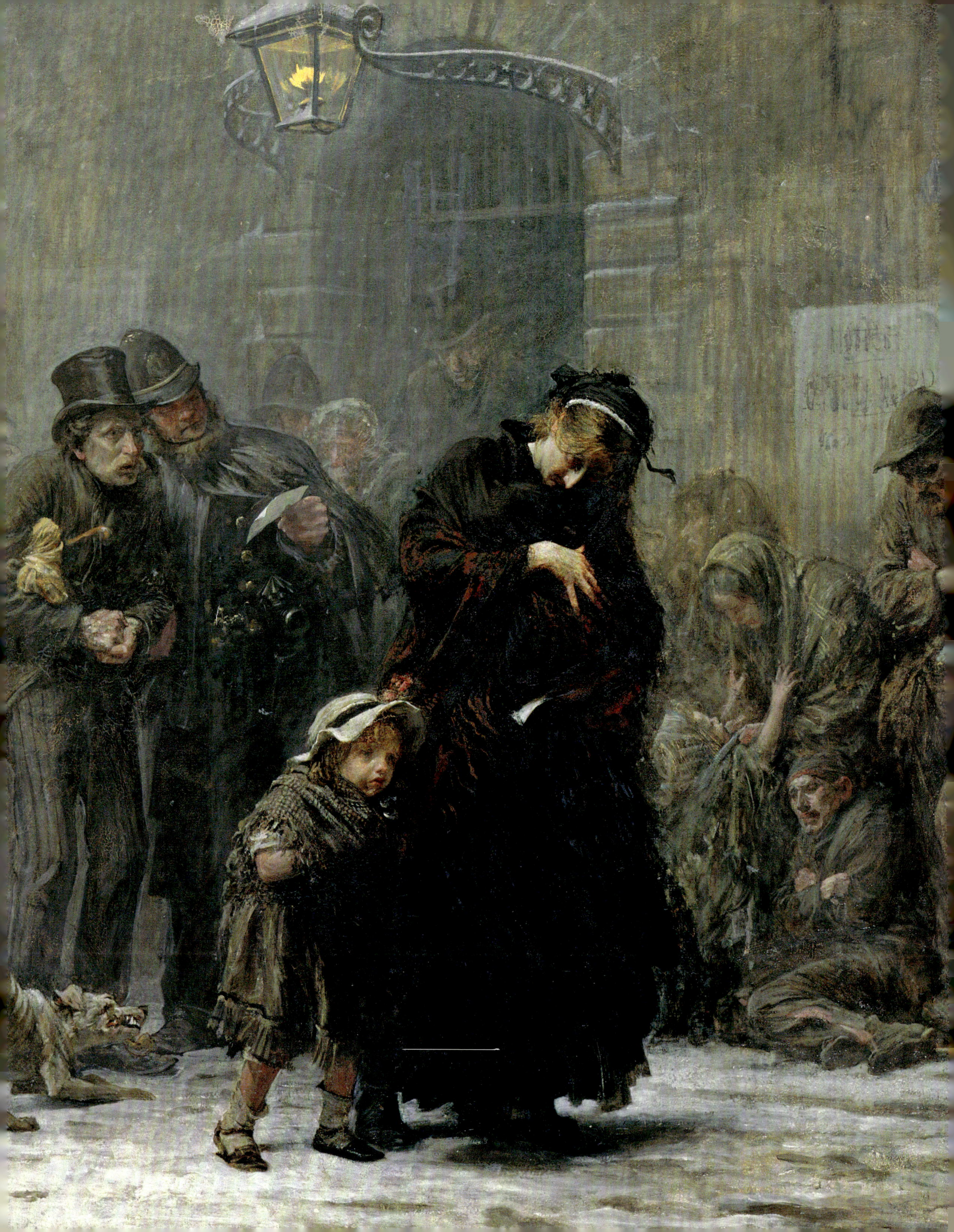

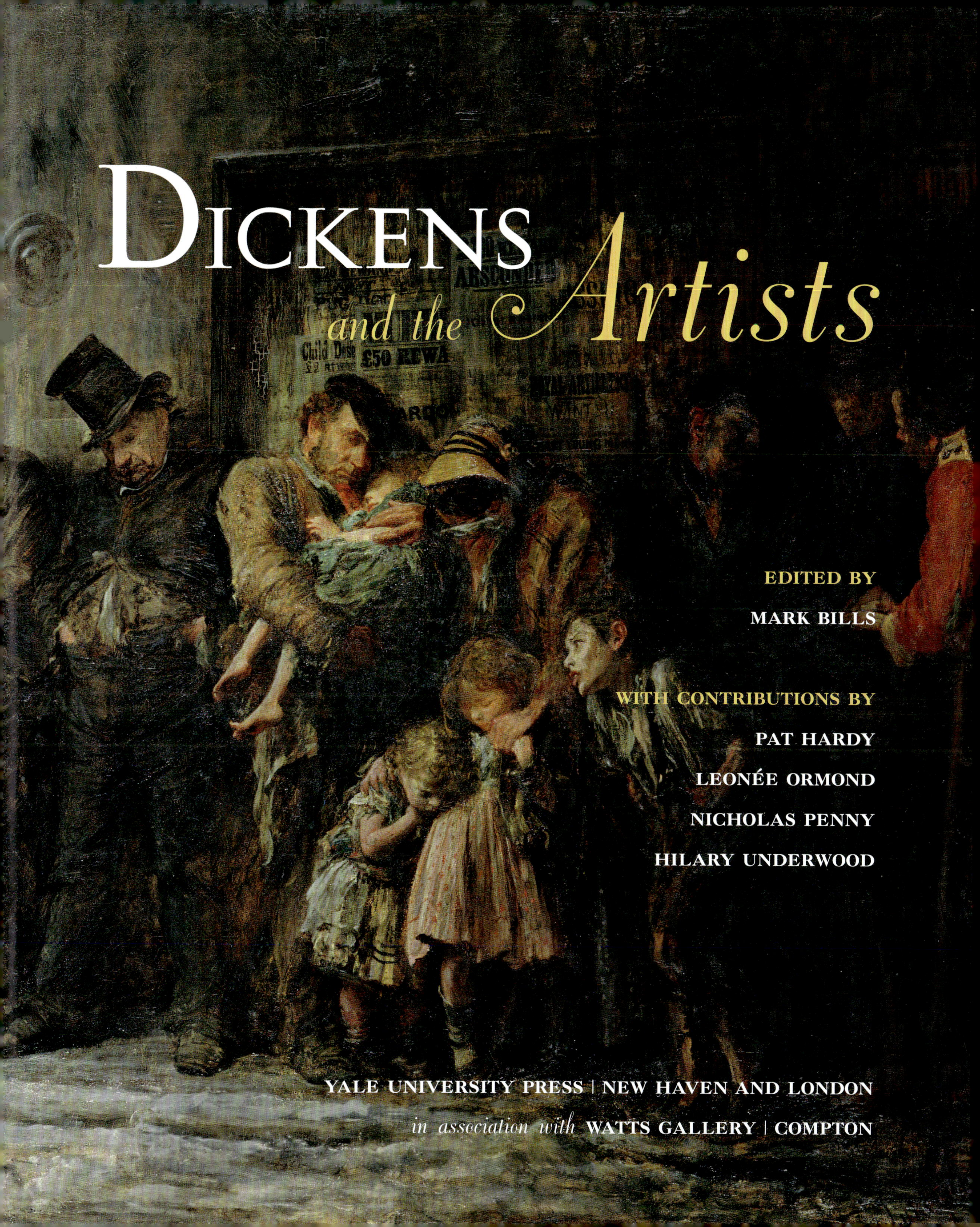

DICKENS *and the Artists*

EDITED BY

MARK BILLS

WITH CONTRIBUTIONS BY

PAT HARDY

LEONÉE ORMOND

NICHOLAS PENNY

HILARY UNDERWOOD

YALE UNIVERSITY PRESS | NEW HAVEN AND LONDON

in association with WATTS GALLERY | COMPTON

WATTS
GALLERY

First published by Yale University Press in association with Watts Gallery on the occasion of the exhibition *Dickens and the Artists*, 19 June – 28 October 2012

Printed in Italy by Conti Tipocolor SrL, Florence
Designed by Catherine Bankhurst
Index created by Meg Davies (Fellow, Society of Indexers)

Library of Congress Cataloging-in-Publication Data

Dickens and the artists / edited by Mark Bills ; with contributions
by Pat Hardy, Leonée Ormond, Nicholas Penny and Hilary Underwood.
pages cm
Dickens and the Artists has been written to accompany the exhibition of the same name at Watts Gallery, Compton, Surrey, from 19 June until 28 October 2012.
Includes bibliographical references and index.
ISBN 978-0-300-17602-5 (alk. paper)
1. Dickens, Charles, 1812-1870--Criticism and interpretation.
2. Dickens, Charles, 1812-1870--Friends and associates. 3. Art, Victorian--Great Britain--Themes, motives. 4. Art and literature--Great Britain--History--19th century. 5. Art and society--Great Britain--History--19th century.
I. Bills, Mark, editor of compilation. II. Watts Gallery.
N7483.D498D53 2012
709.41'09034--dc23

2012003428

Frontispiece: Sir Samuel Luke Fildes, *Applicants for Admission to a Casual Ward* (detail of fig. 103)
Pages vi and viii: Photographs of Charles Dickens taken by John and Charles Watkins, probably late 1850s

CONTENTS

Foreword — vii
Perdita Hunt

Dickens 2012: Celebrating Dickens's Bicentenary — ix
Florian Schweizer

List of Lenders and Sponsors — x

Acknowledgements — xi
Mark Bills

Introduction — 1
Mark Bills

PART THE FIRST: DICKENS AS ART CRITIC

Dickens and Philistinism — 11
Nicholas Penny

Dickens and Contemporary Art — 35
Leonée Ormond

PART THE SECOND: THE INFLUENCE OF DICKENS ON THE ARTISTS

Dickens Subjects in Victorian Art — 69
Hilary Underwood

Dickens and the Painting of Modern Life — 111
Mark Bills

Dickens and the Social Realists — 155
Pat Hardy

Select Bibliography — 183

Index — 184

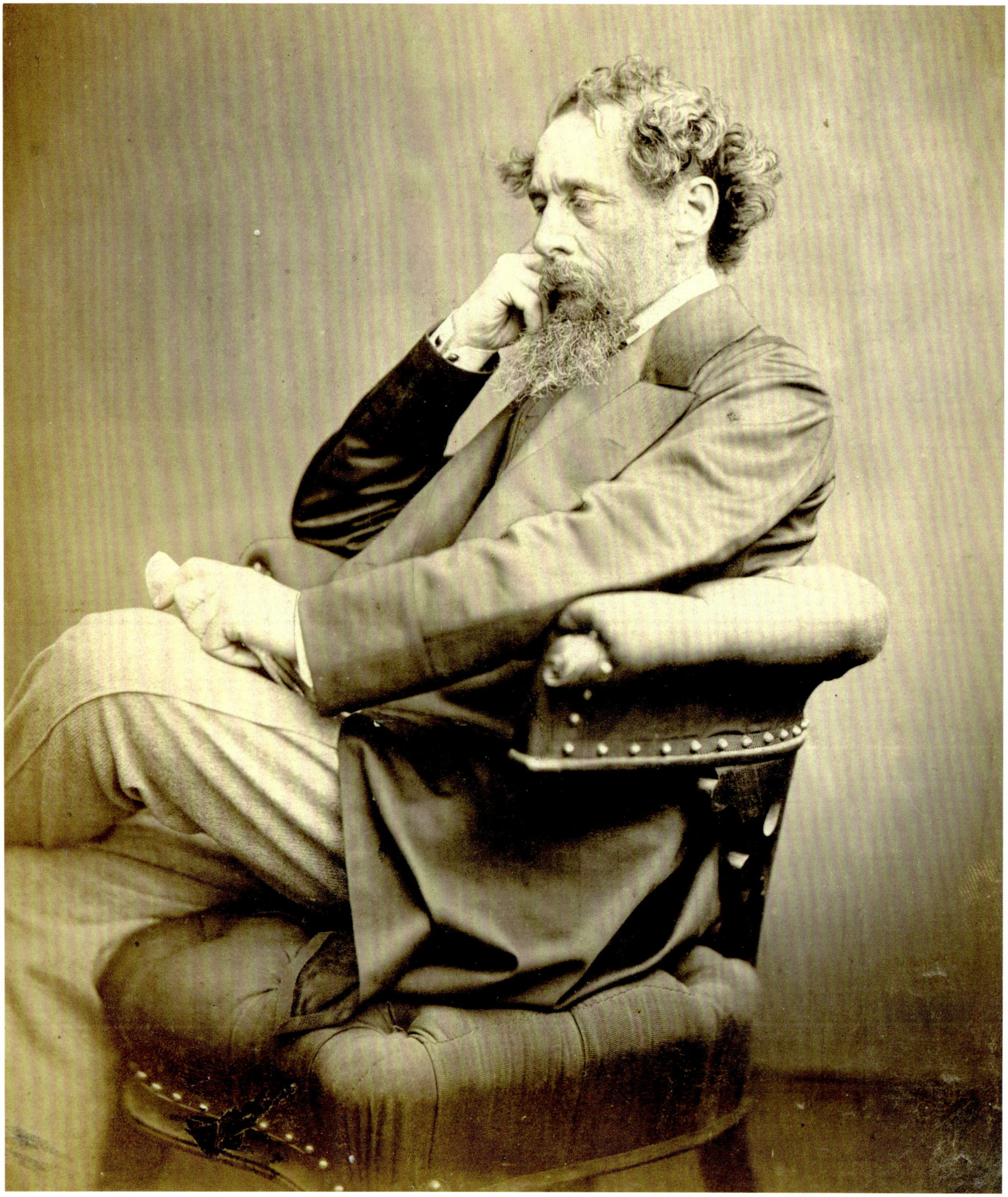

FOREWORD

In reviewing the role of Watts Gallery for another century following its major restoration, it was appropriate to revert to the vision of its founders, who saw Watts Gallery as an opportunity to promote the understanding and appreciation of G. F. Watts and Mary Seton Watts in the context of the nineteenth century.

The exhibition of *Dickens and the Artists* is an excellent example of this founding vision and takes further the aspiration of the current Trustees to establish Compton as a centre for exploring Victorian art, social history, craft and design. Watts and Mary Watts, through their legacy in Compton, demonstrated the ideas, beliefs, society and art of the nineteenth century. The Chapel, the Pottery, Limnerslease (Watts's house and studio), the hostel for apprentice potters and the Gallery represent a campus where the public and students can research and enjoy the values, context and contemporary resonance of the past.

We are extremely grateful to Nicholas Penny, Director of the National Gallery, who built on the momentum of his excellent Watts Lecture given in 2010, which now appears as an essay in this book. We are also very grateful to the institutional and private lenders who have made this exhibition possible.

As we ponder the impact of social realism depicted by great artists of the nineteenth century it is interesting and sometimes chilling to note the resonance with the twenty-first century. We hope that through our work at Watts Gallery, and our plans for bringing Watts's house and studio in to the public domain, the public will be able to draw from the past – the literature, ideas, art and society – to inform our thinking, learning and experience for the future.

Perdita Hunt
Director of Watts Gallery

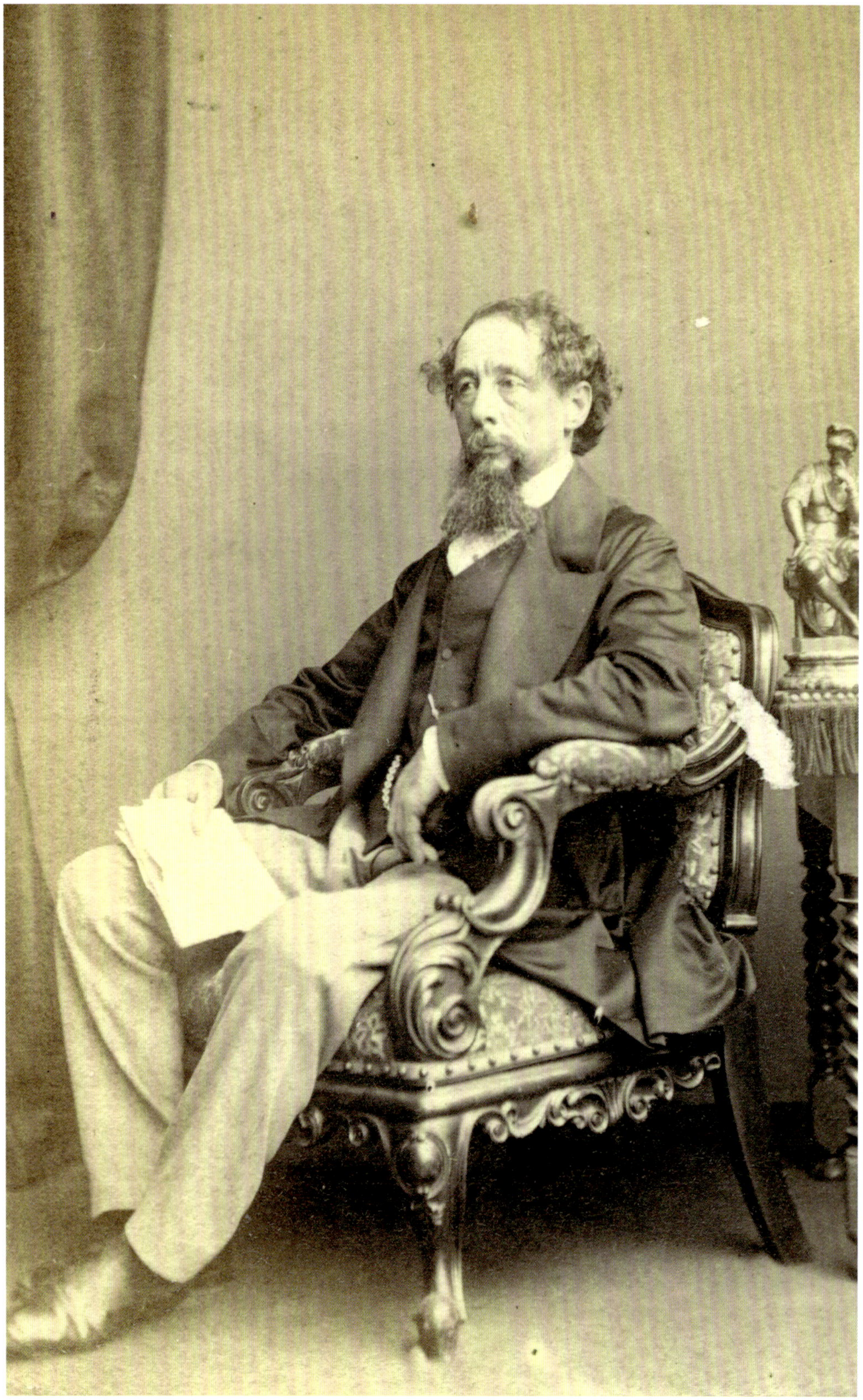

DICKENS 2012

CELEBRATING DICKENS'S BICENTENARY

A critic of the young Dickens once said the writer 'would go up like a rocket and come down like a stick'. In 2012, as we are celebrating the bicentenary of the author's birth, one thing seems to be sure: that rocket will not come down again. One hundred and seventy-five years after he first shot to fame at the age of twenty-five, Charles Dickens continues to be regarded as one of the world's finest authors and storytellers and one of the most influential figures this country has ever produced. I am delighted that Dickens 2012, our campaign to bring together partners from the creative industries from around the world to celebrate the Victorian author, is widely recognized as one of the great cultural initiatives in this important year for London and the UK. Internationally Dickens continues to be one of the most influential ambassadors for British culture, and in 2012 readers, authors, actors and artists around the world are honouring Dickens with a vast programme of bicentennial projects that I am sure will be as memorable as Dickens's own creations.

Against the background of budget cuts within the arts and culture sector, it is an extraordinary achievement that all Dickens 2012 initiatives and projects are scheduled to be delivered in the bicentenary year. It clearly shows the dedication and commitment to Dickens among those who work in the heritage and creative industries. Dickens 2012 demonstrates how much can be achieved through partnerships and collaborative projects: many of the Dickens activities that people take part in during 2012 are the result of organizations working together to deliver outstanding, innovative and inspiring programmes and exhibitions.

Dickens and the Artists explores the significant connection between Charles Dickens and visual art. Not only is Dickens an immensely visual writer, he admired artists, many of whom he counted as close friends. He also had an enormous influence on artists and for the first time this connection will be explored through an exhibition held at the recently restored Watts Gallery in Compton, Surrey. It is fitting that Dickens 2012 brings fresh perspectives on Dickens, who continues to fascinate a new and growing audience.

Dr Florian Schweizer
Director, The Charles Dickens Museum
Project Director, Dickens 2012

LIST OF LENDERS AND SPONSORS

Watts Gallery is deeply grateful to all its generous donors and benefactors including:

Heritage Lottery Fund
The Deborah Loeb Brice Foundation
The Isabel Goldsmith Patino Foundation
Garfield Weston Foundation
The George John & Sheila Livanos Charitable Trust
Richard Ormond CBE
Esmee Fairbairn Foundation
Sir Siegmund Warburg's Voluntary Settlement
English Heritage
An Anonymous Donor
Christopher Forbes
J. Paul Getty Jnr Charitable Trust
The Ingram Trust
The Foyle Foundation
Professor Rob Dickins CBE
The Linbury Trust
Art Fund
David Pike
Guildford Borough Council
The Robert Gavron Charitable Trust
Hamish Dewar Ltd
Peter Harrison Foundation
The John Ellerman Foundation
The Finnis Scott Foundation
The Restoration Fund
The Wolfson Foundation
The Mercers' Company
KPMG Foundation
The Pilgrim Trust
Miklos and Sally Salamon
Surrey Hills LEADER
The Anson Charitable Trust
The Billmeir Charitable Trust
The Monument Trust
Surrey County Council
Man Group PLC Charitable Trust
The Henry Moore Foundation
John Lewis OBE
Wates Foundation
The Michael Marks Charitable Trust
The Rothschild Foundation
The Foundation for Sport and the Arts
The de Laszlo Foundation
Oxford Exhibition Services
The Michael Varah Memorial Fund
Spencer Wills Trust
The Fenton Arts Trust
The Hazelhurst Trust
Community Foundation for Surrey
Robert Freidus & Ellie Packer
Nevill Keating Pictures
The Carole & Geoffrey Lawson Foundation
Rupert & Robin Hambro
Hilary Bachelier-Carasco
The Derek Hill Foundation
The Barbara Whatmore Charitable Trust
The Golden Bottle Trust
The Paul Mellon Centre for Studies in British Art
The John S. Cohen Foundation
The Evelyn Charitable Settlement
The Idlewild Trust
The Bishop of Guildford's Foundation
Lloyds TSB Foundation for England & Wales
The Rayne Foundation
The Leche Trust
Welton Foundation
Christopher Gridley
John George
and all those who wish to remain anonymous

ACKNOWLEDGEMENTS

The Watts Gallery is most grateful to all those who have contributed to the publication and exhibition *Dickens and the Artists*. My thanks go to the authors who have contributed their time and expertise to this project: Nicholas Penny, who first developed his material as the annual Watts lecture in 2010; Professor Leonée Ormond, who has been most helpful in suggesting items for exhibition; and Pat Hardy and Hilary Underwood, who have contributed much new material. I would like to thank the staff of Yale University Press, particularly Catherine Bankhurst and Sally Salvesen, the Paul Mellon Centre for Studies in British Art, who contributed to the costs of the publication, and Colin Grant, who copyedited and proofread the book. Hilary Bachelier-Carasco has always been generous in his aid to studies in Victorian art and his support of Watts Gallery. Thanks to Terry Parker, who always locates so many new and interesting pieces of relevant archive. Thanks too to Alex Werner, who was very generous with his time and expertise, and to Professor Michael Slater, who contributed the title of the exhibition as well as advice.

I would like to thank all staff at Watts Gallery who contributed to the exhibition and its associated events. In effect that means everyone. In particular thanks go to Mary McMahon, Glynis Paxton, Janet Wilkinson and Dr Desna Greenhow who worked on the exhibition. Thanks too to the trustees of Watts Gallery who guide and support our work here. Lenders have been essential and most generous in their loans. The support of Florian Schweizer of the Dickens Museum has meant that we could have important works relating to Dickens. Thanks are due to the Victoria and Albert Museum for their loans from the important John Forster collection, and to Alison Smith and Tate Britain, as well as to Bradford Museums and Galleries, London Metropolitan Archives, Museum of London, National Portrait Gallery, Royal Holloway College, Royal Pavilion Brighton and Sheffield Museums and Galleries. Thanks to many individuals who have helped, including private collectors. I am grateful for the help of Ron Lander and Henry Sotheran Limited, London, Simon Edsor of the Fine Art Society, Coutts and Pieter Van der Merwe. The University of Surrey is an important partner and I am particularly grateful to Greg Tate for his development of the conference *Dickens and the Visual Imagination*. Finally, thank you to all those who thought that Dickens and the visual arts was a good idea for a book and an exhibition.

Mark Bills
Curator of Watts Gallery

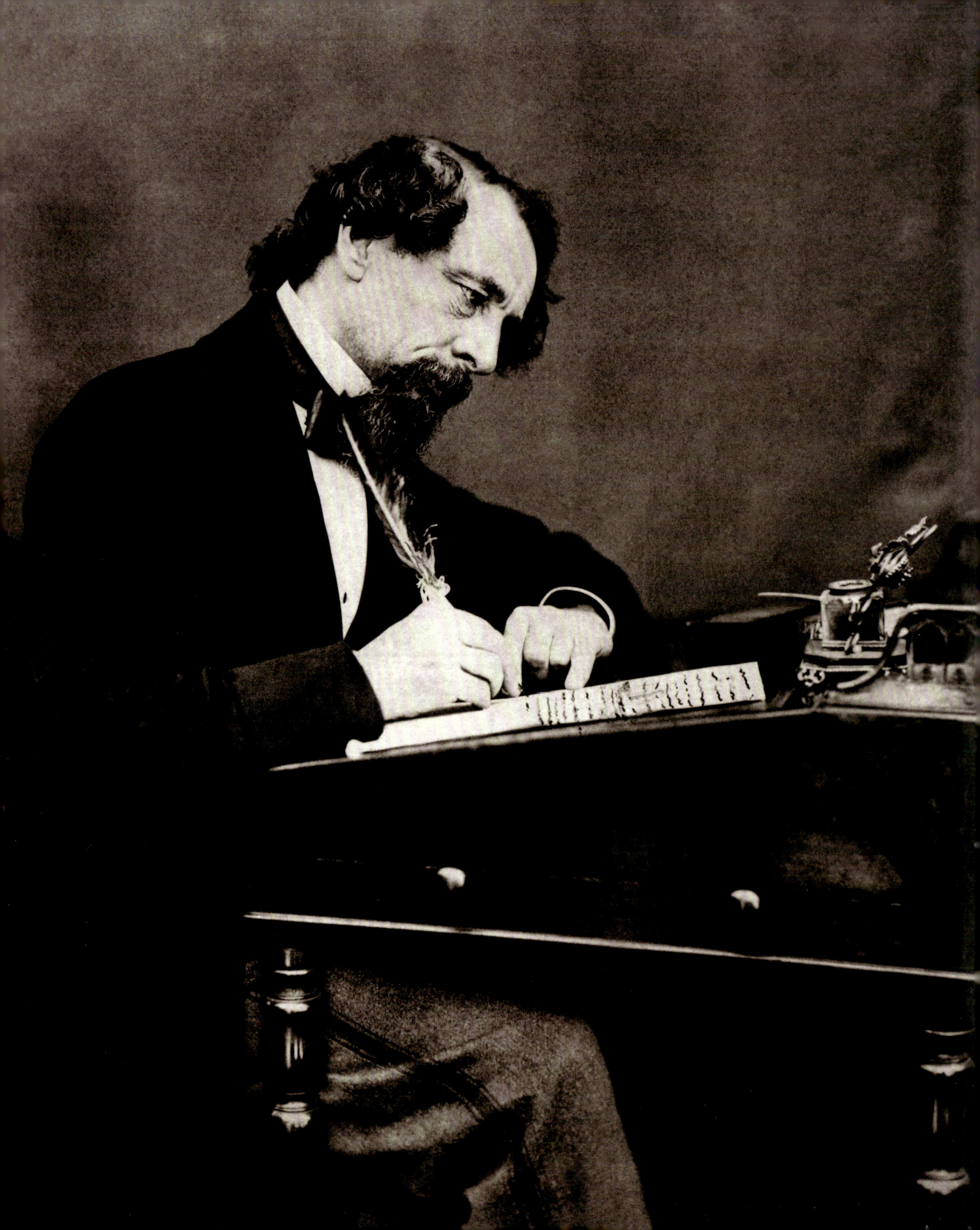

INTRODUCTION

MARK BILLS

> There is no writer, in my opinion, who is *so* much a painter and a black-and-white artist as Dickens.[1] (Vincent Van Gogh, March 1883)

> He had no doubt a strong natural instinct for art, and there are in many of his books descriptions of sunsets, storms, river scenes, old cathedral towns, and landscapes, scenes of sweet and peaceful content, or of dark clouds and sinister suggestion, which only a writer with an innate feeling for artistic effect could possibly have described, and he had also a very just and accurate eye, and a judgement that was entirely his own, and owed nothing to any outside opinion.[2]

Kate Perugini, the daughter of Charles Dickens, wrote the latter words about her father in 1903. Herself an artist and twice married, each time to an artist, she knew the strength and limitations of Dickens's writing on art. Anyone who has read a novel by Dickens knows what a remarkably visual writer he is, but Kate Perugini was in a unique position to understand what the author felt about art and artists. For although Dickens was a very visual writer and had a large number of artist friends, he didn't write very much about art, even though he must have thought quite a lot about it.

His novels, unlike those of William Makepeace Thackeray and Wilkie Collins, do not have main characters as artists or plots set amid the art world. We meet the charmingly amateur miniature painter Miss La Creevy in *Nicholas Nickleby*, who declares 'Ah! The difficulties of Art, my dear, are great' and puts portraits into two categories, 'the serious and the smirk'.[3] The less pleasant Henry Gowan is encountered in *Little Dorrit*, but dabblers aside, artists are rare in Dickens's works. A short story entitled 'The Ghost of Art', which appeared in his weekly journal *Household Words*, comically gives a first-person account of a lawyer living in Temple Bar with an interest in painting. He meets an artist's model who grows an expressive beard, an image that haunts and taints his viewing of pictures. At the beginning of the story Dickens perhaps gives us a little of himself:

FIG. 1
(George) Herbert Watkins, *Charles Dickens*, 1858, photograph. Rob Dickins Collection, Watts Gallery Archive

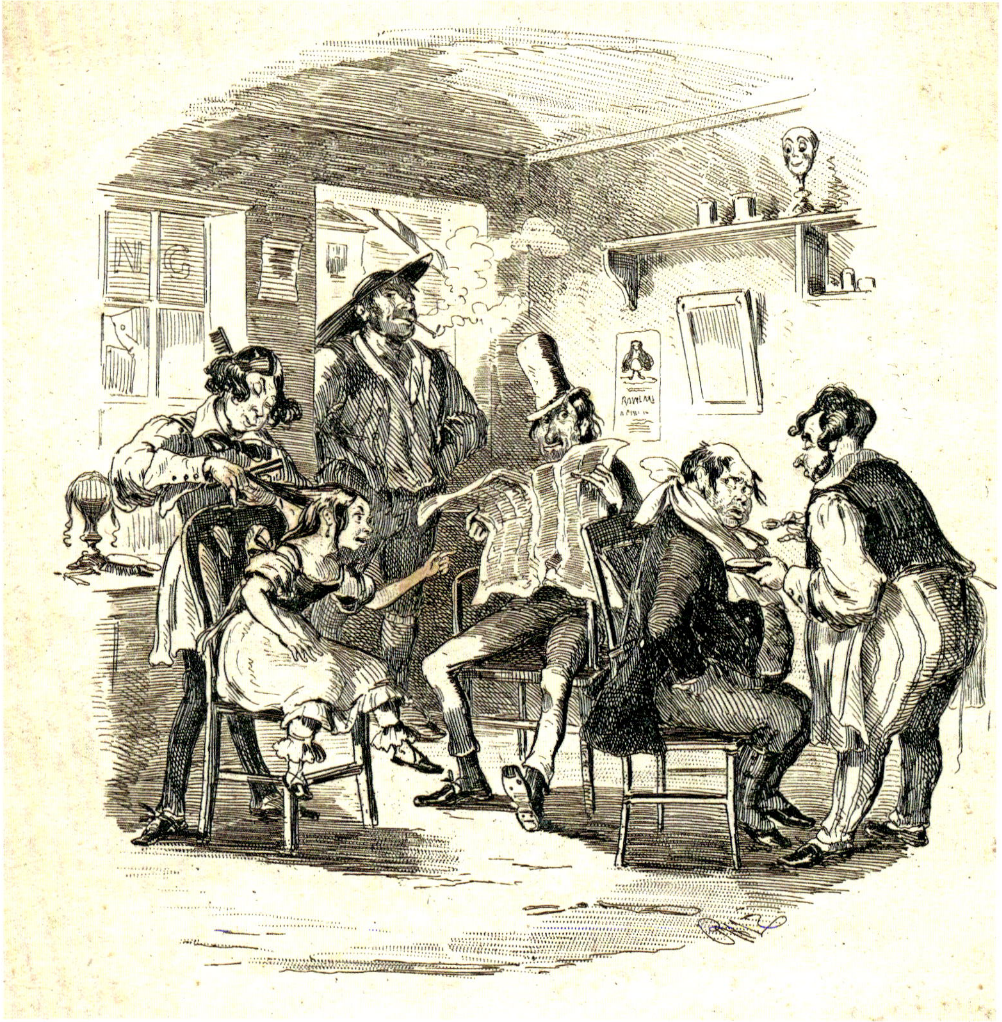

FIG. 2
Hablot Knight Browne, 'Great excitement of Miss Kenwigs at the hair dresser's shop', 1838, etching. Original illustration from *Nicholas Nickleby*

> It is necessary that I should observe that I have a great delight in pictures. I am no painter myself, but I have studied pictures and written about them. I have seen all the most famous pictures in the world; my education and reading have been sufficiently general to possess me beforehand with a knowledge of most of the subjects to which a Painter is likely to have recourse; and, although I might be in some doubt as to the rightful fashion of the scabbard of King Lear's sword, for instance, I think I should know King Lear tolerably well, if I happened to meet with him.[4]

Unlike Dickens, though, the character expresses the view of those who slavishly followed the accepted taste of the day:

> I go to all the Modern Exhibitions every season, and of course I revere the Royal Academy. I stand by its forty Academical articles almost as firmly as I stand by

> the thirty-nine Articles of the Church of England. I am convinced that in neither case could there be, by any rightful possibility, one article more or less.[5]

Dickens also used *Household Words* for a more direct criticism of the art that appeared on the Academy walls in 'Old Lamps for New Ones', the now notorious piece about John Everett Millais' painting, *Christ in the House of His Parents* (see pp. 53–4).[6] It cannot be ignored, but it has often been wrongly taken as the defining text of Dickens as an art critic. His daughter Kate Perugini, in her articles on her father's artistic taste, sought to explain the severity of his judgement of visual art by the fact that he was such a visual writer. She calls it 'the excessive realism of his mental vision', the great and vivid imagination of the author:

> That he always *saw* what he had read of, or heard about, even when he was quite a child, is pretty certain. Thus the picture in his own mind of any subject which attracted him was often so vivid as to preclude the possibility of its being conceived in any other way than the one his own fancy had created, and it was perhaps this curious mental faculty that caused him to write so severe a critique of Millais' 'Carpenter's Shop'.[7]

Dickens developed a very personal taste in art that reflected his own writing and is perhaps nowhere better illustrated than in the control that he exerted over the illustrators who created the plates for his novels. The illustration, 'Great excitement of Miss Kenwigs at the hair dresser's shop' by Hablot Browne (fig. 2), depicts a lively scene from *Nicholas Nickleby* and Dickens was keen that it was realized in the way that he had imagined it. The level of detail is revealed in the author's instruction to the illustrator that he depict the 'underbred attendant with his hair parted down the middle, and frizzed up into curls at the sides'.[8]

Such 'mental faculty' perhaps both marred and enhanced the way he saw art. There was clearly an intense interest, which is only to be expected in a writer who was so profoundly affected by the visual world. In his writings and particularly his letters we can discover something of his personal opinions. More publicly in his travelogue *Pictures from Italy* we find his views on the Old Masters, a subject discussed in this book by Nicholas Penny in his essay 'Dickens and Philistinism'.

On contemporary art Dickens held his own opinions but must have been swayed by his strong friendships with artists such as Daniel Maclise, William Powell Frith, Augustus Egg, Frank and Marcus Stone, and Clarkson Stanfield, to name but a few. The Dickens scholar, Leonée Ormond, explores his view of the art being created in his lifetime and his associations with artists in her essay 'Dickens and Contemporary Art'.

Dickens was also very interested in the great illustrators of the day, revealing much about the author's opinions on art. In two essays, one on George Cruikshank, the other

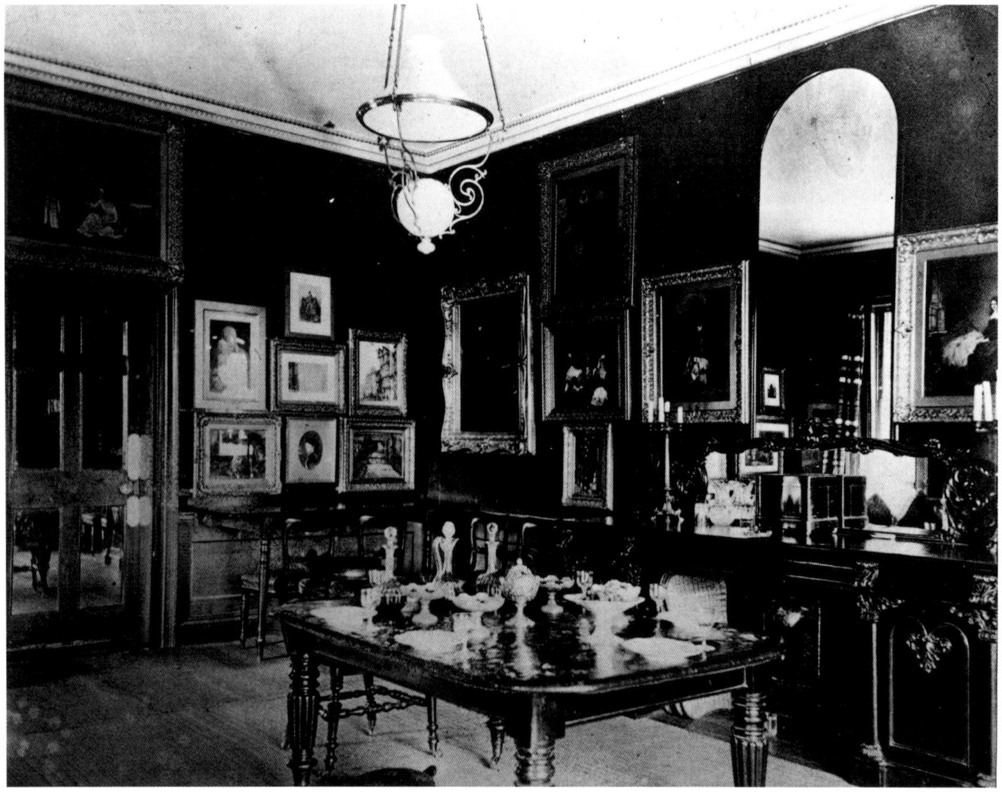

FIG. 3
Dickens's Dining Room at Gad's Hill showing his art collection. Watts Gallery Archive

on John Leech, Dickens expresses his attitude that great illustration is on a par with great art and writes of the absurdity of their exclusion from the Royal Academy.[9] Although it is not the focus of this book to discuss the illustrations in Dickens's novels, it does examine paintings inspired by his novels. Throughout his lifetime, in particular, the scenes and characterizations in his novels moved a number of artists to paint them, and Hilary Underwood's essay 'Dickens Subjects in Victorian Art' discusses this phenomenon.

The influence of Dickens was not limited to such 'literal translations' and was felt in the paintings of modern life that flourished in the mid-nineteenth century and the social-realist movement that followed shortly after his death. In his essay on Cruikshank Dickens's comparison of him to William Hogarth is an important one, confirming Dickens's admiration of the eighteenth-century master as well as giving a sophisticated reading of the artist's popular visual storytelling. It underlines his influence on artists who were part of this strong narrative tradition and who looked to contemporary literature for their sources. My essay 'Dickens and the Painting of Modern Life' considers these painters, particularly William Powell Frith, and the influence Dickens had upon them. As the critic John Ruskin wrote of Frith's great *Derby Day*, 'it is a kind of a cross between John Leech and Wilkie, with a dash of daguerreotype here and there, and some pretty seasoning with Dickens' sentiment'.[10]

FIG. 4
Sir Samuel Luke Fildes, 'Houseless and Hungry' (detail of fig. 104)

FIG. 5
Sir Samuel Luke Fildes, 'The Empty Chair, Gad's Hill – Ninth of June, 1870', wood engraving. From *The Graphic* (December 1870). Charles Dickens Museum, London

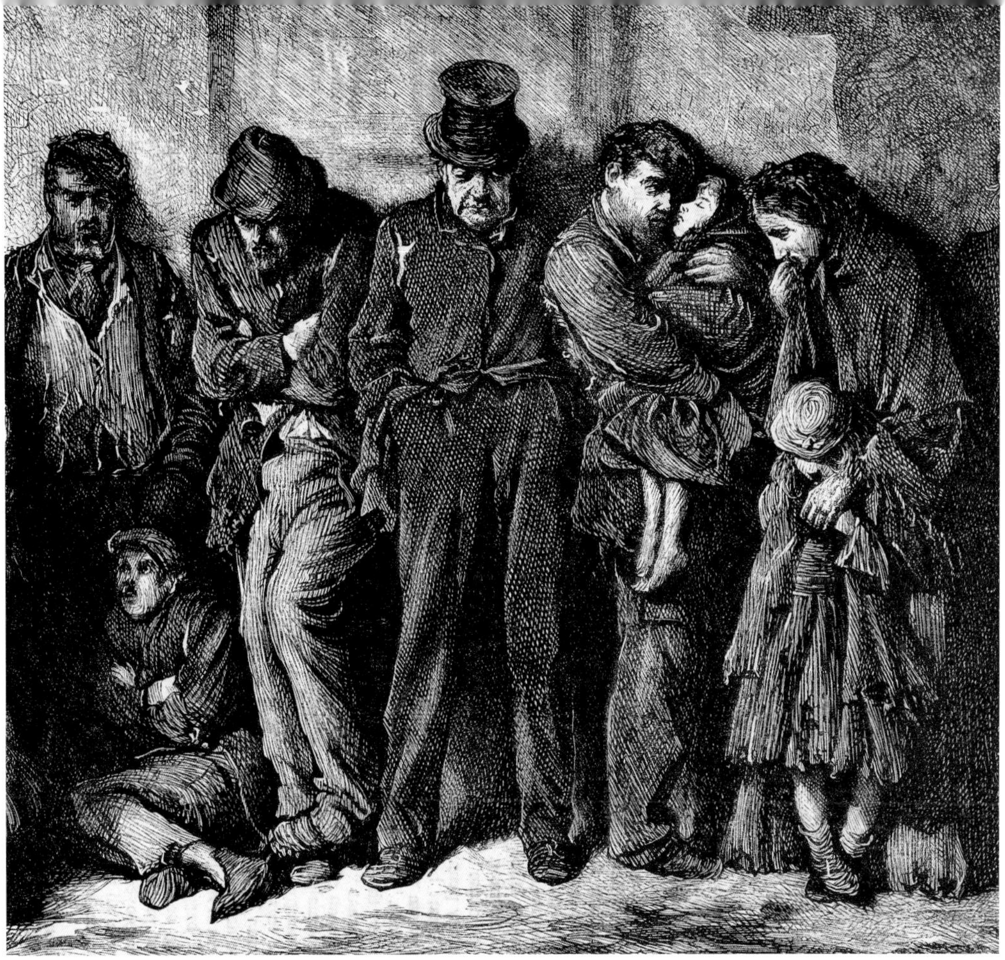

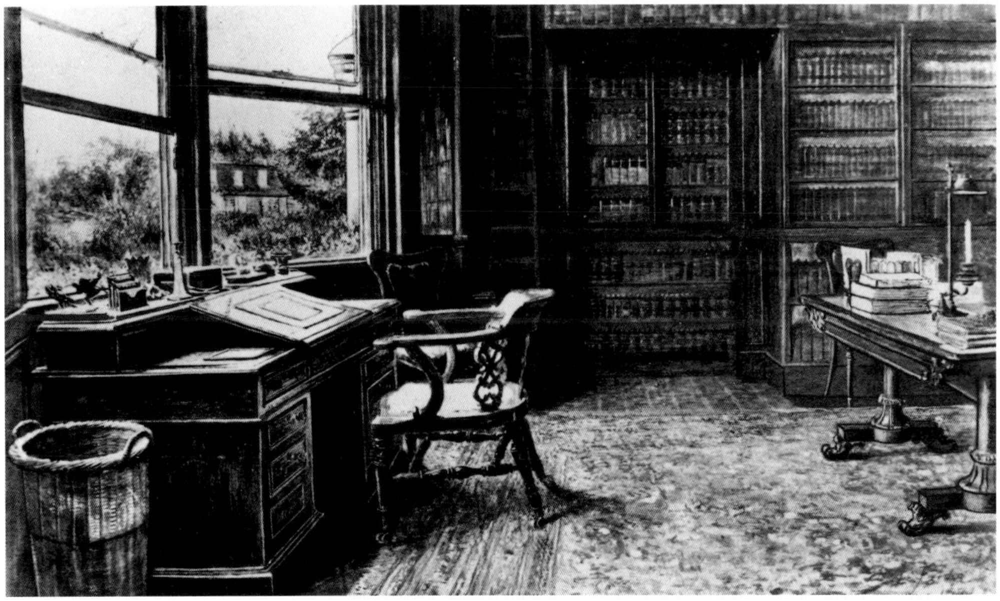

In her essay, 'Dickens and the Social Realists', Pat Hardy looks at a later group of artists, Frank Holl, Hubert Herkomer and Luke Fildes (figs 4, 5), who radically explored Dickens's social issues in their paintings. The social-realist paintings and illustrations were hugely influential, and Vincent Van Gogh saw direct parallels between the writer he so admired and these haunting depictions of the poor and dispossessed:

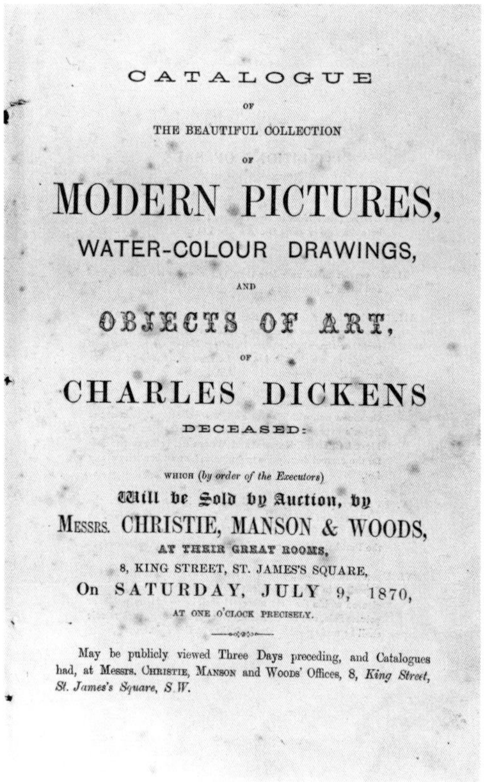

CATALOGUE

OF

THE BEAUTIFUL COLLECTION

OF

MODERN PICTURES,

WATER-COLOUR DRAWINGS,

AND

OBJECTS OF ART,

OF

CHARLES DICKENS

DECEASED:

WHICH (*by order of the Executors*)

Will be Sold by Auction, by

MESSRS. CHRISTIE, MANSON & WOODS,

AT THEIR GREAT ROOMS,

8, KING STREET, ST. JAMES'S SQUARE,

On SATURDAY, JULY 9, 1870,

AT ONE O'CLOCK PRECISELY.

May be publicly viewed Three Days preceding, and Catalogues had, at Messrs. CHRISTIE, MANSON and WOODS' Offices, 8, *King Street, St. James's Square, S.W.*

FIG. 6
Dickens art sale catalogue, 1870. Watts Gallery Archive

> For me the English black-and-white artists are to art what Dickens is to literature. They have exactly the same sentiment, noble and healthy, and one always returns to them . . . I am organizing my whole life so as to do things of everyday life that Dickens describes and the artists I've mentioned draw.[11]

In his lifetime and just after his death, there was a great eagerness to know the opinions of Charles Dickens. His taste in art was sought by artists and the general public alike and the sale of the author's pictures on Saturday afternoon 9 July 1870 was eagerly reported (fig. 6). Many newspapers and journals, including *The Times*, listed all the items in the sale and the event was reported at length. 'When "Dolly Varden," for which Dickens is said to have paid Frith £20, was put up,' the *Birmingham Daily Post* wrote, 'there was quite a cheer. Mr. Agnew bid 1,000 guineas.'[12] This huge amount for such a modestly scaled picture was indicative of the fame of Dickens and the visualization of this particular Dickens character.

Dickens and the Artists has been written to accompany the exhibition of the same name at Watts Gallery, Compton, Surrey, from 19 June until 18 October 2012. There is still great interest in Dickens's opinion of art exactly two centuries after the artist's birth. His enormous influence on art has not been fully investigated and it is the intention of this book of essays with its accompanying exhibition to celebrate and explore this important strand of art history in the bicentenary year of Dickens's birth, 2012.

NOTES

1. Quoted in Pickvance 1974, p. 26.
2. Perugini 1903, p. 129.
3. *The Life and Adventures of Nicholas Nickleby*, ch. 10, paras 6 and 12.
4. Charles Dickens, 'The Ghost of Art', *Household Words: A Weekly Journal, Conducted by Charles Dickens*, vol. 1, no. 17, 20 July 1850, p. 385. The story concludes (p. 387): 'Need I add more of my terrific fate? It HAS haunted me ever since. It glares upon me from the walls of the Royal Academy, (except when MACLISE subdues it to his genius,) it fills my soul with terror at the British Institution, it lures young artists on to their destruction. Go where I will, the Ghost of Art, eternally working the passions in hair, and expressing everything by beard, pursues me. The prediction is accomplished, and the victim has no rest.'
5. Ibid.
6. Charles Dickens, 'Old Lamps for New Ones', *Household Words*, vol. 1, no. 12, 15 June 1850, pp. 265–7.
7. Perugini 1903, p. 129.
8. Dickens quoted in Graham Reynolds, 'Charles Dickens and the World of Art,' *Apollo*, no. 91 (June 1970), p. 426.
9. Dickens 1911, p. 150.
10. John Ruskin, *Notes on Some of the Principle Pictures: Exhibited in ... the Royal Academy ...*, London, 1858.
11. Vincent Van Gogh, September 1882, quoted in Pickvance 1974, p. 26.
12. *Birmingham Daily Post*, Monday July 11 1870.

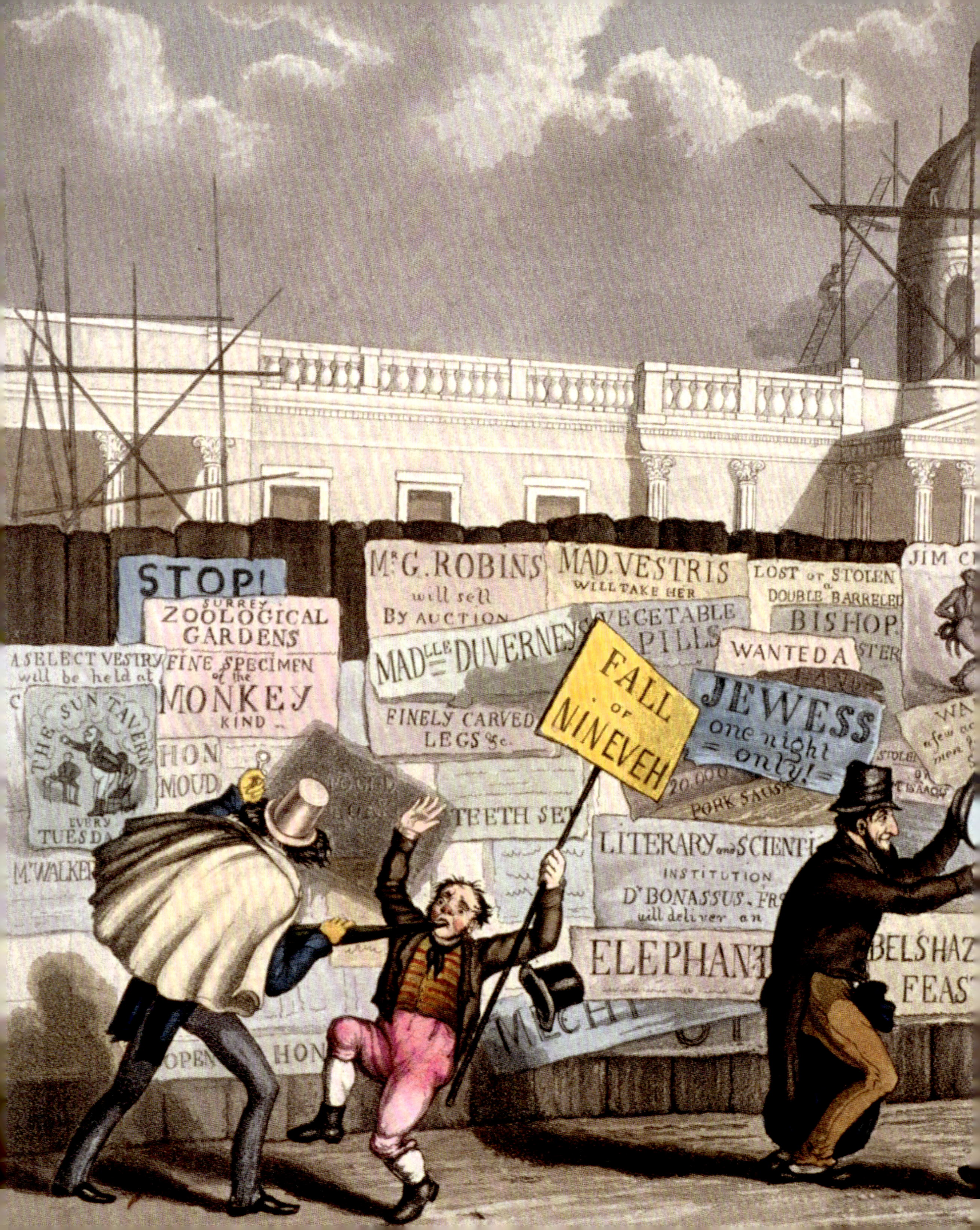
STOP!
SURREY ZOOLOGICAL GARDENS
A SELECT VESTRY will be held at
THE SUN TAVERN
EVERY TUESDA
FINE SPECIMEN of the MONKEY KIND
Mr G. ROBINS will sell By AUCTION
MAD. VESTRIS WILL TAKE HER
LOST or STOLEN a DOUBLE BARRELED BISHOP
JIM C
VEGETABLE PILLS
MADlle DUVERNEY
WANTED A
JEWESS one night = only! =
FALL OF NINEVEH
FINELY CARVED LEGS &c.
TEETH SET
PORK SAUS
LITERARY and SCIENTI
INSTITUTION
Dr BONASSUS, FR
will deliver an
ELEPHANT
BELSHAZ FEAST
Mr WALKER
HON
MOUD
OPEN
HON

PART THE FIRST

DICKENS *as Art Critic*

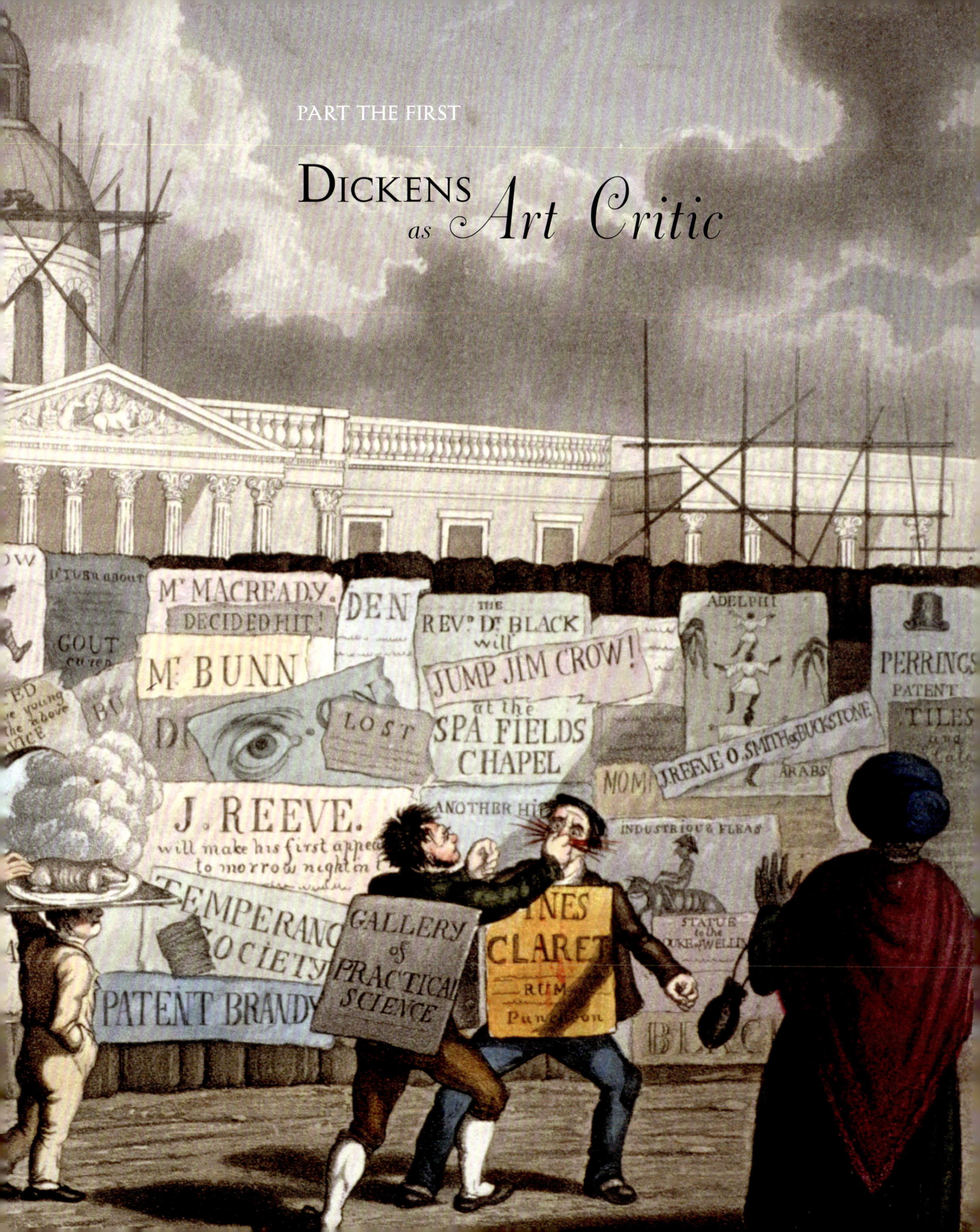

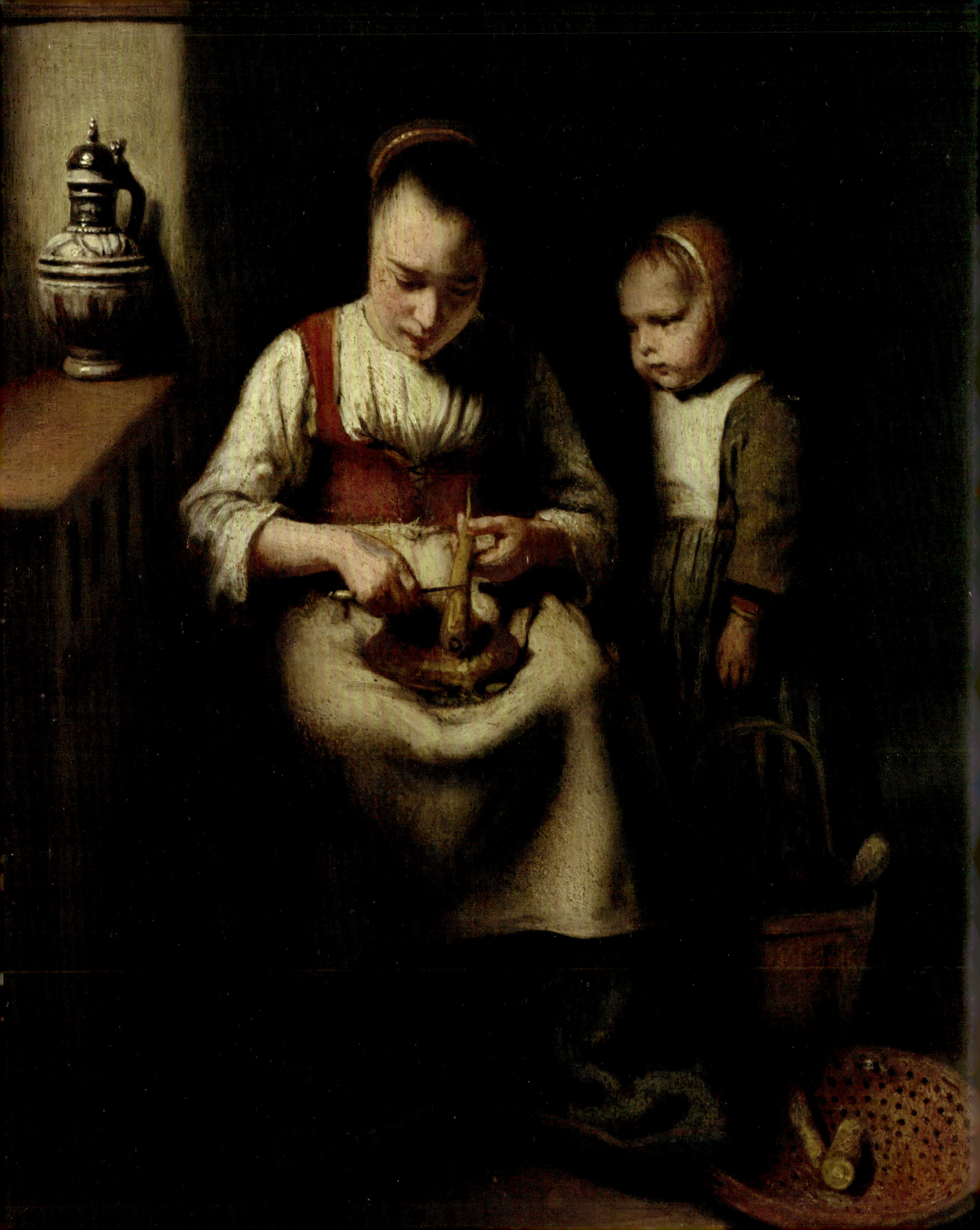

Dickens AND PHILISTINISM

NICHOLAS PENNY

The earliest published image of the Greek Revival building by William Wilkins that stretches across the north side of Trafalgar Square is a jocular engraving that shows it under construction in 1836, with the dignity of its architecture masked (as it so often is today) by hoardings covered with noisy advertising in front of which are enacted some of the violent encounters, familiar to Mr Jingle and Oliver Twist, of London's streets (fig. 8). The print implies that cultural institutions, and especially the National Gallery, are detached from the sordid realities of modern urban life, although in fact, as we shall see, common people flocked to the Gallery, which, unlike the Royal Academy, did not charge for admission.

The Royal Academy moved into the east wing of Wilkins's building in 1837 and the National Gallery occupied the west, opening its doors to the public on 5 April 1838. In the same month the first instalment of *Nicholas Nickleby*, Dickens's third novel, appeared. Together with most of London's fashionable society, Dickens visited the Royal Academy's summer exhibitions in order to see 'those beautiful shiny portraits of gentlemen in black velvet waistcoats, with their fists doubled up on round tables, or marble slabs . . . and all the ladies who are playing with little parasols, or little dogs, or little children' (in the words of Miss La Creevy in his new novel).[1] In 1839 he was able to admire there his own glamorous portrait by Daniel Maclise (fig. 9), which was engraved for the frontispiece of *Nicholas Nickleby* when it appeared in book form in October of the same year. But if Dickens ever turned left on entering the portico and strolled round the National Gallery, there is no evidence that he gave any attention to the small collection of masterpieces it then contained.

He must, of course, have known that Old Master paintings were almost as much favoured as wall furniture in London's most fashionable houses as 'beautiful shiny portraits' and silk hangings and looking glass. But the parody of high society romance that Kate Nickleby is obliged to read to the languid Mrs Wititterly does not progress beyond Lady Flabella's '*mouchoir* of finest cambric, edged with richest lace, and emblazoned at the four corners with the Flabella crest', and the 'golden salver gorgeously chased' on which she receives a billet-doux. The 'silken damask, the hue of Italy's

FIG. 7
Nicholas Maes, *A Woman Scraping Parsnips, with a Child Standing by her* (detail of fig. 19)

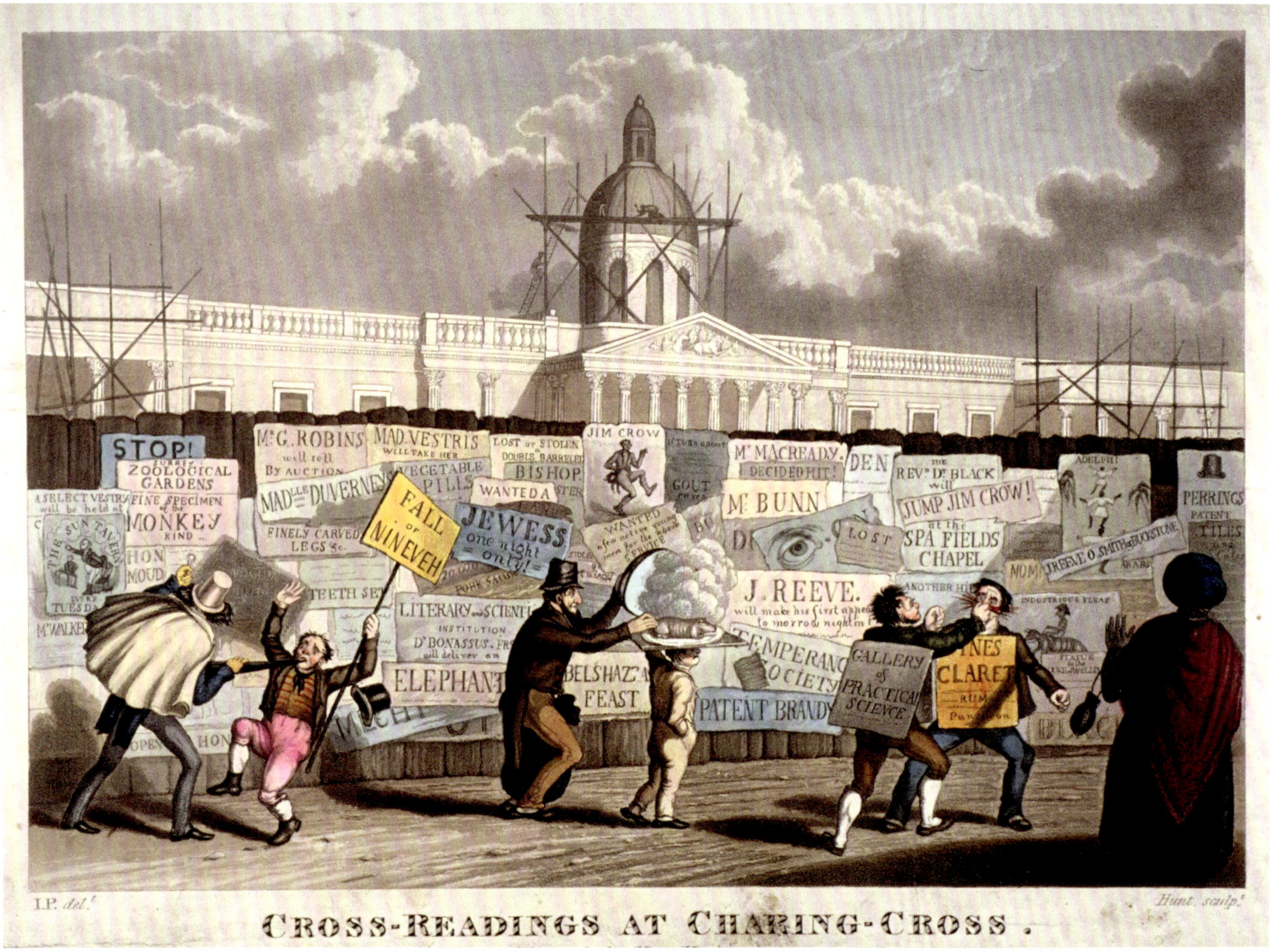

firmament' concealing the door of her ladyship's boudoir, is mentioned but no pictures.[2] William Makepeace Thackeray in 'Codlingsby', his deadly parody of Benjamin Disraeli's *Coningsby*, knew exactly the alliterative hyperbole that would have been appropriate: 'Giorgione the gorgeous, Titian the golden, Rubens the ruddy and pulpy (the Pan of painting), some of Murillo's beautiful shepherdesses, who smile at you out of the darkness like a star, a few score first class Leonardos.'[3]

By 1847, when Thackeray's parody appeared in *Punch*, Dickens had travelled to Italy (he was there in 1844–5), had published his *Pictures from Italy* (early in 1846) and knew something of these artists. *Pictures from Italy* seeks to gratify middlebrow readers by its impatience with the pretensions of connoisseurship and the mindless reverence of guidebooks, but Dickens expressed enthusiasm for easily accessible masterpieces – notably, in Venice, Titian's *Assunta* (1516–18; Santa Maria Gloriosa dei Frari) then in the Accademia Gallery, and Tintoretto's *Paradiso* (after 1588) in the Doge's Palace – and, in Parma, disapproval (also, in fact, conventional) of Correggio's 'heaps of

ABOVE
FIG. 8
I.P., *'Cross-readings at Charing-Cross'; view of the National Gallery in Trafalgar Square shown under construction, with boarding in front of it covered with advertisements, London*, 1835, aquatint, collage. London Metropolitan Archives

RIGHT
FIG. 9
Daniel Maclise, *Charles Dickens*, 1839, oil on canvas. Tate, London

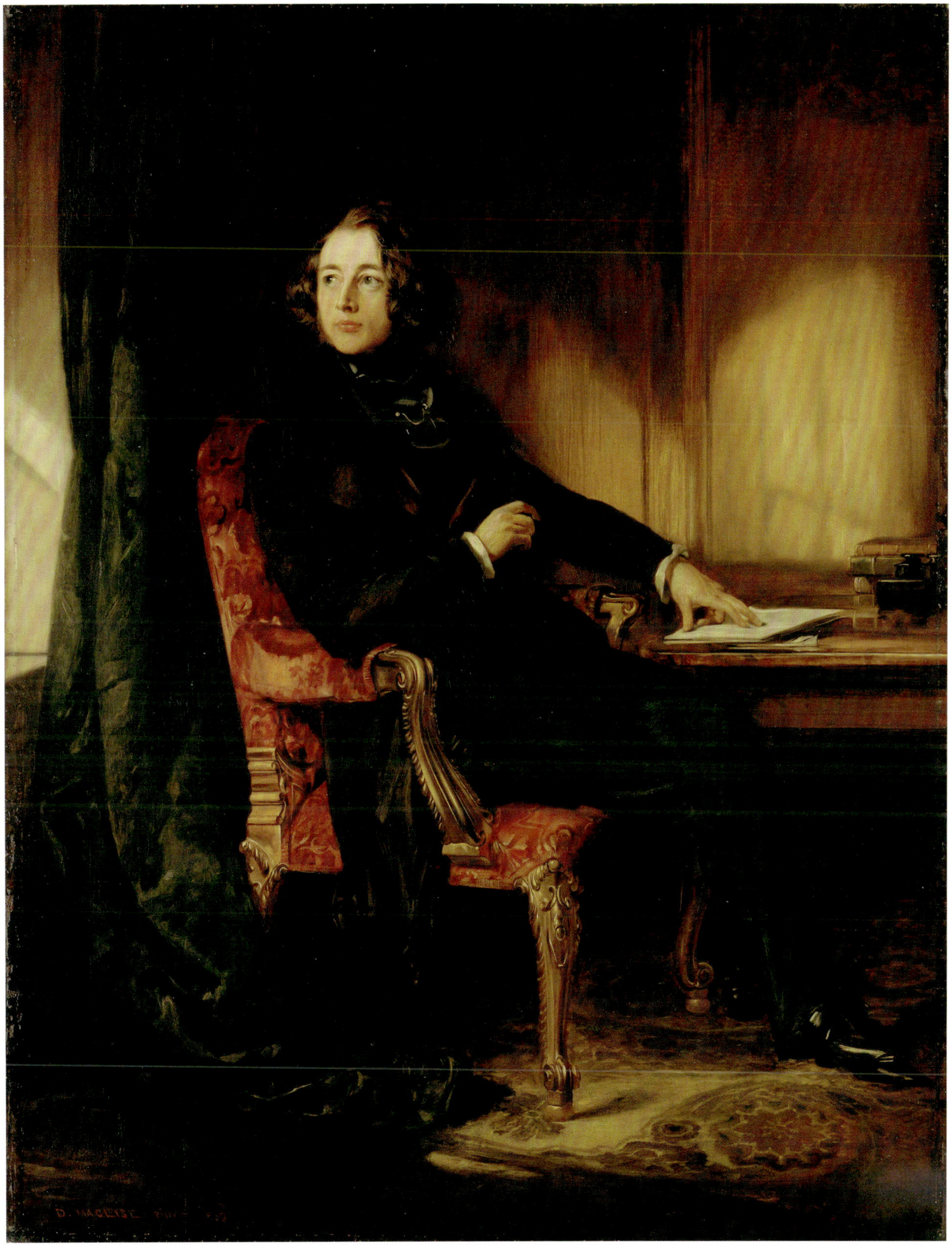

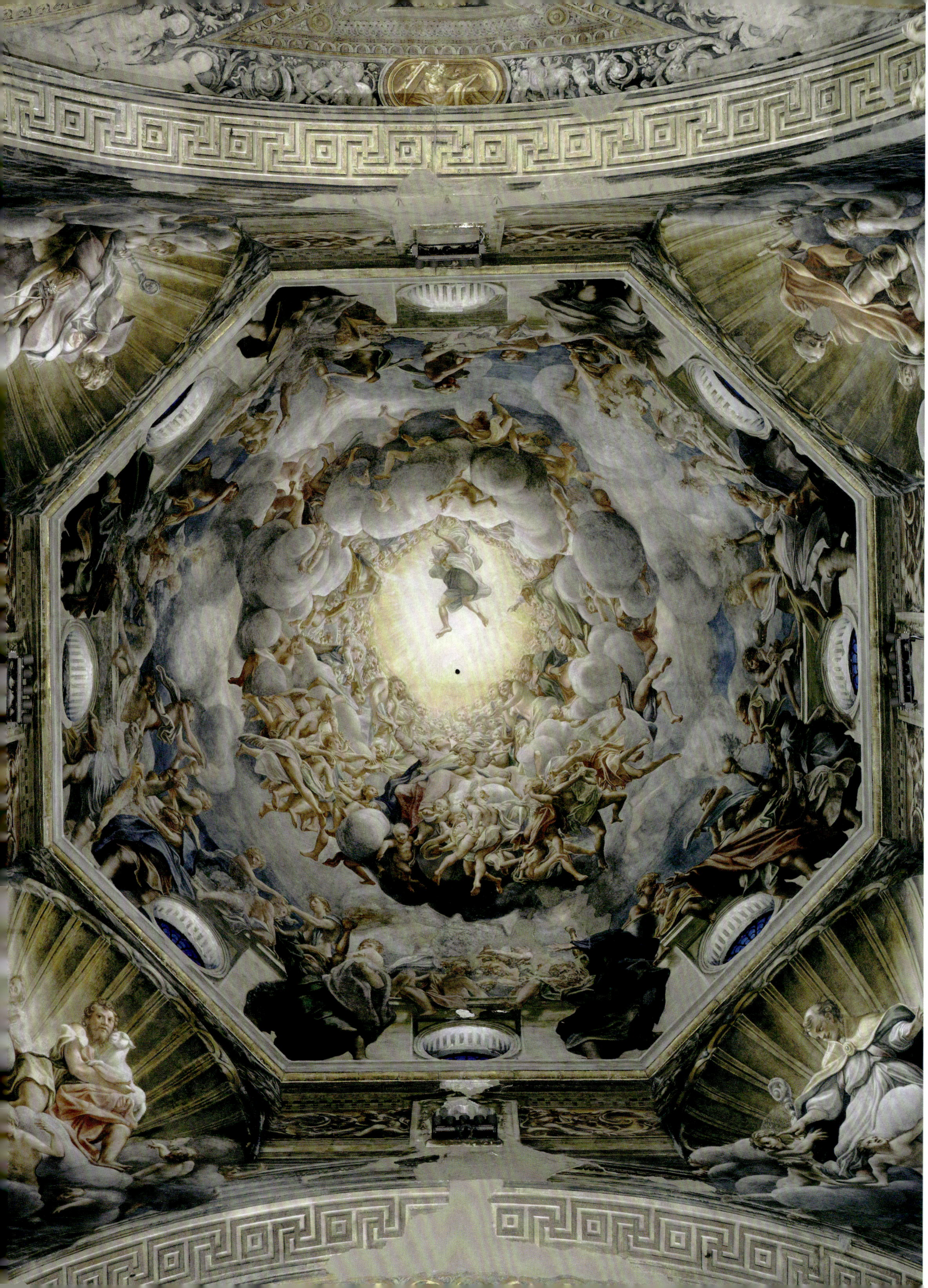

LEFT
FIG. 10
Antonio Allegri Correggio, *Assumption of the Virgin*, from the ceiling of the dome, 1526–30, fresco. Duomo of Parma, Italy

RIGHT
FIG. 11
Antonio Allegri Correggio, *The Vision of St John on Patmos*, 1520–23, fresco. San Giovanni Evangelista, Parma, Italy

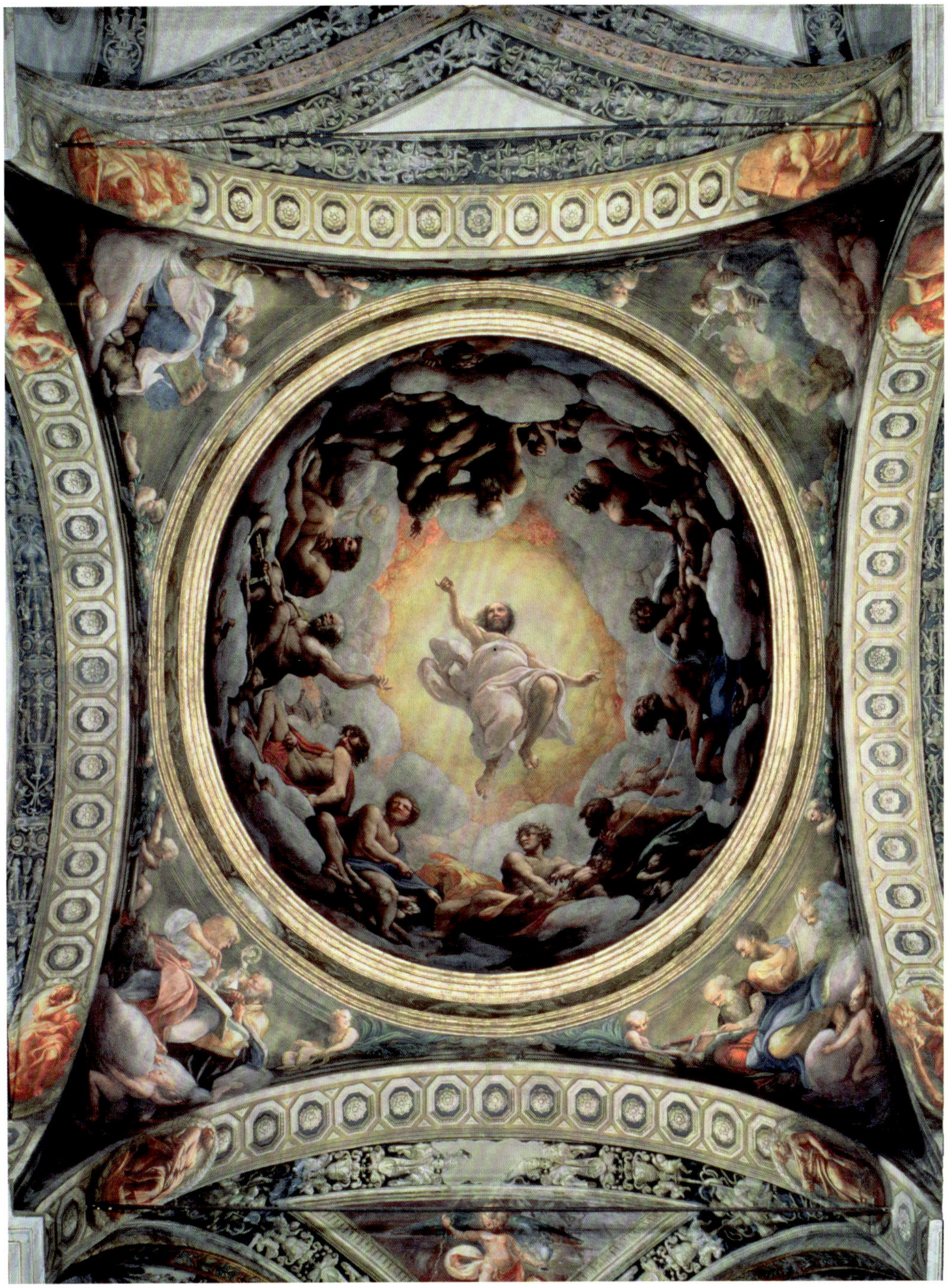

foreshortened limbs, entangled and involved and jumbled together' in his ceiling paintings (figs 10, 11).[4] And yet no mention is made of the paintings by these artists that were easily available to his readers in Trafalgar Square, not even Titian's *Bacchus and Ariadne* (1520–23), Correggio's *Madonna of the Basket* (fig. 12) or Tintoretto's *St George and the Dragon* (*c.*1555), which were among the most remarkable recent acquisitions made for the national collection.

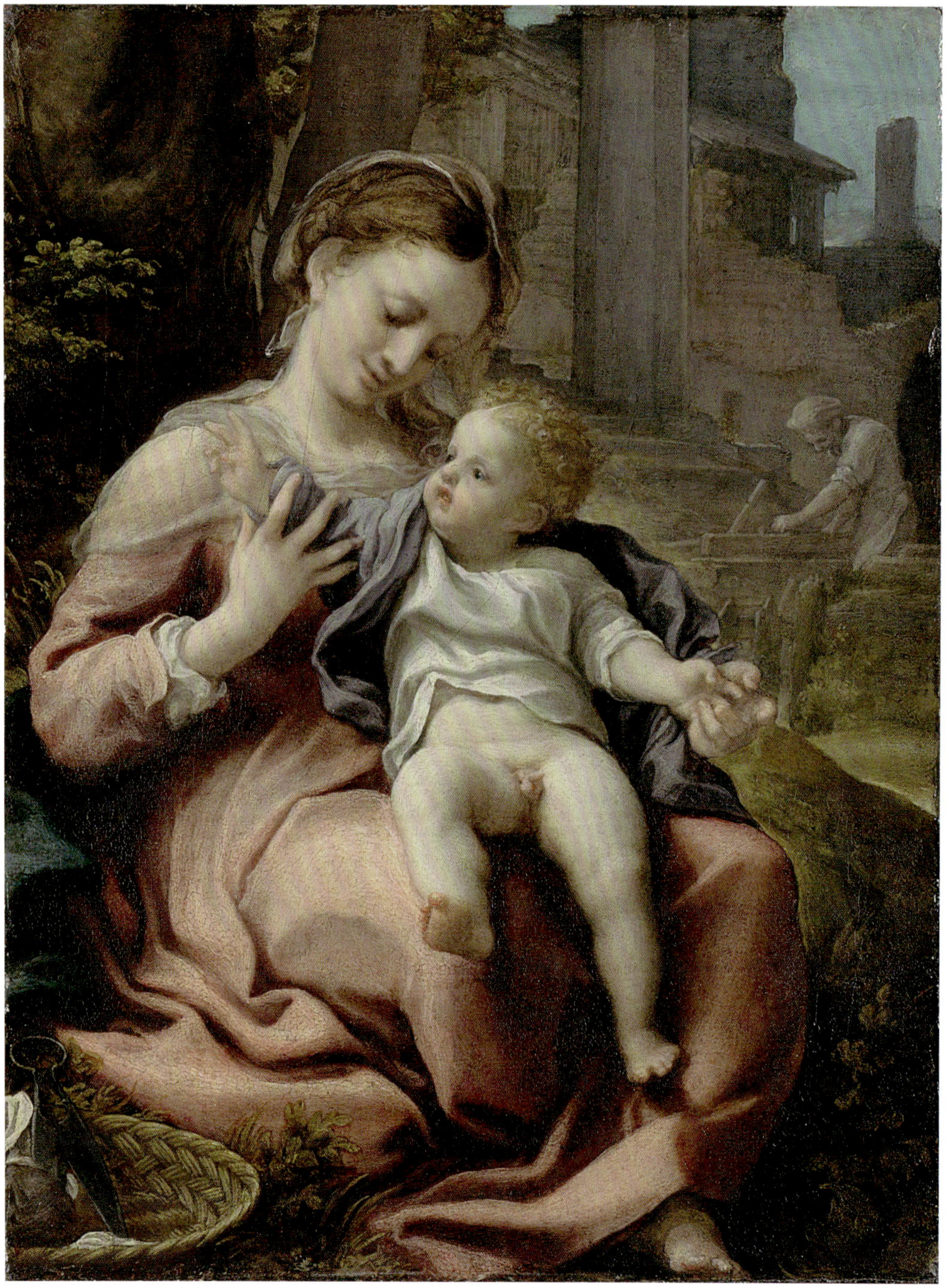

FIG. 12
Antonio Allegri Correggio, *Madonna of the Basket*, *c.*1524, oil on wood. The National Gallery, London

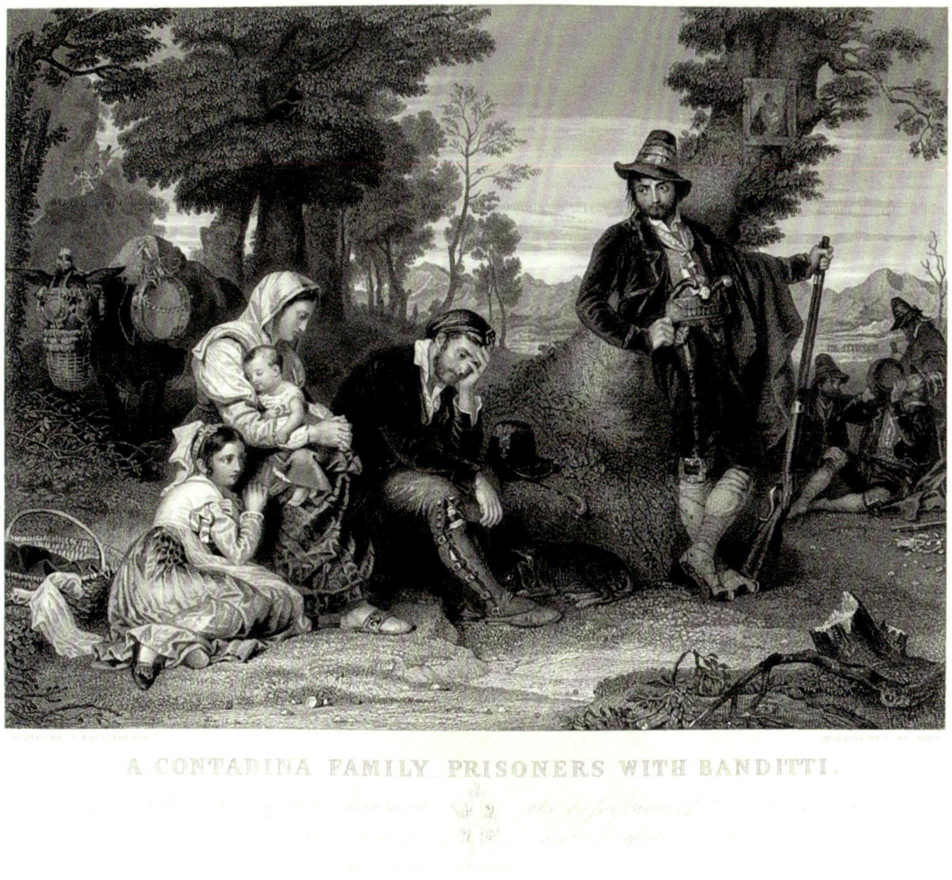

FIG. 13
Edward Smith, after C. L. Eastlake, *A Contadina Family … Prisoners with Banditti*, 1846, engraving, published by Joseph Hogarth, London

Although Dickens seems to have given little if any attention to the Italian Old Masters to be seen in London, he was familiar with the paintings of Charles Eastlake, who served as Keeper of the National Gallery between 1843 and 1847. Eastlake was the leading British painter of fierce brigands and distressed *contadine* (peasant girls) – the latter more convincing than the former – which he had sent to London during his long residence in Rome (fig. 13). When Dickens surveyed the artist's models loitering on the Spanish Steps, he claimed he knew he had seen them before somewhere – it was, he soon realized, in London's exhibitions. The man 'in a brown cloak, who leans against a wall, with his arms folded in his mantle, and looks out of the corners of his eyes: which are just visible beneath his broad slouched hat. This is the assassin model.'[5]

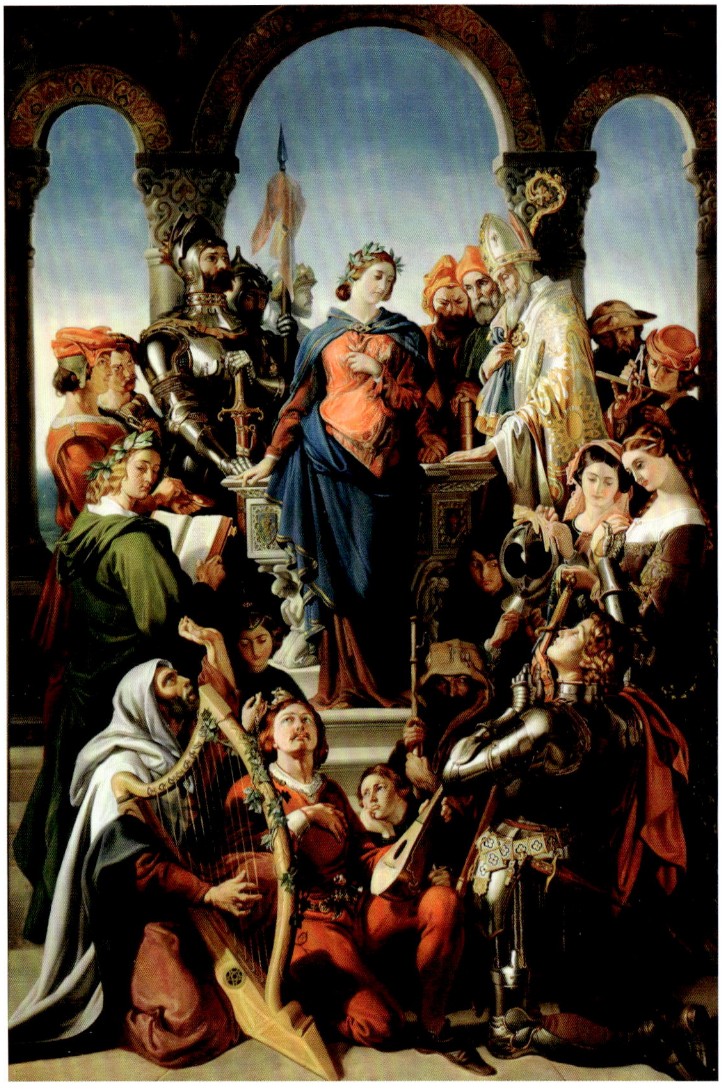

FIG. 14
Daniel Maclise, *The Spirit of Chivalry*, 1858, oil on canvas. Museums Sheffield

In August 1845, soon after his return to London, Dickens was persuaded to publish in the *Shilling Magazine* a puff for *The Spirit of Chivalry* (fig. 14), which his friend Maclise was exhibiting as a cartoon for a fresco to be painted in the House of Lords. The subject was congenial to Maclise, who had been seduced by the medievalizing aspirations of his friends and patrons in the Young England movement. The creator of Sir Mulberry Hawk and Lord Fredrick Verisopht, not to mention the Lady Flabella, must have swallowed hard before taking up his pen to praise this hymn to nobility. Dickens next tried his hand at art criticism nearly five years later when he published, on 15 June 1850, a violent invective against the Pre-Raphaelites in his new two-penny weekly publication, *Household Words*. These two deplorable efforts, the former forgotten, the latter cited by every art historian writing about British art in this period, show no understanding of the growing awareness of medieval or early Renaissance art across Europe, which was

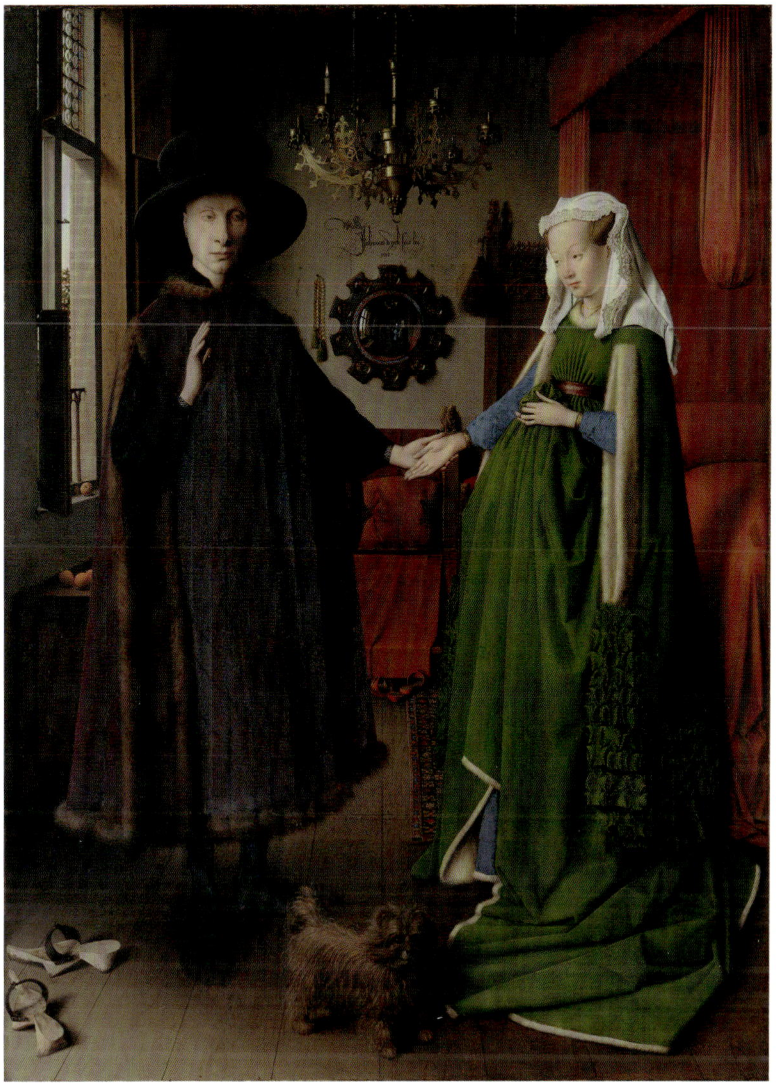

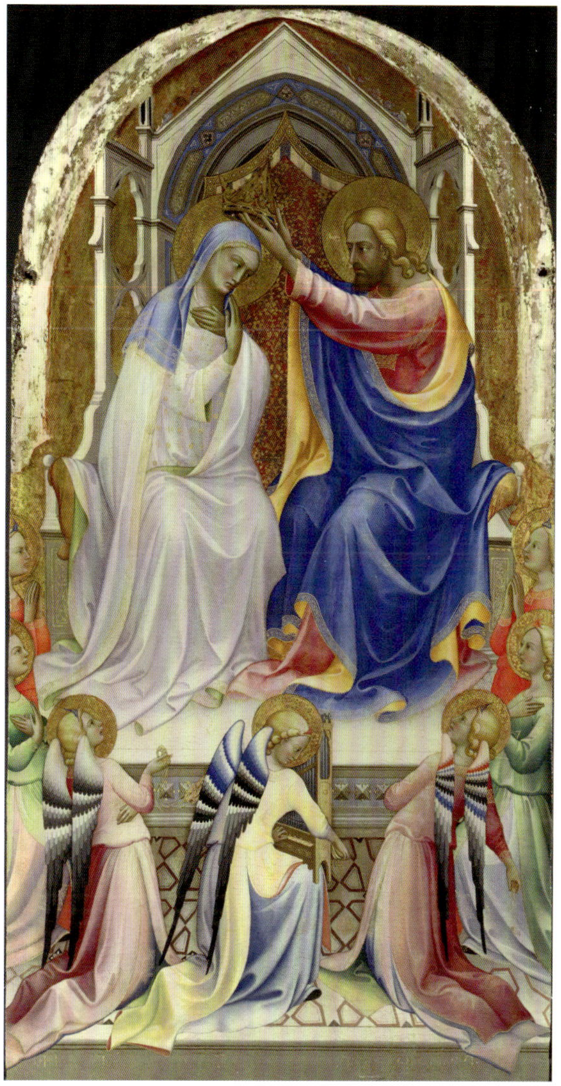

FIG. 15
Jan Van Eyck, *The Arnolfini Portrait*, 1434, oil on oak. The National Gallery, London

FIG. 16
Lorenzo Monaco, *The Coronation of the Virgin*, 1407–9, egg tempera on wood. The National Gallery, London

a precondition both for Maclise's fresco and for the innovations of Millais and his friends. Dickens seems not to have noticed the exponents of Purismo in Italy or the work of the Nazarenes in Rome. More significantly, he had no idea of the decisive influence exercised by two of the most notable recent acquisitions by the National Gallery: Jan van Eyck's *Arnolfini Portrait* (fig. 15), purchased in 1842 (displayed 1843), and the outer panels of Lorenzo Monaco's *Coronation of the Virgin* (fig. 16), donated (as by Taddeo Gaddi) in 1848, the former inspiring the exhausting detail and the latter the archaic stiffness that so offended the bland ideal of beauty and the decorous sentiment to which he was attached.

Art reviews were not to be a major feature of *Household Words*, but on 13 September 1856 the leading contribution – appearing directly below the name of Charles Dickens (in the heading) and certainly with his full approval – was an anonymous article, in fact

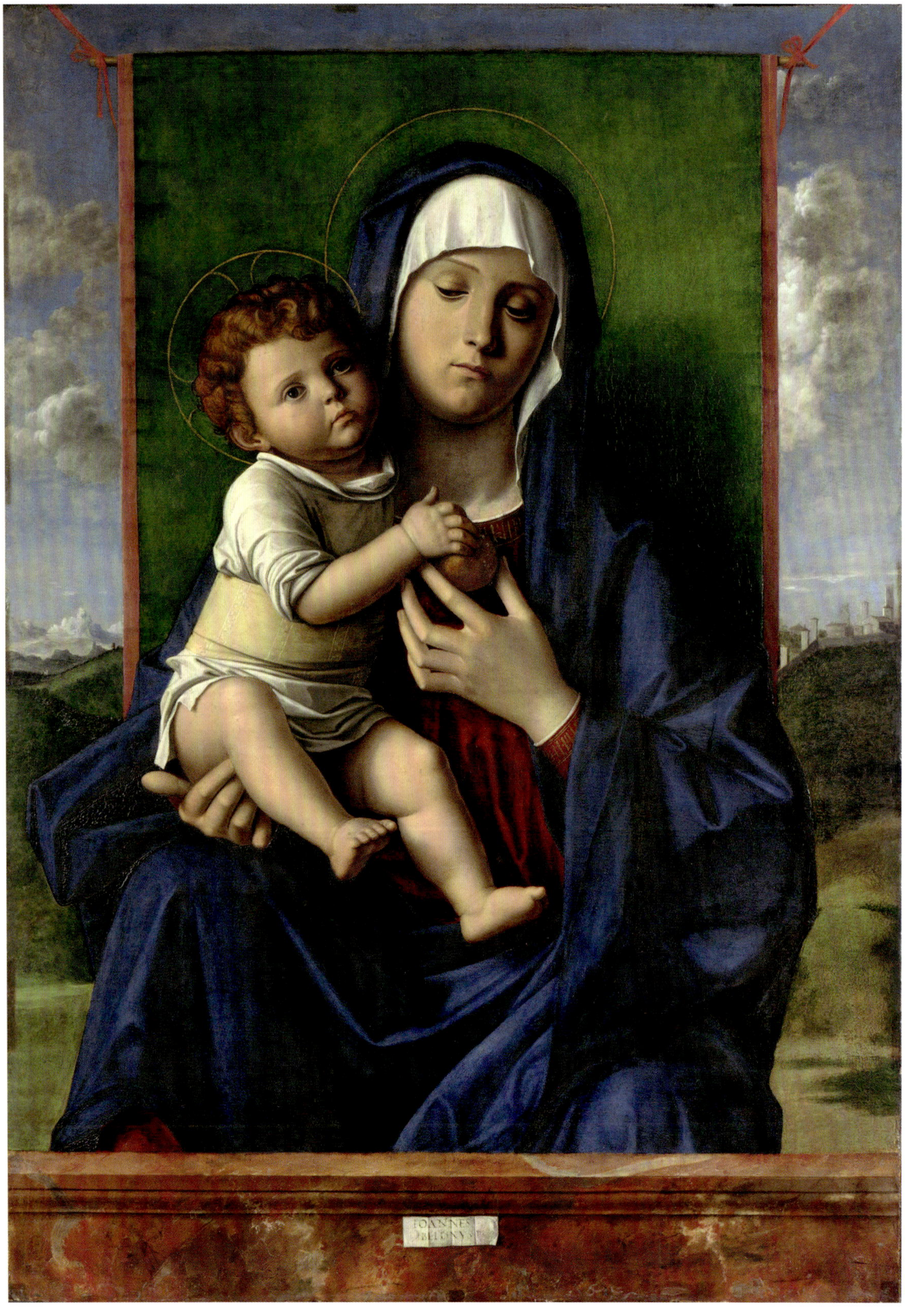

written by Dickens's young friend Wilkie Collins and entitled 'To think, or be thought for?' The pretext for the article was a controversy in the correspondence columns of *The Times* concerning a picture by 'the old Venetian painter Bellini', recently acquired for the National Gallery (workshop of Giovanni Bellini, *The Virgin and Child*, often called 'The Madonna of the Pomegranate'; fig. 17). The collector and connoisseur William Coningham (donor of the panels by Lorenzo Monaco) claimed that the picture had been so 'daubed over' as to be worthless, whereas Gustav Waagen, director of the Berlin picture gallery and a friend of Eastlake (now Sir Charles, the former keeper who had been appointed as the National Gallery's first director in the previous year), defended it as an excellent example of Bellini's work.

> Surely the bewildered visitor to the National Gallery, standing opposite the Bellini with Doctor Waagen on his right hand begging him to admire it, and Mr Coningham on his left entreating him to despise it, must end, in mere self-defence, in shaking both the critical gentlemen off, and judging for himself, not of the Bellini only, but of every other picture in the collection as well.[6]

There is a deliberate confusion here between assessment of condition and authorship, which are obviously a matter for experts, and assessment of artistic success, here reduced to 'knowing what one likes'. The common man, having thrown off the English connoisseur and the German doctor, is then invited to Rome in order to join the author in questioning the merits of a 'confusion of naked knotty-bodied figures, sprawling up or tumbling down' the wall of the Sistine Chapel.[7]

Collins is especially offended by the idea of a sublime style as expounded by Sir Joshua Reynolds, for whom Michelangelo's figures represent a 'superior order of being'. He redefines the classic as the enduringly popular, that which can always be depended on to fill the pit and the gallery – not Milton or Poussin, therefore, but 'the tragedy of Hamlet' and 'the Don Giovanni of Mozart'.[8] The polemic concludes with an indignant glance at 'authority standing drearily and persistently aloof from all popular sympathy' – presumably a reference to the superior manner of the new director – 'purchasing pictures for the National Gallery of England, for which, in nine cases out of ten, the nation has no concern or care'.[9]

Such an extreme attack, not only on the National Gallery's acquisitions but on the idea of authority in matters of taste, requires an explanation. It owed nothing to Wilkie Collins's father, the painter William Collins. From the pious memoirs of him published in 1848 by Wilkie himself his father emerges as an 'uncompromising' supporter of the 'high station' assigned to the Old Masters, who felt that the Royal Academy would suffer were it to neglect to learn from the National Gallery.[10] The best explanation is that Wilkie Collins understood that Dickens would welcome an article that repeated more loudly his own disappointment before Michelangelo's *Last Judgment*, his disdain

FIG. 17
Giovanni Bellini, *The Virgin and Child*, probably 1480–1500, oil and tempera on wood. The National Gallery, London

for connoisseurs trembling with excitement over 'minute details of expression' long departed from Leonardo's *Last Supper*, and his conviction that it was wrong to admire deviations from ordinary proportions in the body or natural expression 'in spite of high critical advice' from Reynolds or the like.[11] Above all we must suspect that Wilkie Collins was transferring to another art form his indignation that the novel was considered in many quarters to be a form of popular entertainment rather than great literature.

Collins's aversion to connoisseurs and collectors found expression again four years later in *The Woman in White*, which Dickens published in *All the Year Round*, the successor to *Household Words*. One of the characters in this novel, Frederick Fairlie Esquire of Limmeridge House, employs his Swiss valet to prevent either daylight or family members disturbing his selfish, valetudinarian seclusion:

> I was reclining, in my usual state, surrounded by the various objects of art which I have collected about me to improve the taste of the barbarous people in my neighbourhood. That is to say, I had the photographs of my pictures, and prints, and coins and so forth, all about me.[12]

For Wilkie Collins philanthropy (in this case the donation of reproductions to the 'Institution at Carlisle') was merely an act of vanity and condescension that did nothing to redeem the repellent and unhealthy practice of hoarding, and fondling in private, old prints and coins and paintings.

In the same volumes of *All the Year Round* that saw the publication of *The Woman in White* in 1860 a series of sprightly satirical pieces were published by 'Our Eye Witness', the pseudonym of Wilkie Collins's younger brother, Charles Allston Collins, who had previously enjoyed some success as a Pre-Raphaelite painter. In the months when these articles appeared he was engaged to Dickens's daughter Kate, whom he married in July. Dickens was not happy about the marriage, although he did think highly of the pieces by 'Our Eye Witness'. The younger Collins, having, on 26 May, ridiculed London's public statues, especially those in Trafalgar Square, including the 'inconceivably foolish' column for Nelson,[13] turned his attention to the National Gallery on 16 and 23 June. He was perplexed by the institution's huge popularity with the uneducated sections of society and facetiously proposed that an irresistible force of suction drew whole families, 'children, babies and all, from distances even as remote as Hoxton or Camberwell'.[14] He even noticed a 'weary old labourer in a white smock frock who must have come from Kingston or Watford'.[15]

The great altarpiece of the Martyrdom of Saint Sebastian by Antonio and Piero del Pollaiuolo (fig. 18) had recently arrived in the Gallery and Collins claims to have observed 'a char-woman and her little girl, the child asking who was St Sebastian, and the char-woman replying that she didn't know'.[16] He also met a man in a 'greasy coat

FIG. 18
Antonio and Piero del Pollaiuolo, *Martyrdom of Saint Sebastian*, 1475, oil on wood. The National Gallery, London

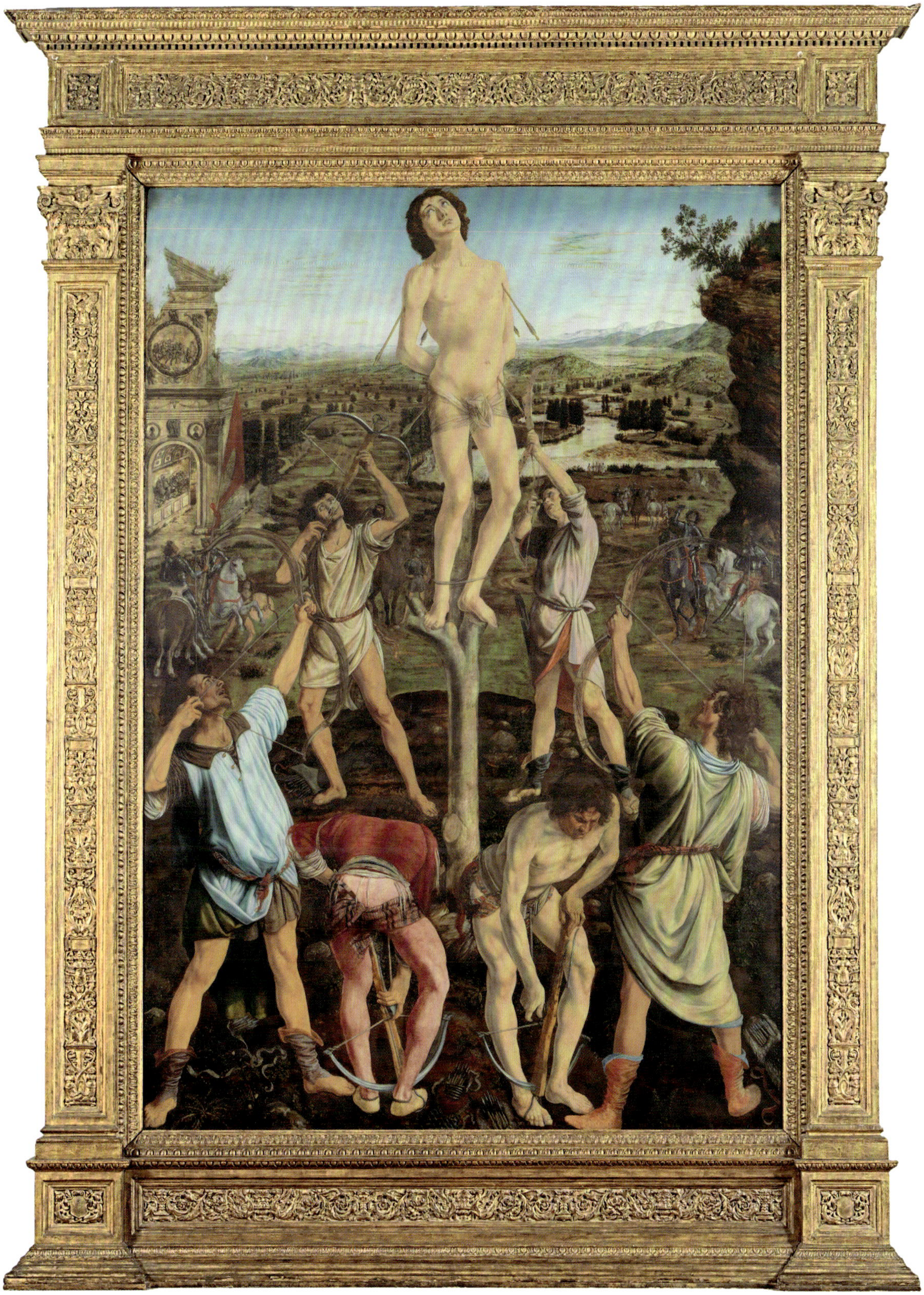

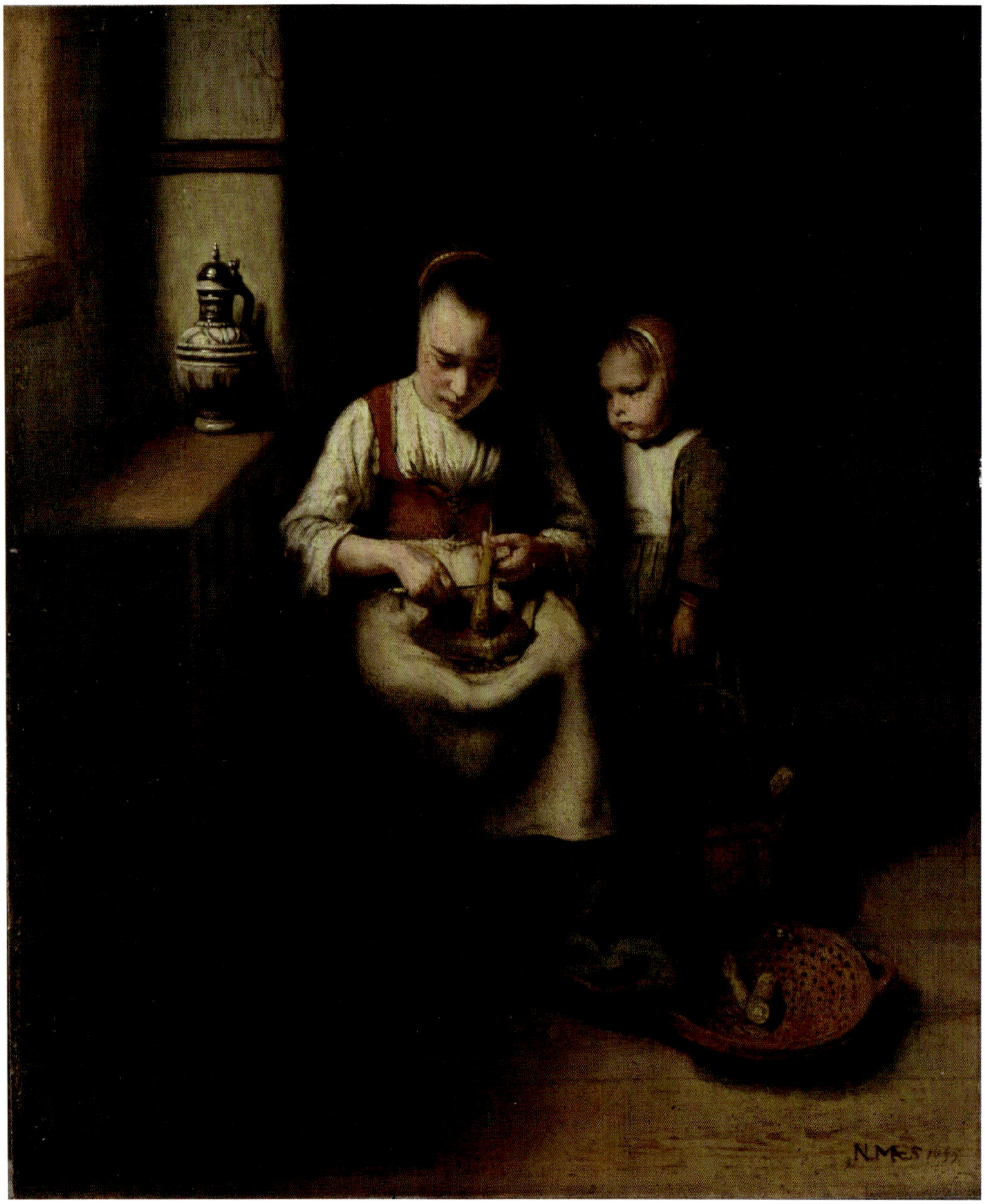

FIG. 19
Nicholas Maes, *A Woman Scraping Parsnips, with a Child Standing by her*, 1655, oil on oak. The National Gallery, London

and cap' directing his friend's attention to a Dutch painting of a girl scraping parsnips (the fine painting by Nicolaes Maes dated 1655; fig. 19), 'this here, George, is a pictur' of a old woman mending a pen'.[17] Would Dickens have participated in this type of mockery? He was in favour of the poor being allowed to enter parks and museums on Sundays and, in his puff for Maclise's *Spirit of Chivalry*, had claimed that he had seen 'ignorant, unlettered, drudging men, mere hewers and drawers' marvelling at its beauty – although if he was simply recording a plain fact, he would not have adopted biblical language.[18] In *Pictures from Italy* he describes a party 'brought over from London, fifteen or twenty strong, by contract' (an early, pre-railways example of the package holiday), which includes a Mr Davis, who, tracing ancient Roman inscriptions with the ferrule of his umbrella, says 'with intense thoughtfulness, "Here's a B you see, and there's a R, and this is the way we goes on in" '.[19] This is a specimen of the humour in which *Punch* specialized that enabled the half-educated or half-cultivated to feel superior to the uneducated or uncultivated – often enough, however, half-sympathizing with them.

For the most part the Eye Witness's account of the National Gallery takes the form of an imaginary tribunal presided over by the ghost of Sir George Beaumont and by Professor Waghorn (obviously intended for Gustav Waagen, who was so closely associated with Eastlake). Beaumont (who was, as Collins must have known, a generous patron of his father) stands for the taste of the connoisseurs who had first supported the Gallery and whose influence was responsible for the acquisition of a 'Susanna assaulted by two mahogany elders' and other specimens of the Bolognese School in the 1840s. Waghorn, on the other hand, is to blame for filling the Gallery with specimens, as if it were a natural history museum, and these included numerous paintings made before 1500, hardly any of which Charles Collins considered to be of any value.

Collins strongly objected to the transfer of Robert Vernon's gift of modern British pictures to temporary accommodation in South Kensington. Moreover, he had, 'that very morning, in walking down St James's Street, seen a pair of photographs from two pictures by a living French painter which gave him greater pleasure than nine-tenths of the works of the Old Masters'.[20] The photographs, one depicting gladiators and the other the assassination of Caesar, must have been those of popular paintings by Jean-Léon Gérome published by the great art dealer Goupil & Cie. Dickens might well have shared this enthusiasm, for he had been struck by the merits of Paul Delaroche and his followers. But perhaps of more significance than the paintings Dickens liked or owned and his relations with living artists (topics that are admirably analysed by Leonée Ormond on pp. 35–64) is the attitude towards the visual arts that can be detected in some remarkable passages in his novels. These extend considerably the prejudices that found expression in the publications by Dickens and his circle surveyed so far.

> He turned the white-legged horse round the street corner, and sought one shining window from among those at the back of the house. Associated with it was a certain stately presence, a gloved hand, the remembrance how the feathers of a beautiful bird's wing had been showered down upon the floor, and how the light white down upon a robe had stirred and rustled, as in the rising of a distant storm. These were the things he carried with him as he turned away again, and rode through the darkening and deserted parks at a quick rate.[21]

Mr Carker in *Dombey and Son* (1846–8) is a keen observer of beauty, whose urge to possess it is an urge to humiliate and even to destroy, hence the suggestions of a bird 'winged' and of quivering prey. He is no idle dilettante, a type found elsewhere in Dickens, notably in the figure of Eugene Wrayburn in *Our Mutual Friend*, who is possessed by a similarly destructive obsession. Carker is as industrious as Dickens. The passage above is taken from a chapter that opens with an account of his evening employment before riding home:

> Frequently, when the clerks were all gone, the offices dark and empty, and all similar places of business shut up, Mr Carker, with the whole anatomy of the iron room laid bare before him, would explore the mysteries of books and papers, with the patient progress of a man who was dissecting the minutest nerves and fibres of his subject.[22]

When riding through the 'darkening and deserted parks', Carker is on his way to his villa in the 'green and wooded country' near Norwood, described in an earlier chapter, as 'of no pretensions as to size . . . beautifully arranged and tastefully kept . . . a house of refinement and luxury'.[23] A long, slow, silent tracking shot begins with the smooth slopes of the lawn, 'the graceful forms of ash and willow', the conservatory, the rustic veranda, and then takes us inside, noting the rich colours of walls and carpets, the 'choice prints and pictures too; in quaint nooks and recesses there is no want of books; and there are games of skill and chance set forth on tables – fantastic chess-men, dice, backgammon, cards and billiards.'[24] We should here imagine those laboriously intricate, white and pink-stained ivory chess pieces imported into Britain from India in the first decades of the nineteenth century.

> And yet amidst this opulence of comfort, there is something in the general air that is not well. Is it that the carpets and the cushions are too soft and noiseless, so that those who move or repose among them seem to act by stealth! Is it that the prints and pictures do not commemorate great thoughts or deeds, or render nature in the poetry of landscape, hall, or hut, but are of one voluptuous cast – mere shows of form and colour – and no more? Is it that the books have all their gold outside, and that the titles of the greater part qualify them to be companions of the prints and pictures? Is it that the completeness and the beauty of the place are here and there belied by an affectation of humility, in some unimportant and inexpensive regard, which is as false as the face of the too truly painted portrait hanging yonder, or its original at breakfast in his easy chair below it? Or is it that, with the daily breath of that original and master of all here, there issues forth some subtle portion of himself, which gives a vague expression of himself to everything about him?

It is Mr. Carker the Manager who sits in the easy chair. A gaudy parrot in a burnished cage upon the table tears at the wires with her beak, and goes walking, upside down, in its dome-top, shaking her house and screeching; but Mr. Carker is indifferent to the bird, and looks with a musing smile at a picture on the opposite wall.

'A most extraordinary accidental likeness, certainly', says he.

Perhaps it is a Juno; perhaps a Potiphar's Wife; perhaps some scornful Nymph – according as the picture dealers found the market, when they christened it. It is the figure of a woman, supremely handsome, who, turning away, but with her face addressed to the spectator, flashes her proud glance upon him.

It is like Edith.

With a passing gesture of his hand at the picture – what! a menace? No; yet something like it. A wave as of triumph? No; yet more like that. An insolent salute wafted from his lips? No; yet like that too – he resumes his breakfast, and calls to the chafing and imprisoned bird, who coming down into a pendant gilded hoop within the cage, like a great wedding-ring, swings in it, for his delight.[25]

No dwelling place in any novel by Dickens is so emphatically a work of art, yet is also the den of an anatomist and voluptuary who, whether 'dissecting the minutest nerves and fibres' or relishing the recollection of female haberdashery, is an enemy of the human heart. We are to link Carker with his good taste to 'canker', 'carcass' and 'incarceration'. It is not hard to imagine the paintings of a 'voluptuous cast' – there was much of this description produced in the decades immediately before the publication of this novel: William Etty's female nudes in rich Venetian settings come most easily to mind, and the 'gaudy parrot' also suggests the flashy paintings by Thomas Lawrence's followers.

The literary devices suggest both Dickens's attachment to popular melodrama and his increasing interest in complex poetic meaning. Thus the use of the portrait as surrogate and (prospective) trophy is familiar from fairy stories and horror films. However, Dickens not only expects his readers to know how absurdly varied were the titles assigned to pictures by dealers and auctioneers, but also to know what he had surely noticed in Italian palaces, how similar old paintings of women might be portraits, historical figures or allegories, or more than one thing – a portrait of a woman, as Cleopatra, say, or as a saint or a virtue. The three identities here correspond to the fluctuating fantasies directed at the socially exalted, at the wife of his employer and at a woman who disdains his advances. Parrots had been a common enough prop in female portraiture for several centuries and were still in favour (Maclise had exhibited a portrait of a woman with a parrot at the Royal Academy in 1844[26]). But here woman and parrot are separated and parallel: one in a cage, the other an effigy in captivity. Carker's brief soliloquy is about as subtle as the text that spells out the villain's thoughts in a silent film, but the ominous and metaphorical status accorded to the gilded hoop, on which the camera settles and focuses, more than makes up for that crude redundancy.

The next passage comes from *Bleak House*, which appeared between March 1852 and September 1853. It describes the London house of Sir Leicester Dedlock, Baronet. It is as comfortable within as it is dreary – that is, plain and Georgian – without.

> As warm and bright as so much state may be, as delicately redolent of pleasant scents that bear no trace of winter as hothouse flowers can make it; soft and hushed, so that the ticking of the clocks and the crisp burning of the fires alone disturb the stillness in the rooms; it seems to wrap those chilled bones of Sir Leicester's in rainbow-coloured wool. And Sir Leicester is glad to repose in dignified contentment before the great fire in the library, condescendingly perusing the backs of his books, or honouring the fine arts with a glance of approbation. For he has his pictures, ancient and modern. Some, of the Fancy Ball School in which Art occasionally condescends to become a master, which would be best catalogued like the miscellaneous articles in a sale. As, 'Three high-backed chairs, a table and cover, long-necked bottle (containing wine), one flask, one Spanish female's costume, three-quarter face portrait of Miss Jogg the model, and a suit of armour containing Don Quixote.' Or, 'One stone terrace (cracked), one gondola in distance, one Venetian senator's dress complete, richly embroidered white satin costume with profile portrait of Miss Jogg the model, one Scimitar superbly mounted in gold with jewelled handle, elaborate Moorish dress (very rare), and Othello.'
>
> Mr Tulkinghorn comes and goes pretty often; there being estate business to do, leases to be renewed, and so on. He sees my Lady pretty often, too; and he and she are as composed, and as indifferent, and take as little heed of one another, as ever. Yet it may be that my Lady fears this Mr Tulkinghorn, and that he knows it. It may be that he pursues her doggedly and steadily, with no touch of compunction, remorse, or pity. It may be that her beauty, and all the state and brilliancy surrounding her, only gives him the greater zest for what he is set upon, and makes him the more inflexible in it. Whether he be cold and cruel, whether immovable in what he has made his duty, whether absorbed in love of power, whether determined to have nothing hidden from him in ground where he has burrowed among secrets all his life, whether he in his heart despises the splendour of which he is a distant beam, whether he is always treasuring up slights and offences in the affability of his gorgeous clients – whether he be any of this, or all of this, it may be that my Lady had better have five thousand pairs of fashionable eyes upon her, in distrustful vigilance,

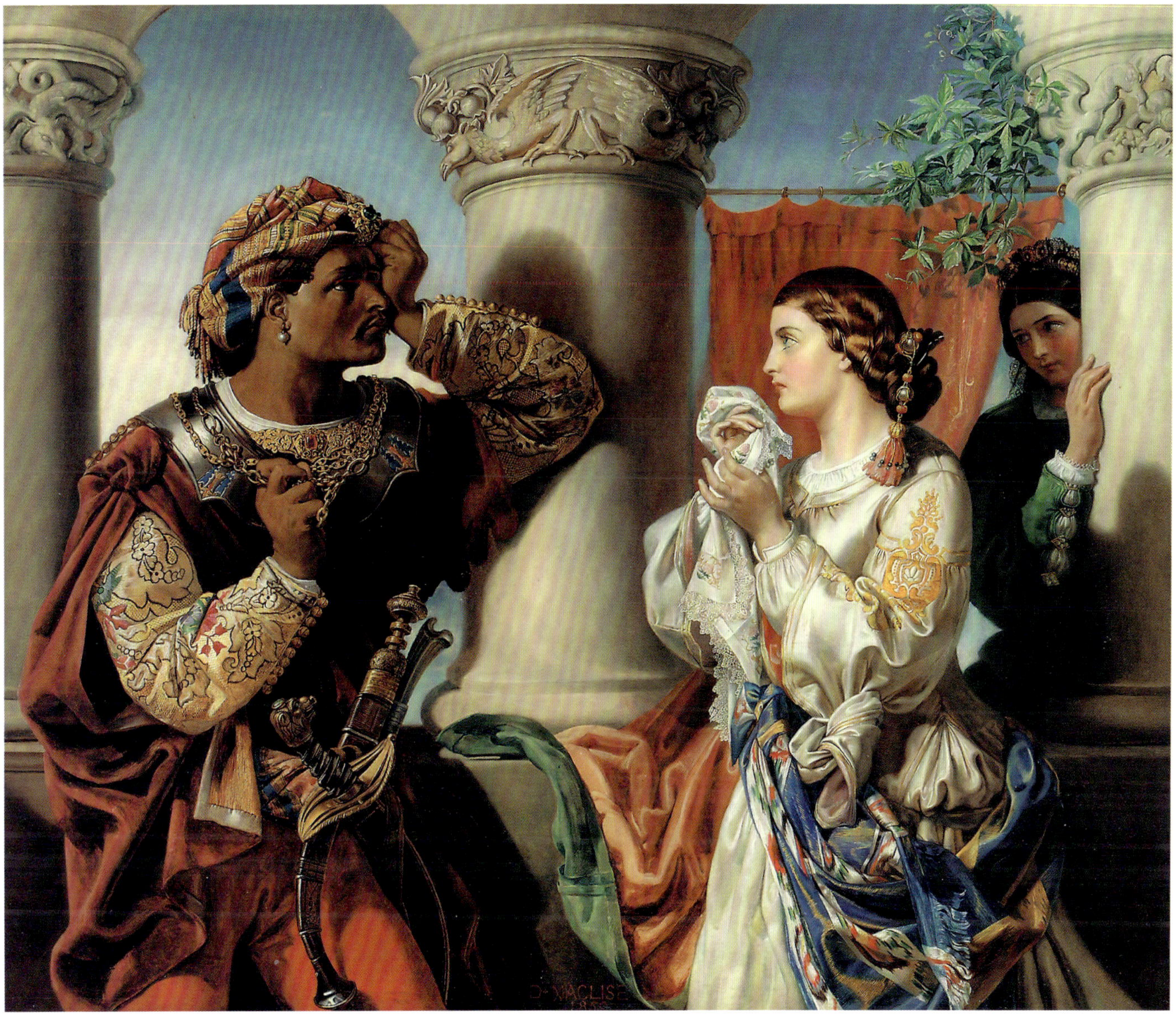

FIG. 20
Daniel Maclise, *Othello and Desdemona*, 1867, oil on panel. Private collection

than the two eyes of this rusty lawyer with his wisp of neckcloth and his dull black breeches tied with ribbons at the knees.[27]

To the hasty reader the description of Sir Leicester's paintings may seem like a gratuitous diversion, satirizing an aspect of contemporary painting. One wonders how well it was received by his friends – by Maclise, for example, who painted an *Othello and Desdemona* (slightly later, however; fig. 20), and especially by Charles Robert Leslie (who had supplied the frontispiece for a cheap edition of the *Pickwick Papers* in 1847). Leslie had on several occasions taken subjects from Cervantes (one example of which had found its way into the National Gallery[28]). But the subjects of the paintings (like those of the paintings within Hogarth's paintings) are carefully selected. For Sir Leicester is a man blinded by antiquated ideals, a Don Quixote of sorts, and he is also blind, as Othello was blind, to the fact that a subordinate of his is working to destroy his marriage.

Dickens slows down the narrative pace, enumerating the comforts accessible to Sir Leicester's ponderous mind, before moving rapidly to other parts of the house and tracing Sir Leicester's lawyer, the villain of a real modern tragedy, whose attire – 'dull black breeches tied with ribbons at the knees' – is old-fashioned but not fancy dress. The author's urgent, repetitive probing at the villain's motives (the device recalls the attempts to define Carker's gesture) contrasts sharply with the superficial priorities of the painters.

The pretensions of artists who would place themselves on a par with Cervantes and Shakespeare are punctured by reducing their productions to the accessories that litter their studios, and the suggestion is also made that paintings themselves are furniture, a sort of comforting commodity – wall ornaments for the affluent – that, together with fine bindings (a point of connection with Carker's suburban villa), can be contemplated with complacency. And of course it is true that paintings, even great paintings, may not only hang in the home of a Sir Leicester but be made with such a consumer in mind. The pleasures they provide are indeed less consistently exalted than those available from poetry or music that cannot be possessed.

The third interior is that of Bleak House itself, the home of the virtuous Mr Jarndyce, and is described in the words of his ward Esther Summerson, with laborious syntax mimicking her first exploration of it.

> It was one of those delightfully irregular houses where you go up and down steps out of one room into another, and where you come upon more rooms when you think you have seen all there are, and where there is a bountiful provision of little halls and passages, and where you find still older cottage-rooms in unexpected places, with lattice windows and green growth pressing through them. Mine, which we entered first, was of this kind, with an up-and-down roof, that had more corners in it than I ever counted afterwards, and a chimney (there was a wood fire on the hearth) paved all around with pure white tiles, in every one of which a bright miniature of the fire was blazing. Out of this room, you went down two steps, into a charming little sitting-room, looking down upon a flower-garden, which room was henceforth to belong to Ada and me. Out of this you went up three steps, into Ada's bedroom, which had a fine broad window, commanding a beautiful view (we saw a great expanse of darkness lying underneath the stars), to which there was a hollow window-seat, in which, with a spring-lock, three dear Adas might have been lost at once. Out of this room, you passed into a little gallery, with which the other best rooms (only two) communicated, and so, by a little staircase of shallow

> steps, with a number of corner stairs in it, considering its length, down into the hall. But if, instead of going out at Ada's door; you came back into my room, and went out at the door by which you had entered it, and turned up a few crooked steps that branched off in an unexpected manner from the stairs, you lost yourself in passages, with mangles in them, and three-cornered tables, and a Native-Hindoo chair, which was also a sofa, a box, and a bedstead, and looked, in every form, something between a bamboo skeleton and a great bird-cage, and had been brought from India nobody knew by whom or when.[29]

This perfectly captures a child's breathless marvelling at the size, complexity and history of a country house – perhaps in reality not very large. Scale, distance and time are indeed almost as confused here as in *Alice in Wonderland*: the window seat that might swallow a little girl, the puzzling oriental object stranded among mangles, the multiplied miniature reflections of a fire, the great expanse of starlit sky.

Mr Jarndyce lives in neither a grand old mansion nor a showy new one, but in a comfortable, rambling, picturesque but spotlessly clean home, united of course with nature. As for the art to be seen there:

> Our sitting-room was green; and had, framed and glazed, upon the walls, numbers of surprising and surprised birds, staring out of pictures at a real trout in a case, as brown and shining as if it had been served with gravy; at the death of Captain Cook; and at the whole process of preparing tea in China, as depicted by Chinese artists. In my room there were oval engravings of the months – ladies haymaking in short waists, and large hats tied under the chin, for June – smooth-legged noblemen, pointing, with cocked-hats, to village steeples, for October. Half-length portraits, in crayons, abounded all through the house; but were so dispersed that I found the brother of a youthful officer of mine in the china-closet, and the grey old age of my pretty young bride, with a flower in her bodice, in the breakfast room. As substitutes, I had four angels, of Queen Anne's reign, taking a complacent gentleman to heaven, in festoons, with some difficulty; and a composition in needle-work, representing fruit, a kettle, and an alphabet.[30]

Dickens delighted in the incongruous medley of objects that might be found in sale-rooms or in antique shops, also in the often banal if poignant decor of the fairly recent past (the home of Mrs Whimple in *Great Expectations* is an example, and Captain Cook is found dying there as well), but this is entirely plausible as an inventory of the relics of 'olden times' mingled with cast-offs of the previous generation or so, which would then have been found in a country house.

Half a century later prints of pastoral subjects after Stubbs and pastel portraits by John Russell were to become collector's items, as would, soon after, quaint seventeenth-century needlework samplers and, in due course, Chinese export paintings. The 'surprising and surprised birds' may even have been plates by Audubon, then regarded primarily as records of natural history, like the stuffed fish, although that was also a trophy. What is important to notice is that the charitable, lovable and emphatically chaste Mr Jarndyce not only sleeps in a very simple bedroom, with the window open all the year round (and with a cold bath at the ready), but lives without the visual arts, or rather with art that has no strong aesthetic appeal, only charming, quaint, curious things acquired by others and retained out of family sentiment or genial indifference.

Virtue in Dickens comes in many forms, of course, and when Bella Rokesmith, towards the end of *Our Mutual Friend*, is conducted by her husband to the magically transformed Boffin mansion, she finds the whole staircase 'tastefully ornamented' with flowers and then enters an indoor garden with an aviary full of exotic birds 'more gorgeous in colour than the flowers'. There are also 'gold and silver fish, and mosses, and water lilies and a fountain'.[31] *Our Mutual Friend* was published between 1864 and 1865. Textile patterns were still highly horticultural; ferns – real, carved and cast – proliferated inside as well as outside; and glass domes protecting stuffed humming birds had become popular. But it is striking that no work of art is mentioned here, except for an ivory jewel casket. Eventually, Bella reaches the nursery. The original illustration by Marcus Stone includes in this sacred place a Parian Ware statuette reclining on a slender rococo chimney piece with an exotic landscape behind. But the text avoids all specificity and merely describes it as 'garnished as with rainbows' – the focus is softened so that this too seems like nature rather than art.[32] The fine arts, including contemporary painting, are associated with heartless sensuality or complacent affluence, whereas nature alone is deemed worthy of supplying a setting for virtue, even when it inherits great wealth.

Whatever these passages reveal about Dickens's attitude to the visual arts, it is also striking how his descriptive techniques anticipate the cinema, the great popular visual art form of the twentieth century. It is also surely true that his imagery could be much more complex and subtle in allusion and suggestion than can have suited the mass readership (and audience) he secured. But that is surely also true of both *Don Giovanni* and *Hamlet*.

NOTES

1. *Nicholas Nickleby*, ch. 10, para 12.
2. *Nicholas Nickleby*, ch. 28, paras 6–9.
3. William Makepeace Thackeray, *The Works of William Makepeace Thackeray*, vol. 7: *Burlesques* (New Century Library; London, 1900), p. 21. 'Codlingsby' was first published as part of 'Punch's Prize Novelists' in *Punch*, 3 April – 9 October 1847, which was reprinted as *Novels by Eminent Hands* in Thackeray's *Miscellanies: Prose and Verse*, vol. 2 (London, 1856). The passage in question comes from para 2, 'Chapter XXIV', part III.
4. Dickens 1846, p. 91. All these passages are fully discussed in Leonée Ormond, 'Dickens and Painting: The Old Masters', *Dickensian*, vol. 79 (1983), pp. 130–51.
5. Dickens 1846, p. 187.
6. *Household Words*, 13 September 1856, vol. 14, no. 338, p. 193.
7. Ibid., p. 195.
8. Ibid., p. 194.
9. Ibid., p. 197.
10. Wilkie Collins, *Memoirs of the Life of William Collins, Esq., R.A.* (2 vols; London, 1848), vol. 1, pp. 296–7 (letter to Sir David Wilkie, 17 April 1828). See also the note on p. 296.
11. Dickens 1846, pp. 135, 208.
12. Wilkie Collins, *Woman in White*, as published in *All The Year Round*, 21 April 1860, pp. 26–7.
13. *All The Year Round*, 26 May 1860, pp. 163–8.
14. *All the Year Round*, 16/23 June 1860, p. 257.
15. Ibid.
16. Ibid.
17. *All the Year Round*, 16/23 June 1860, p. 258.
18. *Journalism*, vol. 2, p. 77.
19. Dickens 1846, pp. 185, 186.
20. *All the Year Round*, 23 June 1860, p. 256.
21. *Dombey and Son*, ch. 46, 5th para from close.
22. *Dombey and Son*, ch. 46, para 1.
23. *Dombey and Son*, ch. 33, para 2.
24. Ibid.
25. *Dombey and Son*, ch. 33, paras 2–7.
26. Daniel Maclise, *Girl with a Parrot*, 1844, oil on canvas (RA no. 165).
27. *Bleak House*, ch. 29, paras 2 and 3.
28. Leslie exhibited subjects from *Don Quixote* at the Royal Academy in 1844 (no. 351), 1849 (no. 141) and 1855 (no. 95; one painting formerly in the National Gallery, *Sancho Panza in the Apartment of the Duchess*, 1843–4, is now in Tate Britain).
29. *Bleak House*, ch. 7, para 46.
30. *Bleak House*, ch. 7, para 47.
31. *Our Mutual Friend*, Book 4, ch. 11, 10th and 7th paras from close.
32. *Our Mutual Friend*, Book 4, ch. 12, 11th paras from close.

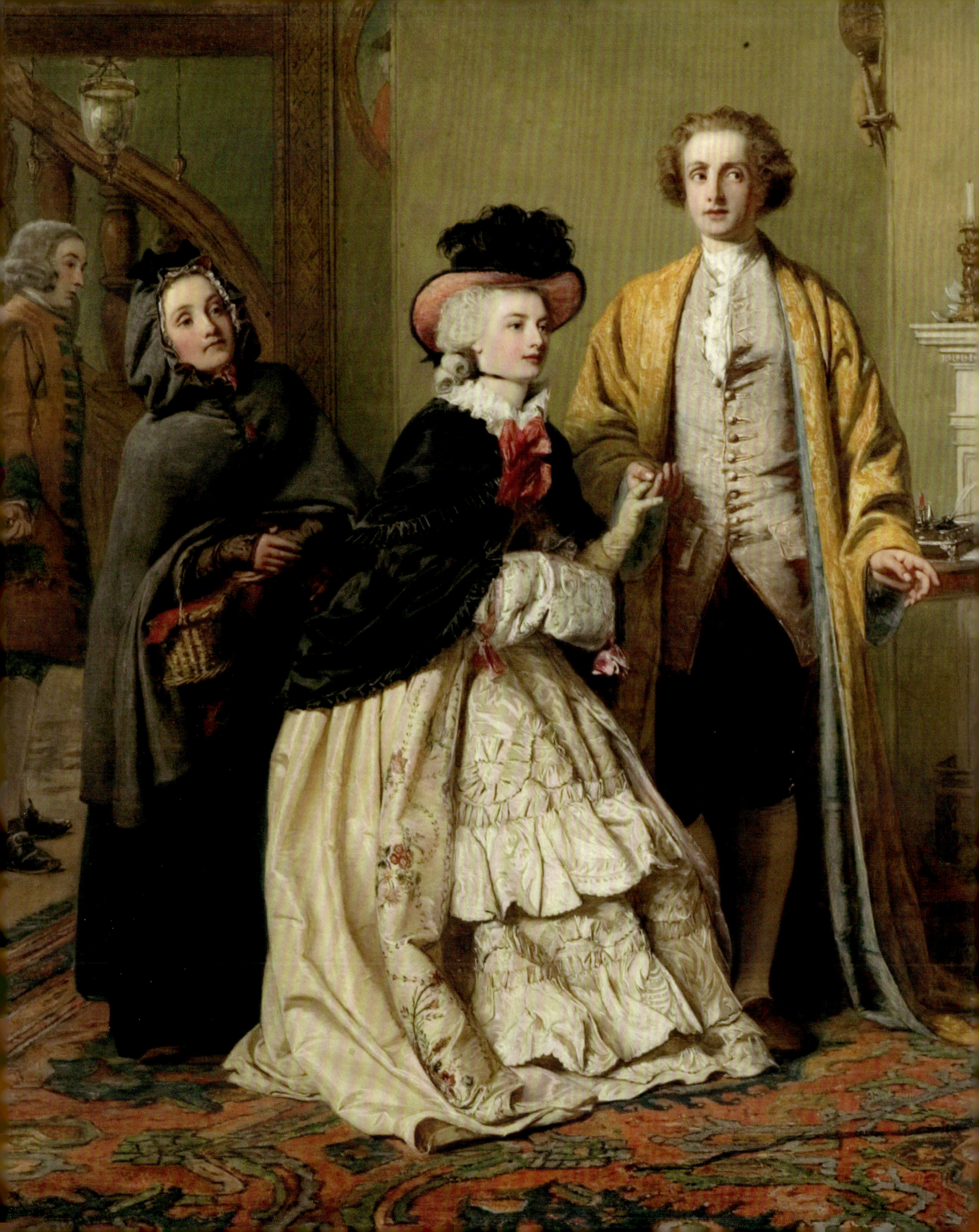

Dickens AND CONTEMPORARY ART

LEONÉE ORMOND

We do not know exactly when Charles Dickens first visited the annual exhibition of the Royal Academy. Before 1837 this took place at Somerset House. Then for the next thirty years the Academy shared the National Gallery's building in Trafalgar Square, before moving to its present premises in Burlington House. Dickens certainly knew the Academy by 1834 when he wrote in *Sketches by Boz* of a shopkeeper, 'who, in his large white neckcloth and formal tie, looked like a bad "portrait of a gentleman" in the Somerset House exhibition'.[1] Miss La Creevy, the artist character in *Nicholas Nickleby*, published five years later, gives a jaundiced account of a typical display of portraits:

> Look at the Royal Academy! All those beautiful shiny portraits of gentlemen in black velvet waistcoats, with their fists doubled up on round tables, or marble slabs, are serious, you know; and all the ladies who are playing with little parasols, or little dogs, or little children – it's the same rule in art, only varying the objects – are smirking.[2]

According to the actor William Macready, Dickens was annoyed that William Makepeace Thackeray had been invited to the Royal Academy banquet in 1840 when he had not. A year later, he encouraged the painter Daniel Maclise, recently elected a full member of the Royal Academy, to procure an invitation for him, only in order to turn it down. Dickens's wife Catherine attended the private view in that year, but Dickens was not with her. Writing to his friend John Forster on 3 May 1841, Dickens explained that he was unable to attend the exhibition with him, describing the Academy, not entirely seriously, as 'that hallowed spot on which the eyes of Europe and the beating hearts of the civilised world are unalterably fixed'.[3] Dickens is satirically describing the opening of the Summer Exhibition, which became synonymous with the start of the fashionable London season.

Five years later, we find Dickens attending the opening of the exhibition with Macready, both being guests at the annual banquet. It was at this time, in the 1840s, that many of Dickens's views on contemporary art were formed. One artist had, however,

FIG. 21
William Powell Frith,
Mr Honeywood Introduces the Bailiffs to Miss Richland as his Friends (detail of fig. 36)

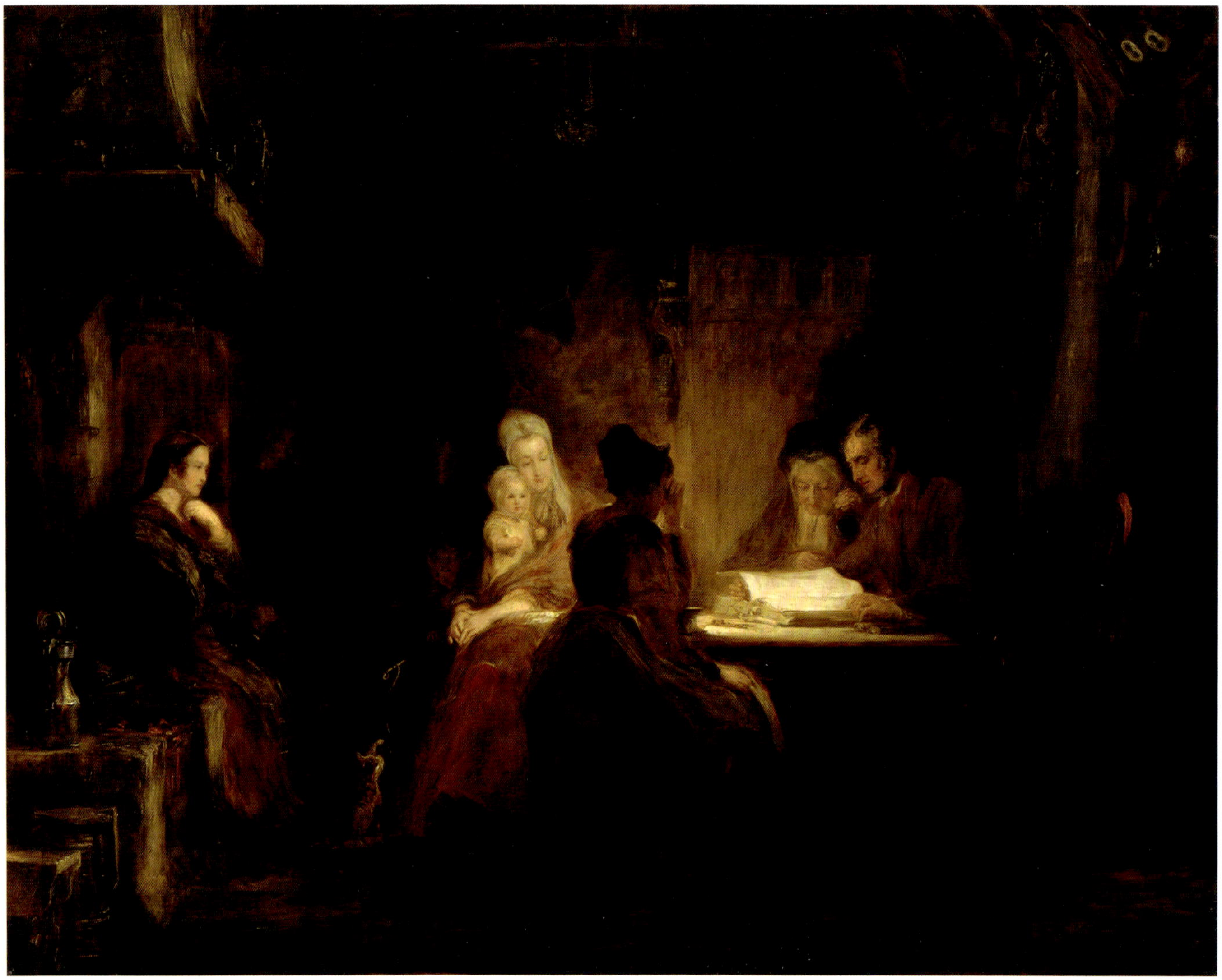

FIG. 22
David Wilkie, *The Cotter's Saturday Night*, 1837, oil on panel. Glasgow Museums

already exercised a considerable effect on his approach to painting. This was the Scottish painter Sir David Wilkie, with whom Dickens had become friendly in the mid-1830s. Dickens's daughter Kate Perugini says that Wilkie was the first artist whom her father knew 'intimately', speaking of him as 'a typical Scotchman of the yellowish red-haired type – very bony and very angular'.[4] Both Dickens and Wilkie, in their respective arts, sought to achieve a genuinely popular style in order to express human emotion. In a speech given after Wilkie's death in 1840, Dickens presents him as a painter who had abandoned the reverence for the antique, characteristic of the eighteenth century, for the representation of the scenes of his own day.

> I think of him as one . . . who has left behind him unwonted fire, who has left an undying and imperishable name, who made the cottage hearth his grave

theme, and who surrounded the lives, and cares, and daily toils, and occupations of the poor, with dignity and beauty: who indeed found 'books in the running brooks, sermons in stones, and good in everything'.[5]

Wilkie was much influenced by the work of Dutch artists of the seventeenth century, and in his fiction Dickens refers directly or indirectly to Dutch genre paintings, often when he creates interior scenes lit by fires and candles. In *David Copperfield*, for example, describing a cabin on the boat that will take the Micawber family to Australia, he evokes the atmosphere through the eyes of the first-person narrator. David looks into the darkness and, 'as my eyes became more accustomed to the gloom . . . I seemed to stand in a picture by OSTADE'.[6]

Wilkie gave Kate Dickens a drawing of a mother and child, a sketch for his painting *The Cotter's Saturday Night* (fig. 22). This hung in her husband's bedroom at Devonshire Terrace and remained in his possession after his separation from his wife. Two engravings by Wilkie were also in Dickens's collection, one of them from *The Rent Day* (1809; private collection) and the other from *The Reading of a Will* (1820; Neue Pinakothek, Munich). Such crowded and dramatic scenes evidently appealed to the novelist, who preferred Wilkie's early genre paintings to the historical works on which the artist was engaged at the time of their friendship. He admired Wilkie both as a man and as a painter, and the respect was mutual. The novelist was a quarter of a century younger than the painter, but at the Nickleby dinner of 1839 Wilkie gave a moving tribute to his friend, speaking of 'the reality of Dickens's genius, and how there had been nothing like him issuing his novels by part since Richardson issued his novels volume by volume, and how in both cases people talked about the characters as if they were next-door neighbours or friends'.[7]

At much the same time Dickens formed a friendship with another artist, Clarkson Stanfield. Like Wilkie, Stanfield, born in 1793, was some years older than Dickens. As a younger man he had been a sailor, both on merchant ships and in the Royal Navy. Much of Stanfield's work was in the theatre, where he was a successful scene painter, but by the time of his meeting with Dickens, he had also built up a considerable reputation as a landscapist and marine artist and had been elected to full membership of the Royal Academy in 1835. 'Stanny', as Dickens called him, became one of the novelist's closest friends. Pieter van der Merwe explains: 'Despite, or more probably because of, the differences in their ages, gifts and temperaments, the novelist found in Stanfield's undemanding company, open simplicity and general good humour, a temporary relief from the problems generated by his own far more complex personality and relationships.'[8]

Stanfield enjoyed the exuberance of the Dickens circle and was an 'imperturbable foil to its more mercurial temperaments'.[9] At the time of the painter's death in 1867, Dickens told Stanfield's son: 'No one of your father's friends can ever have loved him more dearly than I always did, or can have better known the worth of his noble character.'[10]

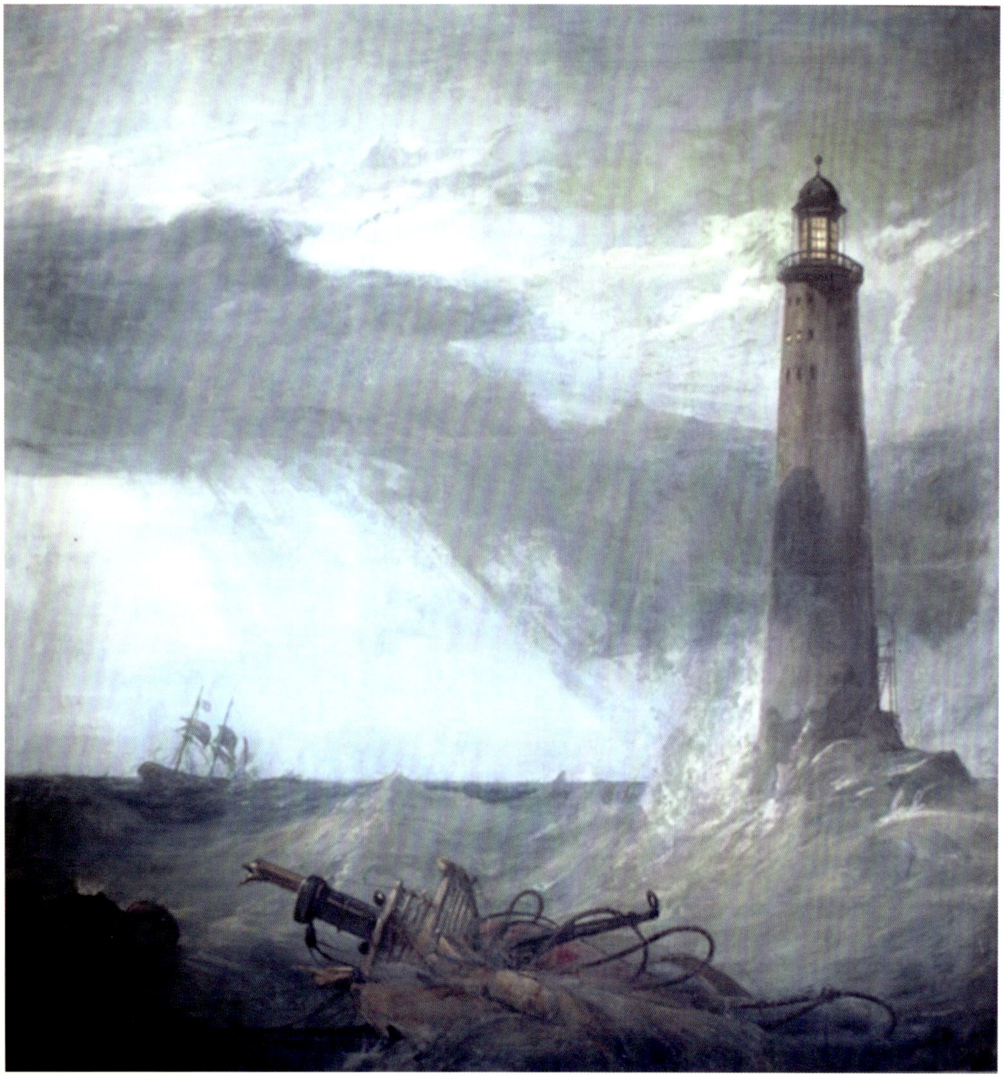

FIG. 23
Clarkson Stanfield, *Eddystone Lighthouse against a Stormy Sea*, *c.*1850, watercolour. Charles Dickens Museum, London

Writing to Dickens at the same time, Stanfield's widow assured him that he was the one among Stanfield's friends whom 'he most affectionately loved and to the last'.[11]

Stanfield was closely involved with the amateur theatrical performances organized by Dickens. He was to have taken a part in the production of *Every Man in his Humour* (1598) by Ben Jonson in 1845 but gave it up to concentrate on the staging. In 1851 he contributed one scene to the performance of Edward Bulwer-Lytton's *Not so Bad as We Seem*. The backdrops painted for *The Lighthouse* by Wilkie Collins, staged at Dickens's home in Tavistock House, London, in 1855, were Stanfield's most important contribution to the theatricals. Warned that his health would suffer if he painted large pictures, Stanfield disobeyed the advice and provided two works, the scene in the interior of the lighthouse and a panorama showing the Eddystone Lighthouse against a stormy sea, now in the Charles Dickens Museum, London (fig. 23). It is said to have

FIG. 24
Clarkson Stanfield, *Logan Rock with Dickens, Stanfield, Maclise and Forster*, 1842, watercolour and body colour on brown paper. Victoria and Albert Museum, London

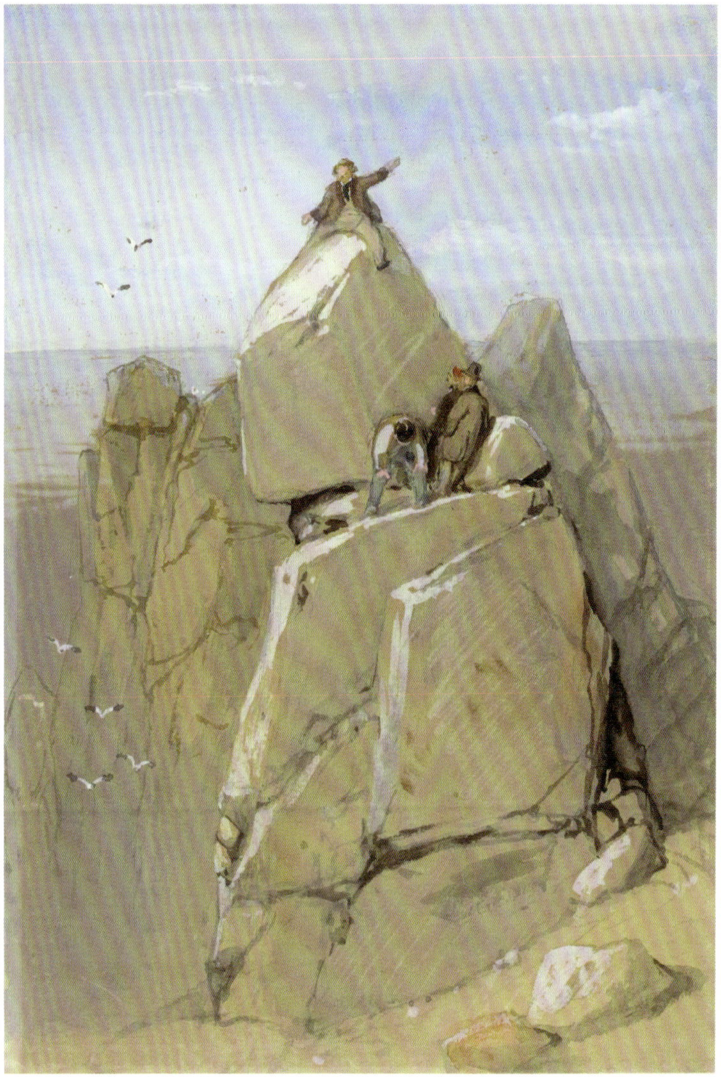

been Stanfield who persuaded Dickens to include the Eddystone Lighthouse scene, 'with a raging sea and a transparent light. He enters into the project with the greatest delight, and I think we shall make a capital thing of it'.[12] The artist's last backdrops for Dickens came in 1857 when he painted two sets for *The Frozen Deep* by Wilkie Collins (revised by Dickens), 'A Cavern on the Coast of Newfoundland' and 'A Hut in the Arctic Regions'. Dickens kept the central sections of both works for his own collection, but they are at present untraced.

As well as their theatrical collaboration, Stanfield also contributed illustrations for Dickens's Christmas books, two for *The Chimes* in 1844, one for *The Cricket on the Hearth* in 1845, three for *The Battle of Life* in 1846 and two for *The Haunted Man* in 1848. The frontispiece to the cheap edition of Dickens's *American Notes*, his recollections of his journey through America in 1842, is another work by Stanfield and showed *The S.S.*

Britannia at Liverpool Embarking Charles Dickens. Stanfield would have been the illustrator for *Pictures from Italy* of 1846, but having read part of the book, he found its anti-Catholic bias offended his own religious beliefs; he was a devout Roman Catholic.

Apart from the play sets that he owned, Dickens was also the possessor of a number of more intimate sketches by Stanfield of himself and his friends. In the autumn of 1842 Dickens, Stanfield, Daniel Maclise and John Forster took a holiday together in Cornwall, travelling around the countryside in an open coach. Dickens owned two watercolours by Stanfield that date from this journey. One shows *The Land's End* (private collection) and the other, which hung in the dining room at Gad's Hill, Higham, was *The Logan Rock* (fig. 24), depicting the four men on top of the rock, with Forster on the summit waving his arm. Thanking Stanfield, Dickens wrote of 'your most beautiful present, which I shall frame conspicuously and prize, most highly'.[13]

Dickens much admired Stanfield's easel work. On his way to Italy in 1844 he passed scenes that Stanfield had painted, telling him that, when he saw the bridge of Avignon, he thought that '[b]eautiful as it undoubtedly is, you made it fifty times better'.[14] Dickens was thinking of Stanfield's *Avignon on the Rhone* (untraced), shown at the Royal Academy in 1840. When he spoke at the Royal Academy dinner or wrote about the exhibitions, Dickens was careful to mention Stanfield's paintings. In 1853, for example, he referred to *HMS Victory Towed into Gibraltar* (*c.*1852; V&A), a scene after the Battle of Trafalgar with Nelson's flagship painted against the background of the Rock of Gibraltar. For Dickens this was 'the noble picture'.[15] Stanfield's best-known painting in his lifetime, *The Abandoned*, was exhibited in 1856 (now missing) and showed a wrecked ship tossed by the waves. The idea for the picture was drawn from 'The Voyage', a story published in 1819 by Washington Irving that dwells on concepts of despair and contemplates the anxiety of those waiting fruitlessly for the sailors' return. Dickens, like many others, thought the painting 'magnificent'.[16]

Dickens published an obituary for Stanfield in *All the Year Round* on 1 June 1867. There he spoke of his friend as 'the man famous in all countries for his marvellous rendering of the waves that break upon her [England's] shores, of her ships and seamen, of her coasts and skies, of her storms and sunshine, of the many marvels of the deep'. Turning to the personal, Dickens wrote: 'He was the soul of frankness, generosity, and simplicity. The most genial, the most affectionate, the most loving and the most lovable of men.'[17]

It was probably through Stanfield that Dickens met the artist's friend and sometime rival, David Roberts, known for his paintings of the landscapes, buildings and ruins of Europe and the Near East. Roberts, like Stanfield, had worked as a scene painter, and in 1851 he contributed an act drop for one of the Dickens productions, *Not so Bad as We Seem*. Roberts became a friend of the Dickens family and gave Dickens a small oil painting, *A Recollection of the Desert on the Approach of the Simoon* (fig. 25), a study of the Sphinx. The message on the back of the painting explains that it was presented 'as a mark of respect & admiration for his talent & work by his very sincere friend & admirer David Roberts R.A. Jany 1st 1850'. Dickens encountered Roberts in Rome in

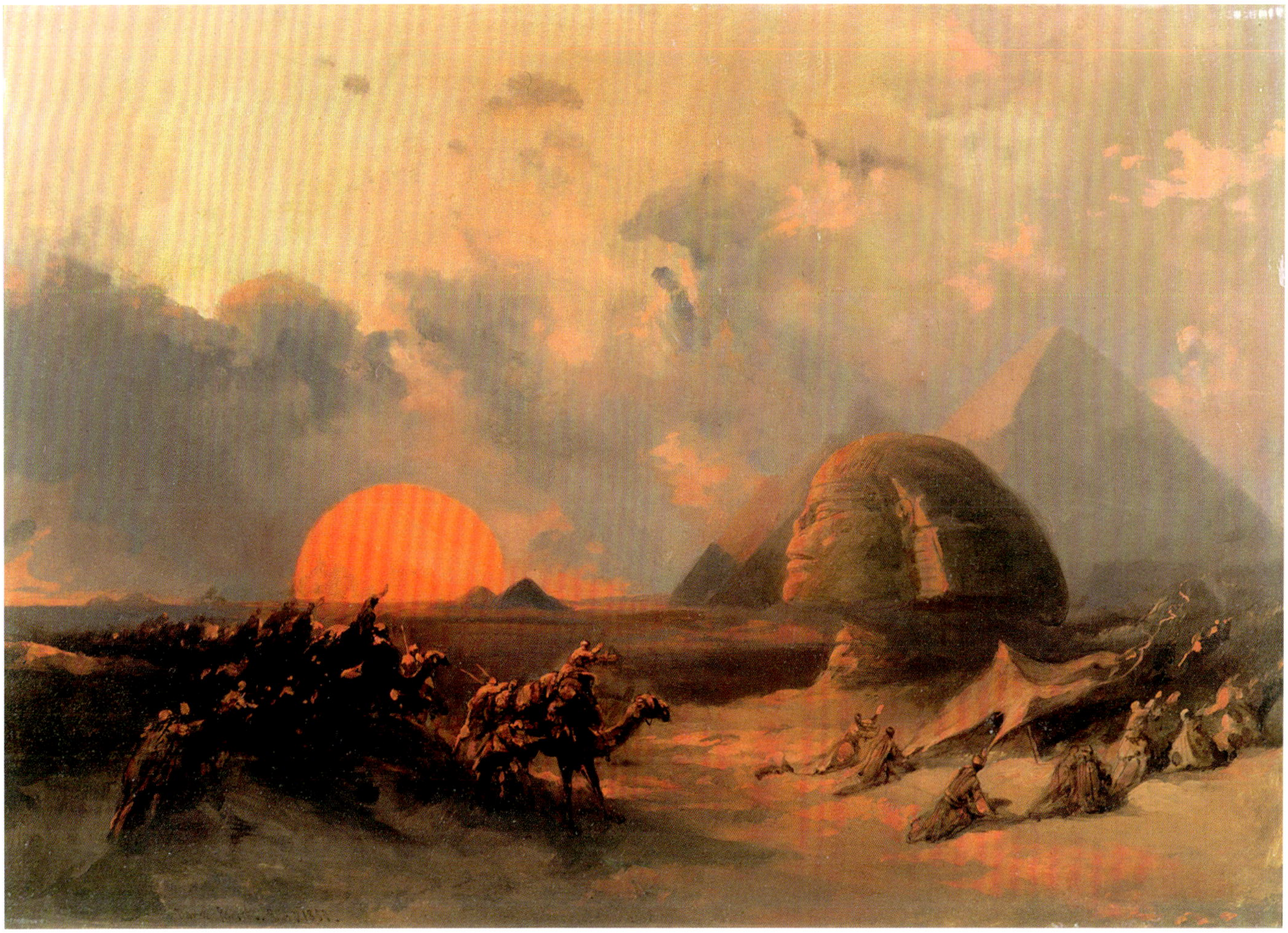

FIG. 25
David Roberts, *A Recollection of the Desert on the Approach of the Simoon*, 1842–9, oil on panel. Private collection

December 1853 when Dickens 'smoked and drank punch' with him. Roberts, Dickens reported, was then painting in St Peter's every day with Louis Haghe, the water-colourist and illustrator.[18]

Wilkie, Stanfield and Roberts were all older men than Dickens. The Irish artist Daniel Maclise, whom Dickens met in 1838, was in fact six years older than the novelist but pretended to be younger. Born in Cork in 1806, Maclise came to London in 1827 and was already a successful painter of historical and literary subjects when Dickens and he were introduced, probably by Harrison Ainsworth, in 1838. Maclise had been elected an associate of the Royal Academy in 1835 and became a full member in 1840. Dickens and Maclise, or 'Mac' as Dickens called him, spent a good deal of time together. One demonstration of the friendship was that Maclise, like Stanfield, contributed illustrations to the Christmas Books, in his case to *The Chimes* and *The Cricket on the Hearth*. There are even suggestions that Dickens took the name for the villainous Bill Sikes (originally spelt Sykes) in *Oliver Twist* from Sir Francis Sykes who had initiated an action (later abandoned) against Maclise, whom he accused of adultery with his wife.

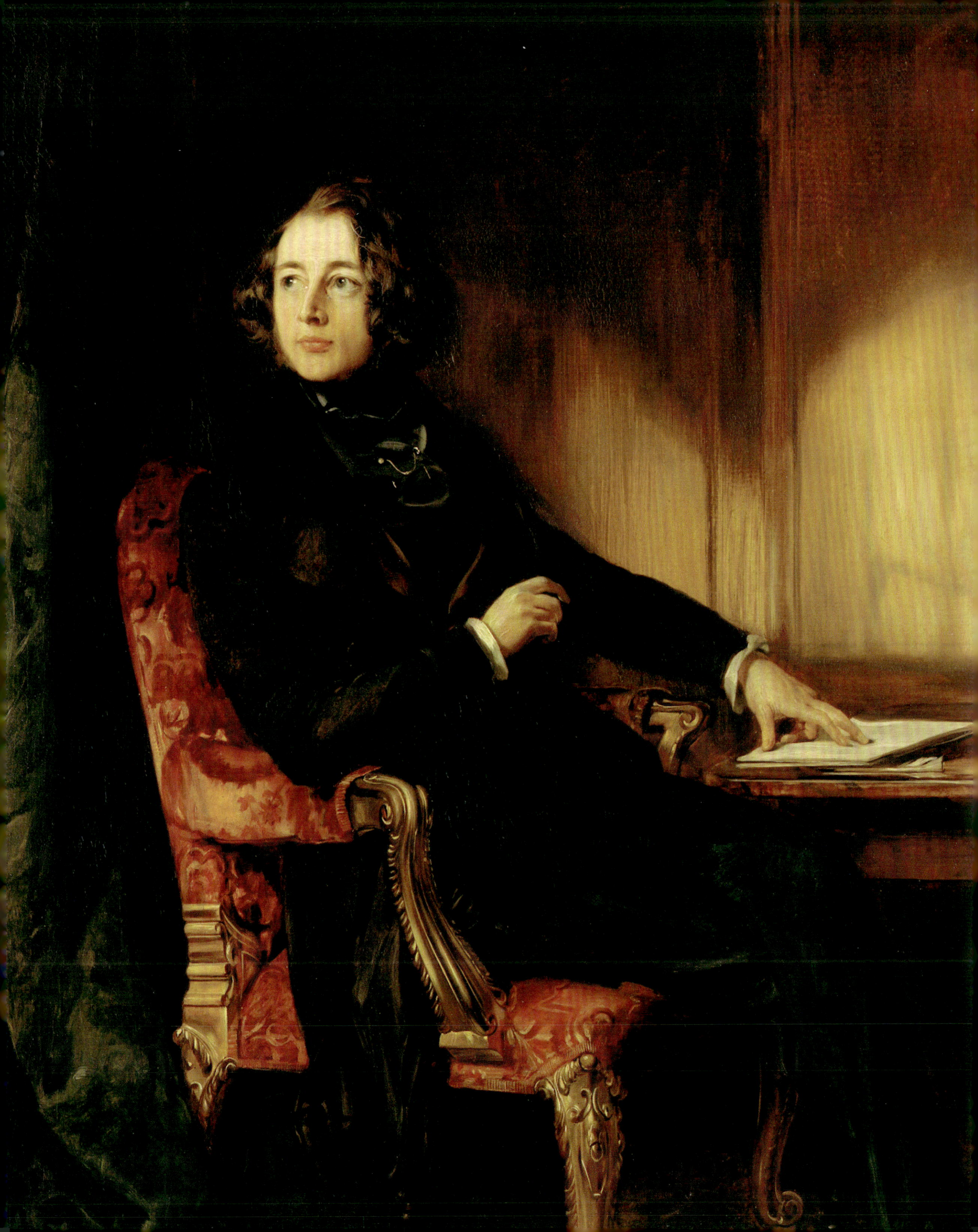

LEFT
FIG. 26
Daniel Maclise, *Charles Dickens* (detail of fig. 9)

RIGHT
FIG. 27
Daniel Maclise, *Dickens's Four Elder Children*, 1842, watercolour. Charles Dickens Museum, London

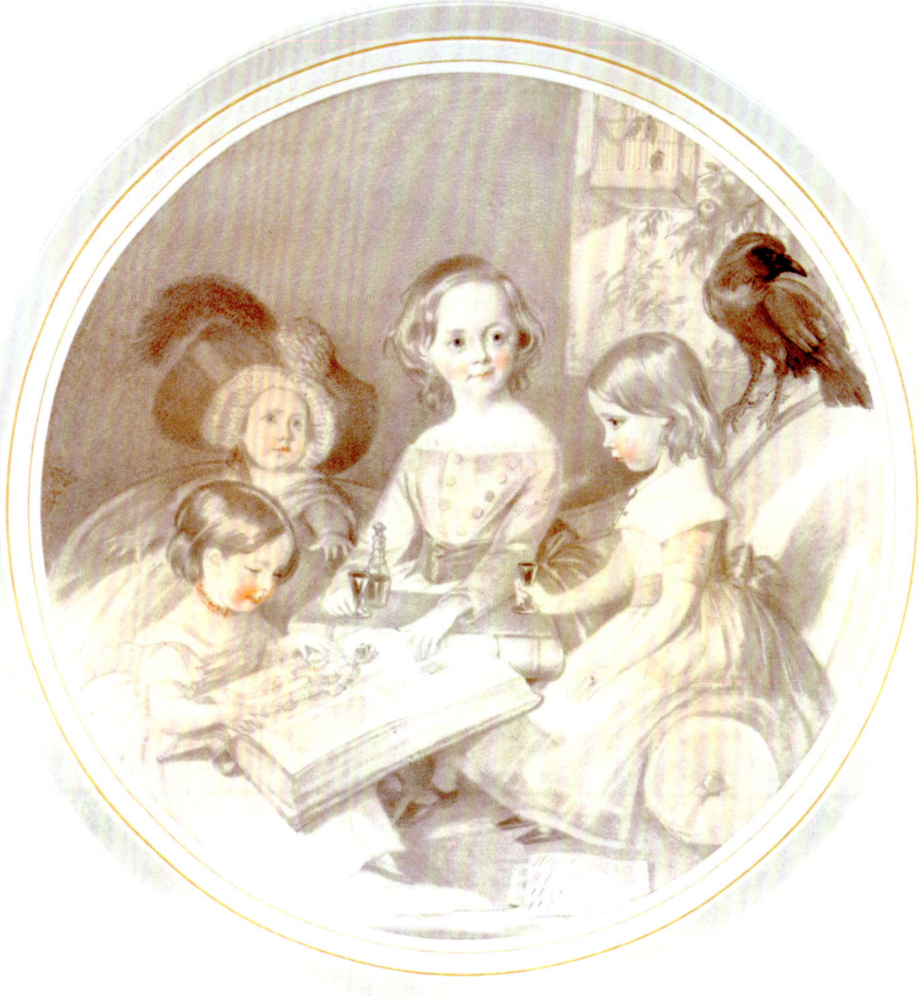

In 1839 Maclise painted what many regard as the finest portrait of Dickens, the 'Nickleby' portrait, now in the National Portrait Gallery (fig. 26). Commissioned by Dickens's publishers, Chapman and Hall, it was engraved as the frontispiece for the final episode of *Nicholas Nickleby*. It shows the novelist at his desk, his head turned to the light as though caught in a moment of inspiration. In June 1839 Dickens told a friend that 'Maclise has made another face of me, which all people say is astonishing'.[19] It seems likely that Maclise gave the painting to Dickens, although it has been argued that it was presented to him by Chapman and Hall.

Other Maclise portraits of the Dickens family include a painting of Catherine Dickens, dated 1846, at the Charles Dickens Museum in Holborn, and a watercolour of the four eldest Dickens children (fig. 27) painted for Catherine to take with her on

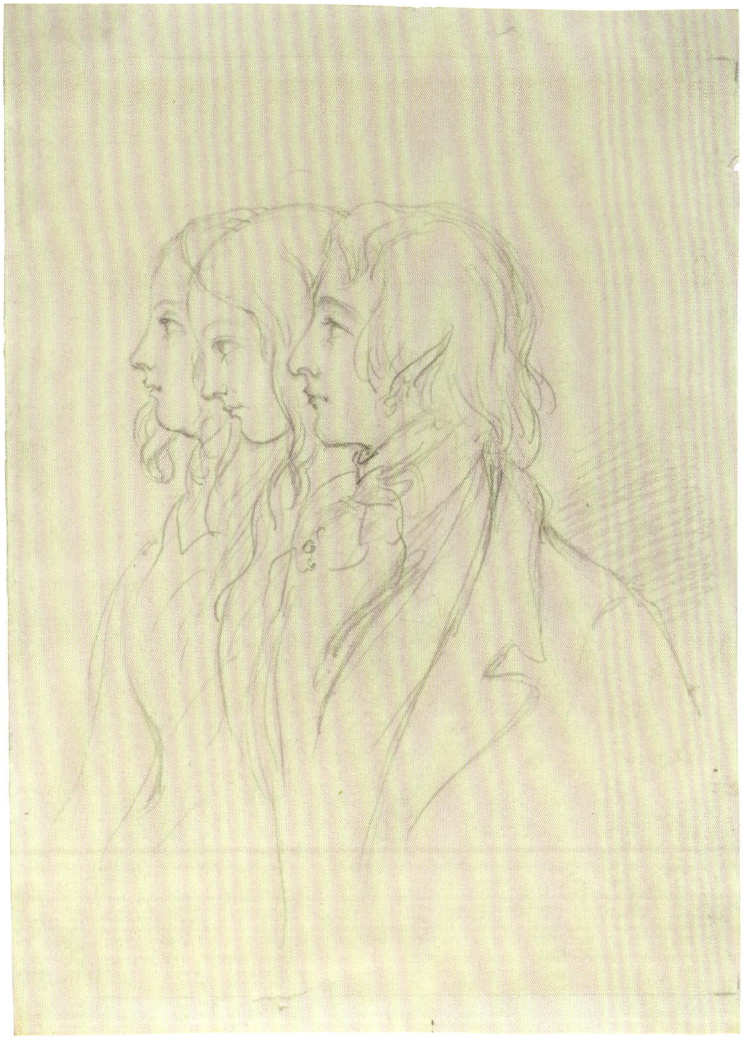

LEFT
FIG. 28
Daniel Maclise, *Charles Dickens, his wife, nee Catherine Thomson Hogarth, and his wife's sister Miss Georgina Hogarth*, 1843, graphite on paper. Victoria and Albert Museum, London

the American tour of 1842. A drawing of Dickens with Catherine and her sister Georgina Hogarth, dating from 1843, is in the Victoria and Albert Museum (fig. 28). Georgina Hogarth is also the model, posed as a maiden with a pitcher of water, for the painting *Waterfall at St Nighton's Kieve* (fig. 29), which Maclise worked up from drawings of the waterfall near Tintagel, sketched on the Cornish expedition of 1842. Dickens told the American writer C.C. Felton that Maclise and Stanfield 'made such sketches . . . in the most romantic of our halting-places, that you would have sworn we had the Spirit of Beauty with us, as well as the Spirit of Fun'.[20] Dickens bought the painting, and it is generally believed that he did so anonymously through a friend, believing that, if he made an open offer, Maclise would insist on giving it to him or 'set some preposterous price upon it, which he can by no means afford to take'.[21] Maclise was unable to attend the party when Dickens unveiled the picture and is said to have been put out when he discovered the truth.

RIGHT
FIG. 29
Daniel Maclise, *Waterfall at St Nighton's Kieve, near Tintagel in Cornwall*, 1842, oil on canvas. Victoria and Albert Museum, London

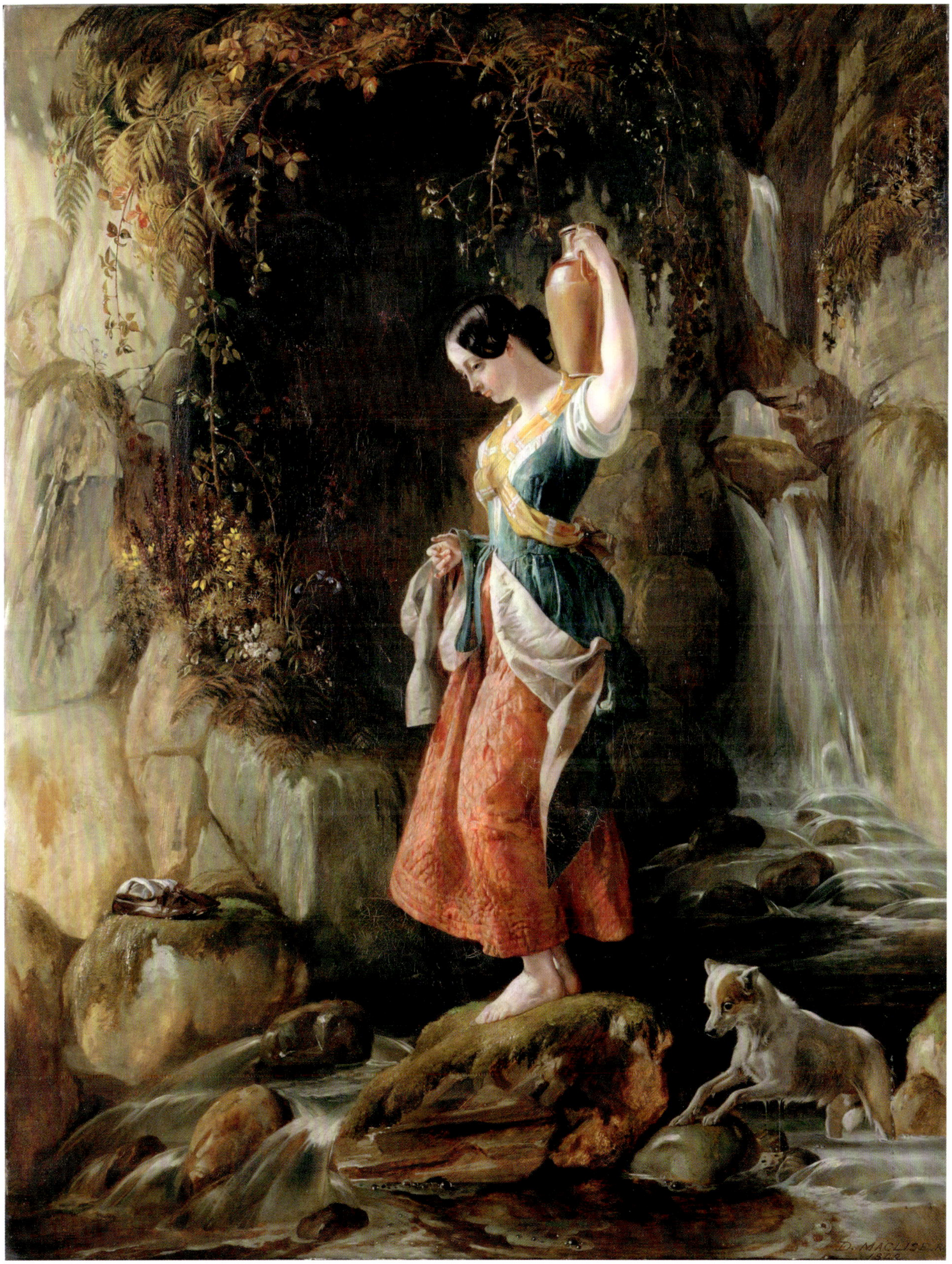

Unlike Thackeray, Dickens did not, on the whole, review art exhibitions, either in his journals or in those to which he contributed. However, the friendship with Maclise led to the publication of 'The Spirit of Chivalry in Westminster Hall' in *Douglas Jerrold's Shilling Magazine* in August 1845. Maclise had submitted designs to the competition for the decoration of the rebuilt Palace of Westminster. One was a projected fresco, *The Spirit of Chivalry* (fig. 30), where a female figure symbolizing chivalry is surrounded by representatives of medieval culture. Dickens liked the direct and universal appeal of the work and praised its nobility. He drew attention to the fact that

> ignorant, unlettered, drudging men, mere hewers and drawers, have gathered in a knot about it (as at our back a week ago), and read it, in their homely language, as it were a Book. In minds, the roughest and the most refined, it has alike found quick response; and will, and must, so long as it shall hold together.[22]

The completed fresco is now in the House of Lords.

Other Maclise paintings that Dickens is known to have admired include *The Serenade* of 1842 (Baylor University, Texas), a picture of a Venetian troubadour, which became the subject of a poem by Robert Browning, and *The Play Scene from Hamlet* of the same year (Tate). When Dickens saw *The Play Scene*, he told the artist that it was '*[w]onderful* . . . it amazed, even me'.[23] He thought it 'a *tremendous* production. There are things in it, which in their powerful thought, exceed anything I have ever beheld in painting'.[24]

Dickens and Maclise became partially estranged, for reasons that have never been entirely clear. One cause of complaint, on Dickens's side, was that Maclise was not always prepared to drop everything and do as Dickens demanded. In November 1840, for example, Dickens invited Maclise to join him for 'a great, London, back-slums kind of walk tonight, seeking adventures in knight errant style'.[25] Maclise found the sights and smells of crowded dwellings and of impoverished people more than he could bear and retired feeling ill. Dickens disparaged the evenings that Maclise spent at the Royal Academy and failed to understand the professional duties of an Academician. For him the Academy, which meant so much to Maclise, was 'the water bottle'.[26] Dickens started to describe Maclise as a 'discursive' and 'eccentric' painter and even suggested that Maclise's work had become hard, blaming the painter's long sight, which 'deprived any distant object he looked at of the mystery and charm which often add so much beauty to a world seen through more short-sighted eyes'.[27] Maclise was not interested in taking part in the Dickens theatricals, although he did paint John Forster dressed for his role as Kitely in the performance of *Every Man in his Humour*. Maclise's biographer, Nancy Weston, argues that Dickens also disparaged Maclise as an Irishman. Dickens destroyed the letters sent to him by Maclise after the artist's death, claiming that Maclise, like Dickens himself, would have wished private things to remain private, so that it is not possible to chart their gradual estrangement.

FIG. 30
Daniel Maclise, *The Spirit of Chivalry* (detail of fig. 14)

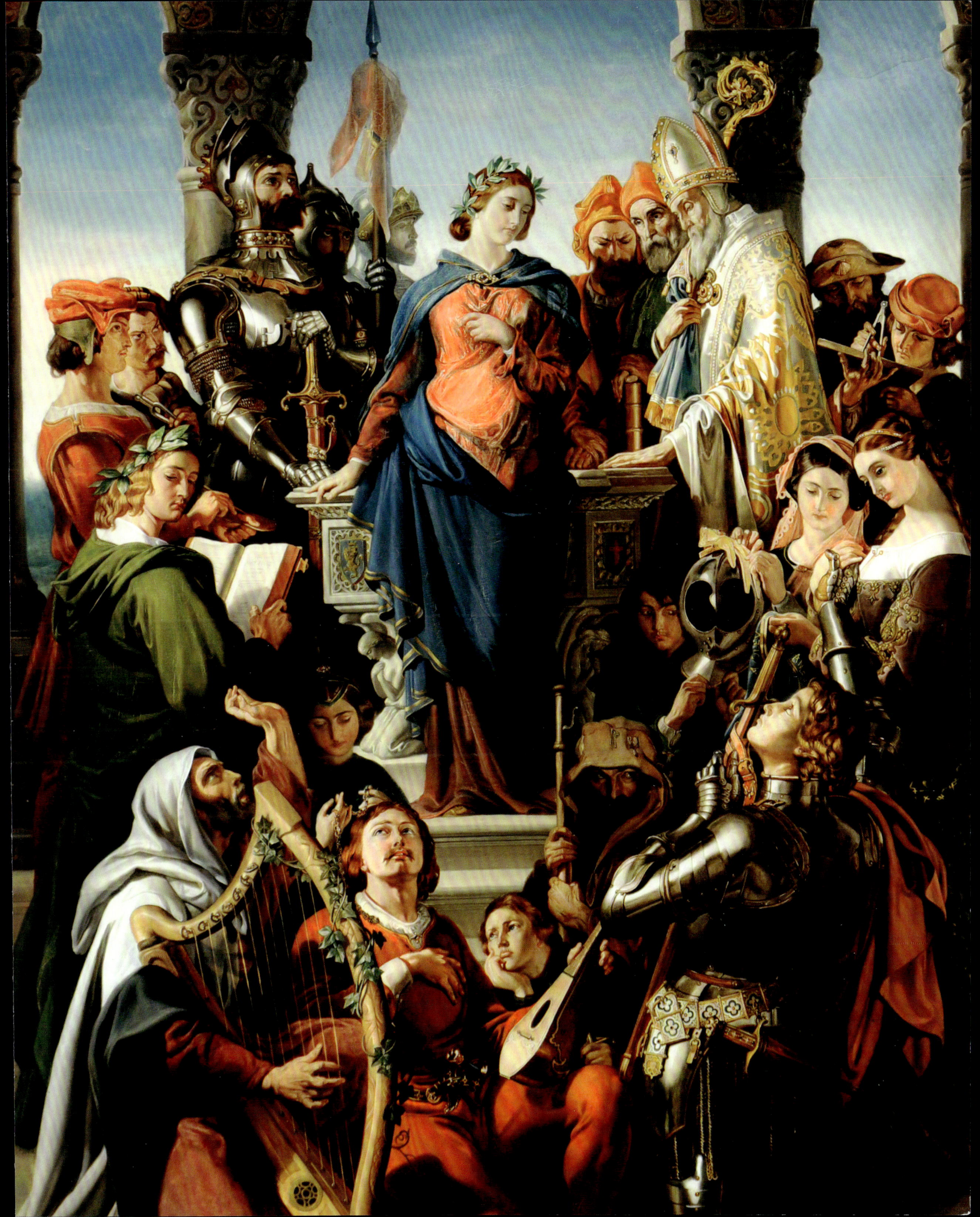

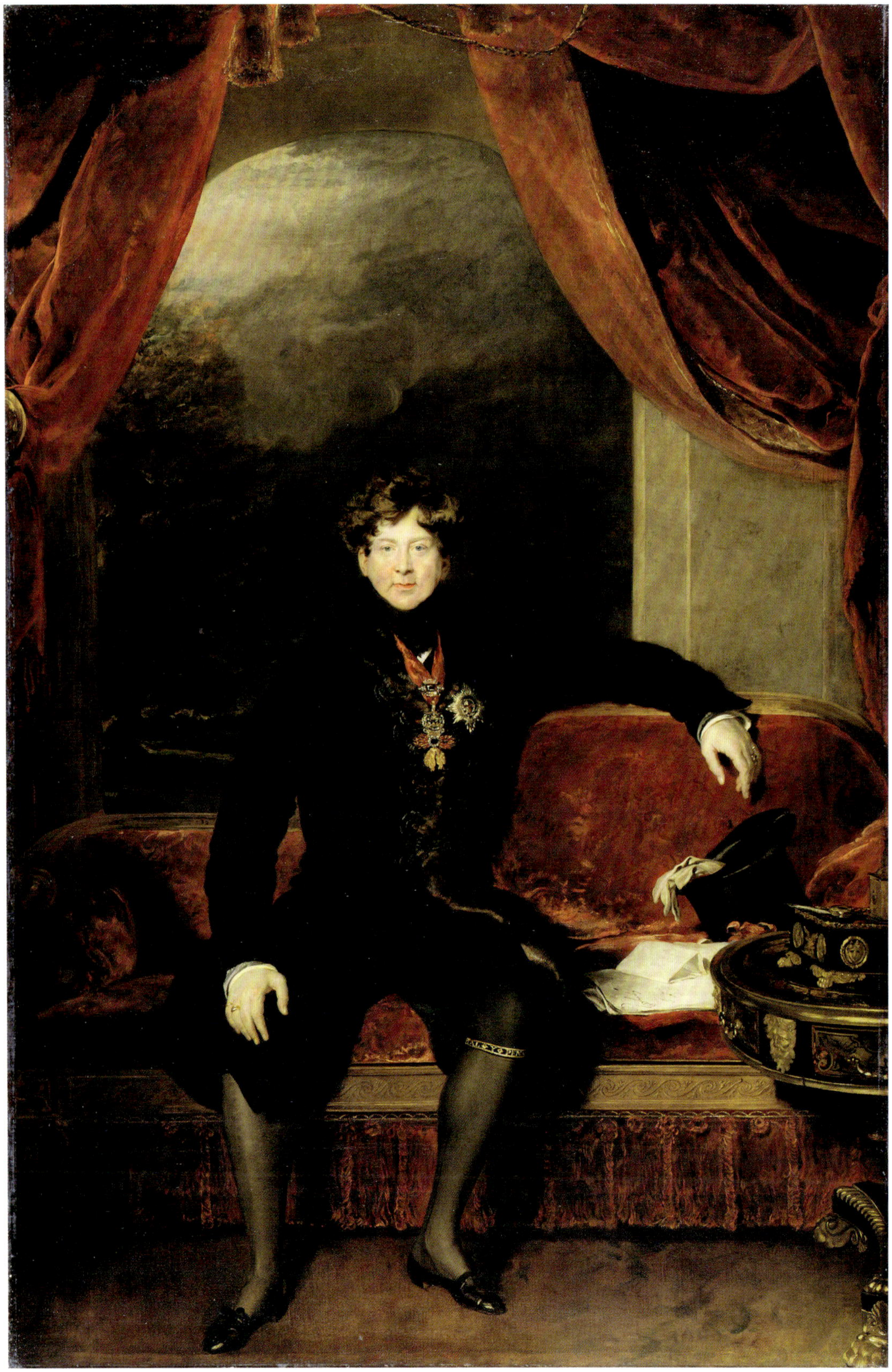

Maclise died on 25 April 1870, only months before Dickens himself. Dickens delivered the address for his old friend (who had been buried on that day) at the Royal Academy Dinner on 30 April. All ideas of coolness between them were forgotten:

> Of his genius in his chosen art I will venture to say nothing here, but of his prodigious fertility of mind and wonderful wealth of intellect, I may confidently assert that they would have made him, if he had been so minded, at least as great a writer as he was a painter. The gentlest and most modest of men, the freshest as to his generous appreciation of young aspirants, and the frankest and largest-hearted as to his peers, incapable of a sordid or ignoble thought, gallantly sustaining the true dignity of his vocation, without one grain of self-ambition, wholesomely natural at the last as at the first, 'in wit a man, simplicity a child', no Artist of whatever denomination, I make bold to say, ever went to his rest leaving a golden memory more pure from dross, or having devoted himself with a truer chivalry to the Art-Goddess whom he worshipped.[28]

Dickens's belief that the truth of Maclise's painting appealed to both the educated and the uneducated was entirely consistent with his dislike of what he regarded as pretension and dishonesty in art. A particular bugbear was the portrait of George IV in private dress by Sir Thomas Lawrence (fig. 31), now in the Wallace Collection, but presumably known to the author through the production of popular prints. Old Mr Turveydrop in *Bleak House* dresses in imitation of this portrait, and Dickens can have had little respect for a king who represents a standard of excellence for such a consummately selfish character. The image recurs in *Little Dorrit* where Mr Tite Barnacle, in his cravat and tightly buttoned coat, 'seemed to have been sitting for his portrait to Sir Thomas Lawrence all the days of his life'.[29]

Dickens's belief that conventional portraiture was not to be trusted was lifelong. In the same novel Dickens describes a portrait of the unlikeable Mr Casby as a boy of ten, 'disguised with a haymaking rake, for which he had had, at any time, as much taste or use as for a diving-bell; and sitting (on one of his own legs) upon a bank of violets, moved to precocious contemplation by the spire of a village church'.[30] Dickens's reaction to idealized figures posing as rustics reflects his abhorrence for the whole concept of the 'artist's model'. From his time in Rome in 1845, when he disliked the sight of professional models congregating for hire around the Spanish Steps, Dickens felt that the authenticity of a work of art was impugned if figures were drawn from men and women whose characters were entirely different to those whom they were paid to represent. This prejudice runs through Dickens's work, as in his mock-Gothic story 'The Ghost of Art', published in *Household Words* in July 1850, where he describes a scene on a Thames steamboat when the lawyer of the story, with a passion for the fine arts, recognizes a familiar face. He realizes that he knows the face from Royal Academy exhibition pictures. When he meets the man again two years later, he is sporting 'a long

FIG. 31
Sir Thomas Lawrence, *Portrait of George IV*, 1822, oil on canvas. Wallace Collection, London

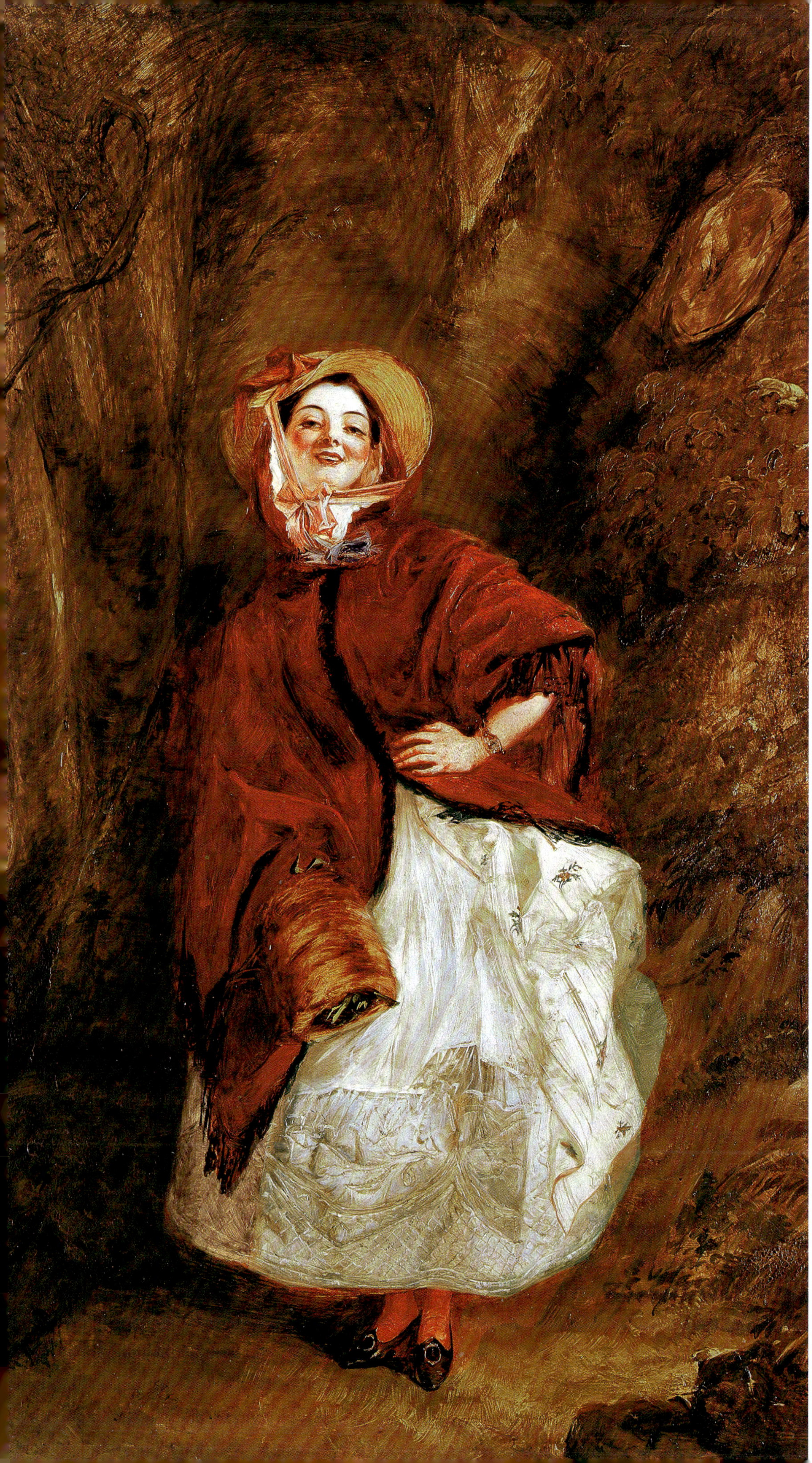

FIG. 32
William Powell Frith,
Dolly Varden, 1842,
(detail of fig. 70)

dark beard', because, he explains, 'I am the Ghost of Art!'. When 'The German taste came up', the model lost his living, but now he is 'ready for the taste'.[31] The model then strikes a series of poses, 'Severity', 'Benevolence', 'death', 'Romantic character', 'Jealousy' and 'Despair', all of them expressed by the beard alone. He promises to haunt the lawyer. 'Go where I will,' the lawyer says, 'the Ghost of Art, eternally working the passions in hair, and expressing everything by beard, pursues me. The prediction is accomplished, and the Victim has no rest.'[32] The story has its comic side, as the model describes his work, with hired armour, costumes, accessories and furniture 'that one 'ud think the public know'd the wery nails in by this time'.[33]

Not surprisingly, Dickens describes paintings that are themselves as predictable as the models and their accoutrements. Like Thackeray in his reviews of current exhibitions, Dickens complains in this story of the endless literary subject matter, heading the list with the most popular source of all, Oliver Goldsmith's *Vicar of Wakefield* (1766): 'I could have taken my affidavit that he belonged to the Vicar of Wakefield's family. Whether he was the Vicar, or Moses, or Mr Burchill, or the Squire, or a conglomeration of all four, I knew not.'[34] Other repetitive subjects for paintings cited here are as follows: 'Alfred the Great, Gil Blas, Charles the Second, Joseph and his Brethren, the Fairy Queen, Tom Jones, the Decameron of Boccaccio, Tam O' Shanter, the Marriage of the Doge of Venice with the Adriatic, and the Great Plague of London.'[35] A perusal of the Royal Academy catalogues for this period will confirm the accuracy of Dickens's judgement.

The novelist writes in much the same vein in *Bleak House* (1852–3). Sir Leicester Dedlock's library contains what the narrator describes as works of the 'Fancy Ball School'. As in the model's account of his work in 'The Ghost of Art', the accessories dominate the scene and are listed like items in a catalogue: ' "Three high-backed chairs, a table and cover, long-necked bottle (containing wine), one flask, one Spanish female's costume, three-quarter face portrait of Miss Jogg the model, and a suit of armour containing Don Quixote." '[36] Among the better-known painters of such subjects were Charles Robert Leslie and William Powell Frith. On the whole, Dickens approved of Leslie's work and he sat to the painter, in the role of Captain Boabdil in *Every Man in his Humour*, following private theatricals in 1846. However, seeing the Paris International Exhibition in 1855, Dickens reported that even 'Leslie's Sancho wants go'.[37] This was *Sancho Panza in the Apartment of the Duchess* (1843–4), now in Tate Britain. Frith became a good friend of the novelist, who commissioned two works from him, both subjects from his own novels, *Dolly Varden* from *Barnaby Rudge* (fig. 32) and *Kate Nickleby at Madame Mantalini's* (untraced). For all Dickens's mockery of the literary subject picture, it was these works by Frith that he singled out, not the scenes of contemporary life for which Frith is best known today.

Contemporary landscapes and paintings of rural scenes were, as his daughter noted, more to Dickens's taste than subject paintings. He admired the rustic genre pictures of William Collins, father of his friend the novelist Wilkie Collins, and wrote of the

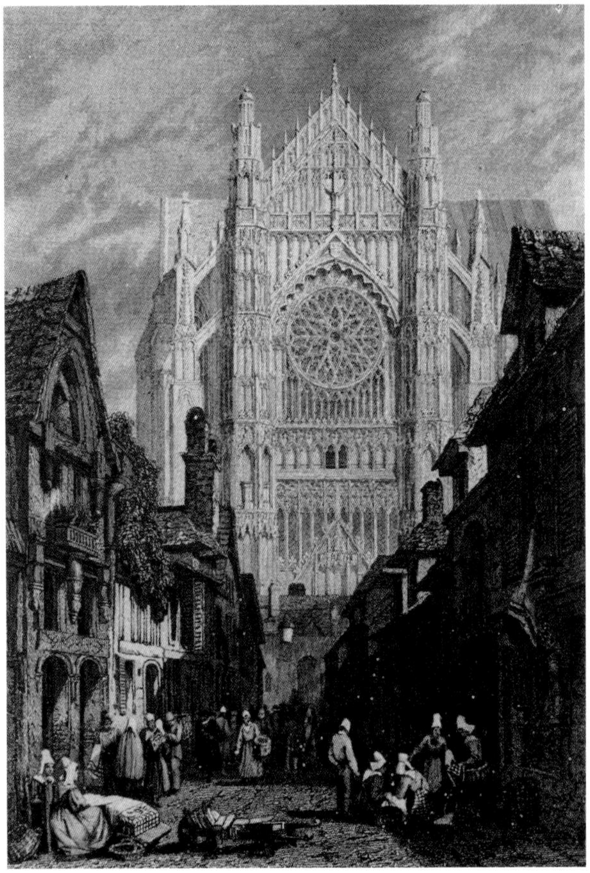

FIG. 33
Samuel Prout, *Beauvais Cathedral*, 1880, hand coloured aquatint, a print of the painting in the Dickens art sale catalogue, 1870, no. 11. Watts Gallery Archive

elder Collins as 'one of the most famous painters of English green lanes, and coast pieces'.[38] Dickens commissioned a painting from Collins, *Ischia Bay of Naples* (untraced), for which he paid £100. According to Kate Perugini, her father had a taste for watercolour pictures with their 'luminous purity' and 'open-air effect'.[39] He bought two topographical examples, Samuel Prout's *Beauvais Cathedral* (untraced; print, fig. 33) and William Callow's *Old House, High Street, Tewkesbury* (1849; untraced). The Callow cost him eight guineas at the Old Water Colour Society exhibition in 1849. The young painter Marcus Stone, son of another artist friend Frank Stone, remembered seeing it as a boy, hanging in the dining room of Dickens's House in Devonshire Terrace, together with *Moss Roses* or *Roses in a Blue and White Jug* by William Henry Hunt (untraced).[40] Kate Perugini tells us that the colour of Hunt's watercolours particularly appealed to him: '[T]he brightness and transparency of treatment in Hunt's work delighted him.'[41]

Kate Perugini also relates that Dickens admired J.M.W. Turner's early work but not his later, more experimental, paintings. This is entirely consistent with her statement that her father 'did not like great masses of paint heaped upon a canvas, thinking that painters like other artists should have "the art to hide the art", and that nothing

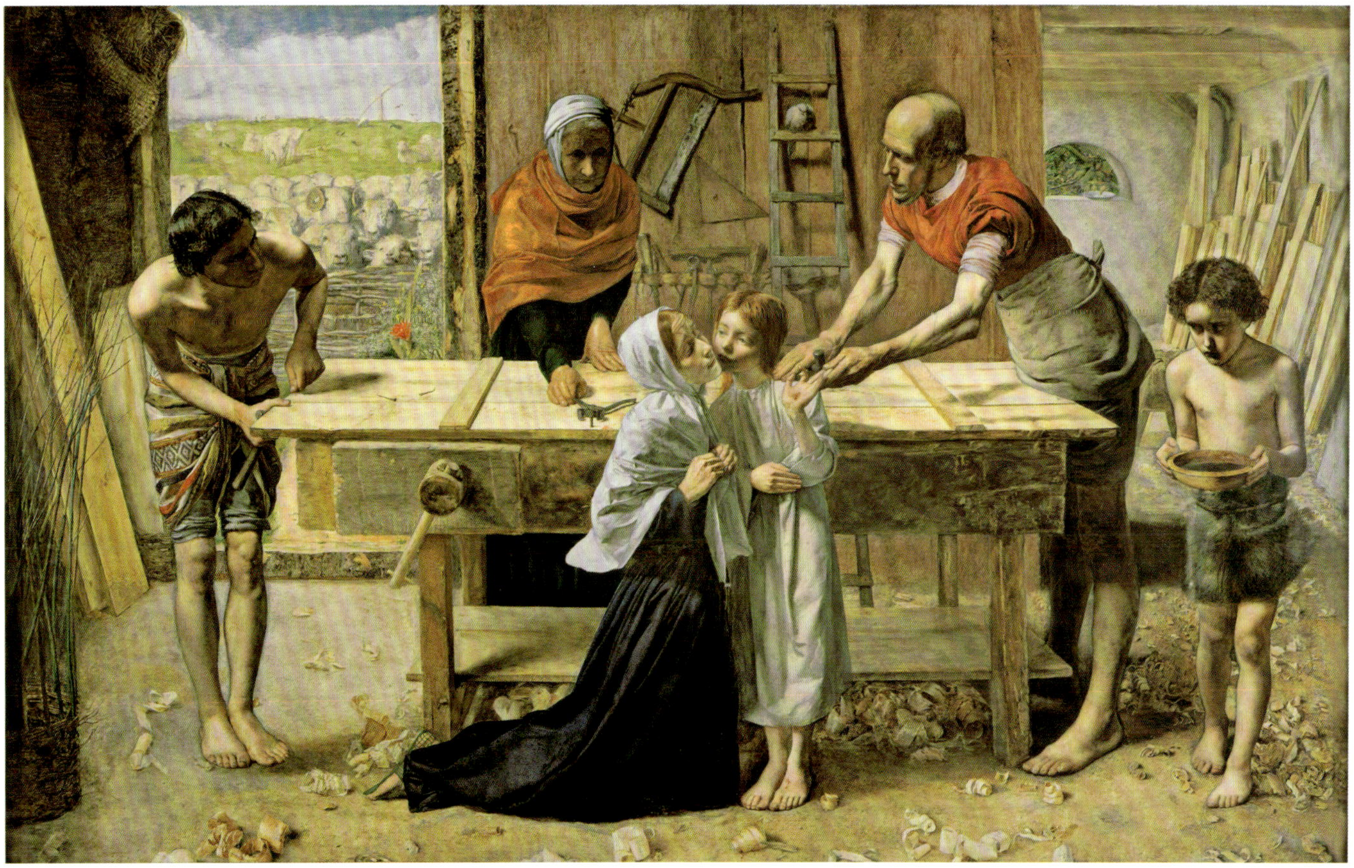

FIG. 34
John Everett Millais, *Christ in the House of his Parents ('The Carpenter's Shop')*, 1850, oil on canvas. Tate, London

in their pictures, however broadly and nobly treated, ought to overstep the modesty of nature'.[42] Dickens may have visited Turner's own gallery, as some of his references to the painter's work date from a time before Turner's death, after which a selection of his paintings was always on public display. On seeing the Niagara Falls, Dickens thought of Turner: 'Nothing in Turner's finest water-colour drawings, done in his greatest day, is so ethereal, so imaginative, so gorgeous in colour, as what I then beheld.'[43]

One of Dickens's few published reviews of a Royal Academy exhibition was published as the leading article in his own journal, *Household Words*, on 15 June 1850. This was the famous (indeed notorious) commentary on the Pre-Raphaelite Brotherhood, the meaning of whose signature, 'PRB', had just been revealed. The Brotherhood had been founded two years before, by a group of young men committed to a new kind of truth to nature, a heightened intensity in which the scenes are painted with vivid exactitude and in direct light. They were, ironically enough, keen Dickensians. Some early Pre-Raphaelite works also had an elaborate programme of religious symbolism, and the twenty-year-old John Everett Millais' *Christ in the House of His Parents ('The Carpenter's Shop')* (fig. 34) was among them. The child Jesus has hurt his hand on a nail, prefiguring the crucifixion, as do the wood and tools that surround him. The dove behind suggests the baptism of Christ, while the sheep in the background recall Christ's role as the shepherd of men.

Dickens hated it. In the first place, after his long stay in Italy in 1844 and 1845, he was an admirer of the work of Raphael and reacted passionately against a movement that appeared to be anti-Raphaelesque. Many years later, another Pre-Raphaelite brother, William Holman Hunt, denied that such an attack was intended, insisting that he and his friends were objecting to the influence of Raphael's later works rather than to his art in general. In 1851 Dickens sprang to Raphael's defence:

> Raphael . . . was fed with a preposterous idea of Beauty – with a ridiculous power of etherealising, and exalting to the very Heaven of Heavens, what was most sublime and lovely in the expression of the human face divine on Earth – with the truly contemptible conceit of finding in poor humanity the fallen likeness of the angels of GOD, and raising it up again to their pure spiritual condition.[44]

Dickens's comments on Millais' painting are usually cited whenever writers need to illustrate the ferocity of anti-Pre-Raphaelite criticism:

> You behold the interior of a carpenter's shop. In the foreground of that carpenter's shop is a hideous wry-necked, blubbering, red-headed boy, in a bed-gown; who appears to have received a poke in the hand from the stick of another boy with whom he has been playing in an adjacent gutter, and to be holding it up for the contemplation of a kneeling woman, so horrible in her ugliness, that (supposing it were possible for any human creature to exist for a moment with that dislocated throat) she would stand out from the rest of the company as a Monster, in the vilest cabaret in France, or the lowest gin-shop in England.[45]

Such comments can be compared to Dickens's criticism of Italian paintings he disliked in *Pictures from Italy*, published in 1846. The Giulio Romano frescoes in the Palazzo del Tè in Mantua horrified him, and he wrote of the scene where Jove overthrows the Titans: 'The figures are immensely large, and exaggerated to the utmost pitch of uncouthness; the colouring is harsh and disagreeable.'[46] The damaged Correggio frescoes in the cupola of the cathedral in Parma, showing the ascension of the Virgin from a ring of apostles, angels and saints struck him even more powerfully: 'Heaven knows how beautiful they may have been at one time. Connoisseurs fall into raptures with them now; but such a labyrinth of arms and legs: such heaps of foreshortened limbs, entangled and involved and jumbled together: no operating surgeon, gone mad, could imagine in his wildest delirium.'[47] These passages echo Dickens's critique of the two 'almost naked' carpenters in Millais' painting: 'Such men as the carpenters might be undressed in any hospital where dirty drunkards, in a high state of varicose veins are received. Their very toes have walked out of Saint Giles's.'[48]

At first glance, this might seem an odd line of attack from the writer who was to begin serializing *Bleak House* two years later. Jo, the crossing sweeper in that novel, and the brickmaker's family belong to that poorest class who, Dickens apparently felt, were inappropriate subjects in a work of art. Some explanation for an apparent contradiction comes from Kate Perugini writing in 1903. She states that her father's judgement of 'biblical, historical, or romantic' works was 'interfered with' by 'the excessive realism of his mental vision, for that he always *saw* what he had read of, or heard about, even when he was quite a child, is pretty certain'.[49] Dickens was anxious that religious painting should not reduce 'every mystery of our religion to some literal development in paint and canvas':[50]

> [T]he shock of seeing it so misrepresented (as it doubtless appeared to him) came upon him as a surprise and a pain, and without waiting to inquire of himself the real reason of his dislike to the work he wrote a very harsh and hasty criticism upon it, a criticism that I have reason to believe he regretted having published in later years.[51]

Dickens was by no means the only critic to dislike Millais' painting. Like many people in 1850, he had never contemplated the childhood of Christ in the realistic style adopted by Millais. Several critics detected a Catholic or High Church flavour in Pre-Raphaelite painting, but that does not seem to have been a factor in Dickens's response. Rather, he laid stress on the physical horrors of the people in the painting. Several of Dickens's friends were painters in a very different style from Millais, and Dickens may have felt that he was defending those artists whom he knew and admired.

The review attracted considerable attention and has done so ever since. Dickens never withdrew his statements, although he soon found himself in the same circles as Millais. Through Wilkie Collins, a close friend of both men, a dinner took place on 29 January 1855, which resulted 'in removing all estrangement, and in making Dickens understand and express his sense of the power of Millais' genius and character'.[52] Dickens sent Millais an article from *Household Words* about the London Fire Brigade, which was relevant to the work that Millais was preparing for the Academy of that year, *The Rescue* (National Gallery of Victoria, Melbourne), a scene of a fireman rescuing two young girls.

However, according to Holman Hunt, Dickens sent with the article a letter that 'needlessly and ungraciously endorsed the sentiments of the original violent article, and so again alienated the confidence of our circle from him'.[53] Dickens wrote hoping that 'a word frankly said may make it pleasanter':

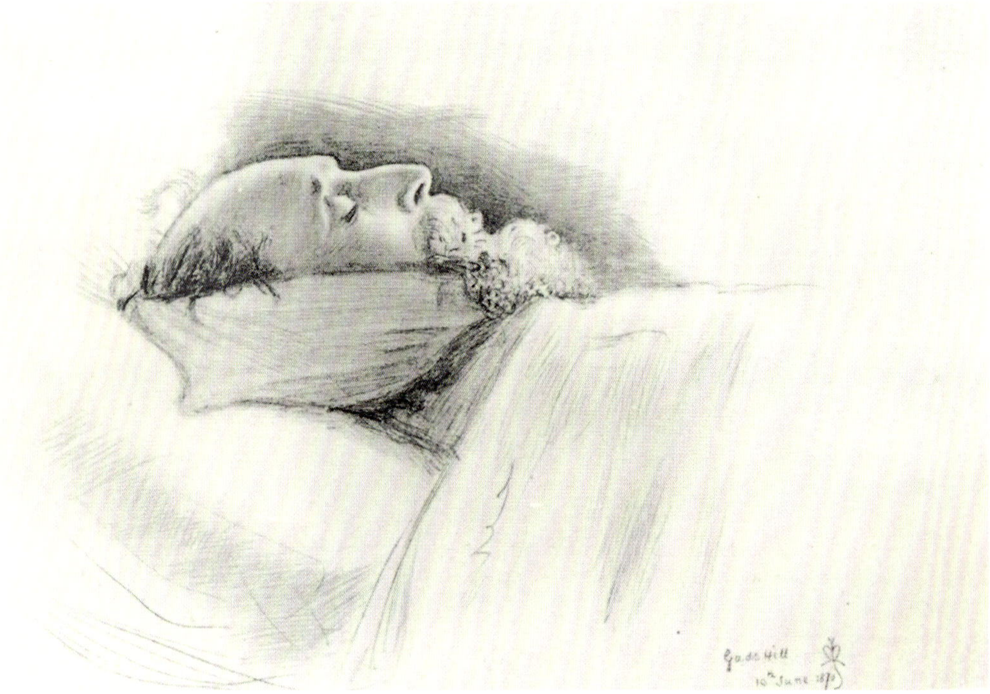

FIG. 35
John Everett Millais, *Charles Dickens on his Deathbed, 10th June 1870*, 1870, drawing. Charles Dickens Museum, London

> Objecting very strongly to what I believe to be an unworthy use of your great powers, I once expressed the objection in this same journal. My opinion on that point is not in the least changed, but has never dashed my admiration of your progress in what I suppose are higher and better things. In short, you have given me such great reasons (in your works) to separate you from uncongenial associations, that I wish to give you in the return one little reason for doing the like by me. And hence this note.[51]

In the face of this renewed criticism, the courteous and good-humoured Millais behaved impeccably. He remained a friend of the novelist and was even called in to draw Dickens's head on his deathbed (fig. 35).

Holman Hunt had a somewhat uneasy correspondence with Dickens in 1858. A story, 'Calmuck' by Robert Brough, had appeared in *Household Words*, and Hunt was convinced, probably rightly, that one of the characters was an unfavourable portrait of himself.[55] He protested, but Dickens sensibly argued that to publish an apology would 'suggest to the public what they have not the faintest idea of'.[56] However, he told Hunt later that he much regretted publishing something that had caused such concern to 'a brother artist'.[57] In his autobiography Hunt fails to mention this incident, implying that he first met Dickens in 1860 when Charles Collins, an associate of the Pre-Raphaelite group, a close friend of Millais and the brother of the novelist Wilkie Collins, married

Dickens's daughter, Kate. At the wedding reception Dickens, seeing Hunt studying the David Roberts painting of the Sphinx, remarked: 'You will not find anything in that picture to suit your particular taste, but I admire it.'[58] Hunt, true to his Pre-Raphaelite principles, could not resist telling Dickens that he himself had recently visited the Great Sphinx and found Roberts's rendering inaccurate. The artist had placed the setting sun in the south. Dickens retorted by telling Hunt that it was the sunset that he particularly admired. Hunt responded that, for religious reasons, the Sphinx was placed to face the rising sun and that Roberts had got his facts wrong. To this Dickens replied that he liked the painting 'as a poetic conception'.[59]

This argument did not prevent Dickens and Hunt from becoming friends. In the same year as the wedding Dickens gave Hunt practical advice about the sale of his *Finding of the Saviour in the Temple* (1854–60; Birmingham City Museum and Art Gallery). The novelist failed to see the painting, which Hunt came to regret, as Dickens 'never had again the opportunity of learning how far we differed or agreed in the purpose I was carrying out in the picture, of attempting to realize the actual history of the divine Man'.[60]

There is some evidence to suggest that Dickens's view of the art of his own day was more negative than he cared to admit in public. While working on *Little Dorrit* in 1855, he spent six months in Paris. His time there coincided with the 1855 Exposition Universelle, which included a large section devoted to contemporary art with exhibits from twenty-eight countries. Nearly three hundred English works were shown in the Galerie Anglaise, the largest group after that representing French art. Photographs show the crowded gallery, with works hanging two or three deep on the walls, and sculptures in the central area.

French critics declared themselves disappointed by the English display. As Laure Chabanne has shown, they associated English art with the painters of the romantic period, including Turner, Constable, John Martin and Thomas Lawrence.[61] Even David Wilkie and William Etty, who had both died comparatively recently, were missing. A range of paintings with literary, historical and genre subjects, by artists including Charles Robert Leslie, Thomas Webster, William Mulready, Charles West Cope and William Powell Frith, drew forth persistent complaints of dullness and of a lack of spirit and inspiration. These were small works intended for private collections, rather than the large history paintings popular in France.

The reaction of Dickens to the works in the English gallery, expressed in a letter to John Forster of November 1855, mirrors that of the French critics: 'There is a horrible respectability about most of the best of them – a little, finite, systematic routine in them, strangely expressive to me of the state of England itself . . . [I]n English art, as in English government and social relations', he argued, form and convention took 'the place of living force and truth.' He had 'praised and admired with great diligence; but it was of no use. I could not make anything better of it than what I tell you'.[62] The *Journal l'Union* makes the same point, arguing that the English ideal of beauty, as it

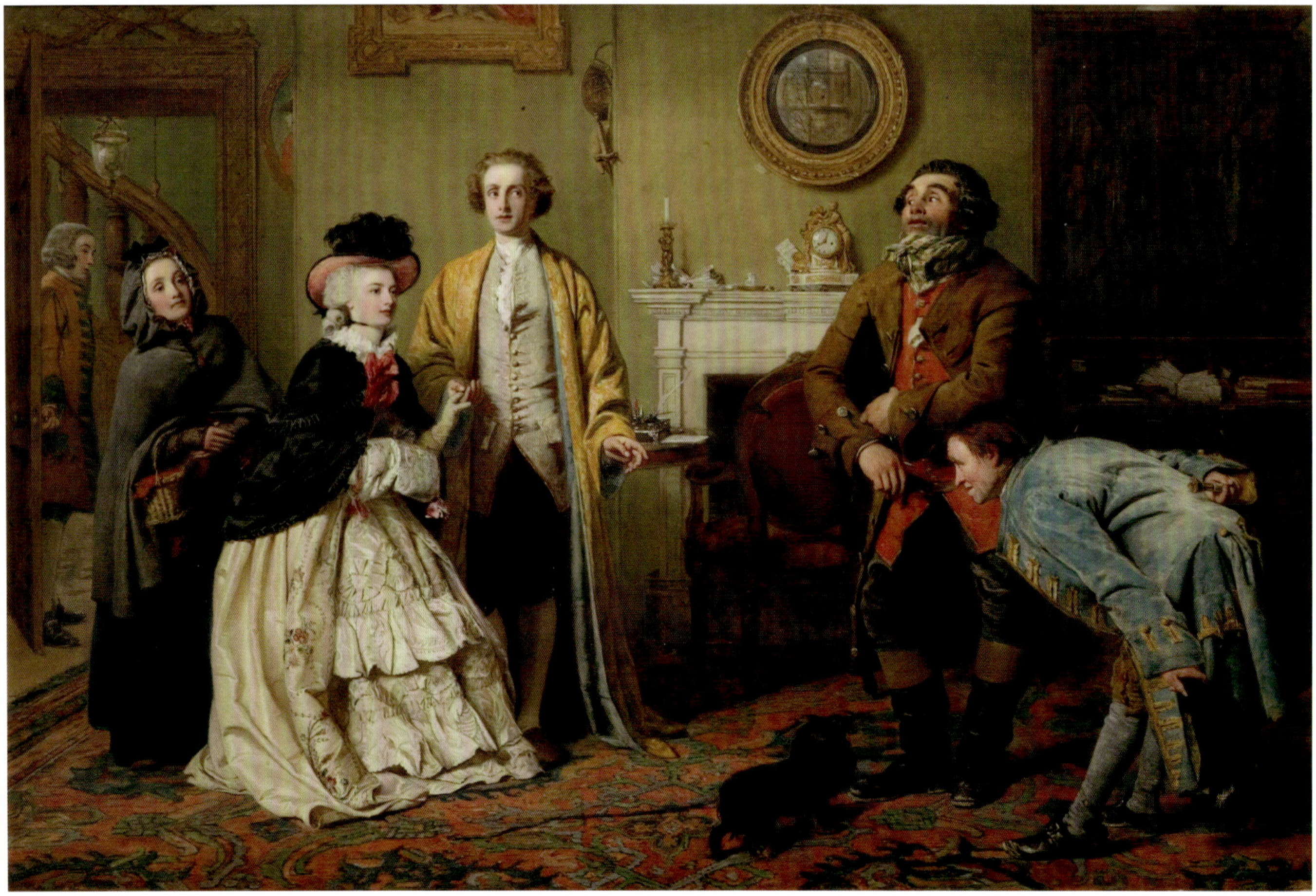

FIG. 36
William Powell Frith, *Mr Honeywood Introduces the Bailiffs to Miss Richland as his Friends*, 1850, oil on canvas. Victoria and Albert Museum, London

appears in these paintings, is 'cold, strong, and correct', even in such a work as Thomas Uwins's *Vintage in Medoc* (untraced), where more spirit was clearly called for.[63]

Dickens requested Forster not to disclose his views to others as '[f]riendship is better than criticism, and I shall steadily hold my tongue. Discussion is worse than useless when you cannot agree about what you are going to discuss.'[64] In confidence, he told his friend that even artists whom he normally admired, including Leslie, Mulready and Stanfield, did not show at their best. Stanfield's contributions were, he decided, like stage sets and he particularly disliked Mulready's *The Whistonian Controversy* (1843; private collection), yet another scene from *The Vicar of Wakefield*. This representation of a discussion about William Whiston's condemnation of remarriage by widowed priests of the Church of England, at a table with a brightly coloured rug, struck Dickens as 'two old men talking over a much-too-prominent table-cloth'. Reading 'the French explanation of their proceedings' left him 'dis-satisfied'.[65] Although both Mulready and Stanfield showed in strength, Mulready with his *The Wolf and the Lamb* (1819–20; Royal Collection), a scene of a bully trying to cow his victim, and Stanfield

FIG. 37
Augustus Leopold Egg, *Peter the Great Sees Catherine, his Future Empress, for the First Time*, photograph of untraced painting. Watts Gallery Archive

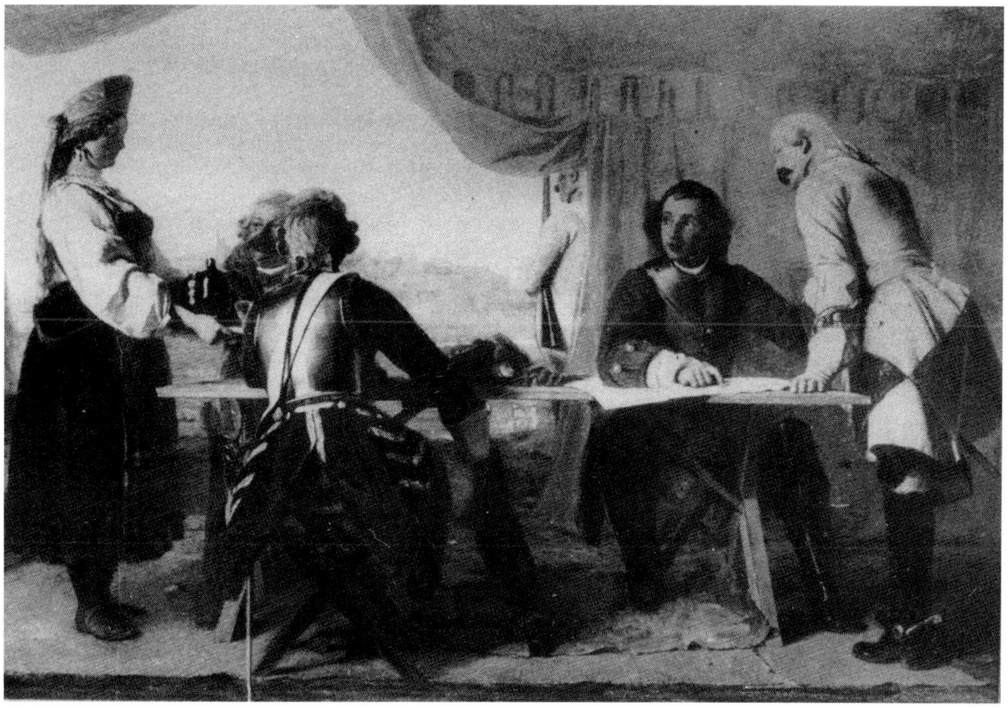

with *The Battle of Roveredo* (1846; Royal Holloway College), neither impressed Dickens. One of Stanfield's vivid sea pieces, *A Dutch Dogger Carrying Away her Sprit* (1846; V&A), did attract favourable attention in Paris, where the British landscapes were preferred to the historical and literary subjects.

According to Dickens, the British artists who came 'out the best' in the exhibition were Frith, E.M. Ward and Augustus Egg.[66] Frith exhibited three works with subjects from literature or from the lives of writers. Of the three, Dickens liked best a comic scene from Oliver Goldsmith's *Good-Natured Man* (1768), *Mr Honeywood Introduces the Bailiffs to Miss Richland as his Friends* (fig. 36). Ward, whom Dickens thought 'a very witty, brilliant man', exhibited three pictures whose subjects are related to capital punishment, a topic that particularly interested Dickens at this time.[67] He praised *The Royal Family of France in the Prison of the Temple in 1792* (1851; Harris Museum and Art Gallery, Preston). With its local subject, this work was singled out by some French critics who complained that it resembled a commonplace bourgeois interior, with the father asleep after a good lunch. Dickens told Forster that he had 'always thought' Egg's *Peter the Great Sees Catherine, his Future Empress, for the First Time* (fig. 37) a good painting and noted that 'foreigners evidently descry a sudden dramatic touch that pleases them'.[68]

There are some surprising absences in Dickens's commentary, although Forster only quotes part of the letter, which is now missing. Most surprisingly, he does not mention his friend, Edwin Landseer, who showed several works, including *The Sanctuary*

(1842; Royal Collection), a scene of peace and tranquillity as the exhausted stag reaches safety. Dickens's daughter tells us that 'for Edwin Landseer my father had a peculiarly enthusiastic admiration', believing that, like Maclise, he would have excelled in any walk of life.[69] This feeling of admiration increased with the years, and Dickens recognized that Landseer's affectations were a result of nervousness rather then hubris. In the year after the exhibition Dickens wrote an article, 'The Friend of the Lions', in *Household Words*. He was supporting Landseer's appeal for the lions in the London Zoo to be given more living space. In his article Dickens claims to have sat to Landseer in the role of a rat-catcher 'with an awful Bulldog much too near us'.[70] There is no evidence that Dickens actually sat, and the description is probably a joke.

The early Pre-Raphaelite masterpieces by John Millais and William Holman Hunt aroused curiosity among the French public, who were fascinated by the accurate representation of foliage and flowers in Millais' *Ophelia* (1851–2; Tate) and Holman Hunt's *Our English Coasts, 1852 (Strayed Sheep)* (1852; Tate). The extraordinary detail provoked some laughter and seemed to many to be characteristically British. As noted above, we do not have a complete copy of Dickens's letter to Forster, but it would not be surprising if he deliberately ignored these two paintings.

A number of artists visited Paris for the prize-giving ceremony, and Dickens dined with Landseer, Leslie and William Boxall, together with three others, at the Palais Royale. It may have been on this occasion that he noted that English artists seemed to have

> a fixed idea that there is no natural manner but the English manner (in itself so exceptional that it is a thing apart, in all countries); and that unless a Frenchman – represented as going to the guillotine for example – is as calm as Clapham, or as respectable as Richmond-hill, he cannot be right.[71]

Forster, not quoting directly, records Dickens's commentary on his conversations with English artists, who told him that they 'found French nature all wrong' and that French pictures were 'theatrical'. Dickens responded by reminding them that the French were 'a demonstrative and gesticulating people' and that they were recording the truth about '*an immense part of the world*'.[72] These comments were repeated in an article, 'Insularities', published in *Household Words* on 19 January 1856. Here Dickens took English reactions to the French paintings in the Exposition as one example of the narrow-minded insularity that he detected in so many of his fellow countrymen.

By contrast with his negative comments on the British exhibition, Dickens found the extensive French display (which included 1,800 oil paintings) exciting and challenging: 'There are no end of bad pictures among the French, but, Lord! the goodness also! – the fearlessness of them; the bold drawing; the dashing conception; the passion and action in them!'[73] Unfortunately, these paintings are unidentified, as are those in the Belgian section, where Dickens found the 'best landscape . . . the best portrait, and the best scene of homely life, to be found in the building'.[74]

In the years before the Exposition Universelle, Dickens had expressed his admiration for two works by French artists, both frescoes rather then easel paintings. On his way to Italy in 1844 Dickens visited the cathedral in Avignon where he saw a group of frescoes by Eugène Devéria. These included *The Adoration of the Kings* and *The Disciples at Emmaus* (1838). Writing to Maclise, then at work for the Westminster competition, Dickens told him: 'I hardly think you allow enough, for the brightness and brilliancy of colour which is commonly achieved on the continent, in that same fresco painting. I saw some – by a French artist and his pupil – in progress at the cathedral at Avignon.'[75] Three years later, Dickens wrote in praise of Paul Delaroche's *Hemicycle* in the École des Beaux Arts, completed in 1841 and the subject of much praise. It shows, as an example to the students, a group of great masters dating from ancient Greece to the nineteenth century. Dickens told Harrison Ainsworth that he believed it to be 'the greatest work of art in the world'.[76] A third French painter whom Dickens greatly admired was Ary Scheffer, although he did not care much for Scheffer's portrait of himself (1855), now in the National Portrait Gallery.

Writing about her father, Dickens's daughter expressed surprise that, given the number of his artist friends, he did not present more artists in his fiction. She speculates that he disliked the lack of daylight in studios, together with the sedentary life and the constant discussion (in technical terminology) of an artist's work.[77] Apart from the miniaturist Miss La Creevy in *Nicholas Nickleby*, there is only one artist character of importance in his fiction, Henry Gowan in *Little Dorrit*. Unlike Miss La Creevy, Gowan is a nasty piece of work. An undistinguished painter, he trades on his grand relations and friends but fails to convince the public of his genius. Edward Burne-Jones and his studio assistant, T.M. Rooke, agreed that Dickens had captured the essence of the incompetent artist with his 'hasty, impatient touches'. 'He guessed at most things. Very few things he didn't get to the bottom of' was Burne-Jones's verdict on the novelist.[78]

Dickens's taste in art, like so much about him, was frequently unpredictable and idiosyncratic. In *Pictures from Italy* he describes himself as a plain man, not an expert on art, with 'no other means of judging of a picture than as I see it resembling and refining upon nature, and presenting graceful combinations of forms and colours'.[79] Dickens was uneasy with allegorizing high art and had little enthusiasm for the representation of tragic or violent subjects. His daughter recalled that he sought 'great breadth and force in the conception and treatment of a subject, but looked for a certain delicacy and refinement of finish, a combination not always attained by one painter'.[80] She draws attention to Dickens's passion for colour, and for scarlet and pink in particular.

Some idea of the works on the walls of his home at 1 Devonshire Terrace, where he lived from 1851 to 1860, is given by Marcus Stone, who remembered the dining room with its 'charming little collection of pictures . . . to which very few additions were made in later years'.[81] Works by Wilkie, Callow, Maclise, Stanfield, Roberts, William Henry Hunt and Frith hung there, as did a painting by Augustus Egg of Dickens in *Used Up* (fig. 38). Three other paintings illustrated scenes from Dickens's novels: Frank Stone's *Tilda Price*, probably a commission; Thomas Webster's *Dotheboys Hall* or *Squeers's School* of 1848 from *Nicholas Nickleby*; and *Little Nell* of 1851 by Francis Topham from *The Old Curiosity Shop* (fig. 39). The Topham was a gift from the artist, whom, Kate Perugini tells us, Dickens 'greatly admired'.[82] Two of a group of watercolours by Dickens's friend, George Cattermole, also illustrated scenes from *The Old Curiosity Shop*, *Little Nell's Home* (Charles Dickens Museum, London) and *Little Nell's Grave* (V&A). *Nell and the Widow*, a painting by Fanny McIan, was presented to the artist in 1841 and can be seen hanging over the doorway in the photograph of the dining room at Gad's Hill (fig. 3). Kate Perugini reports that Dickens was particularly attached to two studies of cottage interiors by Fanny's husband, the Scottish artist Robert Ronald McIan, a former actor who became a good friend. Belinda Morse believes that one of these may be the watercolour *Interior in the Highlands*, exhibited at the National Institution in 1850.[83]

In 1852 Dickens bought two paintings, *The Novel* and *The Play*, directly from the Royal Academy exhibition. These were the work of a Scottish artist, Robert Hannah. They are at present untraced, but a review in the *Athenaeum* tells us that in *The Novel* one young girl is reading *Bleak House* to another in a carriage by the Serpentine in Hyde Park. In the other painting a young girl is courted by two lovers in a theatre box, while her mother watches Sheridan's *The Rivals*. In the eyes of the reviewer, the two works were 'painted with a clear bright touch, although a trifle hard and lackered'.[84] The colour green was prominent in both works. Dickens liked these paintings enough to lend them to the British display at the Exposition Universelle of 1855.

Among the younger generation of artists, Dickens was friendly with Frederic Leighton, whom he first met in Florence in late 1853 during an Italian jaunt with Wilkie Collins and Augustus Egg. Leighton was working on sketches and drawings for *Cimabue's Madonna Carried in Triumph Through the Streets of Florence* (Royal Collection on loan to the National Gallery, London), which was exhibited at the Royal Academy in 1855 and bought by Queen Victoria.

> He [Dickens] was at once struck not only at the cleverness displayed by Leighton in his art, but with the knowledge he possessed of literature, and the extraordinary versatility he showed in speaking on all the subjects that came under discussion, and he was also greatly taken by the courtly manner and handsome looks of the young man.[85]

Letters from Dickens to Leighton speak of meetings in the 1860s, and Kate Perugini remembered that her father was much impressed by 'the beauty and eloquence' of a

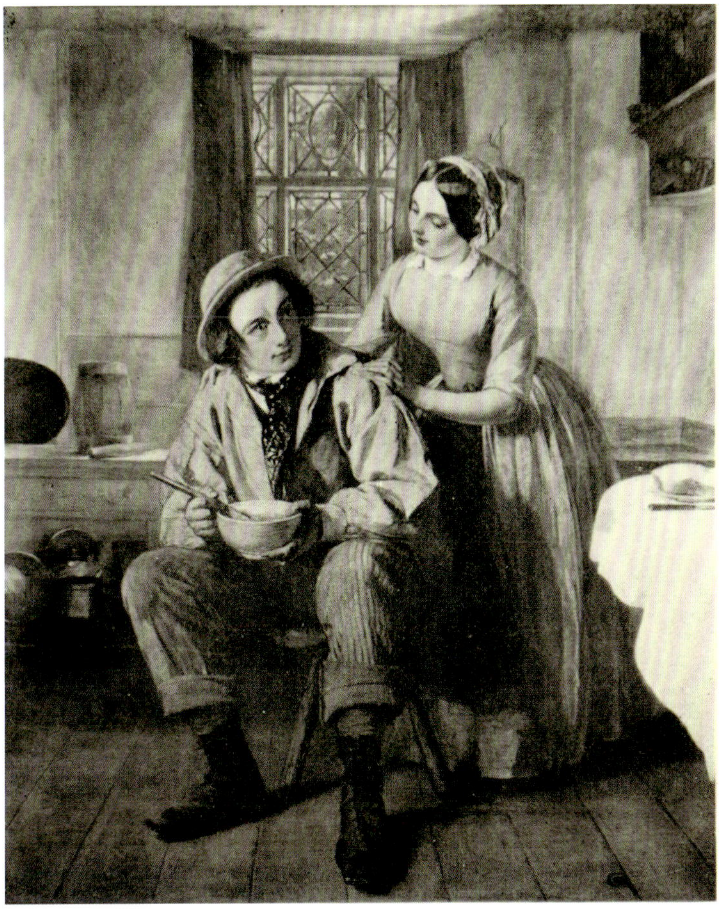

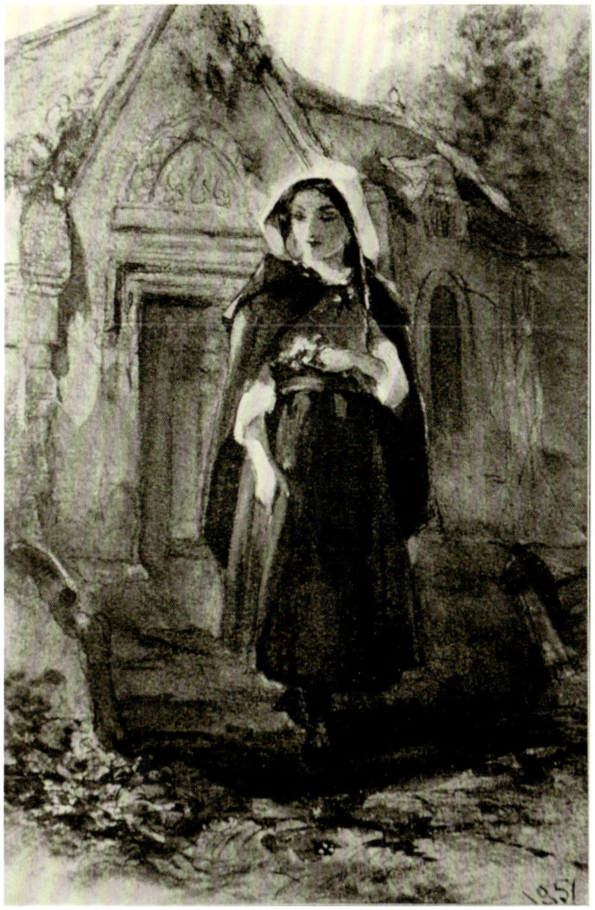

FIG. 38
Augustus Leopold Egg, *Used Up* (otherwise called *Dickens as Sir Charles Coldstream in Used Up*), 1848, oil on canvas. Charles Dickens Museum, London

FIG. 39
Francis Topham, *Little Nell*, 1871, print. Watts Gallery Archive

speech given by Leighton at the Arts Club.[86] Like Thackeray, Dickens predicted that Leighton would become President of the Royal Academy, as he did, after the death of both novelists, in 1878.

Another young artist in whom Dickens took an interest was Marcus Stone. Staying with the writer and his family in Dover in 1852, Stone, who was then twelve, painted a small watercolour portrait of the two surviving daughters, Mamie and Kate. In the same year he drew Jo, the crossing sweeper from *Bleak House*. Delighted, Dickens hung the boy's drawing on the wall. He was not always entirely serious about Stone's work. Frith records Dickens's response to *Rest* (untraced) of 1858, where an old knight lies in an orchard while children offer him apples. '"A capital picture," said Dickens, in his hearty way. "I was delighted to see it. Armour beautifully done. Apples too – only I think the old boy was too far gone for apples. It would require *burnt brandy*, and a good deal of it, to bring *him* to." '[87] After Frank Stone's death in 1859, Dickens gave his son considerable support. Marcus drew the frontispiece for *Little Dorrit* and the illustrations for *Our Mutual Friend*. In 1865 he painted another portrait of Kate Dickens, showing her in profile (private collection). As Lucinda Hawksley has concluded: 'The picture reveals a pretty young woman, pensive but with her lips starting to shape into a slight smile. She fulfils all the ideals of the many women depicted in her father's books as the epitome of feminine beauty.'[88]

Knowing the family as well as he did, Marcus Stone was able to report that Dickens retained the 'same scheme of hanging' found at Devonshire House in his later homes, Tavistock House and Gad's Hill.[89] The photograph of the dining room at Gad's Hill shows the works hanging close together, and often several deep. By then Dickens was adding little to his collection, but there were a few late purchases. In 1866 he bought two works directly from Philip Hermogenes Calderon. One, *The Letter* (1866; private collection), shows a girl sitting on a bed at Hever Castle in Kent, while the other, *Hide and Seek* (untraced), shows children at play. In New York in the late 1860s Dickens bought *Le Garde Champêtre* (untraced) by Eduardo Zamaçois, a Spanish pupil of the French artist, Ernest Meissonier. At the time of the sale of Dickens's collection at Christie's on 9 July 1870, Sir George Scharf described it in his catalogue, now preserved in the National Portrait Gallery, as 'figure under a tree, sunlight on fresh field, tree in shadow'. Many of Dickens's paintings were gifts from the artists, so those that he chose for himself are a better guide to his taste.

However much the young Dickens might have mocked the works on show in the Royal Academy, he later became, as David Roos has shown, closely associated with the institution. He is known to have been a speaker at the annual banquet on five occasions between 1851 and the last weeks of his life in 1870. It is possible that he spoke at banquets before this, but as *The Times* did not report the speeches until 1851, it is not known whether he did so. 'So firmly established was the connection between Dickens and the Royal Academy that he was sometimes even called upon to offer toasts in its honour at other social gatherings.'[90] Speaking at the Royal Academy in 1862, Dickens even reversed his previous judgement on literary subject pictures by stating that it was 'one of the privileges of literature to speak from the walls of this room rather than from the floor' and, giving a predictable list of authors, rather than subjects, declared that 'a host of illustrious writers has been so eloquent in the masterpieces of members of this academy'.[91] In giving these addresses, Dickens consistently asserted the importance of the arts: 'rightly understood, [they] are quite as important to the welfare of the empire as . . . Downing Street or Westminster Hall'.[92] Summing up her father's position, Kate Perugini, herself a painter, declared that he had been

> a real lover of art, but that he undoubtedly had a still greater love of nature, against which he thought that many artists, either from want of reverence for their art, or from want of knowledge, or from a mere whim or affectation, which it was not in his nature to forgive, often very gravely offended.[93]

NOTES

1. *Journalism*, vol. 1, p. 357.
2. *Nicholas Nickleby*, ch. 10, para 12.
3. *Letters*, vol. 2, pp. 277–8.
4. Perugini 1903, p. 164.
5. *Speeches*, pp. 13–14.
6. *David Copperfield*, ch. 57, para 66.
7. John Forster, *The Life of Charles Dickens*, 2 vols (London, 1872), vol. 1, p. 156.
8. Merwe 1979, p. 19.
9. Merwe 1979, p. 19.
10. *Letters*, vol. 11, p. 368.
11. Merwe 1979, p. 19.
12. Merwe 1979, p. 80.
13. *Letters*, vol. 3, p. 418.
14. *Letters*, vol. 4, p. 184.
15. *Speeches*, p. 164.
16. *Letters*, vol. 8, p. 108.
17. *Journalism*, vol. 4, p. 332.
18. *Letters*, vol. 7, p. 201.
19. *Letters*, vol. 1, p. 558.
20. *Letters*, vol. 3, pp. 415–16.
21. *Letters*, vol. 3, p. 396.
22. *Journalism*, vol. 2, p. 77.
23. *Letters*, vol. 3, p. 277.
24. *Letters*, vol. 3, p. 299.
25. *Letters*, vol. 2, p. 152.
26. *Letters*, vol. 2, p. 209.
27. *Letters*, vol. 3, p. 453, and Perugini 1903, p. 129.
28. *Speeches*, p. 422.
29. *Little Dorrit*, ch. 10, para 41.
30. *Little Dorrit*, ch. 13, para 7.
31. *Journalism*, vol. 2, p. 263.
32. *Journalism*, vol. 2, p. 264.
33. *Journalism*, vol. 2, p. 262.
34. *Journalism*, vol. 2, p. 260.
35. *Journalism*, vol. 2, p. 260.
36. *Bleak House*, ch. 29, para 2.
37. *Letters*, vol. 7, p. 743.
38. *Letters*, vol. 9, p. 246.
39. Perugini 1903, p. 164.
40. Collins 1981, vol. 2, p. 184.
41. Perugini 1903, p. 164.
42. Perugini 1903, p. 164.
43. *Letters*, vol. 12, p. 75.
44. *Journalism*, vol. 2, p. 244.
45. *Journalism*, vol. 2, p. 245.
46. Schwarzbach & Ormond 1977, p. 376.
47. Schwarzbach & Ormond 1977, p. 353.
48. *Journalism*, vol. 2, p. 245.
49. Perugini 1903, p. 129.
50. *Letters*, vol. 4, p. 277.
51. Perugini 1903, p. 129.
52. Hunt 1905, vol. 2, p. 185.
53. Hunt 1905, vol. 2, p. 185.
54. *Letters*, vol. 7, p. 517.
55. *Household Words*, 3 April 1858, pp. 365–70.
56. *Letters*, vol. 8, p. 548.
57. *Letters*, vol. 8, p. 555.
58. Hunt 1905, vol. 2, p. 216.
59. Hunt 1905, vol. 2, p. 217.
60. Hunt 1905, vol. 2, p. 191.
61. Laure Chabanne, 'La Lady, le King's Charles et la modernité: les Français et l'école anglaise à l'Exposition universelle de 1855', *Napoléon III et la reine Victoria: Une visite à l'Exposition universelle de 1855* (Compiègne, 2008), p. 81.
62. *Letters*, vol. 7, p. 743.
63. Ormond 1984, p. 17.
64. *Letters*, vol. 7, p. 743.
65. *Letters*, vol. 7, p. 743.
66. *Letters*, vol. 7, p. 743.
67. Perugini 1903, p. 165.
68. *Letters*, vol. 7, p. 743.
69. Perugini 1903, p. 165.
70. *Journalism*, vol. 3, p. 352.
71. *Letters*, vol. 7, p. 744.
72. *Letters*, vol. 7, pp. 743–4.
73. *Letters*, vol. 7, p. 743.
74. *Letters*, vol. 7, p. 743.
75. *Letters*, vol. 4, p. 161.
76. *Letters*, vol. 5, p. 37.
77. Perugini 1903, p. 126.
78. Mary Lago, ed., *Burne-Jones Talking* (London, 1981), p. 142.
79. Schwarzbach & Ormond 1977, p. 378.
80. Perugini 1903, p. 164.
81. Collins 1981, vol. 2, p. 184.
82. Perugini 1903, p. 164.
83. Belinda Morse, *A Woman of Design, A Man of Passion: The Pioneering McIans* (Lewes, 2001), p. 287.
84. Ormond 1984, p. 7.
85. Perugini 1903, p. 167.
86. Perugini 1903, p. 167.
87. Frith 1887, vol. 1, p. 95.
88. Lucinda Hawksley, *Katey: The Life and Loves of Dickens's Artist Daughter* (London, Toronto, Sydney, Auckland and Johannesburg, 2006), p. 208.
89. Collins 1981, p. 184.
90. Roos 1977, p. 101.
91. Roos 1977, p. 102.
92. Roos 1977, p. 101.
93. Perugini 1903, p. 130.

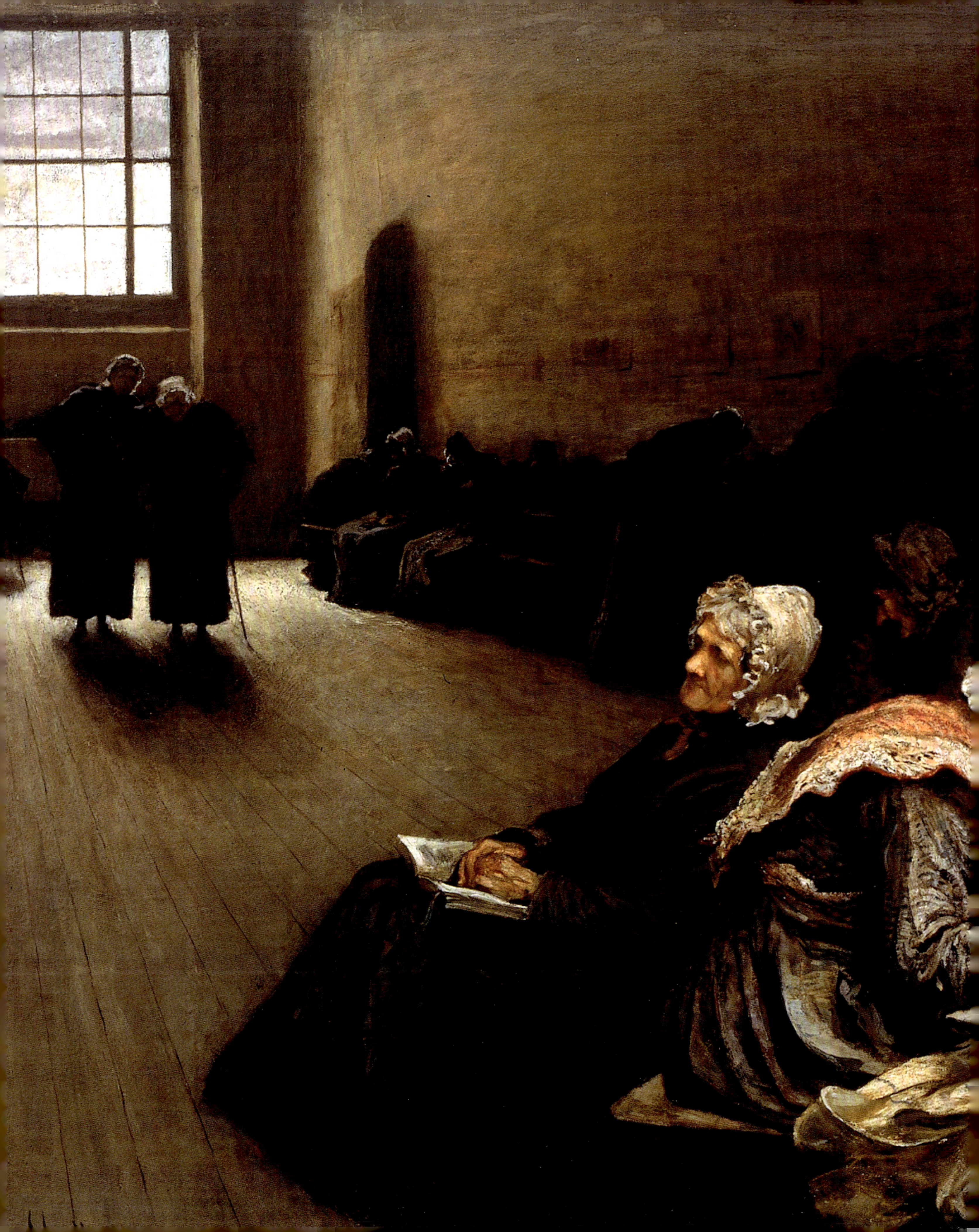

PART THE SECOND

THE INFLUENCE OF DICKENS *on the* Artists

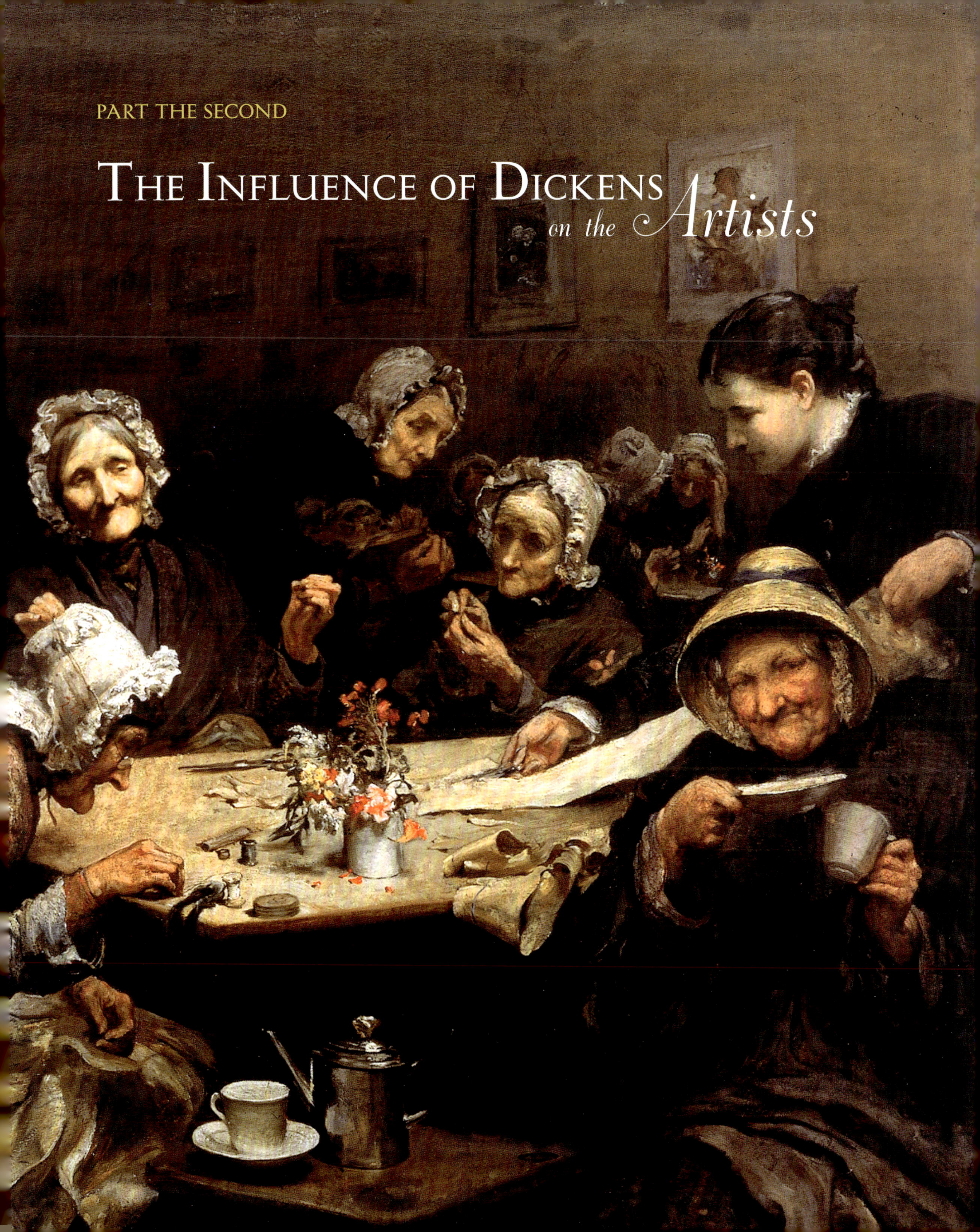

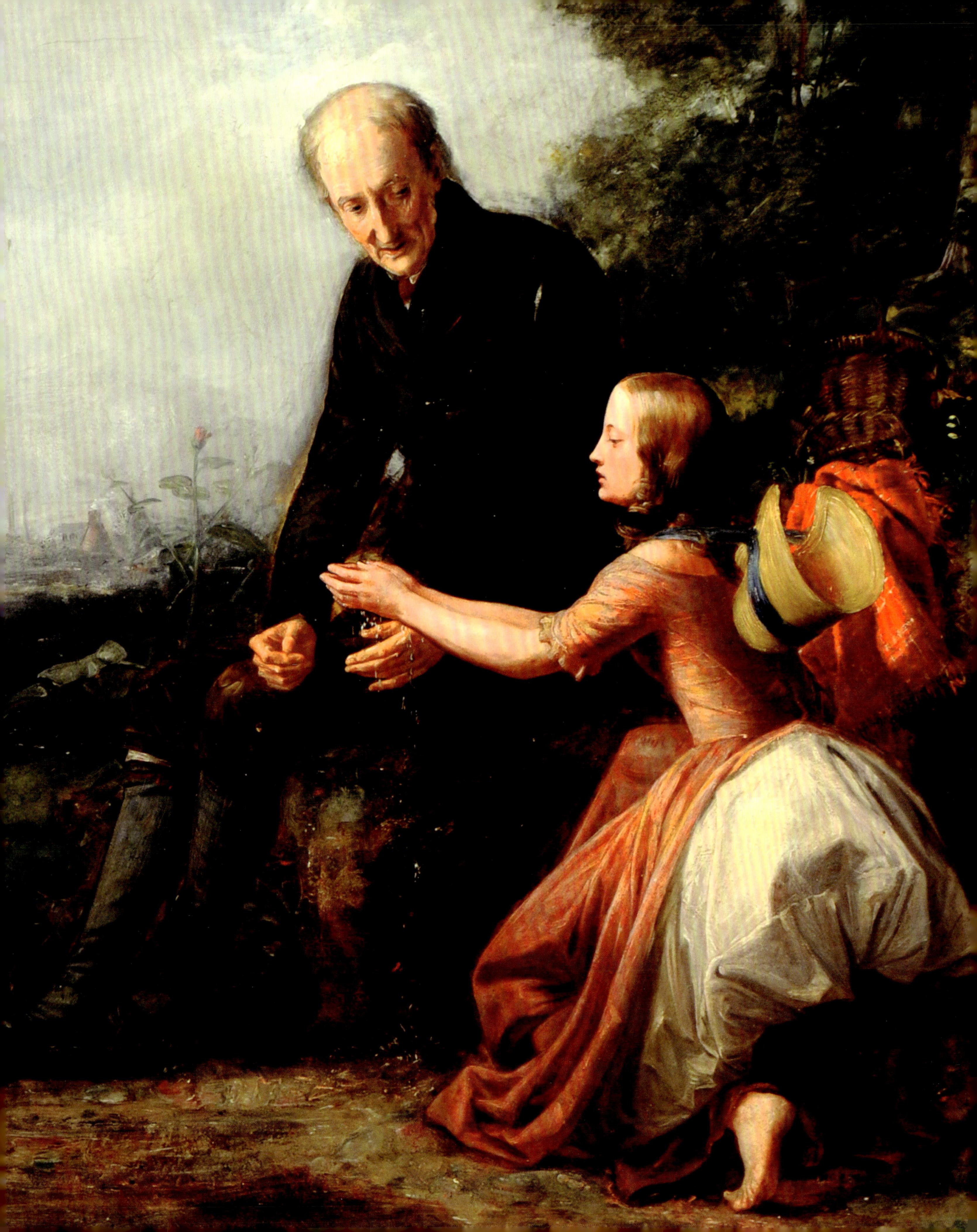

Dickens SUBJECTS IN VICTORIAN ART

HILARY UNDERWOOD

INTRODUCTION

Famous since the success of *Pickwick* in 1836–7 and described as 'the best read writer in the English language' whose death seemed a 'personal loss' to every English home,[1] Dickens has remained enduringly popular. His vivid characterization, the popularity of his novels and their extensive afterlife, particularly in plays, musicals, film and TV, have ensured that many of his characters have attained an almost archetypal presence in modern consciousness. Michael Slater in the *Oxford Dictionary of National Biography* epitomizes what we see as iconic in Dickens today:

> Mr Pickwick and Sam Weller, Oliver Twist asking for more, the Artful Dodger, Fagin, Sikes and the murder of Nancy, the death of Little Nell, Scrooge and Tiny Tim, Mr Pecksniff, Mrs Gamp, Uriah Heep, Mr Micawber hourly expecting something to turn up and Mrs Micawber refusing to desert him – these are some of the main Dickens characters and scenes that have been, and continue to be, drawn on over and over again . . . throughout the English-speaking world to point a moral or adorn a tale, to satirize or celebrate some contemporary figure or state of affairs.[2]

This essay explores painting and sculpture based on Dickens's writings, with a particular focus on works exhibited in major London exhibitions during Victoria's reign. These reveal significantly different patterns of subjects and themes from those favoured in modern culture, because of differences in Victorian social values and artistic conventions. In the mid-Victorian period, when Dickens subjects are most common, fine art was a high cultural form that incorporated popular painting. Its aesthetic permitted the appreciation of subject as well as form. Its public audience was considered to be universal (all classes, all ages and both genders) and its primary market was domestic (fig. 41). As concepts of art and audiences for art changed later in the century, so Dickens subjects also changed and declined. This essay therefore aims to explore what the particular qualities of Victorian Dickens subjects reveal about Victorian society and

FIG. 40
William Holman Hunt, *Little Nell and her Grandfather* (detail of fig. 47)

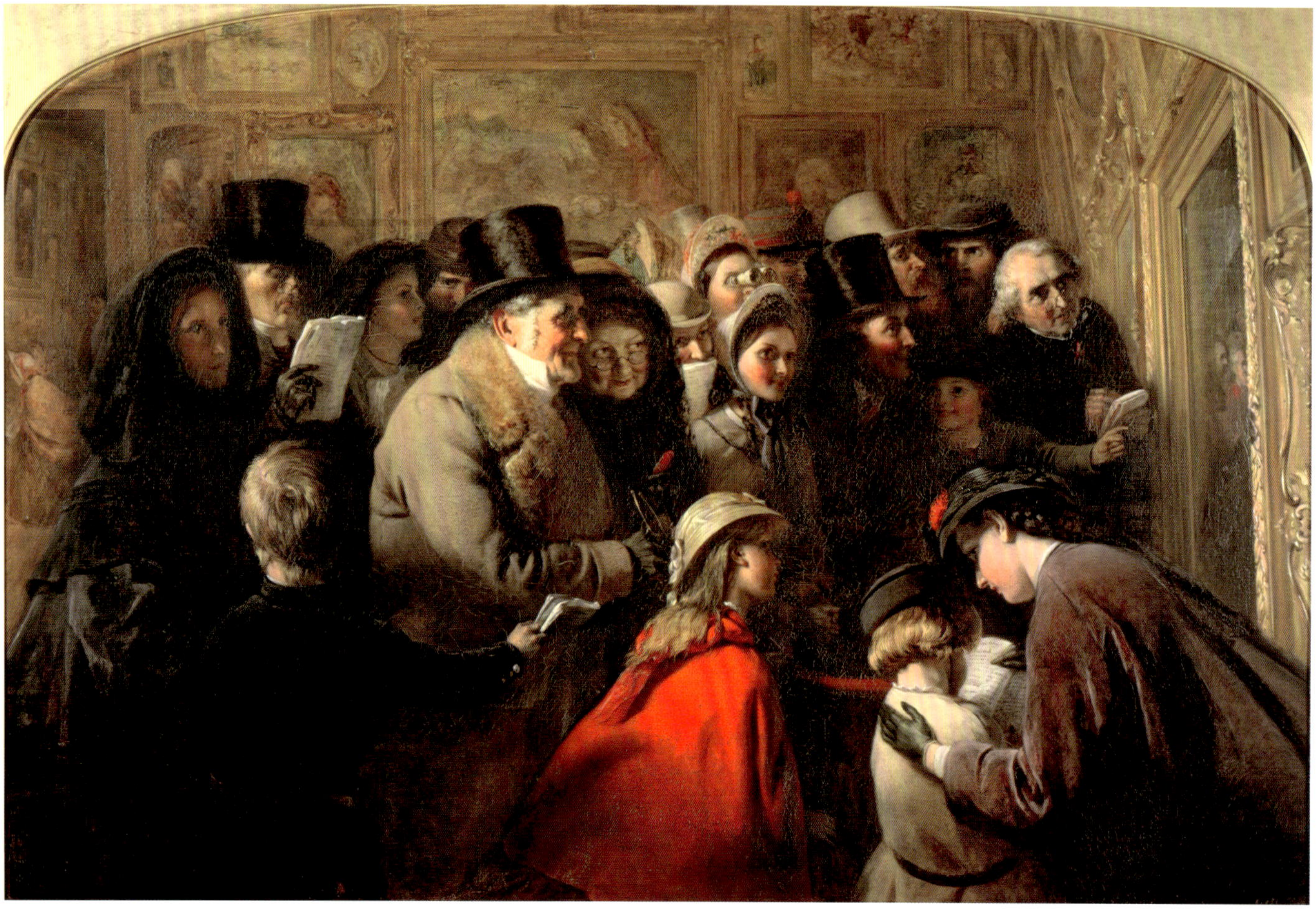

FIG. 41
George Bernard O'Neill, *Public Opinion*, RA 1863, oil on canvas. Leeds Museums and Galleries (City Art Gallery)

Victorian artistic conventions. Dickens subjects are also used to explore the relationship between image and text in literary painting. The story is then taken into the twentieth century, though in a more summary way, with an exploration of Dickens subjects at the Royal Academy.

Individual paintings with Dickens subjects have been discussed in catalogues, exhibitions, books and articles, but mainly those by artists with high reputations today including William Powell Frith, William Holman Hunt and Robert Braithwaite Martineau. Dickens paintings as a group, indeed Victorian literary painting as a whole, has been surprisingly little studied.[3] After Sir Walter Scott, Dickens was the contemporary novelist whose works were most depicted. F.G. Kitton provided a preliminary list of sixty-three British paintings and sculptures with Dickens subjects.[4] Sixteen of these were exhibited at the Royal Academy. A fuller search of exhibition catalogues and indices up until 1900 has so far revealed at least 170 certain exhibited works, of which seventy-one were exhibited at the Royal Academy (RA).

Public interest in Dickens was not just shown by paintings of his works, he was also the subject of numerous exhibited portraits. Many were not directly initiated by

FIG. 42
William Powell Frith, *Charles Dickens in his Study*, 1859, oil on canvas. Victoria and Albert Museum, London

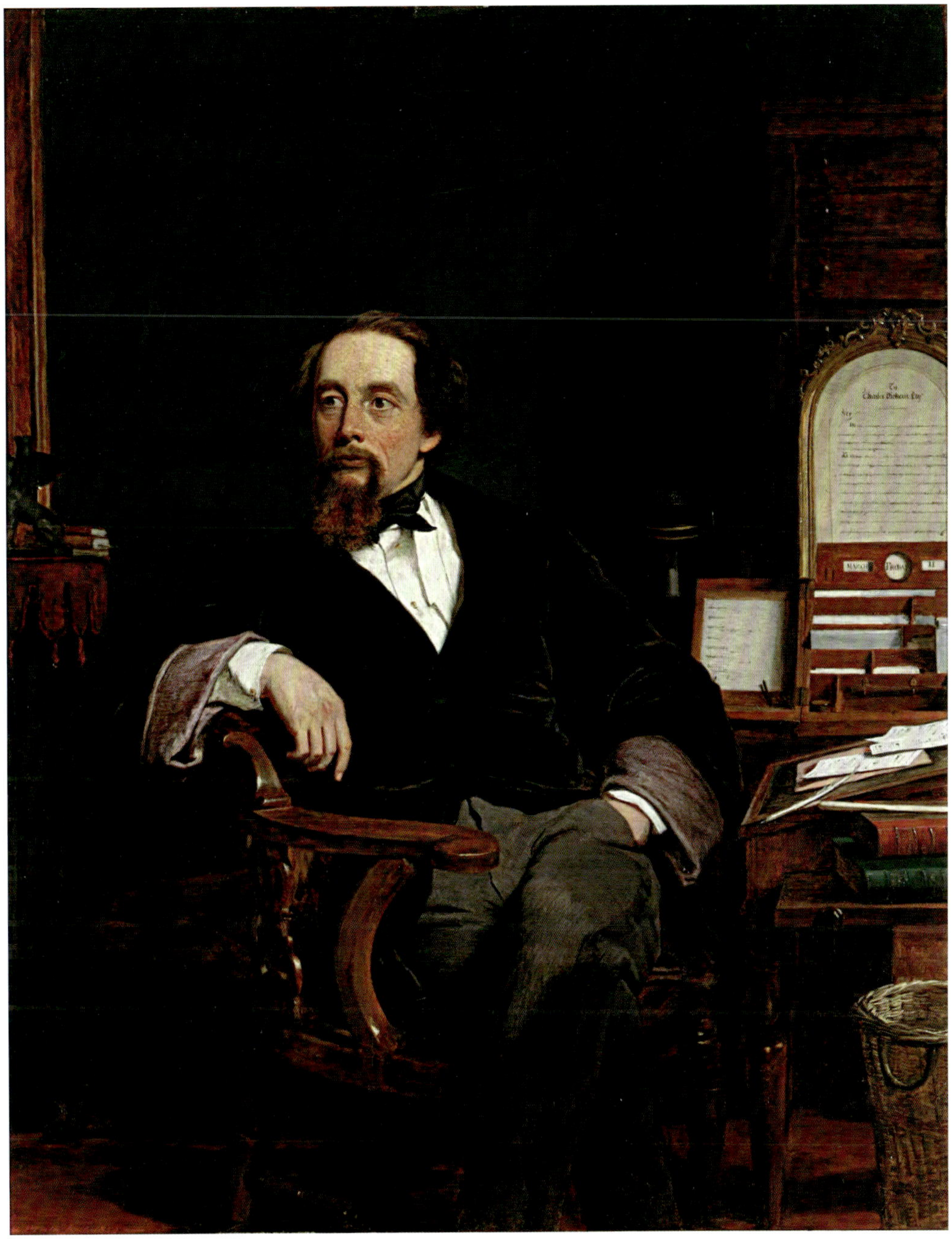

the writer. Frith's portrait, *Charles Dickens in his Study* (fig. 42), was commissioned by Dickens's friend and biographer John Forster. Other portraits were instigated by the artists themselves, for instance Ary Scheffer's portrait of 1855 (National Portrait Gallery, London). The popular interest in Dickens's image is shown by the proliferation of Parian Ware busts of the writer in various sizes.[5] Detailed discussion of Dickens portraiture lies outside the scope of this essay, but it is surveyed elsewhere.[6] Interest in

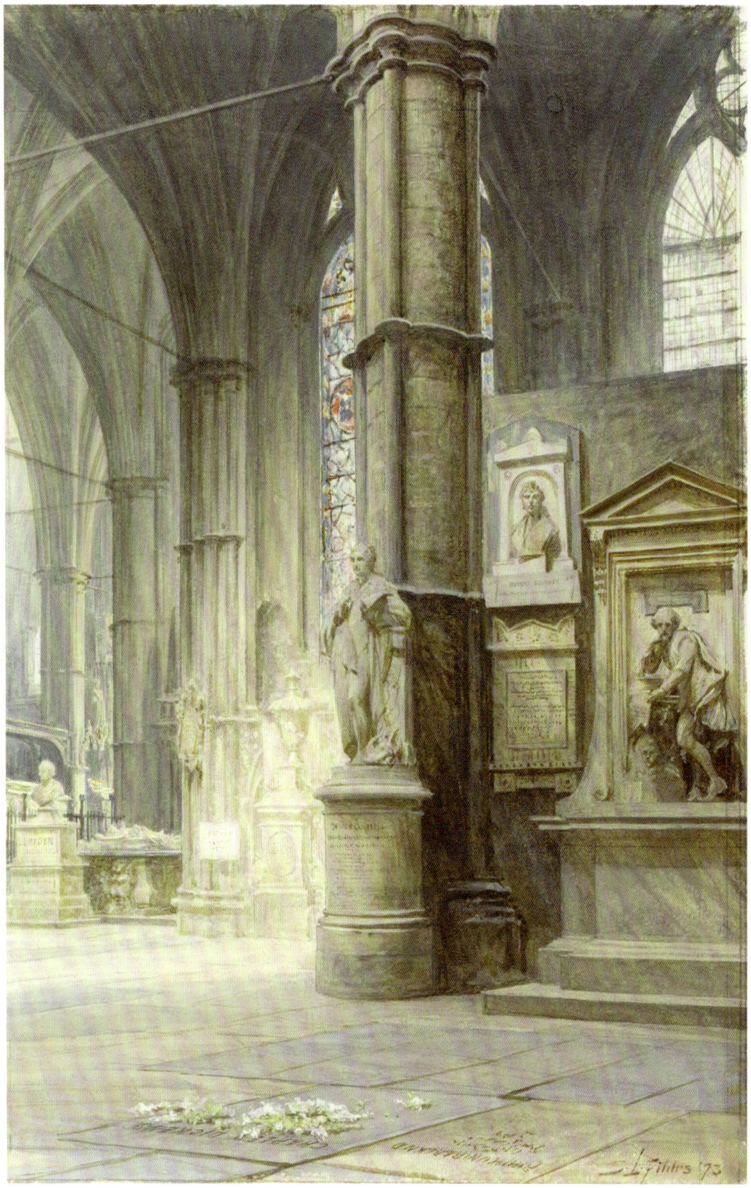

FIG. 43
Sir Samuel Luke Fildes, *The Grave of Charles Dickens, Poets' Corner, Westminster Abbey*, 1873, watercolour. Victoria and Albert Museum, London

Dickens is also revealed by paintings of places explicitly associated with him. There were a number of paintings of his grave in Westminster Abbey, including that by Luke Fildes (fig. 43).[7] Artists produced topographical watercolours of places associated with Dickens. George Ruff senior depicted *Broadstairs, 'Our Watering-place' of Charles Dickens* and R.A. Gill exhibited *Bleak House Broadstairs*. The earliest of these 'landscapes of association' is William Carter's *Sketch on the Spot of Jacob's Island, Southwark, Mentioned by Boz in 'Oliver Twist'* (1843; see pp. 106–7 for a list of exhibition dates and catalogue numbers). Paintings of readers, particularly women readers, are common in nineteenth-century genre paintings, and some refer to Dickens. They include Alfred Barron Clay's

Finishing Bleak House, Selina Forster's *Reading the 'Household Words'* and Solomon Alexander Hart's *Reading Dickens*. Robert Hannah's *The Novel* shows two young ladies in a carriage in Hyde Park reading *Bleak House*, while the footboy behind them eagerly eavesdrops.[8] A further indication of the impact of Dickens on the British psyche is that even in his lifetime his characters became so well known that they could be seen as types rather than just individuals, giving rise to paintings such as James Holmes's *The Streets of London: A Female Dombey* and William Rose's *An Artful Dodger*.

DICKENS LITERARY PAINTINGS: PATTERNS OF PRODUCTION

Dickens subjects began to appear in substantial numbers in the early 1840s. Dickens's initial rise to fame is hinted at by watercolours of *Mr Pickwick and the Spinster Aunt* by H. Richter and of Kate Nickleby by F.T. Baynes. The consolidation of his reputation with *The Old Curiosity Shop* and particularly the appeal of the pathetic heroine Little Nell led to a boom in Dickens subjects, of which at least twenty-two were produced in the first half of the 1840s. *The Old Curiosity Shop* reached a circulation of around 100,000 by the end of its serialization in February 1841[9] and resulted in at least nine exhibited paintings by the end of 1845. *Barnaby Rudge*, completed in November 1841, was less popular as a novel (final circulation 30,000),[10] but its eighteenth-century setting appealed to the pictorial tastes of the 1840s. No less than ten subjects from *Barnaby Rudge* were exhibited by the end of 1845, mainly of the flirtatious Dolly Varden (fig. 45). The continued popularity of Dickens led to a steady production of works based on his novels in the following years. After the initial peak in the early 1840s around fifteen Dickens subjects appeared every five years at the Royal Academy, Society of British Artists and British Institution exhibitions together, with further showings in the watercolour societies and the lesser exhibitions. The half-decade after Dickens's death saw a rise in the number of exhibits, although moderate, to twenty. In the 1890s, as changing tastes in art became more established, numbers of Dickens subjects began to decline dramatically.

Throughout the Victorian period the first pictorial favourites, *The Old Curiosity Shop* and *Barnaby Rudge*, continued to inspire the largest numbers of works, at least forty-five and twenty-eight respectively by 1900. *Dombey and Son* (published 1848), not one of Dickens's most popular works today, was third with at least twenty-two works. Most of these focus on the love between the dying child Paul Dombey and his elder sister Florence. *David Copperfield*, *Bleak House* and *Nicholas Nickleby* gave rise to at least eleven, ten and eight works respectively, and Dickens's remaining novels four or less. Particular characters inspire paintings from otherwise little depicted novels. For instance, three of the paintings drawn from *Our Mutual Friend* portray the relatively minor figure Jenny Wren, the doll's dressmaker.[11] The two paintings based on *Martin Chuzzlewit* (published 1843–4) both represent Betsy Prig and Sarah Gamp.[12] The absence of some subjects that are iconic to modern eyes is striking. Although Dickens's writings actively shaped the British awareness of Christmas from the 1840s on, there are no paintings after *A Christmas Carol*, one of his most popular works today. The seasonality of the subject may have limited its appeal in painting, which tends to be bought for year-round display, although other Victorian genre paintings feature Christmas subjects. Oliver Twist's story was little treated: among only four paintings, Miss Jessie Macleod showed *The Employment of Oliver Twist in the Jew's House* in 1849 and Oliver does not 'ask for more' in art until Alfred W. Strutt's painting at the Academy of 1888. Starveling Oliver, Fagin, Sykes and Nancy are some of Dickens's most dramatic characters and indeed formed the material for some of his most powerful readings. George Cruikshank's definitive illustrations, which derived from traditions of the caricatural grotesque, may have inhibited further pictorial treatment. After the time of Hogarth this tradition was less available to the fine arts, which were increasingly bound by bourgeois realism. Dickens's scenes and characters are also squalid and repulsive, due to his intention to de-glamorize crime, so a further reason for the absence of representations may be the domestic market for art, which encouraged subjects that were appealing, both visually and in sentiment.

Dickens's readings from his own works, which he undertook professionally between 1858 and the end of his life,[13] may have influenced artists in their choice of subjects. For example *Little Dombey*, focusing on the story of Paul and Florence Dombey, was first performed in June 1858 but, despite its popularity, rarely after 1861.[14] After a cluster of paintings following the book's publication in 1847–8, another small batch followed in the early 1860s probably inspired by the readings.[15]

In other cases successful theatrical representations had a measurable effect on Dickens subject paintings. *Bleak House* themes are a clear example and fall into two groups. The first, of four works, was produced between 1853 and 1858, immediately following the book's serialization. In fact, Miss Flora Elizabeth Thomas's *Rosa* was exhibited in February 1853 while the serialization (March 1852–September 1853) was still in progress. The paintings of the reading of *Bleak House* testify to the interest generated by the book: as Dickens said, 'I have never had so many readers.'[16] The second group, of six works, was produced between 1878 and 1891, and was almost certainly prompted by the success of J.P. Burnett's play *Jo, or, Bleak House*, which concerned the ragged crossing sweeper in *Bleak House* and was first produced in the UK in 1876 but never published. Jenny Lee, wife of the playwright, made a career of the title role, in which she was the subject of a theatrical portrait by Henry Macbeth-Raeburn. Four of these six later paintings and sculptures are of *Jo* subjects. None of the earlier ones is.

Sir John Martin Harvey starred as Sidney Carton in *The Only Way*, an adaptation of *A Tale of Two Cities*, playing the role intermittently for over forty years in a hugely successful play first produced in 1899. The 1859 novel generated its first painting as early as 1861. Others followed intermittently.[17] The success of the play prompted a group of early twentieth-century artworks based on the *Tale of Two Cities* at a time when Dickens subjects were increasingly rare: Thomas Benjamin Kennington's *Recalled to Life*, a bust of Martin Harvey in role by George James Frampton and a theatrical portrait by James Jebusa Shannon (fig. 44).

FIG. 44
James Jebusa Shannon, *Sir John Martin Harvey as Sydney Carton in 'The Only Way'*, RA 1904, oil on canvas. Private collection

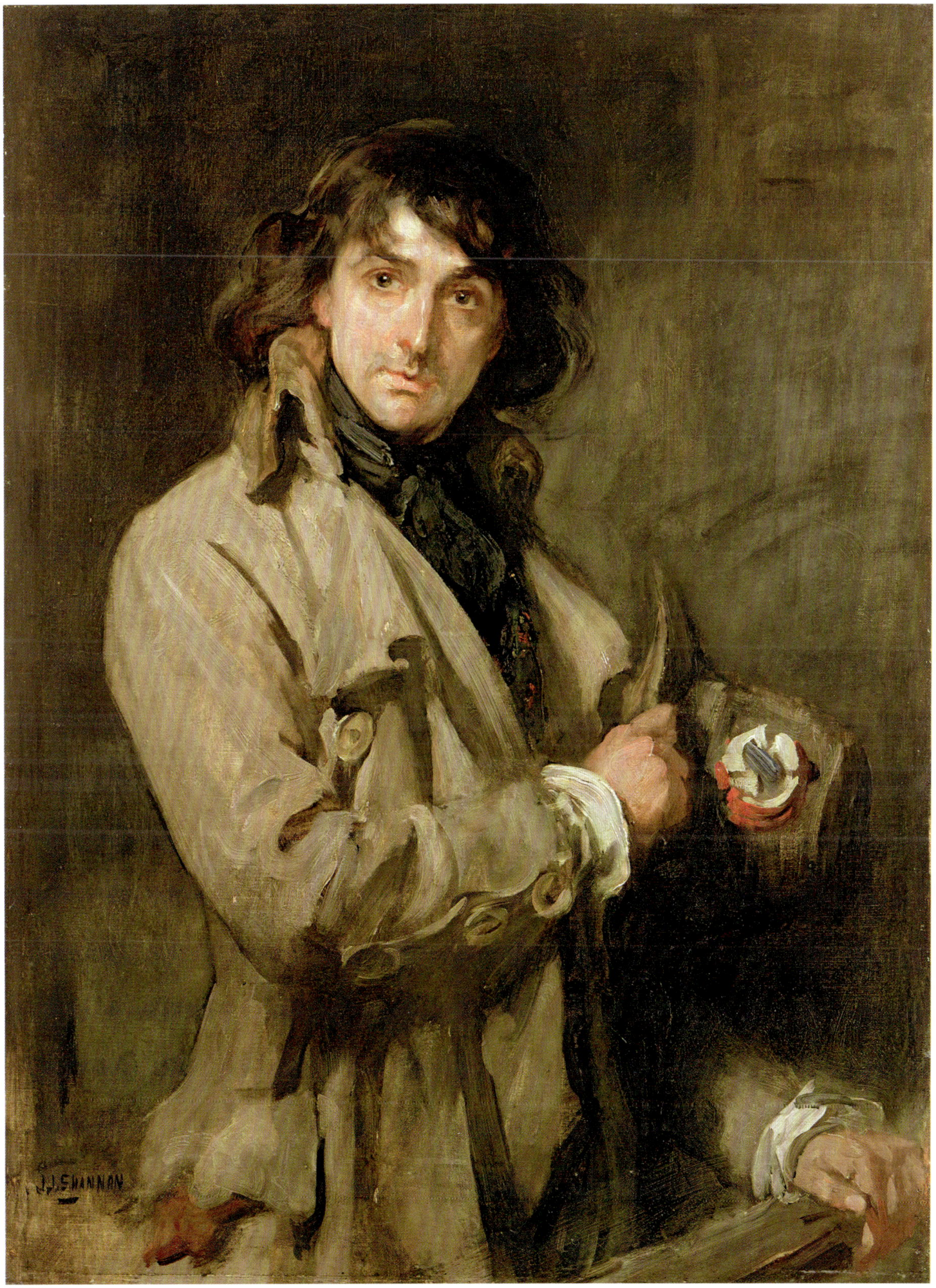
J.J. SHANNON

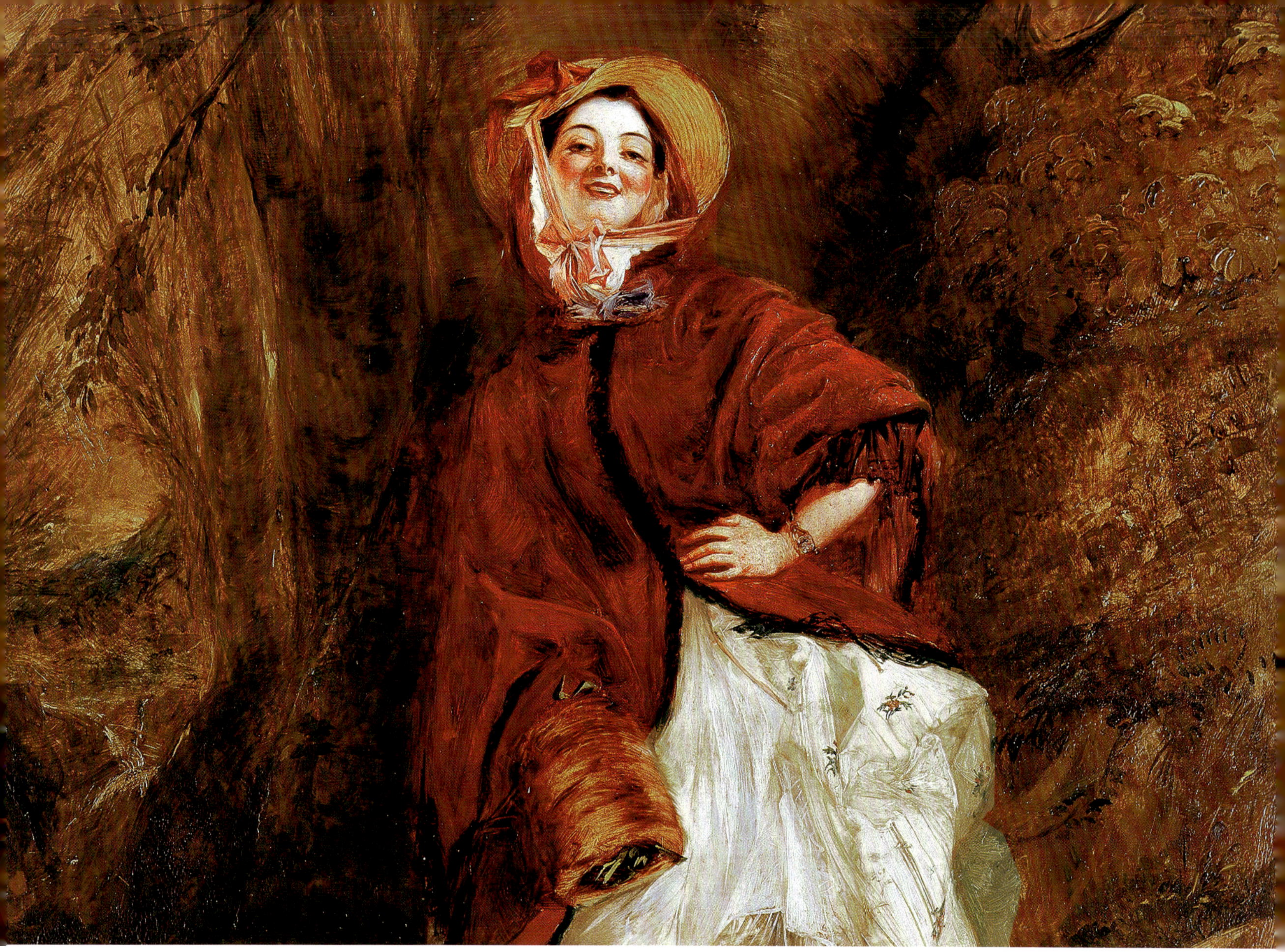

Some of the paintings of Dickens subjects belonged to Dickens himself, either by commission or as gifts from the artist. Frith's second composition of *Dolly Varden* was painted for Dickens,[18] after Dickens had seen and admired the earlier picture of the subject. Dickens also commissioned a picture of *Kate Nickleby* and paid 20 guineas for each. When Dickens saw the completed pictures, he said they were 'exactly what he meant',[19] and they hung in the dining room of his house (see figs 3, 71). Frith also painted two *Little Dorrit* subjects as vignettes for the Library Edition of Dickens.[20] William Gale's *Mr F.'s Aunt* was admired by Wilkie Collins,[21] who wrote enthusiastically to Dickens about it. Dickens replied on 22 May 1857: 'I am very much excited by what you tell me of Mr. F's Aunt, I already look upon her as mine. Will you bring her with you.' Dickens bought the picture through Collins.[22] Charles Robert Leslie painted *Mr Pickwick and Mrs Bardell* for Dickens, and it was engraved for the first cheap edition of *The Pickwick Papers*.[23] Frank Stone painted *Tilda Price*, *Madeline Bray* and *Kate Nickleby* for Dickens. None of these works was exhibited, as was common for small direct commissions.[24] Mrs Fanny

ABOVE
FIG. 45
William Powell Frith, *Dolly Varden* (detail of fig. 70)

RIGHT
FIG. 46
Thomas Faed, *Kate Nickleby*, 1862, oil on canvas. Private collection

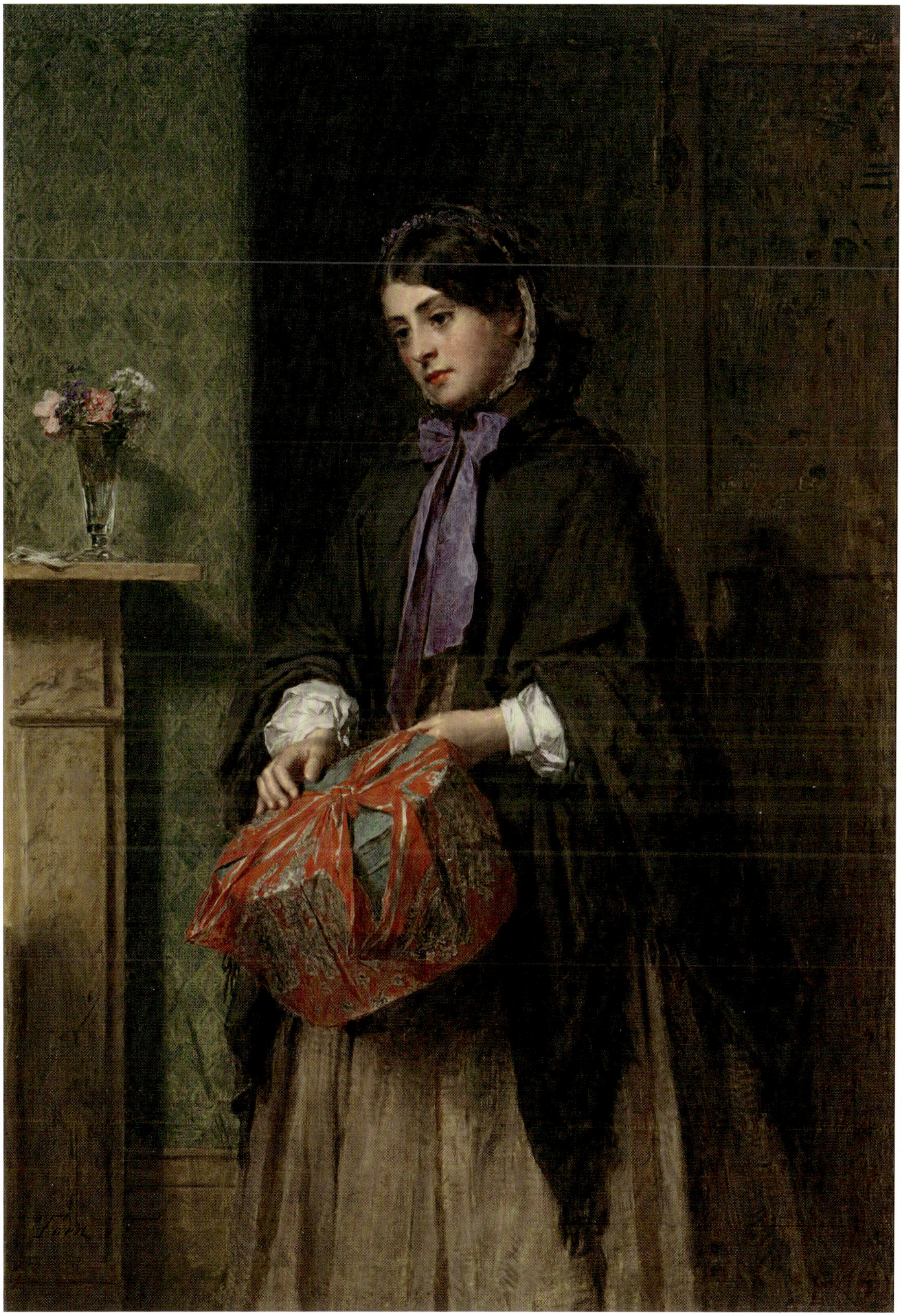

McIan presented Dickens with her *Little Nell Reading the Inscription on the Tombstone*. This selection of works suggests that Dickens had the typical artistic tastes of the early Victorian period in preferring small and finely detailed domestic subjects and 'fancy portraits'. The hyperrealism and more complex narratives developed by the Pre-Raphaelites were not to his taste.

Although relatively large numbers of Dickens subjects were produced and exhibited, the majority of them were minor works. In surviving pictures scenes of one and two figures predominate, and titles suggest that this is true of the majority of works. More complex figure compositions are rare. Exceptions are by Charles Green of the 1870s and 1880s, both autonomous compositions and direct translations into watercolour of illustrations that he produced for the Household Edition of the works of Charles Dickens.[25] Single figures, such as Thomas Faed's *Kate Nickleby* (fig. 46), often relate to the fancy portrait or keepsake tradition: primarily, attractive female images to which title, narrative and 'subject' are loose adjuncts. Many Dickens paintings were produced by little-known artists with small exhibition records. A high proportion of painters of Dickens subjects were women, as can be seen from the works referred to. Almost one fifth of the Royal Academy and British Institution exhibitors of Dickens subjects and almost one third of those in the Society of British Artists were by women. Dickens was perceived as a highly suitable writer for family reading. His works featured attractive potential subjects of women and children, considered more suitable themes for female genre painters, who sometimes found models from within their own family circles. Modern-life subjects involved less investment in research and costuming. These may all have been potential factors in the attraction of women artists and lesser-known artists to Dickens.[26] Other clues suggest the minor status of most Dickens paintings. Large numbers were shown at the Society of British Artists, which was more associated with saleability than prestige. Dickens paintings in the Royal Academy after 1869 often have high catalogue numbers, indicating the later rooms in the Burlington House exhibition, which mainly contained smaller paintings attracting less critical attention. Prices for most Dickens paintings in the British Institution and Society of British Artists exhibitions (given after 1853 and 1855) are moderate.[27] These factors have led to an afterlife in which usually only exhibition titles have survived. The majority of Dickens paintings were little reviewed and have no subsequent history in sale records, exhibitions or public collections.

Major Victorian artists who treated Dickens subjects did so mainly in the form of small or early works, such as Faed's *Kate Nickleby*. Frith saw his *Dolly Varden* paintings of 1842 as important transitional works towards the paintings of modern life that made his name.[28] They are small genre scenes of one of two figures, of which he stated: 'These pictures easily found purchasers, though for sums small enough.'[29] Holman Hunt's first extant exhibited work is *Little Nell and her Grandfather* (fig. 47), but as his involvement in what became Pre-Raphaelitism developed, Hunt did not return to Dickens, despite turning to modern-life genre subjects in the early 1850s.

FIG. 47
William Holman Hunt, *Little Nell and her Grandfather*, 1845, oil on canvas. Museums Sheffield

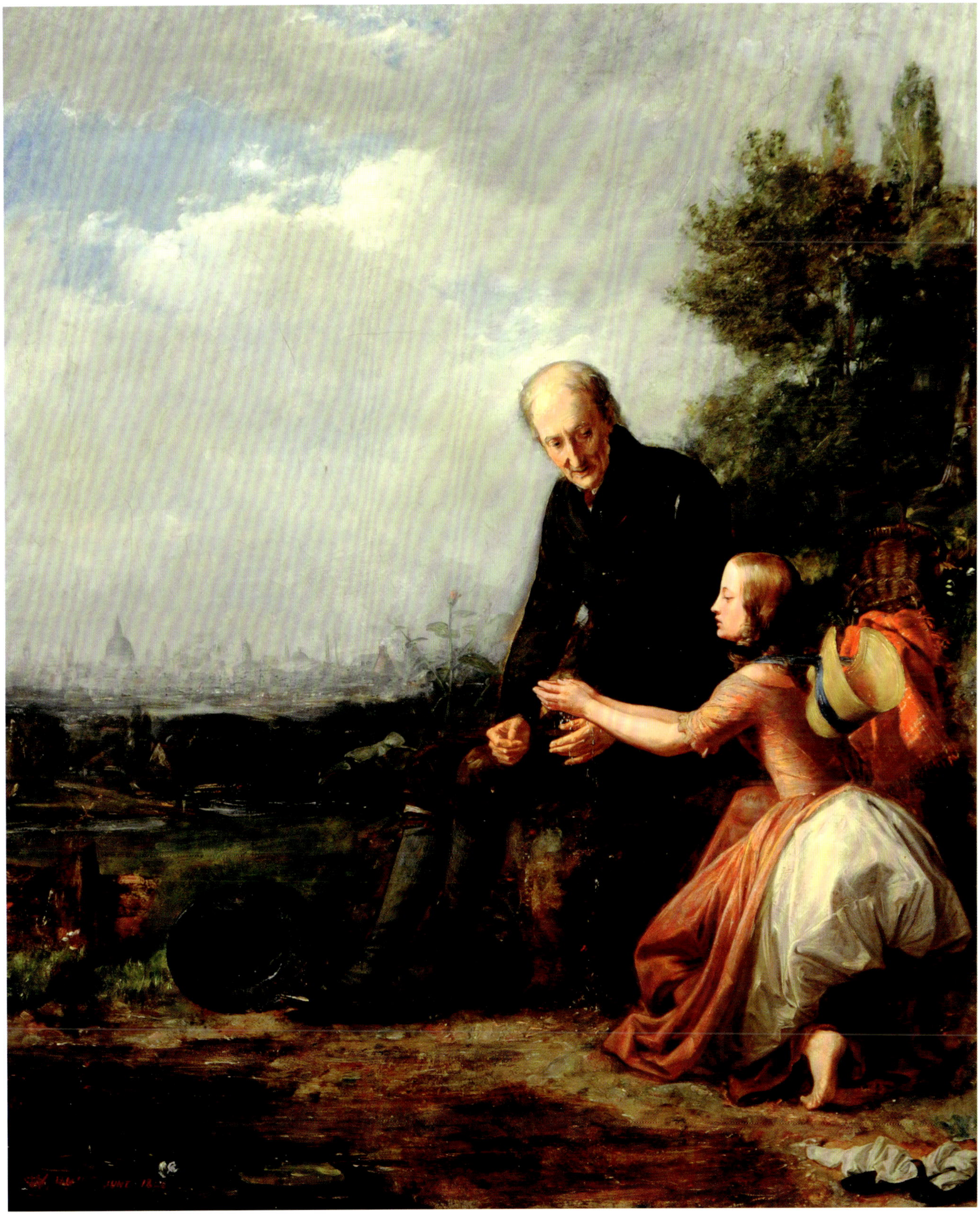

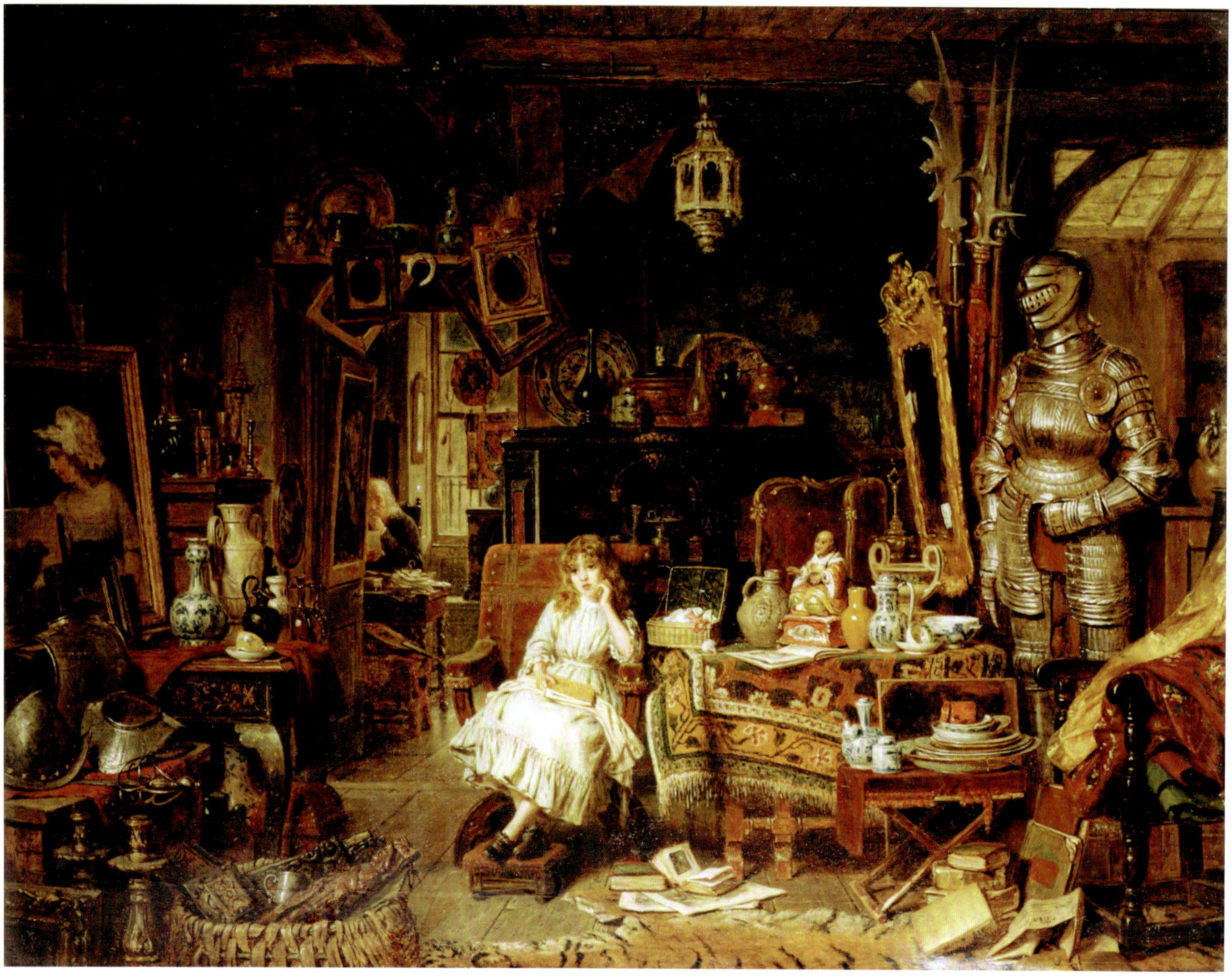

Occasionally Dickens subjects proved successful for their artists. The first version of Frith's flirtatious painting of the laughing Dolly Varden leaning against a tree was originally sold to the private collector Henry Cooper through the dealer Charles Hawker in January 1842. Frith borrowed it back in the spring to show it at the Society of British Artists, and two commissions for replicas resulted.[30] Seven versions of the composition are now known,[31] including the version bequeathed by Dickens's friend and biographer John Forster to the Victoria and Albert Museum (fig. 45) and a smaller version in Tate Britain. John Watkins Chapman was a minor genre painter mainly exhibiting at the Society of British Artists and intermittently at the Royal Academy. He showed Little Nell and her grandfather in *The Old Curiosity Shop* at the Academy of 1888. It was displayed in Gallery 8 and attracted little critical attention, but spawned two closely related versions.[32] One of the three pictures is illustrated here (figs 48, 49).

FIGS 48, 49
John Watkins Chapman, *The Old Curiosity Shop* (or *Little Nell and her Grandfather*), version of RA 1888, oil on canvas. Private collection

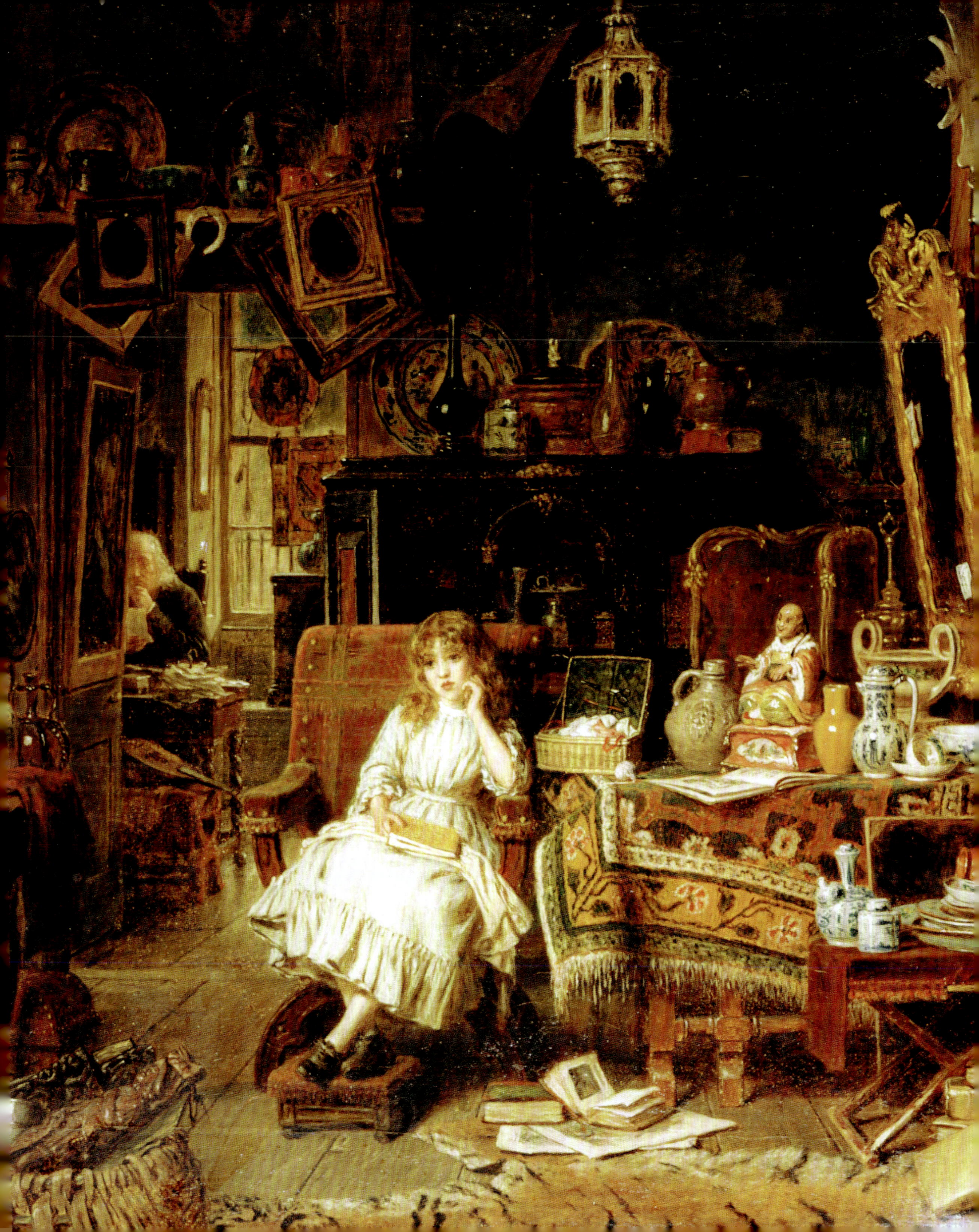

However, Dickens subject paintings may not have proved as saleable as the popularity of Dickens's novels and of the works mentioned above might indicate. Hunt's *Little Nell and her Grandfather* was unsold at the 1846 British Institution and at the 1847 Manchester and Liverpool exhibitions. The artist sold the picture to a Bath dealer only some thirty-five years after it was painted.[33] William Maw Egley's *Florence Dombey in Captain Cuttle's Parlour* (fig. 50) did not receive a London exhibition and remained unsold at nine provincial exhibitions, despite a price reduction from £40 to £15. It was finally sold to a collector in 1898 for £25, ten years after it was painted.[34] These instances could be attributed to individual circumstances: in the first case a young, unknown and inexperienced artist (who spoilt the sky of his painting by using salad oil as a medium), and in the second a painter reaching the end of his career, when literary painting was dropping out of favour. But a further suggestive pattern emerges in Dickens works. Few painters exhibited more than a handful. The prolific genre painter Alfred Joseph Woolmer showed 412 paintings in London between 1829 and 1886, including 355 at the Society of British Artists, but he produced only two Dickens subjects, and those at the height of Dickens paintings in the 1840s: a *Dolly Varden* and a *Five Sisters of York* from *Nicholas Nickleby*, which may be largely an architectural subject. There were no more, although other literary subjects including those from Shakespeare and Tennyson feature strongly in his later output. Kate Perugini, Dickens's painter daughter, showed only five Dickens subjects.[35] The extreme rarity of pictures based on the works of other leading Victorian novelists such as Thackeray and George Eliot suggests a limited market for subjects from contemporary prose fiction.

Dickens subjects were at their most popular in the 1840s, when they were part of a broader taste for literary narrative genre paintings. These were generally drawn from seventeenth- or eighteenth-century novels, from plays by writers such as Molière, Cervantes, Laurence Sterne and Oliver Goldsmith or from the historical novels of Sir Walter Scott. The Sheepshanks and Vernon art collections, given to the nation in 1857 and 1847 respectively, are representative of this phase of taste.[36] Dickens's eighteenth-century *Barnaby Rudge* first opened his work to artistic representation because it fitted in with existing tastes in literary painting. Recent novels with contemporary settings were little represented because of the general belief in the unpicturesqueness of modern dress.[37] The popularity of *The Old Curiosity Shop* broke through this barrier, and the fame and the seriousness of Dickens's modern-life novels and his close links with a circle of genre painters assisted the development of the modern-life genre painting, as Mark Bills argues in his essay. But the growing confidence and ambition of mid-Victorian genre painters may have been a factor in the decline in importance of literary subject matter. From the time of the codification of artistic theory in the Renaissance, 'invention' was used as a measure of the ability of a painter.[38] In early- and mid-Victorian art, with its relatively unsophisticated approach to issues of form, invention was usually equated with originality of subject matter, as Frith makes clear in his reminiscences. He writes of 'a subject which I found and presented to Egg',[39] which he 'much repented

FIG. 50
William Maw Egley, *Florence Dombey in Captain Cuttle's Parlour*, 1888, oil on canvas. Victoria and Albert Museum, London

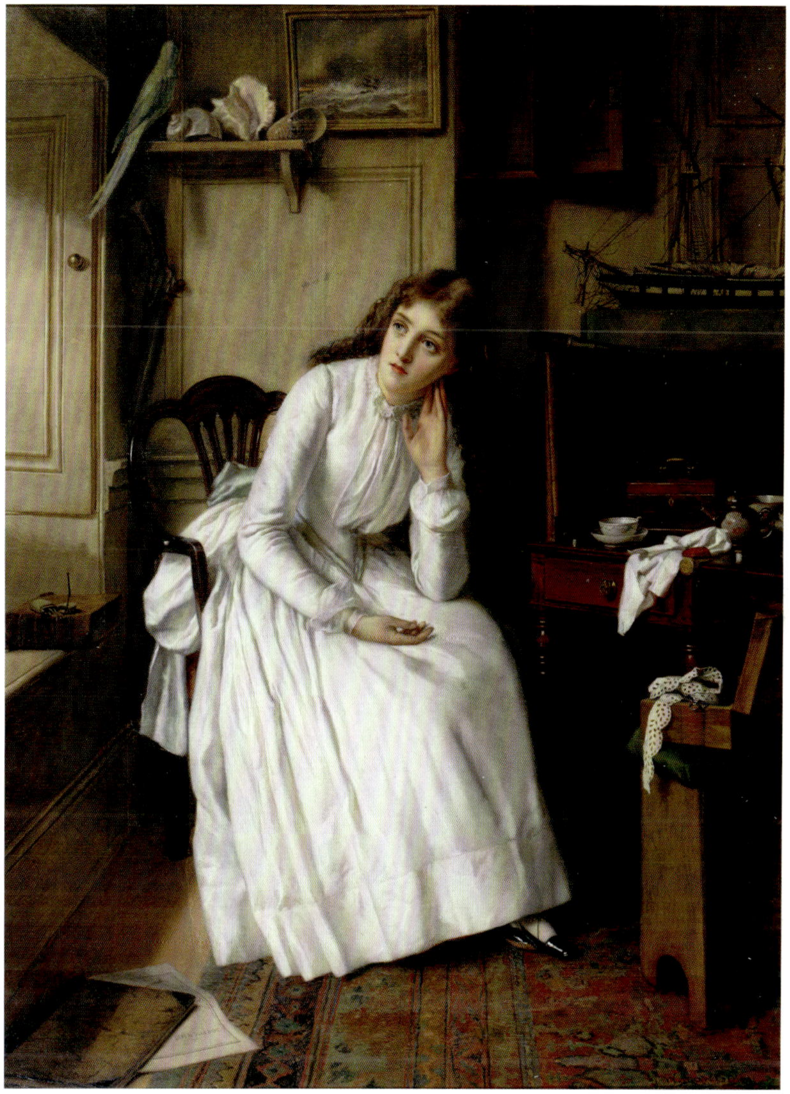

of afterwards'. His friend Dickens described his presentation of this work to Augustus Egg as an 'amazing devil of generosity'.[40] Frith later offered financial rewards for suggestions of useable original modern-life subjects.[41] The Pre-Raphaelites, also pioneering high-status modern-life subjects, shared similar concerns with originality. Holman Hunt and Dante Gabriel Rossetti disputed priority in representing the fallen woman in, respectively, *The Awakening Conscience* (1853; Tate Britain) and *Found* (1854–81; Delaware Art Museum).[42] As ambitious painters moved into the field of modern life, raising the status of modern genre subjects to a sort of high art, they focused more on invention and originality, which could be diminished by being directly illustrative of a fictional text.[43] As Mark Bills shows, most important Victorian modern-life genre painting from Frith to Luke Fildes and Frank Holl is profoundly Dickensian, but it does not depict Dickens subjects.

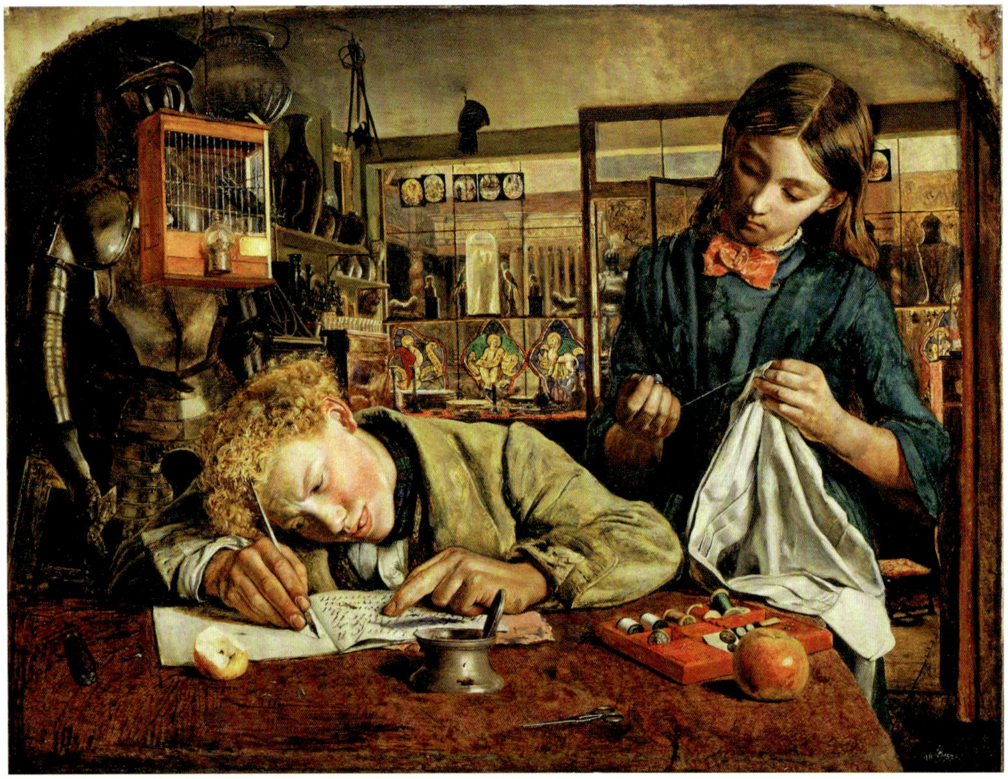

FIG. 51
Robert Braithwaite Martineau, *Kit's Writing Lesson*, 1852, oil on canvas. Tate, London

LITERARY PAINTING: BETWEEN ILLUSTRATION AND GENRE

Literary subject painting has received relatively little attention as a scholarly category. Discussions of artists' literary subjects are included in monographs and the genre sections of survey volumes, and there have been publications on artistic representations of the works of various authors, including Shakespeare, Scott and Tennyson.[44] With the exception of Catherine Gordon's doctoral thesis (see note 3), there has been little discussion of literary subject painting as a separate category in the way that Roy Strong has discussed issues in the re-creation of history in painting.[45] Recent academic study of Victorian genre painting has had an overwhelming focus on original scenes of contemporary life and on what these reveal of the dominant values and ideologies of the Victorians,[46] but in these studies contemporary scenes with literary sources play a minor part.[47] Recent academic concerns with multimodality and adaptation are largely focused on the translation of literary works into the modern media of film and television, within which understanding the mechanisms of Victorian literary painting is recondite and largely irrelevant. The awareness of how literary painting operates in relation to book illustration on the one hand and original genre painting on the other is therefore underdeveloped.

It is revealing to compare Robert Braithwaite Martineau's *Kit's Writing Lesson* (fig. 51) from *The Old Curiosity Shop* with James Collinson's *The Writing Lesson* (fig. 52), which is nearly contemporary but not a literary subject. In the Collinson a young girl guides

FIG. 52
James Collinson, *The Writing Lesson*, 1855, oil on panel. Royal Academy, London

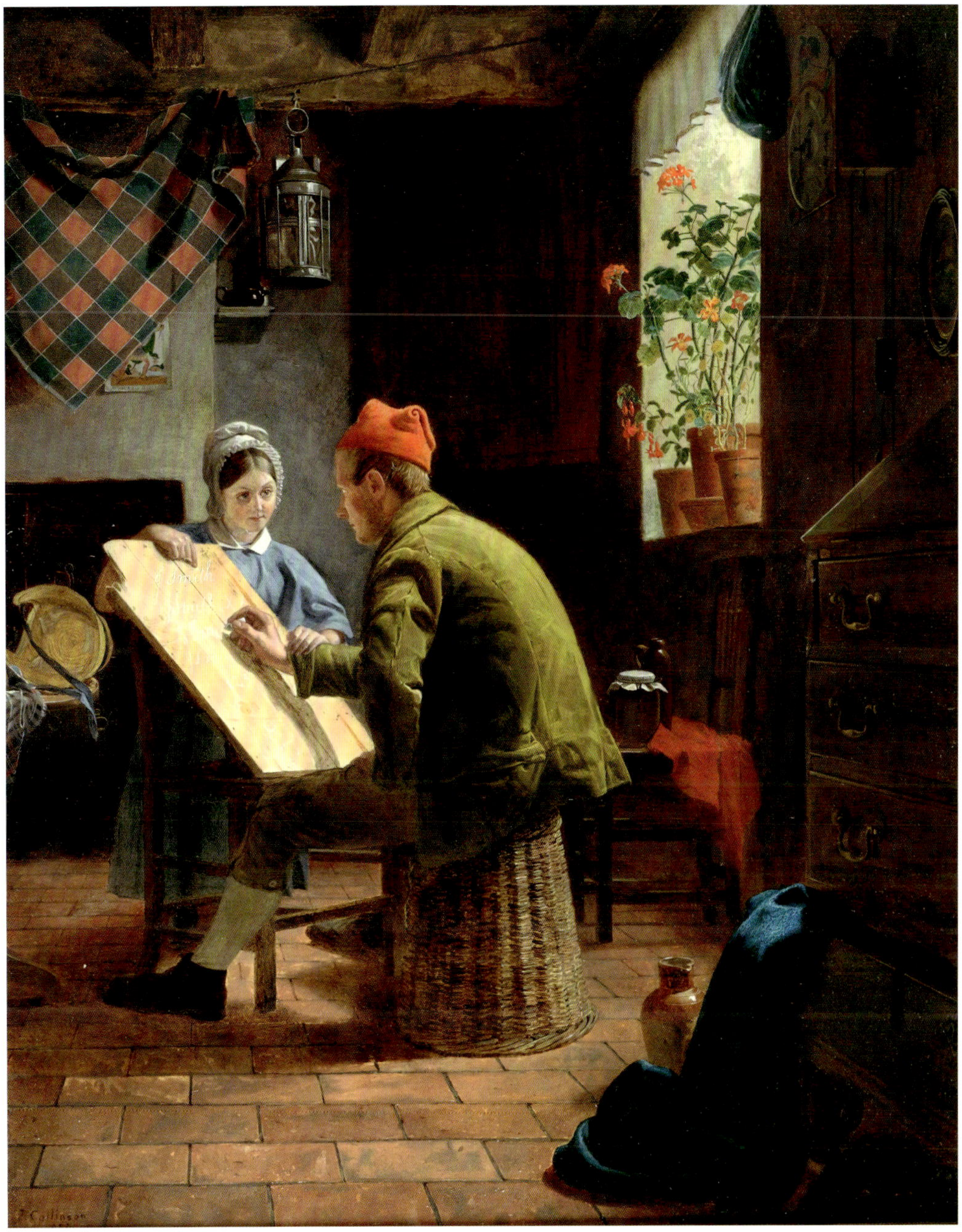

the hand of a working class man as he writes on a board in white chalk. The setting is probably a farmhouse. In the Martineau Little Nell, sewing a shirt for her grandfather, stands over the scratchy pen-work of the young Kit Nubbles, the shop's errand boy. The cluttered interior of the Old Curiosity Shop itself is in the background. Obviously one interpretative strand of Dickens subject paintings (as indeed of Dickens's novels) is to see them in the light of Victorian values and ideologies. The works discussed do address similar themes of working-class literacy, aspiration and self-help, and also reinforce dominant Victorian concepts of female roles. Like George Elgar Hicks's *Woman's Mission* triptych of 1863 (*Guide of Childhood*, *Companion of Manhood* and *Comfort of Old Age*[48]), paintings like Martineau's and Collinson's both reinforce a female ideal of motherly guidance and nurturing, here made to seem more potently natural by being embodied in the actions of young girls. But to deal with the specificity of Dickens and other literary paintings, it is important to explore how they can be read in different ways to non-literary genres.

In the Collinson we know no more of the characters and their history than we can infer from the scene itself, reading or reconstructing the meanings and connotations of clothing and accessories. The girl's blue dress and cap may show that she owes her education to a charity school; the nurtured fuchsias and geraniums parallel the nurturing of literacy and symbolize the responsible, deserving working class. The *Art Journal* reviewer assumed a father and child relationship, which is plausible but an assumption.[49] The anonymity of the figures makes them archetypal, symbolic of an idealized, self-improving working class. They enact 'mythological' social values and relationships in the sense that the cultural theorist Roland Barthes defined the term.[50] It is no accident that the name the man is writing is 'J. Smith'.

In *Kit's Writing Lesson* the underlying themes in the painting are shaped by the framework of a particular narrative. If the figures have less of a universal quality, they can invoke a richness of connotation for informed viewers, which derives from what they as readers know of the characters' past and future. Nell's nurturing goodness is signalled visually by her actions as a teacher, her useful sewing work, her neat hair and modest clothes, and her sweet regular features and downcast eyes. These directly evoke the Victorian female ideal. But they are also indirectly suggested by what the reader knows of Nell's character in the novel as a whole, particularly by her selfless care of her grandfather, which is implicitly what exhausts and destroys her. We can read that back into the painting, where it is symbolized by her sewing of one of her grandfather's shirts. Mary Cowling's work on physiognomy and painting rediscovered the Victorian visual language that Martineau used to convey Kit's clumsy working-class but good-hearted character.[51] We see his large hands, coarse but well-proportioned features, ruddy cheeks and shock of hair. This is supplemented by clues of pose and dress. From the narrative we know that his character is expressed in protective devotion to Nell.

Holman Hunt asserted the importance of the relationship between the whole text and an individual image when he disputed the proper association between textual source and visual representation with Tennyson. Tennyson complained that the tossing hair and wrapping threads in Hunt's *Lady of Shalott* (1886–1905; Manchester Art Gallery) were not explicitly sanctioned in the poem, stating, 'an illustrator ought never to add anything to what he finds in the text'. Hunt argued that the artist had to go beyond the textual information directly related to his immediate subject in order to realize the writer's deeper themes. He created images compatible with the text but had 'only half a page to convey the impression of a weird fate', which the author could work out in

FIG. 53
Robert Braithwaite Martineau, *Kit's Writing Lesson* (detail of fig. 51)

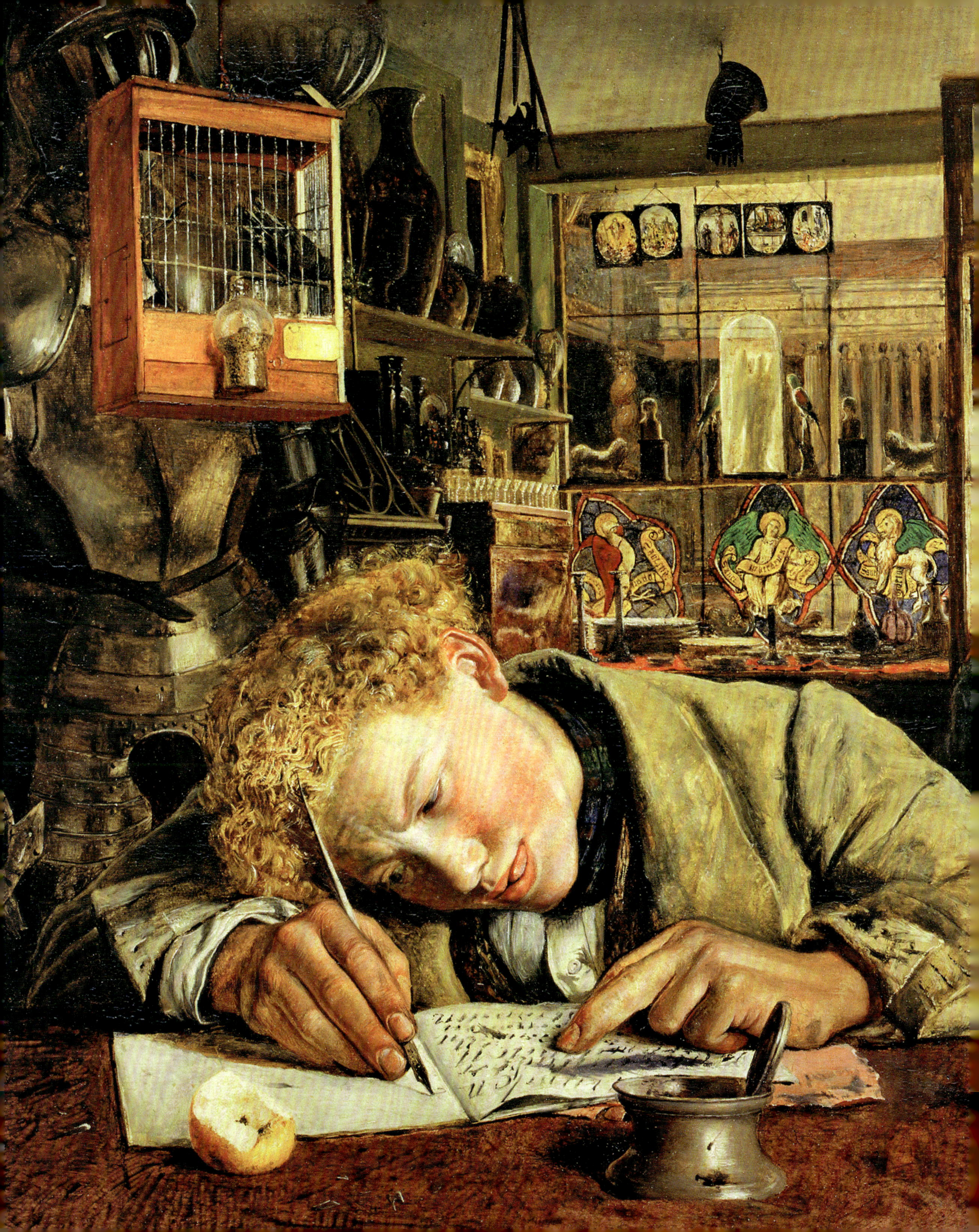

the whole poem. He reminded the poet of 'the difference of requirements in our two arts. In mine it is needful to trace the end from the beginning.'[52]

A literary painting's relationship both to the whole text and the specific passage that inspired it raises interesting issues for *Kit's Writing Lesson*. The incident represented takes place in chapter 3, witnessed by Master Humphrey, the story's original narrator:

> [T]he child came back directly, and soon occupied herself in preparations for giving Kit a writing lesson, of which it seemed he had a couple every week, and one regularly on that evening, to the great mirth and enjoyment both of himself and his instructress. To relate how it was a long time before his modesty could be so far prevailed upon to admit of his sitting down in the parlour in the presence of an unknown gentleman – how when he did sit down, he tucked up his sleeves and squared his elbows and put his face close to the copybook and squinted horribly at the lines – how, from the very first moment of having the pen in his hand he began to wallow in blots, and to daub himself with ink up to the very roots of his hair – how if he did by accident form a letter properly, he immediately smeared it out again with his arm in his preparations to make another – how at every fresh mistake, there was a fresh burst of merriment from the child and a louder and not yet less hearty laugh from poor Kit himself and how there was all the way through, notwithstanding, a gentle wish on her part to teach, and an anxious desire on his to learn – to relate all these particulars would no doubt occupy more time and space than they deserve.

Martineau's painting respects the description of Kit's pose and gestures as he begins to write, but omits the grandfather as well as the narrator who are present. The subject is set after dark, but Martineau's painting suggests the light of the studio rather than lamplight, possibly because the latter is less favourable to Pre-Raphaelite detail, and because Holman Hunt had not yet produced *The Light of the World*, which opened up Pre-Raphaelitism to dim lighting effects. Kit's inkiness is not shown, perhaps through difficulty of representation and pictorial propriety. Nell's needlework is not referred to in the text but is imported from chapter 3, where she sews unspecified items as the narrator and the grandfather talk again. Her needlework skills also feature later in the plot when she mends Judy's dress in the graveyard, which encourages the Punch and Judy men to accept her and her grandfather on their travels. The addition of the needlework to the scene therefore adds a greater depth of reference to the novel and reinforces messages about Little Nell's idealized and doubly nurturing femininity: her actions parallel those of the multi-tasking mother in Charles West Cope's *A Life Well Spent* (private collection), who takes her young children through their lessons while also knitting a sock. What is also and most interestingly omitted from Martineau's picture is the laughter. In Martineau's painting the serious and saintly image of Little Nell, created in the text as a whole, overrides the merriment that dominates this particular scene.

Martineau was a friend and pupil of Holman Hunt, working in his studio in 1851–2, when *Kit's Writing Lesson* was developed, with Hunt's encouragement, from a design he had begun.[53] Martineau was therefore exposed to the particular richness and density of symbolic visual narrative developed by the Pre-Raphaelites around 1850. This was influenced by the work of Hogarth, the revival of Christian artistic symbolism and the symbolic readings of artworks developed by Ruskin.[54] Martineau embodies this understanding in his painting, to a much greater extent than is found in other paintings of Dickens subjects. The jumble of artefacts in the shop, particularly the armour, has a textual sanction: the place was

> one of those receptacles for old and curious things . . . There were suits of mail standing like ghosts in armour here and there, fantastic carvings brought from monkish cloisters, rusty weapons of various kinds, distorted figures in china and wood and iron and ivory; tapestry and strange furniture that might have been designed in dreams. (Ch. 1)

The religious artefacts Martineau depicts in the window include a statuette of a winged angel in a glass dome. Because this is given a luminous prominence, it may be a symbol of Nell herself, who is explicitly seen as angelic elsewhere in the book, for instance by the child in the churchyard (ch. 55). Nell's face in death is described as bearing, as in life, 'the same mild lovely look. So shall we know the angels in their majesty after death' (ch. 71). Less conspicuous, but also possibly symbolic, is the sequence of religious lantern slides hanging above, including images of crucifixion and resurrection, which may also symbolize Nell's redemptive self-sacrifice.

Nell's caged linnet is conspicuous in the picture, hanging above Kit's head. This placing epitomizes Hunt's idea of 'tracing the end from the beginning'. Nell's care for the bird is another symbol of her nurturing qualities and moral worthiness: the caged bird appears as frequently as the pot plant as a natural symbol in Victorian genre paintings of the respectable working class and the deserving poor. Its juxtaposition to Kit in the painting points forward to the way that Kit takes care of it after the flight of Little Nell and her grandfather: he saves it from destruction by Quilp by fighting for it (ch. 13) and nurtures it within his family, to return it to Nell at the end of the story. Implicitly Nell has trained Kit in moral qualities as well as writing. The bird also looks forward to Nell's end. At the crucial moment she is contrasted with the bird: 'Her little bird – a poor slight thing the pressure of a finger would have crushed – was stirring nimbly in its cage; and the strong heart of its child mistress was mute and motionless for ever' (ch. 71). The bird, unmentioned in the text that inspired the painter, has therefore multiple important meanings. The two apples in the painting appear to be Martineau's invention.[55] A whole and perfect apple stands by Nell and a part eaten one by Kit. As apples are traditionally the biblical fruit of the fall of man, Kit's suggests earthly, fallen humanity and Nell's an innocent, 'unfallen' sinlessness.

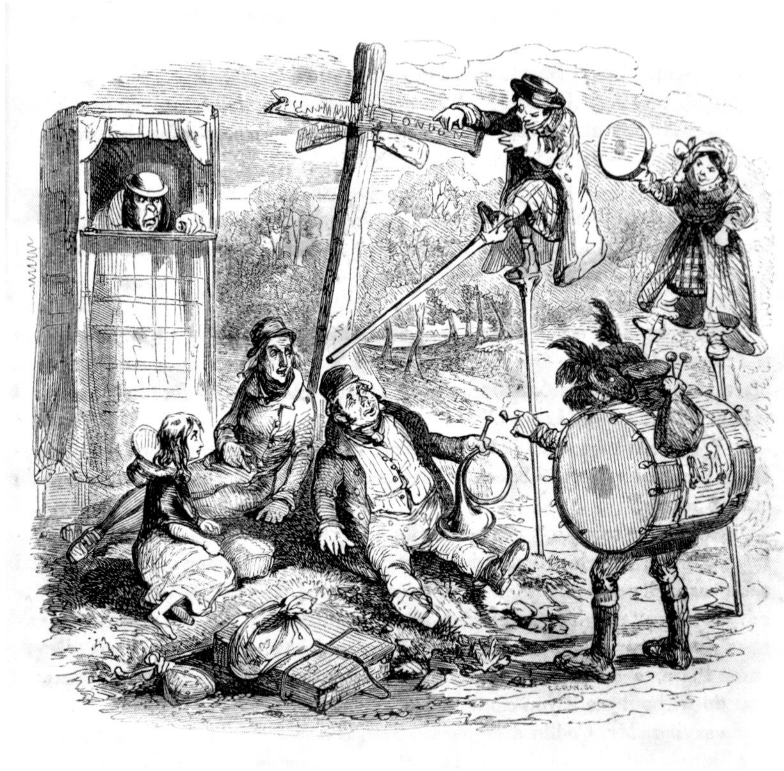

FIG. 54
Hablot Knight Browne, 'Grinder's Lot', 1841, etching. Original illustration from *The Old Curiosity Shop*

DICKENS'S VERBAL STYLE AND VICTORIAN VISUAL STYLE

Artists painting literary subjects must make use of visual clues provided in the text in realizing their settings and characters. Sometimes the prestige of a first illustrator or the development of a representational tradition also determines artists' choices. Dickens gives several indications of Little Nell's appearance and that of her grandfather. In the first chapter of *The Old Curiosity Shop* we learn that Nell is 'a pretty little girl': 'her small and delicate frame imparted a particular youthfulness to her appearance.' She has light brown hair. She is described throughout the book as 'the child', although she is 'nearly fourteen' (ch. 7). The grandfather is a 'little old man with long grey hair' and is much aged with a face 'deeply furrowed and so very full of care', although he is similar to his granddaughter in their 'bright blue eyes', 'spare and slender form' and 'delicate mould' (all ch. 1). The grandfather is also described as having a 'stooping figure, care-worn face and jaded aspect' (ch. 3). The first illustrator, 'Phiz' (Hablot Knight Browne), created cursory renditions that respected these descriptions, as seen in the depiction of the couple in his 'Grinder's Lot' showing the 'exhibitors of the freaks of Punch' (fig. 54). The elderly and old-fashioned grandfather is shown wearing knee breeches and stockings rather than trousers. This tradition is continued in George Cattermole's depictions of Nell and her grandfather in *The Old Curiosity Shop* (fig. 58) and *The Grave of Little Nell* (fig. 55), and is directly echoed in Green's watercolours of 1876 (V&A) and

FIG. 55
George Cattermole, *The Grave of Little Nell*, 1867, watercolour. Victoria and Albert Museum, London

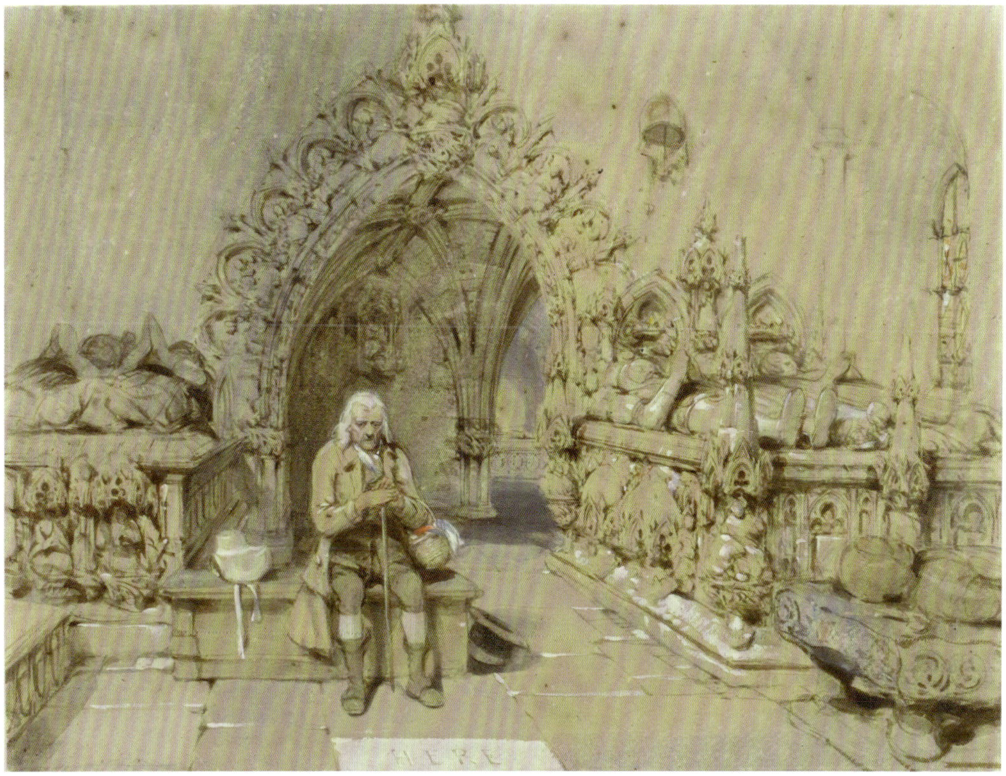

Chapman's painting of 1888 (figs 48, 49) However Holman Hunt's and John Ritchie's grandfathers have short hair, and Hunt's, although slightly built, appears tall, rather than a 'little old man', probably because these artists' detailed renditions depended on the appearance of their models.

Dickens's verbal descriptions are vivid but in his early novels not realistic, even of his heroines. Their qualities can be suggested by the sketchy caricatural style of his early illustrators but are less well served by painters, especially after the mid-century, when solid artistic realism dominates artistic representation. Dickens's descriptions of Little Nell, for instance, emphasize her ethereal, fairy-like quality: Quilp says she is 'so fair, with such blue veins and such a transparent skin, and such little feet' (ch. 9). In the wood she leads, 'printing her tiny footsteps in the moss, which rose elastic from so light a pressure . . . and thus she lured the old man on' (ch. 24). Her room in the shop contains 'a little bed . . . that a fairy might have slept in' (ch. 1). Hunt's slender Little Nell of 1846 captures something of this ethereal quality. However, the insistence on the details of clothing and texture in the later Pre-Raphaelite-influenced paintings of Martineau, Ritchie and James Lobley makes their characterizations inescapably more solid and earthbound. Realism in art became so dominant that when the Household Edition of Dickens was created between 1870 and 1879, Dickens's original illustrators' works were replaced. New illustrations in a more realistic manner were commissioned

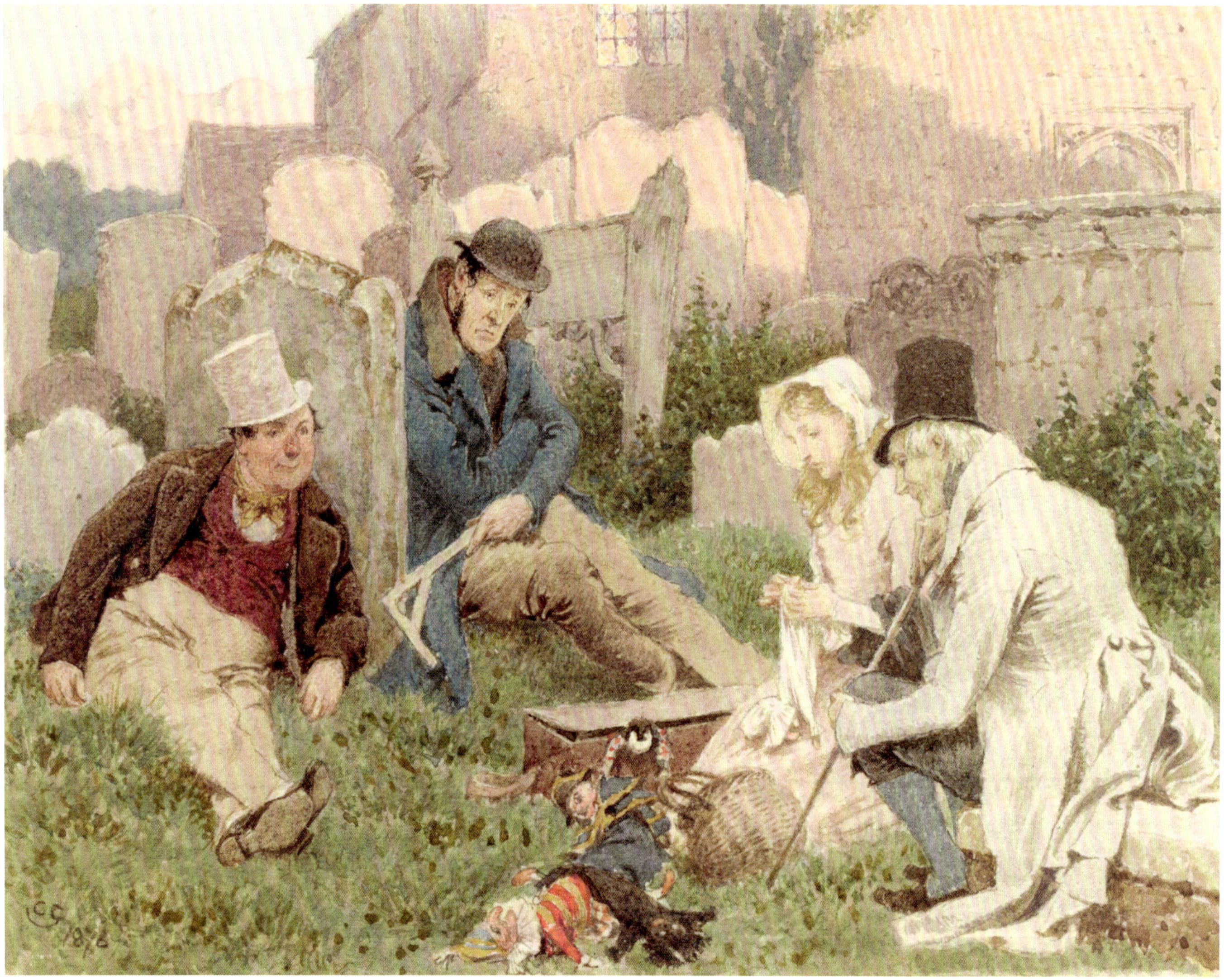

from Frederick Barnard and Charles Green. Green illustrated *The Old Curiosity Shop* in a tonal rather than a linear style. The contrast in realism can be seen in his *Little Nell Mending the Puppet's Dress* (fig. 56) compared with Phiz's illustration of the similar subject, 'exhibitors of the freaks of Punch'. What the realist mode of representation finds hard to convey is the 'Gothic' and metaphorical quality of Dickens's descriptive text. The musty accumulation in the Curiosity Shop is heavy with death, and contrasts with and oppresses the vitality of Little Nell, as the narrator ends the first chapter:

> I had ever before me the old dark murky rooms – the gaunt suits of mail with their ghostly, silent air – the faces all awry, grinning from wood and stone – the dust and rust and worm that lives in wood – and alone in the midst of all this lumber and decay and ugly age, the beautiful child in her gentle slumber. (Ch. 1)

FIG. 56
Charles Green, *Little Nell Mending the Puppet's Dress*, illustration to *The Old Curiosity Shop* from the Household Edition of the Works of Charles Dickens, 1876, watercolour. Victoria and Albert Museum, London

FIG. 57
Samuel Williams, 'The child in her gentle slumber', 1841, etching. Original illustration from *The Old Curiosity Shop*

FIG. 58
George Cattermole, *The Home of Little Nell*, also called *The Old Curiosity Shop*, 1841. Charles Dickens Museum, London

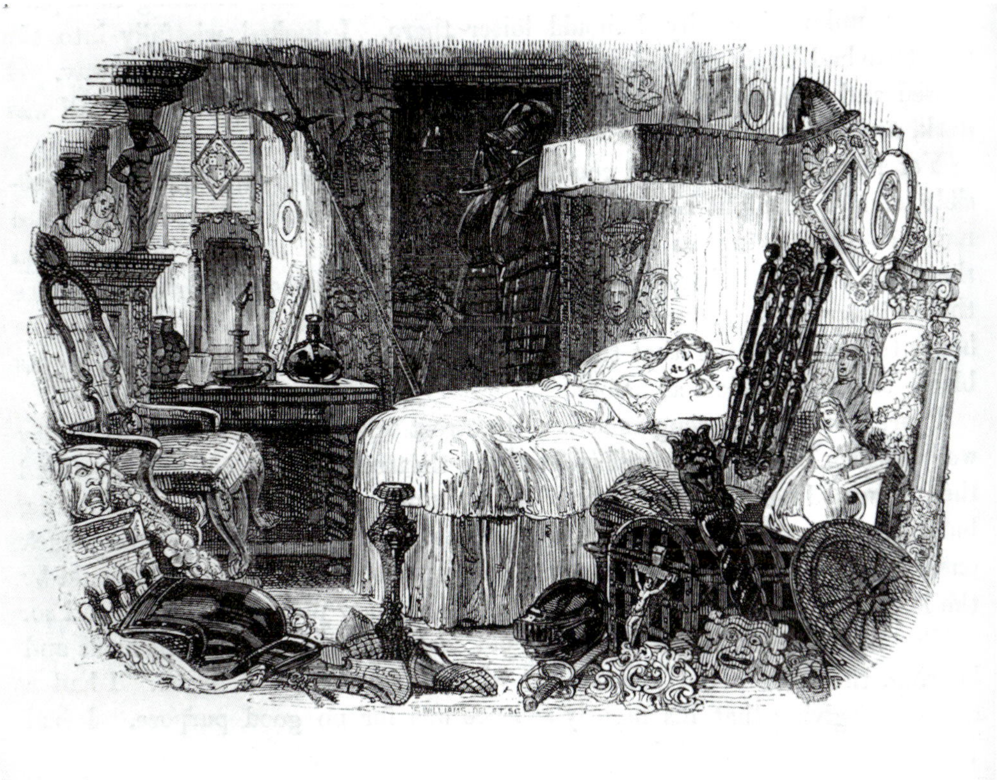

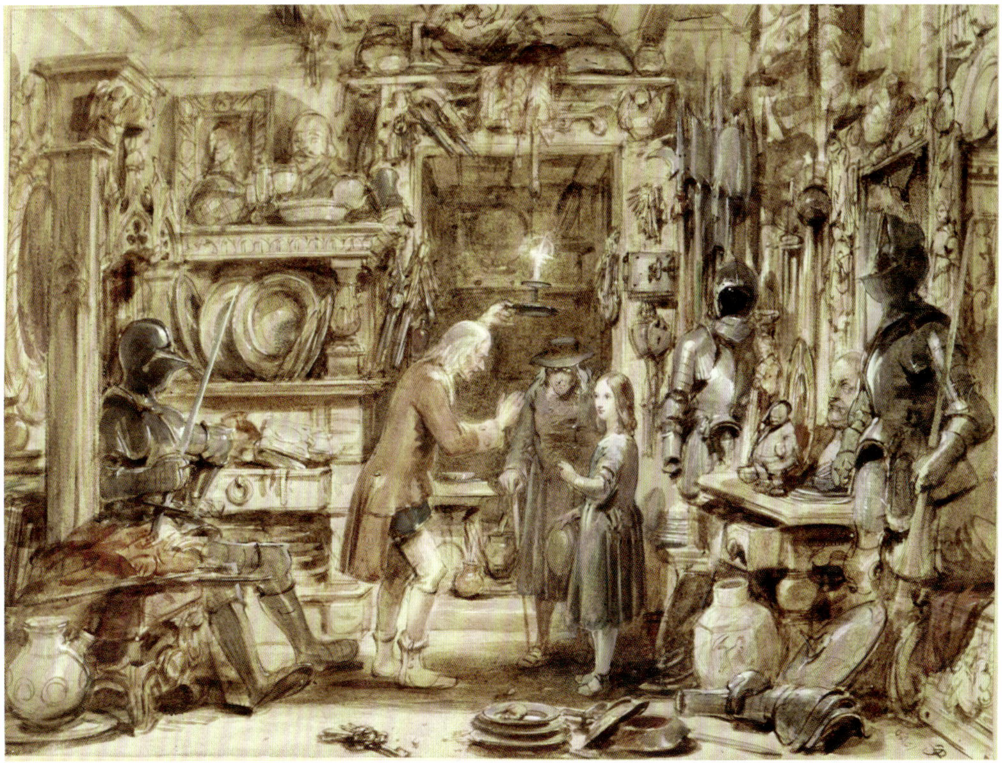

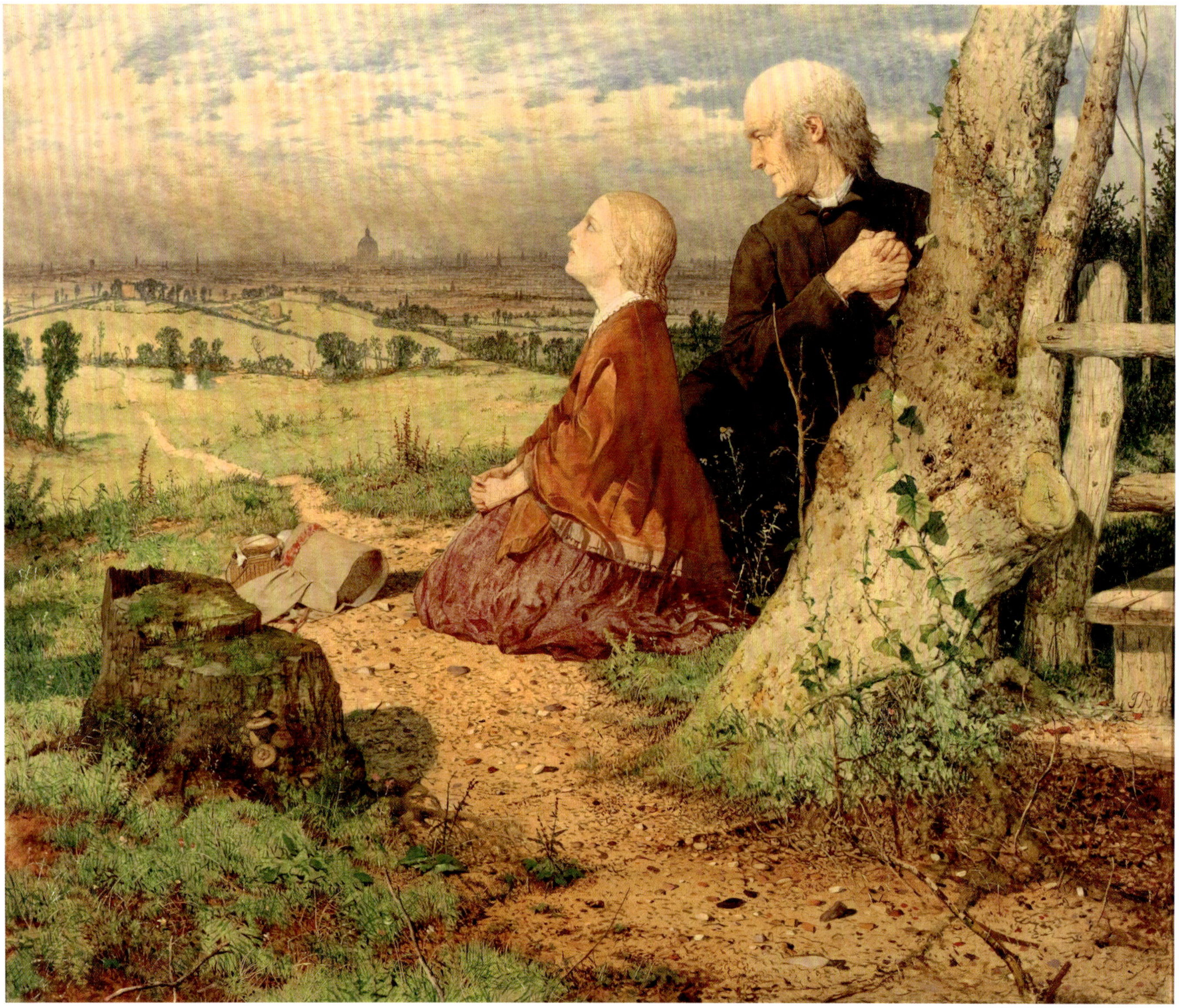

FIG. 59
John Ritchie, *Little Nell and her Grandfather Leaving London*, 1857, oil on canvas. Royal Pavilion and Museums, Brighton & Hove

Later, these images become the stuff of nightmare as Nell returns to bed after a futile wait for her grandfather (ch. 9). Samuel Williams's etching illustrating 'in the midst of all this lumber and decay and ugly age, the beautiful child in her gentle slumber' (fig. 57), and Cattermole's painting of *The Home of Little Nell* (fig. 58) capture something of this Gothic quality, while later interiors such as Chapman's and Martineau's, for all their realism, suggest only carefully composed still life.

Only those early Victorian artists who preserve something of Regency flamboyance in their pictorial style are able to find an equivalent to the verbal vitality of Dickens's early novels. Frith's laughing *Dolly Varden*, with her swaying pose, tumbling satin clothes and setting of feathery painterly foliage, created a hugely popular representation of Dickens's flirtatious heroine partly for this reason.

DICKENS PAINTINGS AND VICTORIAN VALUES

In the Victorian period, partly because of the domestic market for art and the conventions of realism, the overwhelming preference in painting and sculpture was for images of Dickens's heroines and children, rather than the grotesques and caricatures that feature largely in the novels and their original illustrations. For instance, of at least sixty *Old Curiosity Shop* subjects (exhibited and unexhibited), fifty titles refer to Little Nell (sixteen with her grandfather), three to Dick Swiveller, two to the marchioness, one to Kit and only two to Quilp.[56] The subject of the vulnerable and saintly but redemptive child, usually a girl, is central to many of Dickens's earlier novels. It was created and is much depicted because it is also central in early- and mid-Victorian culture. The idealization of childhood innocence commenced by Rousseau and perpetuated in Romanticism was given an early-Victorian pious flavour and touched with the melodramatic fascination for innocence under threat.[57] In the representation of Little Nell we see these themes brought to the fore.

Nell's saintly characteristics are shown in her nurturing aspect, which has already been discussed in regard to Martineau's painting. These qualities are also shown in her care for her grandfather in their wanderings. This is depicted by several artists but most explicitly realized in Holman Hunt's *Little Nell and her Grandfather* (fig. 47). Hunt illustrates the accompanying quotation from chapter 15:

> There was a pool of clear water in the field in which the child laved her hands and face, and cooled her feet before setting forth to walk again. She would have the old man refresh himself in this way too, and making him sit down on the grass, cast the water on him with her hands and dried it with her simple dress.

Nell is also shown as a pious figure. John Ritchie selects a different passage from the same episode for his *Little Nell and her Grandfather Leaving London* (fig. 59):

> The child had repeated her artless prayers once that morning, more earnestly perhaps than she had ever done in all her life, but as she felt all this they rose to her lips again. The old man took off his hat – he had no memory for the words – but he said amen, and that they were very good.

The Copeland Parian statuette of Little Nell (fig. 60) shows her carrying a bible. Her affinity with the church at the end of the book is as much a sign of her piety as a predictor of her death. In Dickens's narrative, on her first entry into the church, she reads a bible and then climbs from the tomb-filled interior to the sunlit top of the tower, which Dickens describes as like 'passing from death to life, it was drawing nearer heaven' (ch. 53). Nell then acts as a guide to the church, which has a clear metaphorical undertone (ch. 55). Nell in the church inspired several paintings, including those by

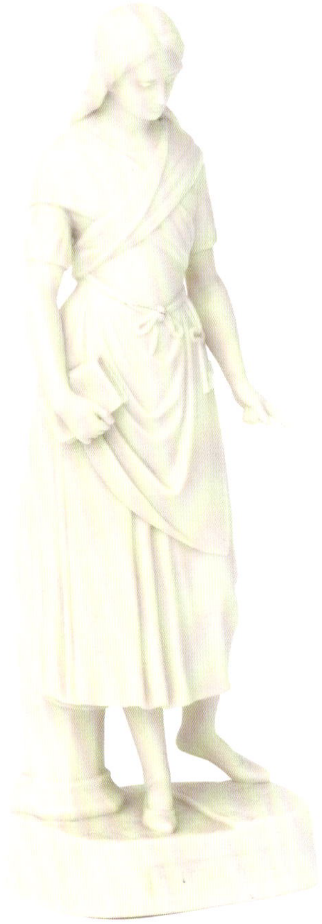

FIG. 60
James Shewood Westmacott, *Statue of Little Nell; Companion to Master Daniel*, 1870, parian ware. Private collection

Miss Mary Pickett, Harold Copping, which shows her sitting alone, Eliza Sharp, which portrays her showing round visitors, and James Lobley.

Lobley represents Little Nell leaving the church (fig. 61). She is shutting and is about to lock the door. The incident depicted is probably in the immediate aftermath of the moment of epiphany on top of the church tower, and can be seen as a more picturesque and complex pictorial equivalent of it. Nell stands in a meditative attitude with one hand to her breast just inside the shadowed old church. Her feet are on a grave slab marked with a cross and her other hand is grasping the ring on the ancient and mouldering door. Dickens creates a deliberate parallel between the interior of the church and the stagnant environment of the Old Curiosity Shop itself. Both of them are an accumulation of material remains with connotations of age and death. Nell is about to step outside into the sunlit churchyard. Lobley's subject therefore parallels Nell's flight with her grandfather at the beginning of the book from the Curiosity Shop into nature, relates to her ascent from the inside the church to the view of the natural world at the top of the tower and foreshadows her departure from the material world to the heavenly sphere at the end of the book.

The pathos of Nell's final decline and death was a major factor in the original huge popularity of *The Old Curiosity Shop* and in its later decline to its status today, 'among

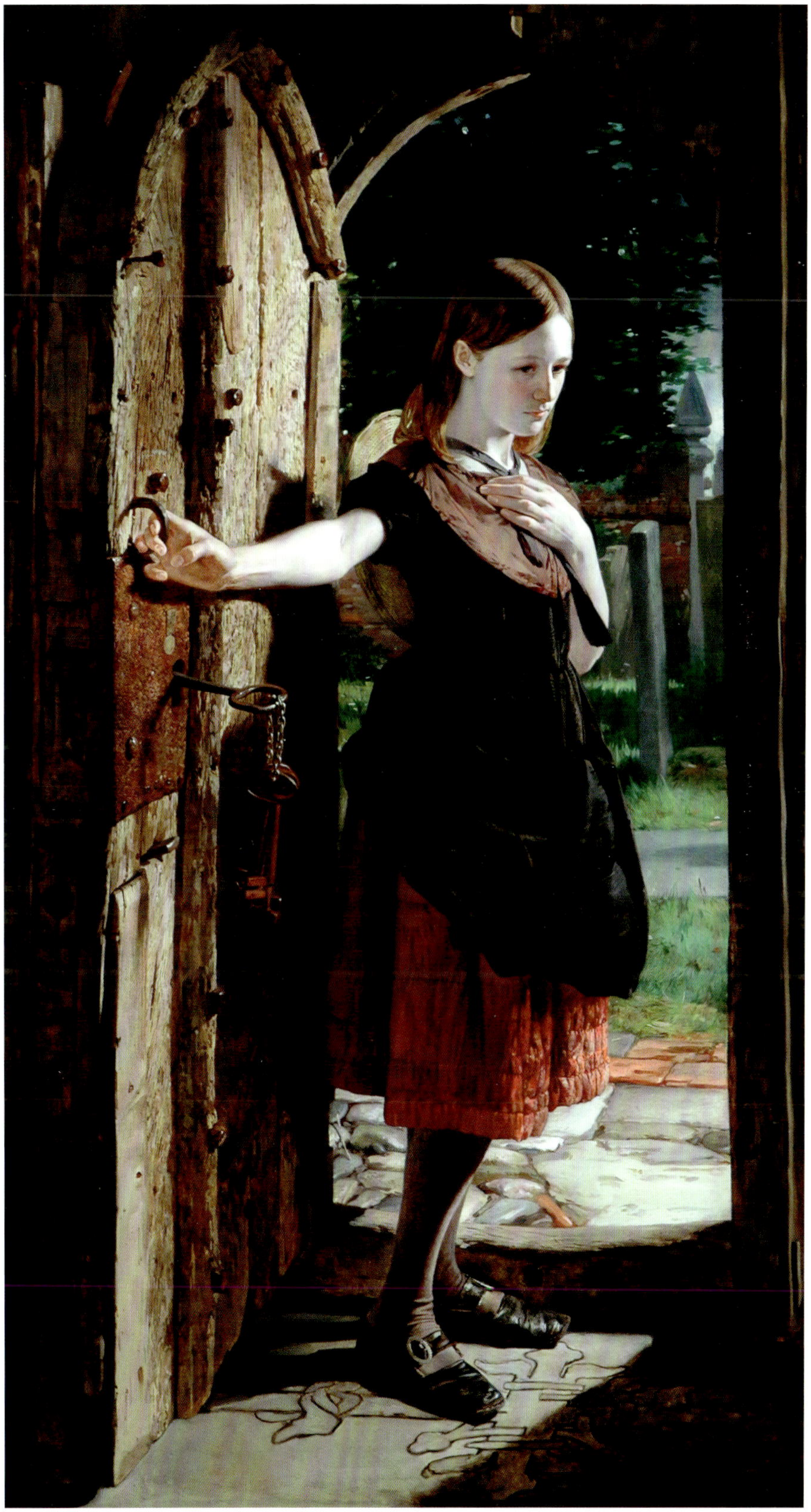

FIG. 61
James Lobley, *Little Nell Leaving the Church (The Old Curiosity Shop)*, 1867, oil on canvas. Bradford Museums and Galleries

the least regarded of Dickens's novels'.[58] The subject of Nell's actual death is surprisingly little represented. The sculptor Edgar George Papworth exhibited *Poor Little Nell: 'No marvel at the silence now.'*[59] However, Nell's death is more frequently referred to indirectly. The sculptor James Bouverie Haydon preferred to show her in death's image, sleep, in *Nell Asleep: Curiosity Shop*. George Cattermole and Herbert Dicksee depict the grandfather at the grave of Little Nell in the church. But the subject that dominates in this area is the association of Little Nell with graveyards, traditionally associated with reflections on mortality. In their wanderings Nell and her grandfather encounter the Punch and Judy men in a graveyard (ch. 16). At the end of the book Nell and her grandfather find refuge in a ruined house in a graveyard, which Nell describes as 'A quiet happy place, a place to live and learn to die in' (ch. 52), regarding the graveyard as her garden. W.A. Atkinson, Mrs McIan (in a work presented by the artist to Dickens),[60] James Lawson Stewart, Miss Clara Cawse, Miss Emily Macirone and John Parker all deal with aspects of this subject. The little sick scholar, whom Nell meets at her first encounter with the schoolmaster (depicted by Mrs McIan), also potentially symbolized Nell's own mortality.

Although Nell's death might have exerted too strong an imaginative power to be represented directly, the illness and deaths of children feature elsewhere in Dickens's writing and in Dickens subject painting. The multiplication of subjects of Paul and Florence Dombey has already been mentioned. Fig. 64 is a late example. Thomas Edward Roberts depicted *The Sick Boy* from *Nicholas Nickleby* looking all day at the sky and his flowers. In the imagination of Dickens and of the Victorians, as we saw in the case of Little Nell, the child is associated with the world of nature, which provides a window into hope and immortality. Themes of sick and dying children, of which these Dickens subjects are a part, are common throughout Victorian art.[61] In an era of high infant and child mortality, which could strike families of all classes without warning, such literary texts and artistic imagery may have provided artistic catharsis for real and feared griefs.[62] The presentation of dying children as saintly and too good for this world in the writings of Dickens and its associated art clearly relates to compensation strategies for the reality of loss.

The Dickens paintings most richly loaded with cultural meanings were produced in the early- and mid-Victorian period, with the 1860s as a period of transition. After that the characters are more simply presented. William Quiller Orchardson's *Little Nell and her Grandfather in the Wood* (fig. 62) is representative of this phase. It came from a Scottish tradition of painting that was less dominated by Hogarthian moral narratives and would exert a considerable influence on London painting in the decade. The incident from Nell and the grandfather's wanderings lacks the stress on nurturing or piety found in the Hunt or the Ritchie. The painting represents the moment when Nell and the grandfather rest in exhaustion. While resting, Nell makes an inner transition from exhaustion and despondency to resolution, through a sense of her responsibility towards her helpless grandfather (ch. 24), a transition impossible to represent in a single still image. Orchardson's choice of a scene without outward action is significant, as is the

FIG. 62
Sir William Quiller Orchardson, *Little Nell and her Grandfather in the Wood*, *c.*1863, oil on canvas. Museums Sheffield

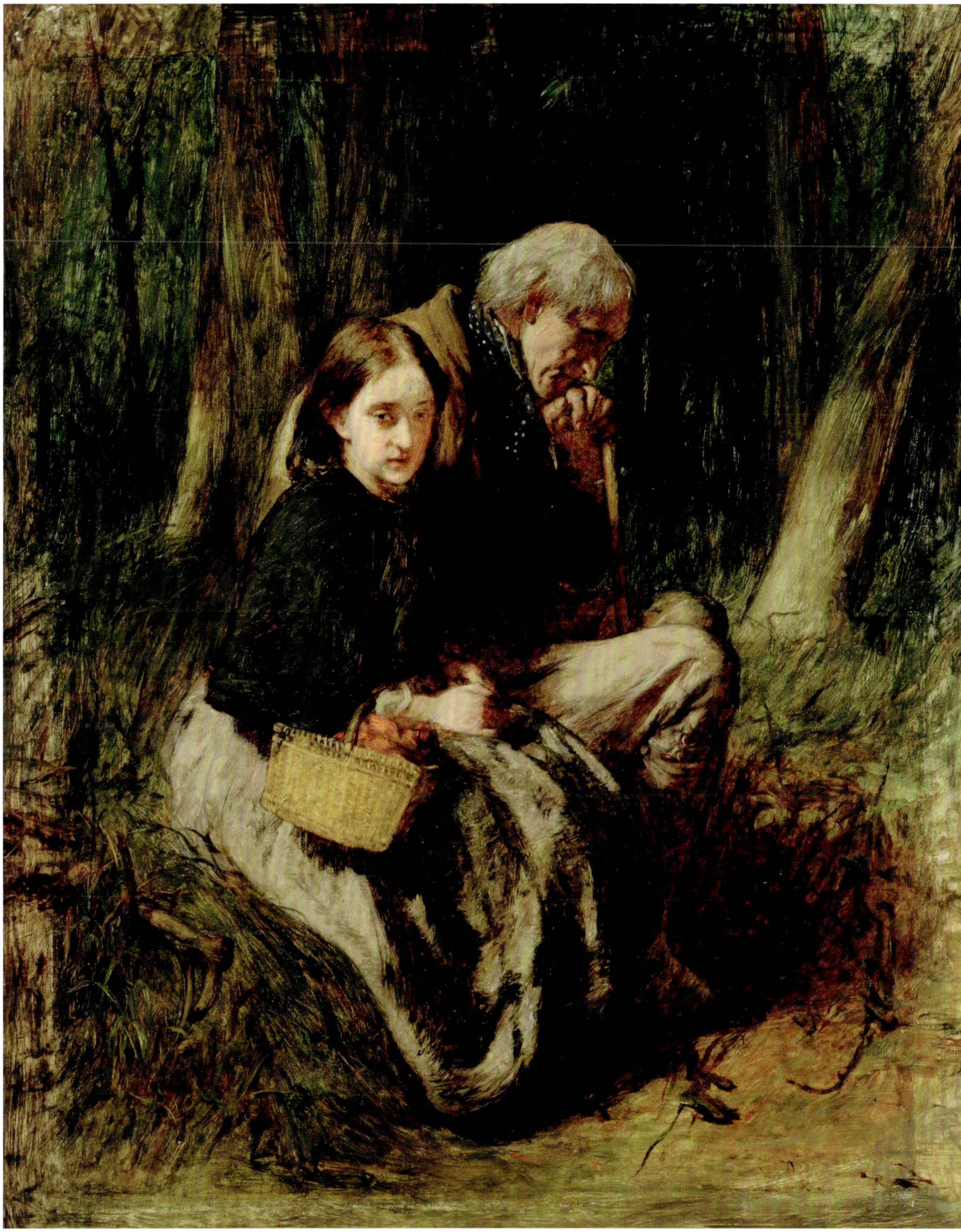

fact that he does not support his title with a quotation. His painting, therefore, is primarily a visual study in Nell's tiredness and despair rather than an attempt to engage directly with wider aspects of the narrative or its morality.

Dickens was a very visual writer, whose narratives often make explicit reference to the act of looking, either by the characters or by the narrator himself. Occasionally artists select passages about looking to underpin their own visual works. W.T. Dennis showed at the Royal Academy of 1847 and the Free Exhibition of 1848 a picture of *Captain Cuttle and Uncle Sol Examining Charts* (*Dombey and Son*, ch. 19). At the Royal Academy of 1848 Frank Williams exhibited *Captain Cuttle Watching the Slumbers of Florence: 'She was sleeping heavily, and moaning in her sleep; and Captain Cuttle, with a perfect awe of her youth, her beauty and her sorrow, adjusted the coat which had covered her, where it had fallen off'* (*Dombey and Son*, ch. 48). In 1852 at the British Institution Miss Clara Cawse showed *Poor Nell: 'There were none to see the frail perishable figure as it glided from the fire and leaned pensively at the open casement; none but the stars to look into the upturned face and read its history'* (*Old Curiosity Shop*, ch. 52). Pictures about looking may be neutral (as in images of Captain Cuttle and charts) but, as in the last two examples, they can have disturbing undertones of voyeurism.

Laura Mulvey opened this issue to academic scrutiny and debate in the essay, 'Visual Pleasure and Narrative Cinema', of 1975.[63] Mulvey claims that 'in a world ordered by sexual imbalance, pleasure in looking has been split between active/male and passive/female. The determining male gaze projects its fantasy onto the female figure.'[64] She distinguishes two overlapping modes of representing women as objects. The first is that of voyeurism, where the gaze distances and is controlling or sadistic, investigating the woman to punish or save her. The second is that of 'fetishistic scopophilia', which presents the woman as a reassuring and beautiful object of display, in an intimate relation to the spectator and often in close-up. Mulvey's concepts can be readily applied to the subjects selected by Williams and Cawse. In the Williams picture we are implicitly voyeurs with Captain Cuttle, while observing his own voyeurism. Florence's uneasy sleep is eroticized by her moaning and by the fallen coat. These implications are neutralized in the text by Captain Cuttle's honourable 'awe' and the mention of her sorrow along with her youth and beauty. The replacement of the fallen coat is both reassuring and disturbing because it causes the watcher to both conceal and touch the passive object of his gaze. In Cawse's picture the absence of onlookers evoked in the text is paradoxically reversed by the imaginative presence of author and reader and made concrete by the viewer's relationship with the depicted figure, to see without being seen being the essence of voyeurism. The descriptive quotation and scale (2ft 5in × 2ft 2in including frame) imply a figure at a window, probably the half-length close-up associated with the keepsake painting or fancy portrait, a genre in which visual pleasure predominates. The title's evocation of the 'frail perishable' figure indicates latent vulnerability and sadism. Mulvey's approach suggests the primacy of the male viewpoint. Dickens had a large female readership and, as here, was much depicted by female artists. Possibly, concepts of passive vulnerable femininity, reinforced by the culture and by representations in literature and art, had become so embedded in Victorian society that women also identified with them, and those women artists who questioned them looked for their subjects elsewhere. However, the popularity of Dickens with female artists suggests further exploration is needed of the female experience of art and literature.

Dickens's novels and Dickens pictures contain many examples of the innocent and vulnerable heroine. Catherine Gordon intimates that this type of subject was commonest between 1830 and 1850.[65] Works like those by Williams and Cawse point to the moral ambivalence in the popularity of this theme. Issues of social and pictorial propriety determine which aspects of the heroine as victim can be translated into pictorial form. Florence Dombey fled from the cruelty of her father to the house of Captain Cuttle. Williams depicted her sleep and in *Florence Dombey in Captain Cuttle's Parlour* (fig. 50) Egley showed her musing the day after her flight, interrupting her womanly mending. Little Em'ly from *David Copperfield* is often represented.[66] Little Em'ly lived in Peggoty's house with her cousin and sweetheart Ham. A pretty and simple girl, she is induced to elope by James Steerforth, who afterwards abandons her. It is interesting that this pathetic figure is much represented by women, but after one depiction of 1850, made while the book was still in serialization (May 1849–November 1850), the remaining depictions were produced between fifteen and twenty years after its publication. Nicholas Nickleby's sister Kate was apprenticed to a dressmaker, Madame Mantalini. She experienced the unwelcome attentions of Sir Mulberry Hawk, which she repelled. Thomas Faed's depiction of Kate Nickleby (fig. 46) is another example of a fancy portrait of a Dickens heroine in which the character and experience of the individual are summed up in a single image. The bandbox in her hand suggests her role at the dressmakers and also her vulnerability. Milliners and dressmakers' assistants were expected to be pretty and well dressed. They delivered finished goods to clients, exposed to the temptations and dangers of the street. Other Victorian genre paintings of milliners, such as E.C. Barnes's *The Seducer* (*c.*1860; Pre-Raphaelite Trust)[67] and Charles Hunt's *A Coffee Stall* (*c.*1860; Museum of London),[68] subject them to unwelcome gazes or advances from predatory middle-class men. As with these anonymous figures, Kate Nickleby's modest downcast gaze in Faed's painting suggests her propriety. Little Nell's vulnerability is expressed in frequent depictions of her wanderings with her grandfather, and by scenes of her waiting at the window for his return (*Old Curiosity Shop*, ch. 9).[69] However, the predatory sexual threat represented by the deformed dwarf Quilp, who makes advances and suggests marriage (ch. 6) and who tells her to sit on his knee and commandeers her bed (ch. 11), remain unpainted. Similarly, the violent assault made by Sir Mulberry Hawk on Kate Nickleby, although dramatic, is unrepresented.

THE DECLINE OF DICKENS SUBJECT PAINTING

Dickens's popularity continued unabated into the twentieth century, but the painting of Dickens subjects almost ceased in the late-Victorian period. There are many causes for this. A minor reason is the period in which Dickens's novels are set. Only two of Dickens's

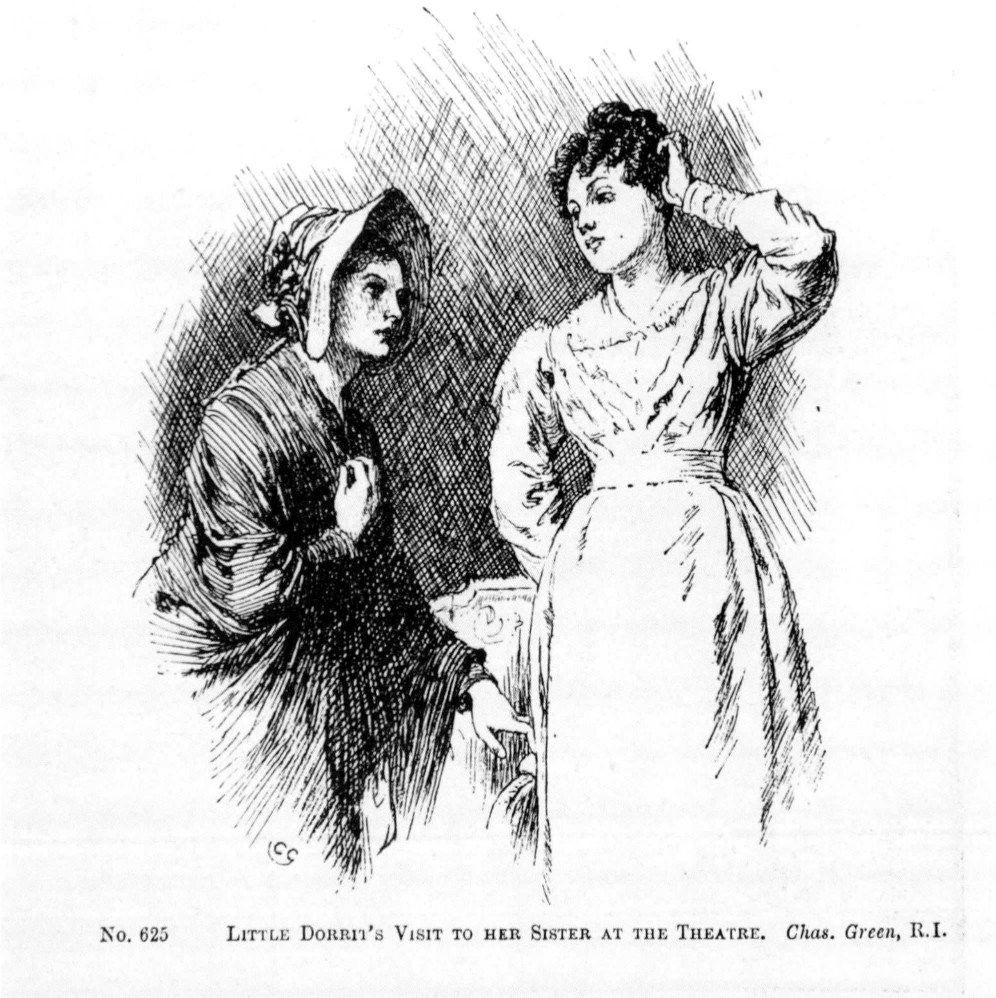

FIG. 63
Engraving of Charles Green, *Little Dorrit's Visit to her Sister at the Theatre*, 1887, watercolour, reproduced in Royal Institute of Painters in Watercolours exhibition catalogue. Watts Gallery Archive

novels have historical settings, the late-eighteenth-century *Barnaby Rudge* and *The Tale of Two Cities*. The remainder broadly relate to the time of their publication from the 1830s to the 1860s. Victorian artists and illustrators worked in a culture of historical accuracy. As the antiquarian and dress historian Frederick William Fairholt declared in 1860, paintings that represented historical characters 'in habits not known until many years after their death . . . are but "painted lies" and cannot be excused any more than history that falsifies fact and dates would be'.[70] As Dickens novels slipped from being contemporary to being 'of the past', artists and illustrators faced tensions between expectations of accuracy and problems of representing a recent past that was not yet picturesque. Quentin Bell in *On Human Finery* suggested that there is a period of time in which the dress of the recent past is so unfashionable as to be unrepresentable.[71] As late as 1862, Faed could depict Kate Nickleby (novel published 1838–9) in contemporary dress, but that soon became incongruous. William Maw Egley noted of *Florence Dombey in Captain Cuttle's*

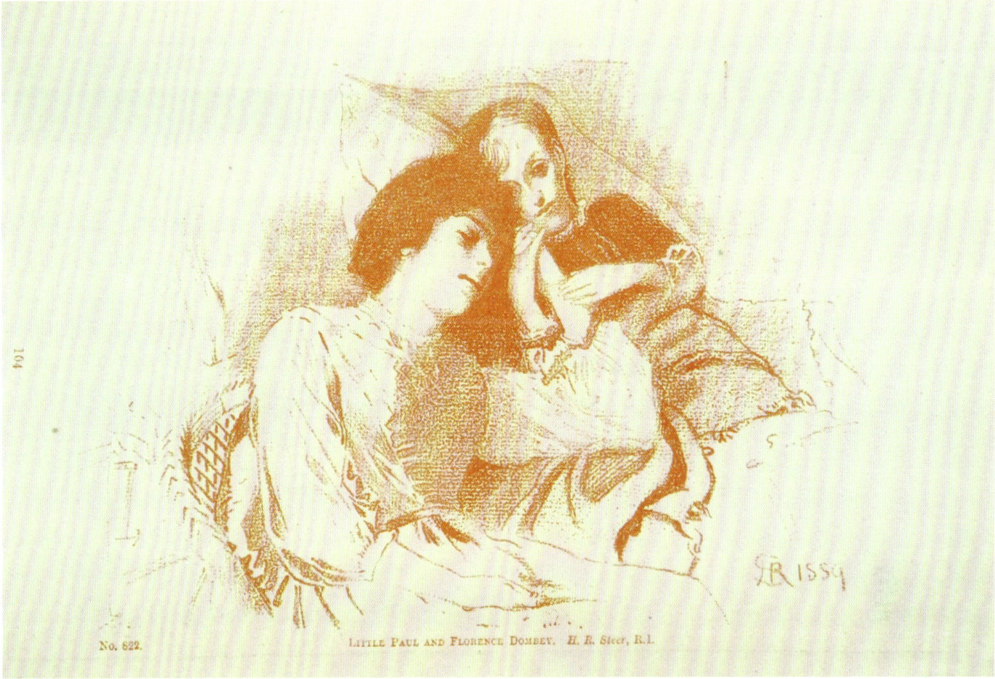

FIG. 64
Engraving of Henry Reynolds Steer, *Little Paul and Florence Dombey*, 1889, watercolour, reproduced in Royal Institute of Painters in Watercolours exhibition catalogue. Watts Gallery Archive

Parlour: 'The costume of that of a young girl in 1848, the date of the publication of *Dombey and Son*.'[72] Although to our eyes the overall line of the clothes is more typical of the fashionable silhouette of about 1890 than the tight waists and bulky petticoats of the late 1840s (compare Hunt's *Little Nell and her Grandfather*, 1846), to contemporary eyes the clothes may have appeared archaic and unfashionable, contributing to the painting's delayed sale. The new illustrations to the Household Edition of Dickens set the earlier novels in the fashions of the late 1830s. Painting followed more slowly. Charles Green was one of the first to reconstruct Dickens's early Victorian world in his *Little Dorrit's Visit to her Sister at the Theatre* (fig. 63). Egley's painting is in the vanguard of the recuperation of this period of fashion in art, which became more popular only in the early twentieth century in the hands of painters such as Leonard Campbell Taylor.

Changing artistic conventions provide the most important reason for the decline in Dickens paintings. Art for art's sake and French-derived naturalist aesthetics rose to dominant positions in England in the last decades of the nineteenth century, and by 1900 their exponents held many key positions in art institutions and as critics. Both aestheticism and naturalism rejected Dickens subjects for slightly different reasons. Aestheticism rejected sentiment, narrative and morality in favour of poetic visual beauty, favouring effects that Walter Pater defined as analogous to music and often preferring a 'vagueness of mere subject'.[73] Although J.A.M. Whistler's aestheticism usually featured contemporary subjects, the movement tended to favour the exotic and ahistorical past. The Grosvenor Gallery (1877–90) was the main home of aestheticism, particularly before 1888. Significantly, it showed no Dickens subjects, although it exhibited many literary paintings. Of around fifty writers whose works were depicted, the overwhelming majority were poets, including the romantics, Tennyson, the Brownings, the Rossettis, Algernon Swinburne and William Morris.[74] Naturalist aesthetics, associated with the 'new critics' such as George Moore and D.S. MacColl, and with 'British Impressionism' and the New English Art Club, favoured value-free, non-narrative realism in contemporary subjects; it is an aesthetic of the eyewitness. Despite the processes of study and contrivance actually needed to create its more elaborate compositions, it rejected the obvious artifice involved in reconstructing a literary subject in a historical setting. The New English Art Club, from its foundation in 1886 until at least the First World War, was increasingly controlled by the naturalists Fred Brown and Henry Tonks, and its members produced no Dickens subjects.

In the twentieth century the Royal Academy remained a traditionalist institution until the 1960s, yet art shown there reflected these changes. Although occasional literary subjects continued to appear (mainly Shakespeare and poetic), they were much reduced in number. The few traditional illustrative Dickens subjects were usually minor works by minor artists. These included Ninian Hurley, who exhibited *A Visit to Pegotty's* (*David Copperfield*) in 1911, and Miss Ethel F. Everett, who showed two *Tiny Tim* subjects in 1912. Once again the high catalogue numbers signalled their display in the later rooms dominated by small and less significant paintings. With G. Sidney Hunt's *Charles Dickens Memorial Stamp* (1911) this atypical cluster of works had probably responded to the *first* Dickens centenary. Other Dickens works reflected the naturalist preference for eyewitnessing, and occasional theatrical portraits showed actors in Dickens roles. Those of Martin Harvey as Sidney Carton have already been mentioned. Robert D. Greenham painted *Edna May Oliver as 'Aunt Betsy Trotwood'* from *David Copperfield* (1937). Some of the last Dickens subjects in the Academy were two paintings by the elderly Royal Academician Frederick Elwell (1870–1958), both entitled *Still Life: The Pickwick Club* (1956 and 1958). A significant and early indication of the new approach is W.H. Humphris's *At a Dickens Character Ball* (1907), another minor work demonstrating clearly both the continuing popularity of Dickens and the growing difficulty of making paintings from his works. Despite the small numbers of these twentieth-century works, their subjects show a shift from Victorian preferences to a modern view of Dickens. Note some of the first *Christmas Carol* subjects and the preference for Pickwick. If one of the meanings of 'Dickensian' is the festive, or jolly, with further associations of tradition and humanitarianism, these aspects seem to have come to the fore in the interwar period, with associations of all that was best in Englishness. When Sir William Hutchison RA chose exceptionally to exhibit a Pickwick subject, *Presenting Jimmy Snodgrass*, at the 1939 Academy on the eve of war, such associations may have been on his mind.

The rejection of Dickens subjects along with the development of elitist concepts of art emerged in aestheticist and realist circles by the 1880s. Oscar Wilde had expressed ambivalent and often disparaging attitudes to Dickens since his school days, admiring his humour and his grotesque caricatures, but loathing his moralizing.[75] Notoriously,

FIG. 65
James McNeill Whistler, *Nocturne: Grey and Gold – Chelsea Snow*, 1876, oil on canvas. Fogg Art Museum

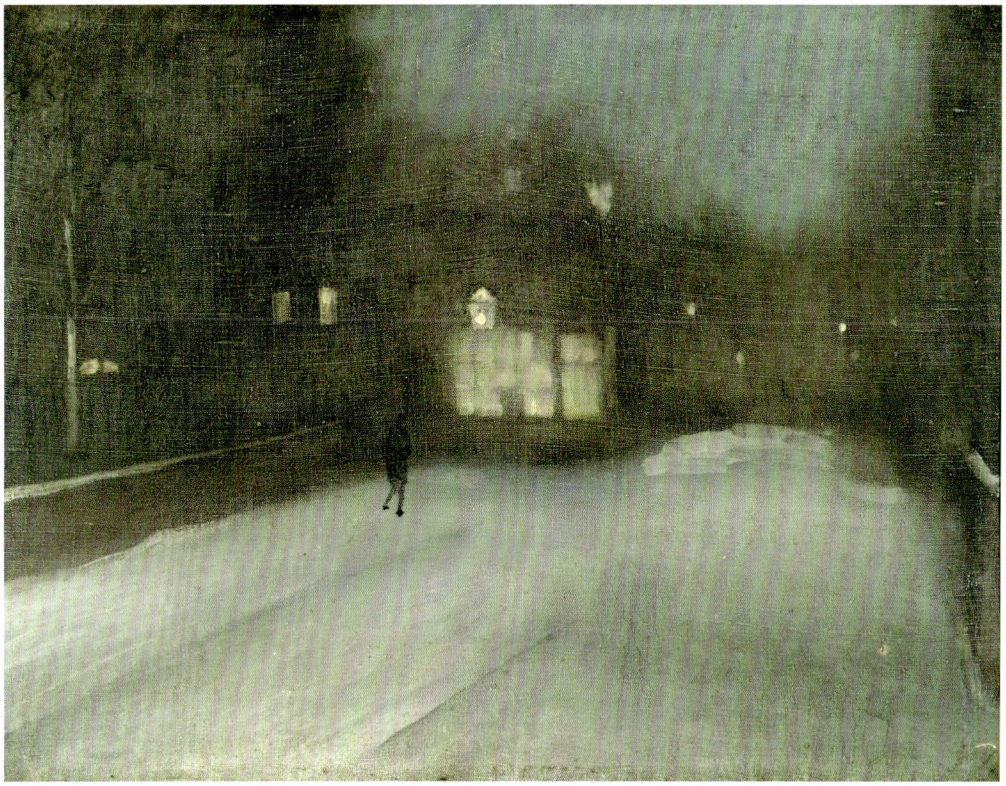

Wilde declared to Ada Leverson while awaiting his second trial in 1895: 'One must have a heart of stone to read the death of Little Nell without laughing.'[76] His provocative reversal of conventional responses marked a rejection of dominant attitudes, partly because they were popular. Whistler, part of this movement, rejected Dickens themes in visual art. The Society of British Artists had been a prime location for Dickens subjects, averaging eight per half-decade. In the period of Whistler's ascendancy and presidency this dropped to zero.[77] In his statement of 1878, 'The Red Rag', Whistler selects a Dickens subject to stand for all that is inartistic and mercenary in painting (although simultaneously betraying that, like Wilde, he was deeply imbued with the works of Dickens). The reference is to Dickens's Trotty Veck, porter, errand runner and main character in the Christmas book, *The Chimes*, and Whistler describes his picture of a 'Harmony in Grey and Gold' (fig. 65) as

> a snow scene with a single black figure and a lighted tavern. I care nothing for the past, present or future of the black figure, placed there because the black was wanted at that spot. All that I know is that my combination of grey and gold is the basis of the picture. Now this is precisely what my friends cannot grasp.
>
> They say, 'Why not call it "Trotty Veck," and sell it for a round harmony of golden guineas?'[78]

EXHIBITION DATES AND CATALOGUE NUMBERS

A list of works in this chapter and their exhibition data. Page references are given for their appearance in the above text.

W.A. Atkinson, *Little Nell and the Two Gravediggers [etc] – The Old Curiosity Shop*: Royal Academy (RA) 1856, no. 1184 (p. 98)

Alfred Barron Clay, *Finishing Bleak House*: British Institution (BI) 1854, no. 435 (p.73)

F.T. Baynes, *Kate Nickleby at her Uncle's Dinner Party* (and quotation): Society of British Artists (SBA) 1839, no. 663 (p. 73)

William Carter, *Sketch on the Spot of Jacob's Island, Southwark, Mentioned by Boz in 'Oliver Twist'*: RA 1843, no. 820 (p. 72)

Miss Clara Cawse, *Poor Nell: 'There were none to see the frail perishable figure as it glided from the fire and leaned pensively at the open casement; none but the stars to look into the upturned face and read its history'*: BI 1852, no. 307 (p. 98)

John Watkins Chapman, *Little Nell and her Grand-father*: RA 1888, no. 677 (p. 80)

James Collinson, *The Writing Lesson*: RA 1855, no. 321 (p. 84)

Charles West Cope, *A Life Well Spent*: probably RA 1862, no. 109 or 110, a pair entitled *The Two Mothers* (p. 88)

Herbert Dicksee, *The Grandfather at the Grave of Little Nell – The Old Curiosity Shop*: RA 1887, no. 1166 (p. 98)

Frederick Elwell, two paintings entitled *Still Life: The Pickwick Club*: RA 1956, no. 546, and 1958, no. 431 (p. 104)

Miss Ethel F. Everett, two *Tiny Tim* subjects: RA 1912, nos 1087 and 1137 (p. 104)

Thomas Faed, *Kate Nickleby*: RA 1862, no. 45 (p. 78)

Selina Forster, *Reading the 'Household Words'*: RA 1858, no. 135 (p. 73)

George James Frampton, *Martin Harvey as Sidney Carton in 'The Only Way'* (bust): RA 1901, no. 1729 (p. 74)

William Powell Frith, *Charles Dickens in his Study*: RA 1859, no. 210 (p. 71)

William Powell Frith, *Dolly Varden*: first version exhibited SBA 1842, no. 193 (p. 94)

R.A. Gill, *Bleak House Broadstairs:* SBA 1872, no. 616 (p. 72)

Charles Green, *Little Dorrit's Visit to her Sister at the Theatre*: Royal Institute of Painters in Watercolours 1887, no. 625 (p. 103)

Robert D. Greenham, *Edna May Oliver as 'Aunt Betsy Trotwood'*: RA 1937, no. 530 (p. 104)

Robert Hannah, *The Novel*: RA 1852, no. 972 (p. 73)

Solomon Alexander Hart, *Reading Dickens*: RA 1873, no. 1021 (p. 73)

James Bouverie Haydon, *Nell Asleep: Curiosity Shop*: RA 1845 (p. 98)

James Holmes, *The Streets of London: A Female Dombey*: SBA 1848, no. 87 (p. 73)

W.H. Humphris, *At a Dickens Character Ball*: RA 1907, no. 1042 (p. 104)

G. Sidney Hunt, *Charles Dickens Memorial Stamp*: RA 1911, no. 1481 (p. 104)

William Holman Hunt, *Little Nell and her Grandfather*: BI 1846 (p. 78)

William Holman Hunt, *The Awakening Conscience*: RA 1854, no. 377 (p. 83)

Ninian Hurley, *A Visit to Pegotty's* (*David Copperfield*): RA 1911, no. 956 (p. 104)

Sir William Hutchison, *Presenting Jimmy Snodgrass*: RA 1939, no. 144 (p. 104)

Thomas Benjamin Kennington, *Recalled to Life*: RA 1900, no. 589 (p. 74)

James Lobley, *Little Nell Leaving the Church*: RA 1867, no. 386 (p. 96)

Henry Macbeth-Raeburn, *Miss Jenny Lee as 'Jo'. 'He was wery good to me, he wos'* [sic]: RA 1886, no. 1010 (p. 74)

Miss Emily Macirone, *Nelly in the Churchyard* (and quotation): RA 1846, no. 747 (p. 98)

Miss Jessie Macleod, *The Employment of Oliver Twist in the Jew's House*: BI 1849, no. 501 (p. 74)

Robert Braithwaite Martineau, *Kit's Writing Lesson*: RA 1852, no. 1286 (p. 84)

Mrs Fanny McIan, *Little Sick Scholar*: RA 1841, no. 79, and Free Exhibition 1848, no. 122 (p. 98)

John Parker, *Little Nell's Garden*: RA 1875, no. 801 (p. 98)

Miss Mary Pickett, *Little Nell in the Old Church – The Old Curiosity Shop*: RA 1898, no. 1299 (p. 96)

William Quiller Orchardson, *Little Nell and her Grandfather in the Wood*: Royal Scottish Academy 1863, no. 198 (p. 98)

H. Richter, *Mr Pickwick and the Spinster Aunt*: Old Water Colour Society (OWCS) 1838, no. 238 (p. 73)

John Ritchie, *Little Nell and her Grandfather Leaving London* (and quotation), 1857: BI 1859, no. 302 (p. 95)

Thomas Edward Roberts, *The Sick Boy*: SBA 1857, no. 86 (p. 98)

William Rose, *An Artful Dodger*: SBA 1869, no. 222 (p. 73)

George Ruff senior, *Broadstairs, 'Our Watering-place' of Charles Dickens*: SBA 1879, no. 608 (p. 72)

James Jebusa Shannon, *Martin Harvey as Sidney Carton in 'The Only Way'*: RA 1904, no. 106 (p. 74)

Eliza Sharp, *Little Nell in the Church*: OWCS 1844, no. 86 (p. 96)

H.R. Steer, *Little Paul and Florence Dombey*: Royal Institute of Painters in Watercolours 1889, no. 822 (p. 103)

James Lawson Stewart, *The End of the Journey. 'A quiet and happy place – a place to live and learn to die in.' The Old Curiosity Shop*: RI 1885, no. 1020 (p. 98)

Alfred W. Strutt, *Oliver Asks for More*: RA 1888, no. 1612 (p. 74)

Miss Flora Elizabeth Thomas, *Rosa*: BI 1853, no. 479 (p. 74)

Alfred Joseph Woolmer, *Dolly Varden*: SBA 1842, no. 148 (p. 82)

Alfred Joseph Woolmer, *Five Sisters of York*: SBA 1846, no. 300 (p. 82)

NOTES

1. [Dickens Obituary], *The Leeds Mercury*, Saturday 11 June 1870, issue 10036, quoting the *Daily News* and the *Telegraph*.
2. Slater 2011.
3. C.M. Gordon, *British Paintings of Subjects from the English Novel 1740–1870* (New York, 1988), a published doctoral thesis, is the main study.
4. Appendix in Kitton 1899, pp. 243–6.
5. Paul Atterbury, ed., *The Parian Phenomenon: A Survey of Victorian Parian Porcelain Statuary and Busts* (Shepton Beauchamp, 1989), *passim*.
6. See F.G. Kitton, *Dickens by Pen and Pencil* and supplement (London, 1890–91), and Richard Ormond, *Early Victorian Portraits, National Portrait Gallery*, 2 vols (London, 1973), vol. 1 (text), pp. 138–45, vol. 2 (plates), cat. nos 255–71.
7. Others by Alfred Johnson (SBA 1881/2, no. 801) and Edith Barrow (Royal Society of British Artists 1891, no. 131).
8. *Athenaeum*, vol. XX, June 1852, no. 1286, p. 680.
9. Slater 2011.
10. Slater 2011.
11. G. Childs (SBA 1871, no. 685), Kate Perugini (RA 1882, no. 842) and Miss Florence Hanham (RA 1892, no. 516).
12. John Scott Carel (BI 1860, no. 175) and John Morgan (RA 1875, no. 154).
13. Slater 2009, ch. 20 ('Stories into scripts: the public readings, 1858') and pp. 461–8.
14. Slater 2009, p. 463.
15. Frederick T. Baynes (RA 1847, no. 592), Siegfried Detlen Bendixon (RA 1847, no. 165), W.T. Dennis (RA 1847, no. 660), Frank W. Williams (RA 1848, no. 863), Thomas Clack (RA 1851, no. 638), Mrs H. Criddle (OWCS 1851, no. 203). Only two of these early paintings show Paul and Florence Dombey. Three works produced around the time of Dickens's readings – by Henry Barraud (SBA 1859, no. 59, and BI 1863, no. 113) and E.C. Barnes (BI 1862, no. 101) – all focus on Paul and Florence Dombey.
16. Charles Dickens, *Bleak House* (London: Bouverie and Evans, 1853), preface, p. x.
17. Auschar Chauncy, BI 1861; Hammond, RA 1886; Fred Barnard, RA 1882; Henry Wallis, RA 1876.
18. Kitton 1899, p. 244.
19. Kitton 1899, pp. 247–7.
20. Kitton 1899, p. 244.
21. Kitton 1899, p. 244. Kitton erroneously states that the work was exhibited at the Royal Academy.
22. Kitton 1899, p. 244.
23. Kitton 1899, pp. 220, 245.
24. Kitton 1899, pp. 178–9, 246.
25. For instance the two compositions of 1876 from *The Old Curiosity Shop* in the V&A.
26. Paintings, prints and sculpture subjects explicitly drawn from Dickens's fictional writing in major Victorian exhibitions classed by gender of artist are as follows: Royal Academy to 1900: 53 male, 18 female; British Institution to 1867: 11 male, 5 female; Society of British Artists to 1893: 45 male, 18 female. Ambiguous titles such as *Great Expectations* or *Nell* have been omitted from this listing.
27. Of 48 priced works illustrating Dickens novels and short stories in the British Institution and Society of British Artists, 13 were priced at 10 guineas (gs) or under, 21 between 10 and 30 gs, and only 3 over 100 gs. The guinea (21 shillings, £1 1s. or £1.10) has been selected as a unit because it was often used for professional transactions in the Victorian era. Price depended on the reputation of the painter and the scale and complexity of the work. Of the works discussed here, Ritchie's *Little Nell and her Grandfather Leaving London* (BI 1859) was priced at £35. The most expensive paintings included a Little Nell subject by John Watkins Chapman (probably not one of those listed here, but likely to be elaborate), priced at £131 5s. (125 gs) (SBA winter 1877/8). More typical are such works as Charles Compton's *A Sketch of Nell – Vide 'Old Curiosity Shop'* (SBA 1855) at £10.
28. Frith 1887, vol. 1, pp. 101–2
29. Frith 1887, vol. 1, p. 102; quoted in Parkinson 1990, p. 96.
30. Parkinson 1990, p. 97.
31. Parkinson 1990, pp. 98–9.
32. The versions are: Wood 1995, vol. 2, reproduced p. 157 as collection of H.D. Lyons, Esq. (this is the RA exhibit); Christie's, London, 19 December 1991, no. 181 (work illustrated figs 48, 49), and Christie's, London, 3 June 1999, no. 67. The latter includes a representation of Kit's writing lesson.
33. Judith Bronkhurst, *William Holman Hunt: A Catalogue Raisonné*, vol. 1 (New Haven and London, 2006), cat. 29, pp. 103–4.
34. Parkinson 1990, pp. 78–9.
35. Including *Bébelle*, RA 1883, no. 68. *Nancy* (Society of Lady Artists 1886) may also be a Dickens subject from *Oliver Twist*. See Lucinda Hawksley, *Katey: The Life and Loves of Dickens's Artist Daughter* (London, 2006), pp. 275, 279.
36. The Vernon Collection was given to the National Gallery and is now in Tate Britain; the Sheepshanks collection was given to the South Kensington Museum, which became the V&A. See Parkinson 1990 and Robin Hamlyn, *Robert Vernon's Gift: British Art for the Nation 1847* (exh. cat., Tate Gallery, London, 1993).
37. Frith 1887, vol. 1, pp. 101, 243.
38. Leonardo considered invention analogous to divine creation, involving the realization of imagined beings and landscapes (Anthony Blunt, *Artistic Theory in Italy 1450–1660*, 4th impression, Oxford, 1978, p. 37). To Joshua Reynolds in the eighteenth century, 'Invention in painting does not imply the invention of the subject for that is commonly supplied by the Poet or Historian' but involves 'the power of representing [a] mental picture on canvas' (Robert R. Wark, ed., *Sir Joshua Reynolds's Discourses on Art*, New Haven and London, 1975, pp. 58–9). By the mid-nineteenth century C.R. Leslie's discussion of 'Invention and Expression' focused on Hogarth, noting that 'most of his subjects are entirely of his own invention' (Charles Robert Leslie, *Handbook for Young Painters*, 3rd edn, London, 1887, pp. 120–1).
39. *Peter the Great's First Sight of Catherine*, RA 1850
40. Frith 1887, vol. 1, p. 157
41. Frith 1887, vol. 2, p. 35.
42. A.I. Grieve, *The Art of Dante Gabriel Rossetti – 1. 'Found'; [and], 2. The Pre-Raphaelite Modern Life Subject* (Norwich, 1976), pp. 10–11 and *passim*.
43. See note 38.
44. Shakespeare is obviously the most frequent inspiration for literary imagery in

British painting, and Shakespearean subjects in art have been well explored, for instance in Geoffrey Ashton, *Shakespeare and British Art* (exh. cat., Yale Centre for British Art, New Haven, 1981); Ross Anderson, ed., *A Brush with Shakespeare: The Bard in Painting, 1780–1910* (exh. cat., Montgomery Museum of Fine Arts, Montgomery, Alabama, 1985); and Jane Martineau, *Shakespeare in Art* (exh. cat., Dulwich Picture Gallery, London, 2003). Particularly in the first half of the nineteenth century, Walter Scott subjects were almost as common. Catherine Gordon (1971, p. 297) records that between 1805 and 1870 over three hundred painters and sculptors exhibited more than one thousand 'Scott' works at the Royal Academy and the British Institution. Jim Cheshire, ed., *Tennyson Transformed: Alfred Lord Tennyson and Visual Culture* (exh. cat., The Collection, Lincoln, 2009).
45. Strong 1978.
46. For instance Cowling 2000.
47. For instance the brief treatment of Martineau's *Kit's Writing Lesson* in Cowling 2000, fig. 34, pp. 50–51.
48. Exhibited RA 1863 under the title *Woman's Mission*. The full title is given in Hicks's Notebooks, see Allwood 1982, p. 55.
49. *Art Journal*, 1855, pp. 175–6.
50. See 'Myth Today' in Roland Barthes, *Mythologies*, selected and translated by Annette Lavers (London, 1972), especially pp. 116ff. and pp. 142–3.
51. Mary Cowling, *The Artist as Anthropologist: The Representation of Type and Character in Victorian Art* (Cambridge, 1989).
52. Hunt 1905, vol. 2, pp. 124–5.
53. Wood 1995, vol. 1, p. 344, and Hunt 1905, vol. 1, p. 302.
54. George P. Landow, *William Holman Hunt and Typological Symbolism* (New Haven, 1979).
55. Apples are associated with mischievous boys in the classroom (chs 24 and 25); Kit takes a handkerchief full of apples to Astley's and hits someone on the head with them (ch. 39), which reinforces this interpretation.
56. Examples exist by Mulready, Morgan, Collinson et. al.
57. For example Patricia Thompson, *The Victorian Heroine, A Changing Ideal 1837–1873* (Westport, 1978); Michael Slater, *Dickens and Women* (London, 1983), ch. 14, 'The Womanly Ideal', and Sara Holdsworth, *Innocence and Experience: Images of Children in British Art from 1600 to the Present* (exh. cat., Manchester City Art Galleries, 1992).
58. Dominic Head, ed., *The Cambridge Guide to English Literature* (Cambridge, 2006), p. 824.
59. Dickens's text in the first book-form publication of *The Old Curiosity Shop* was: 'The solemn stillness was no marvel now.'
60. Kitton 1899, p. 245.
61. They range from Thomas Webster's *Sickness and Health* (RA 1843, no. 128; V&A), and Mrs Alexander Farmer's *An Anxious Hour* (RA 1865; V&A) to Luke Fildes's popular *The Doctor* (RA 1891; Tate Britain). G.F. Watts addressed the topic allegorically in *Death Crowning Innocence* (1886–7; Tate Britain), and George Elgar Hicks depicted an angel bearing the soul of a child to heaven, as its parents in their cottage mourn its body, in *A Cloud with a Silver Lining* (RA 1890; private collection; Allwood 1982, no. 40).
62. John Morley, *Death, Heaven and the Victorians* (Pittsburgh, 1971); James Stevens Curl, *The Victorian Celebration of Death* (London, 1972).
63. First published in *Screen*, Autumn 1975, reprinted in Mulvey 1989, pp. 14–26. See discussion and critique in Gillian Rose, *Visual Methodologies* (London, 2001), pp. 106–16.
64. Mulvey 1989, p. 19.
65. She notes the sudden new popularity in this period of Lucy Ravenswood and Effie Deans subjects, although the Scott novels in which they feature, *The Bride of Lammermoor* and *The Heart of Midlothian*, had been published in 1819 and 1818 respectively: Gordon 1971, pp. 311–15.
66. For instance by Miss Charlotte E. Babb (SBA 1865), Thomas Herbert Maguire (SBA 1873, no. 90), Miss Josephine Saville (SBA 1875, no. 433), Miss Clara Cawse (RA 1850, no. 341) and Henry C. Harrison, sculptor (RA 1872, no. 1534).
67. Reproduced in Cowling 2000, p. 141, fig. 26.
68. This painting bears the date 1881, but its style and costume date it to the earlier period.
69. For instance by Miss Emily Macirone (SBA 1846, no. 660) and Miss Maria Brooks (RA 1875, no. 530), although the latter may represent a scene at Nell's last home rather than at the shop.
70. Frederick William Fairholt, *Costume in England*, 2nd edn (London, 1860), preface, quoted in Strong 1978, p. 55.
71. Quentin Bell, *On Human Finery* (first published 1947; revised and reprinted London, 1992), pp. 66–9 (in ch. 3, 'The Nature of Fashion, pp. 57–89); see p. 68: 'Du Maurier could no more put his *Trilby* into crinolines [set late 1850s, published 1894] than Thackeray could give Amelia a high waist [*Vanity Fair*, set 1815, published 1847].'
72. Quoted Parkinson 1990, p. 78, from the artist's catalogue of his own work, no. 928.
73. Donald L. Hill, ed., *The Renaissance: Studies in Art and Poetry [by] Walter Pater* (originally published London, 1893; Berkeley, Los Angeles and London, 1980), p. 108. See also Elizabeth Prettejohn, *Beauty and Art* (*Oxford History of Art*) (Oxford, 2005), pp. 111–55, and Elizabeth Prettejohn, *Art for Art's Sake: Aestheticism in Victorian Painting* (New Haven and London, 2007).
74. Christopher Newall, *The Grosvenor Gallery Exhibitions: Change and Continuity in the Victorian Art World* (Cambridge, 1995).
75. Wright 2008, p. 54, from Frank Harris, *Oscar Wilde, his Life and Confessions* (New York, 1930), p. 17.
76. Wright 2008, p. 238, from R. Ellmann, *Oscar Wilde* (London, 1987), p. 441.
77. Eight Dickens paintings in 1881–5 and none in 1886–90. Whistler was President of the Society of British Artists from June 1886 to June 1888.
78. James McNeill Whistler, 'The Red Rag' in 'Mr. Whistler, Cheyne Walk', *The World*, 22 May 1878, reprinted in James McNeill Whistler, *The Gentle Art of Making Enemies* (London, 1890), p. 126.

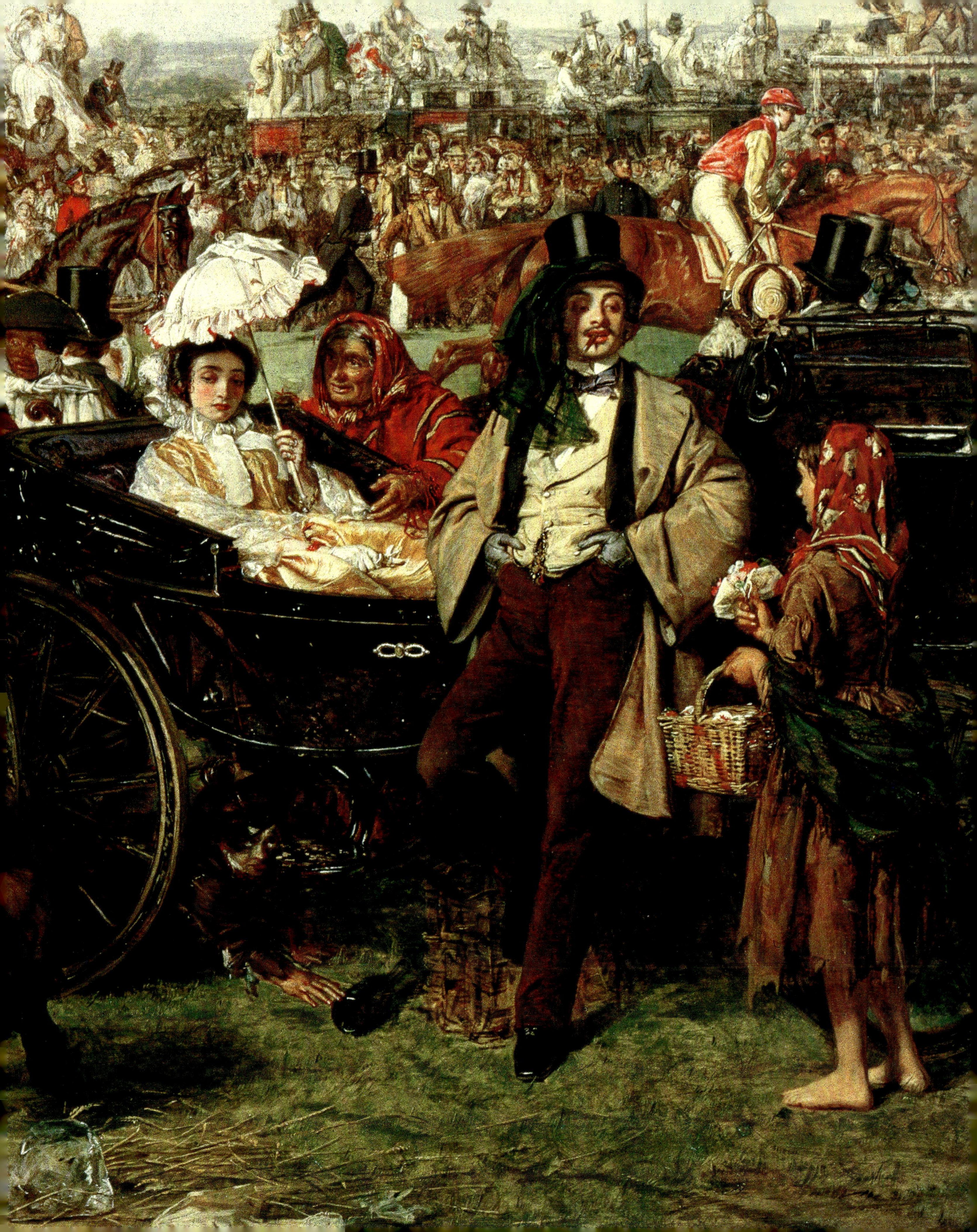

Dickens AND THE PAINTING OF MODERN LIFE

MARK BILLS

FIG. 66
William Powell Frith, *The Derby Day* (detail of fig. 85)

Artists, just like those in other fields, were not immune to the influence of Dickens. In the pages of his novels they found a rich body of writing that evoked and inspired picture making. This was most obviously manifest in the numerous depictions of characters invented by the writer that appeared on the walls of the Royal Academy and elsewhere. This was a phenomenon that Dickens observed directly, and the artist William Powell Frith recalled meeting the author at an exhibition: 'There were some pictures in the exhibition illustrating "Dombey and Son;" I told Dickens of them. "Yes," he said, "I know there are; just go and see them, and tell me what they are like. I don't like to be caught looking at them myself."'[1]

Yet the influence of Dickens on artists was not limited to depictions of his characters, and his writings, art criticisms aside, inspired a style and approach to painting that ran parallel to those of his novels. This can be seen in the modern-life movement that flowered in the 1850s and 1860s when Dickens was at the height of his fame. At the forefront was Frith, a friend of Dickens from whom Dickens had commissioned works and whom he had sat for.[2] Although images of contemporary life were regularly depicted in the pages of novels and illustrated papers and magazines, to have paintings of contemporary life on the walls of the Royal Academy was something quite new in the 1850s. Dickens gave Frith and other artists, such as George Elgar Hicks and John Ritchie, the confidence to depict the world around them, allowing them to raise the subject from the sole preserve of popular art forms. Before *Ramsgate Sands (Life at the Seaside)* (1854; Royal Collection) Frith had been nervous of painting any genre scene that was not masked in historical costume. He recalled: 'One of the greatest difficulties besetting me has always been the choice of subject. My inclination being strongly towards the illustration of modern life, I had read the works of Dickens in the hope of finding material for the exercise of any talent I might possess.'[3] As Frith instinctively knew, the novels of Dickens offered new opportunities for artists and a freedom to explore modern life as a valid subject for his art.

The writings of Dickens and the paintings of Frith have many parallels: one very visual in its literary form, the other very literary in its visual form. In other words, the author's narratives created vivid pictures and the painter's pictures evoked strong narratives. They both shared the same subject, the narratives of modern life, but each art form had its own particular demands and opportunities. When a major Frith retrospective was held at the Guildhall Art Gallery in 2006, critics who reviewed the exhibition exclaimed in their titles, 'A Dickens of a Painter' and 'Dickens, with a Paintbrush'.[4] The critics affirmed what one instinctively sees in such paintings. The narratives and characters of Dickens are clearly evoked in modern-life painting in general and Frith in particular. This essay will explore in greater detail the close parallel between the art of Frith and Dickens and the strong influence Dickens had on a movement in painting.

Dickens and Frith had a number of things in common. Both – one the master of word and the other a master of paint – arose from a shared tradition, even though they worked in different art forms. They were friends and they were both successful, even though Frith remained in awe of the great author.[5] They both grew up with a fascination for a popular British visual tradition that was epitomized by the work of William Hogarth, an artist who combined so many elements that appealed to author and writer. Nor were they alone in their admiration for the eighteenth-century master, for in the Victorian age Hogarth was seen as the father of the British school of painting, as Ruskin affirmed: 'It is from Hogarth that English painting may be truly said to date.'[6] One of the most influential surveys of English painting by Ernest Chesneau in the 1880s acknowledged that Hogarth 'had a decisive influence on the English school, which even to-day continues to cultivate . . . the ground . . . on which this intelligent adventurer in art . . . planted his tent of observation'.[7] The painters of modern life similarly recognized the debt of the English master, Frith writing that Hogarth 'stands *longo intervallo* above any of his successors'.[8]

If Hogarth was admired by painters, he was also esteemed by writers and his influence was felt in both spheres. When William Makepeace Thackeray delivered his series of celebrated lectures on English humorists at Willis's Rooms in 1851, his audience included Charles Dickens, Charlotte Brontë and Thomas Carlyle. One of the lectures concerned Hogarth, and Thackeray admiringly explored the contemporary relevance of the eighteenth-century artist. Although the lectures focused primarily on writers, they emphasized the characteristics and importance of a national school that encompassed both literary and visual forms. They were, according to Thackeray, essentially the same tradition, one echoing the other. 'Masters sent their apprentices,' Thackeray wrote, 'fathers took their children, to see Jack Sheppard or Jonathan Wild hanged, and it was as undoubting subscribers to this moral law that Fielding wrote and Hogarth painted.'[9] If Thackeray's essay described the synergy between certain writers and artists in the eighteenth century, the same, as this essay will argue, can be said of Dickens and Frith and the modern-life school of painting.

Thackeray gave the lectures again at a number of other venues the following year including some in America, where he added a further lecture, 'Charity and Humour',

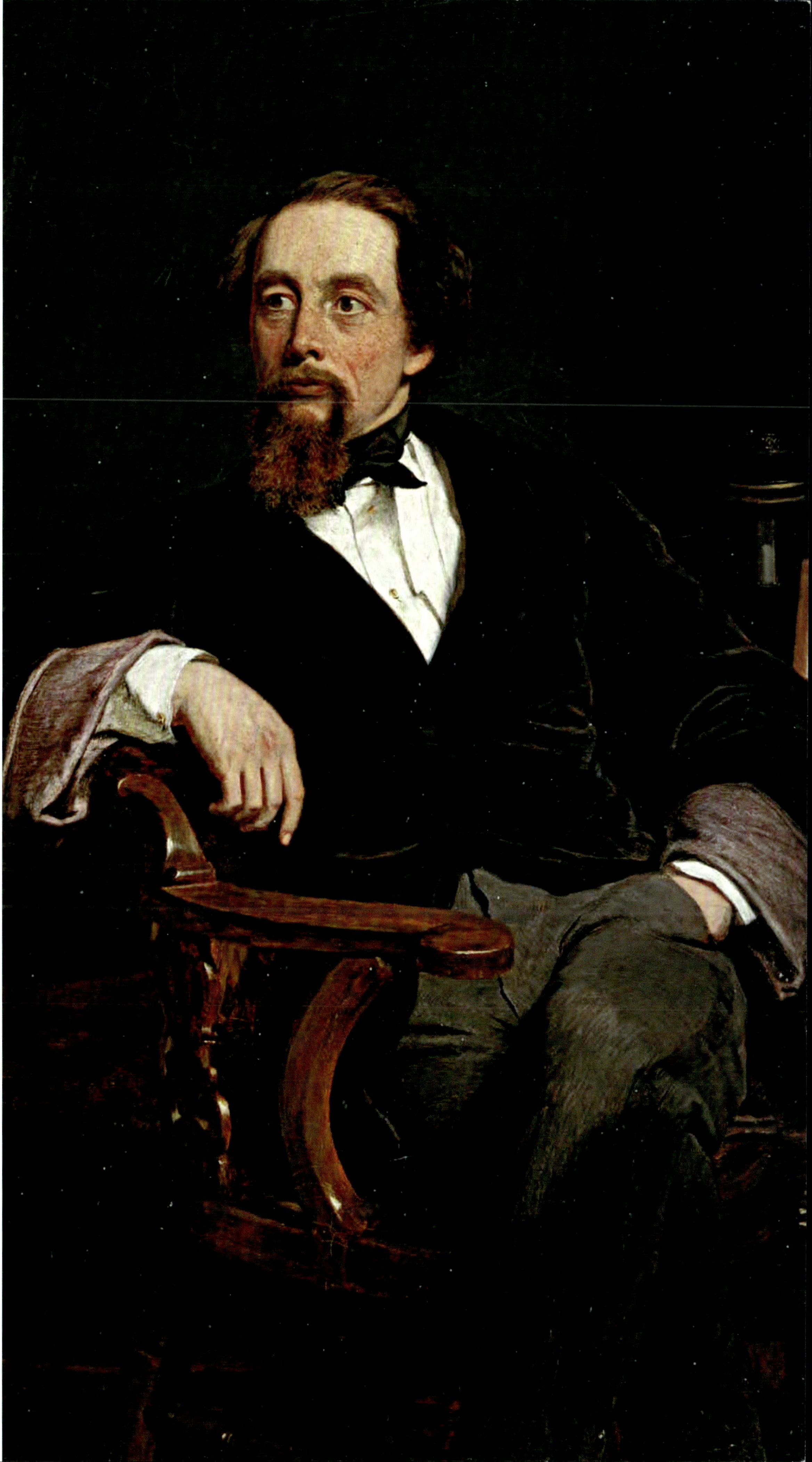

FIG. 67
William Powell Frith, *Charles Dickens in his Study* (detail of fig. 42)

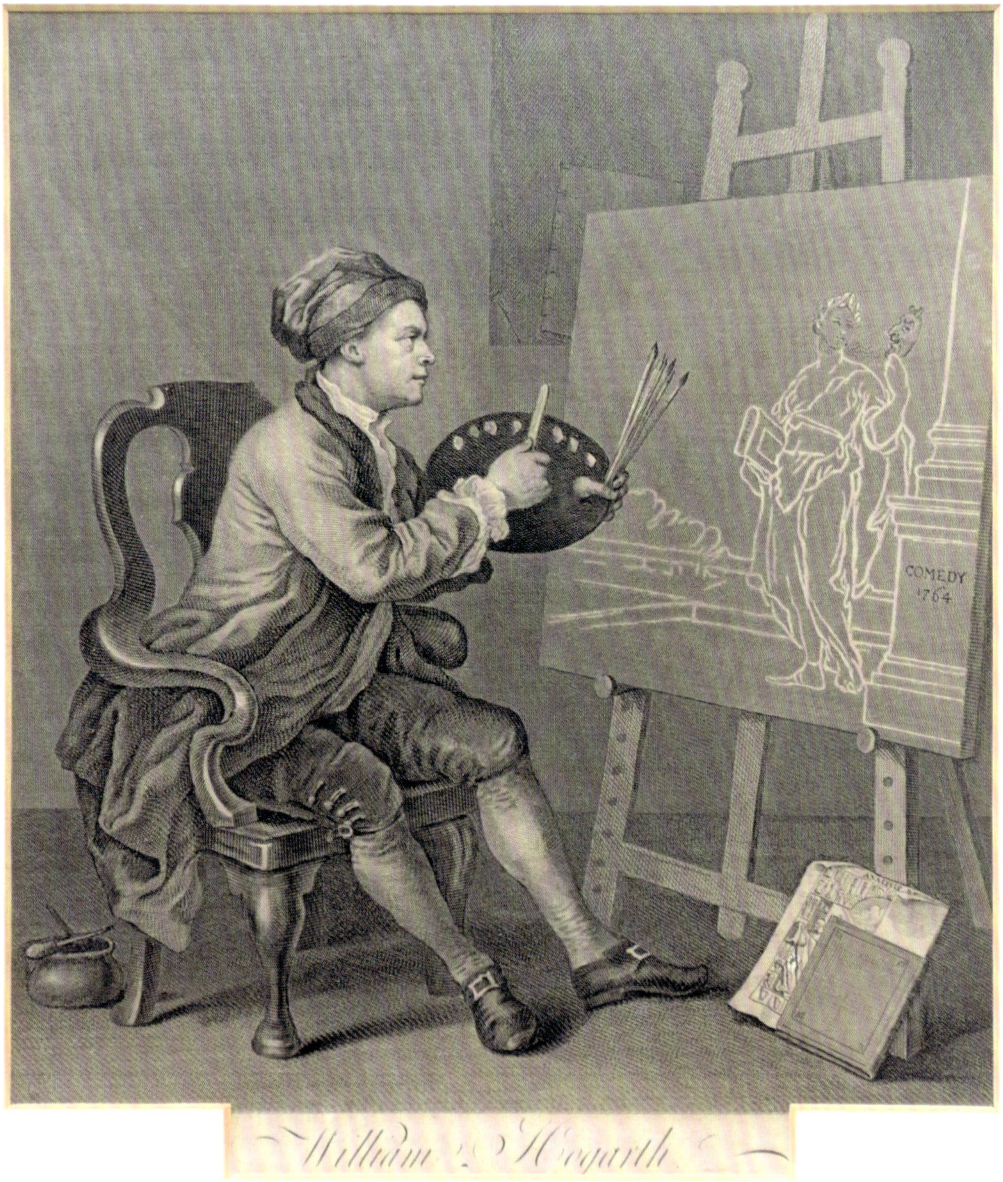

FIG. 68
William Hogarth, *Self-Portrait*, 1764, etching with engraving. Collection of the author

which he repeated in London in March 1855, and brought the series up to date with the addition of Dickens. The lecture did not evade Dickens, who wrote to Thackeray to say 'that I am profoundly touched by your generous reference to me. I do not know how to tell you what a glow it spread over my heart.'[10] The lectures themselves were hugely influential, successfully presenting the importance of Hogarth and what he meant to both artists and writers as the creator of a popular British tradition where moral tales imbued with humour reflected the manners and customs of contemporary life. In updating the survey to include Dickens, Thackeray positioned Dickens not only as the pre-eminent author of his age but as the contemporary leader of this rich tradition.

FIG. 69
The Hogarth Room, reproduced in *The Strand Magazine*, No. VI, July–December 1893, p. 82: 'These Hogarth's ... used to hang on the staircase at Gad's Hill, and after Dickens's death they found a place in the billiard-room, eventually Mr. Yates bought them.' Collection of the author

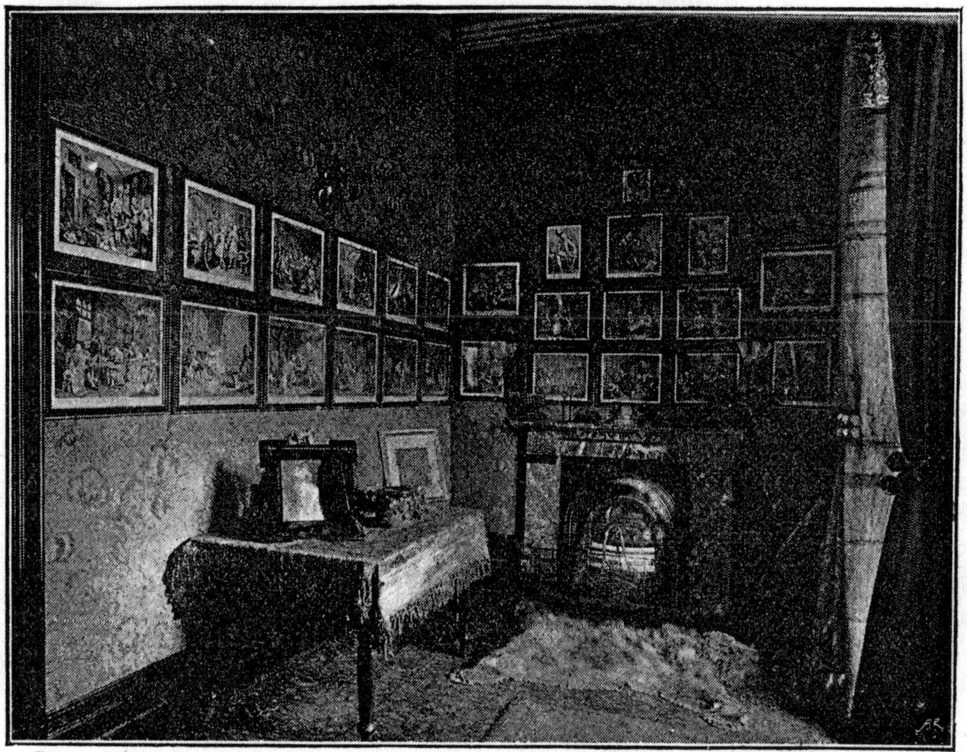

From a Photo. by] THE HOGARTH ROOM. [*Elliott & Fry.*

Dickens's own admiration of Hogarth was profound, and a personal recollection of the author by J.F. Fields noted the works by the eighteenth-century artist that Dickens owned as well as the joy he took in 'reading' them (fig. 69):

> Dickens's admiration of Hogarth was unbounded, and he had hung the staircase leading up from the hall of his house with fine old impressions of the great master's best works. Observing our immediate interest in these pictures, he seemed greatly pleased, and proceeded at once to point out in his graphic way what had struck his own fancy most in Hogarth's genius. He had made a study of the painter's thought as displayed in these works, and his talk about the artist was delightful. He used to say he never came down the stairs without pausing with new wonder over the fertility of the mind that had conceived and the hand that had executed these powerful pictures of human life; and I cannot forget with what fervid energy and feeling he repeated one day, as we were standing together on the stairs in front of the Hogarth pictures, Dr. Johnson's epitaph on the painter.[11]

Although we do not have a complete record of Dickens's enthusiastic readings of Hogarth, there is a long passage in his review of George Cruikshank's *The Drunkard's*

Children (1848) in which he writes in detail about Hogarth's *Gin Lane* (1751). The ostensible reason for the passage is to draw comparisons between Hogarth's work and the Cruikshank series, but this gives way to the author taking the opportunity to expound on Hogarth's print, explaining that he had 'always been inclined to think the purpose of this piece not adequately stated, even by Charles Lamb'. In it Dickens thought that Hogarth was deploying all his artistic skills: the masterly depiction of characters, the scattering of symbolic details throughout to echo the main action, and the creation of a setting to delineate the conditions in which alcoholism arose – the cause not the problem, as he had so admirably described in his 'Gin-Shops' in *Sketches by Boz* (1836). He saw *Gin Lane* to be just as relevant to Londoners of the late 1840s as it was to Hogarth's audience in the 1750s.

> But after one immortal journey down Gin Lane he turned away in grief and sorrow perhaps in hope of better things one day, from better laws, and schools, and poor men's homes and went back no more. It is remarkable of that picture that, while it exhibits drunkenness in its most appalling forms, it forces on the attention of the spectator a most neglected, wretched neighbourhood (the same that is only just now cleared away for the extension of Oxford Street), and an unwholesome, indecent, abject condition of life, worthy to be a Frontispiece to the late Report of the Sanitary Commissioners, made nearly one hundred years afterward.[12]

Hogarth served as an influence for Dickens, Frith and the depiction of modern-life subjects as he did for many Victorian artists and writers, offering a model of an indigenous art form that was both popular and essentially British. Naturally, Hogarth was viewed through the eyes of the time, and although much of his work appealed to nineteenth-century sensibilities, there were elements that were seen as less desirable to imitate, most notably those that were considered crude. For Dickens and Frith Hogarth offered both strong narratives, encompassing humour and tragedy, and moral tales for a contemporary audience. Thackeray stated this plainly in his lecture about the artist:

> It was not by satire of this sort, or by scorn and contempt, that Hogarth achieved his vast popularity and acquired his reputation. His art is quite simple; he speaks popular parables to interest simple hearts, and to inspire them with pleasure or pity, or warning and terror.[13]

The moral narrative was clearly very important to both Dickens and Frith in the development of their art and was one of the central themes of the Thackeray lectures. His concluding paper linked Dickens directly to this tradition of satire and morality:

> If the humorous writers claim to be week-day preachers, have they conferred any benefit by their sermons? Are people happier, better, better disposed to

> their neighbours, more inclined to do works of kindness, to love, forbear, forgive, pity, after reading in Addison, in Steele, in Fielding, in Goldsmith, in Hood, in Dickens? I hope and believe so, and fancy that in writing they are also acting charitably, contributing, with the means which Heaven supplies them, to forward the end which brings you too together.[14]

If the moral dimension of Hogarth was important, the settings and the scope of the narrative were too, centred around London and incorporating the breadth of society from low to high in both poor and affluent districts. Thackeray concluded:

> To the student of history, these admirable works must be invaluable, as they give us the most complete and truthful picture [of] the manners, and even the thoughts, of the past century.[15]

Similarly, modern-life painting meant fidelity to truth in both depiction and narrative, truth in terms of morality as well as of accurate pictorial representation of the surrounding world, a belief in realism above artifice. Hogarth embodied a cornerstone of this belief, which Frith saw as a 'blunt and truthful rendering of nature'.[16] Consequently, Hogarth's paintings were considered to be a faithful portrayal of the life around him.

In Hogarth they also saw a supremely popular artist, one who had appealed to a wide audience. His art did not speak exclusively to connoisseurs, and there was huge demand for the prints after his paintings, just as the next part of a serialized Dickens novel was sought by an eager audience. Frith recalled:

> It would be difficult to convey to the present generation the intense delight with which each new work of Dickens was received; and I can easily believe the story that was current at the time of the sick man, who, lying as was thought on his death-bed, and listening apparently with becoming reverence to the warnings of his clergyman, was heard to mutter as the divine left the room, 'That's all very well. Thank goodness, a new number of "Pickwick" comes out on Wednesday.'[17]

Dickens was, like the great satirists, suspicious of connoisseurship, as Nicholas Penny has rightly discussed in his essay on Dickens and philistinism (pp. 11–33). In satire, connoisseurs are the goggled spectator, half blind, full of pretension and missing the point of the picture they are scrutinizing. Hogarth's feet, in contrast, were seen to be very firmly on the ground, with an art form that was equally attractive to high and low. Dickens felt that to develop one's own opinion was more important than to take blindly the advice of connoisseurs and wrote of his travels in Italy, where he viewed at first hand the work of the Old Masters:

> One of the great uses of travelling is to encourage a man to think for himself, to be bold enough always to declare without offence that he *does* think for himself, and to overcome the villainous meanness of professing what other people have professed when he knows (if he has capacity to originate an opinion) that his profession is untrue.[18]

For a Victorian artist to follow the example of Hogarth was not without its difficulties, given the cultural changes of a hundred years. Critics praised those qualities that were widely perceived as his merits, avoiding the elements that they felt were problematic such as the explicit sexuality, crude behaviour and sharp satire. When Frith chose to paint smart people gambling in *The Salon d'Or, Homburg* (1871; Museum of Art, Rhode Island), it was far removed from the debauchery of Hogarth's rake. 'I think Hogarth would have made a picture of such an incident,' Frith wrote, 'with the addition, perhaps, of matter unpresentable to the present age.'[19] Yet the difficulties of following a Hogarthian model go far deeper than the Victorian conception of decency. The nature of form and depiction that Hogarth adopted was questioned in relation to contemporary painting practice. In particular, the use of satirical forms by fine artists had become problematic with the increasing polarization between 'high' and 'low' art, an important issue in understanding the liberation that Dickens offered to painters of modern life.[20]

In his lectures on the English humorists Thackeray had eloquently expressed that there was a distinct tradition of satire in English art and literature. Yet by the 1840s visual satire had increasingly become the preserve of popular culture, as opposed to an art of the status accorded to Hogarth. The pages of illustrated magazines, most famously *Punch* and *The Illustrated London News* but also many others, rather than the walls of the Royal Academy, carried satirical images and depictions of the modern world. Ironically, eighteenth-century costumes posed the least difficulties for artists and it was easier for an artist to convincingly represent these pictures as 'high' art than those with modern dress. As Frith put it when he first came to tackle the subject of the contemporary world around him, 'I had determined to try my hand on modern life, with all its drawbacks of unpicturesque dress.'[21]

Modern-life painting, therefore, was a problem for critics who considered it a distinctly 'low' subject for a picture. G.F. Watts, the epitome of a Victorian 'high' artist, said:

> To the painter of actualities the materials are ever available and good. There is nothing to prevent the perfect success of another Hogarth. The details of everyday life and the police courts, looked at from a philosophical point of view, furnish subjects perhaps superior, certainly more affecting, than the majority of those treated by the earlier painters. But still the beautiful, the dignified, and the glowing form part of our natural wants, and cannot be given up without regret.[22]

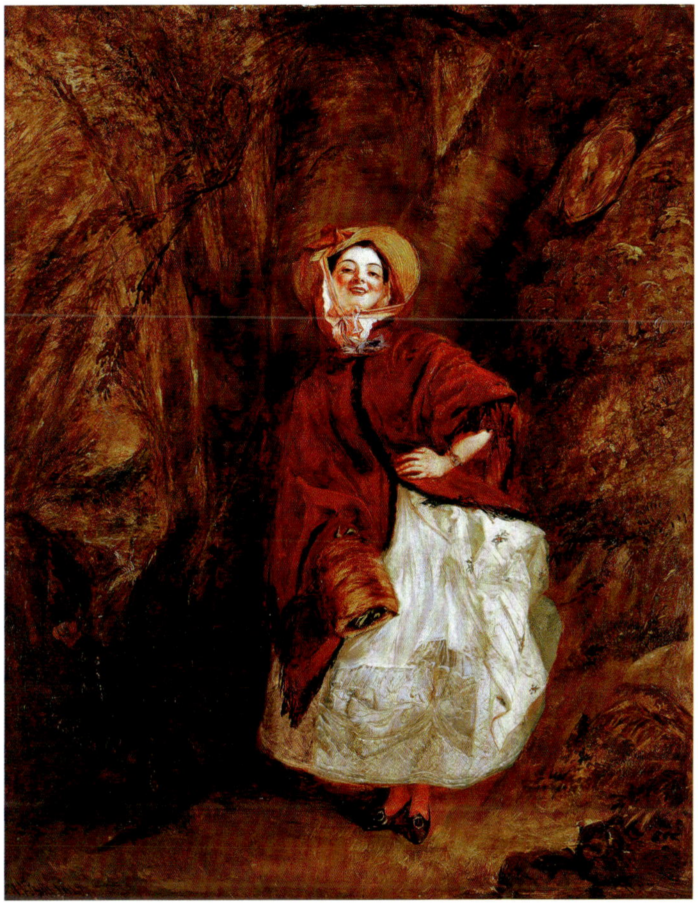

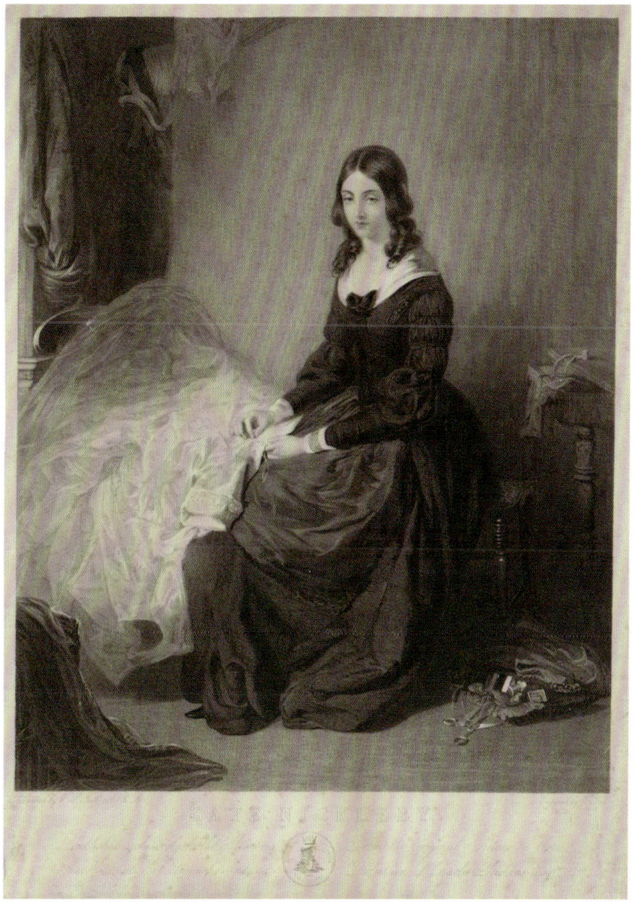

FIG. 70
William Powell Frith, *Dolly Varden*, 1842, oil on canvas. Victoria and Albert Museum, London

FIG. 71
William Holl Jr after William Powell Frith, *Kate Nickleby*, published 1848, stipple engraving. National Portrait Gallery, London

Watts was profoundly interested in the social issues that modern-life painting could offer but ultimately found the 'low' depictions too realistic and unpicturesque. He had himself successfully attempted social-realist painting in the late 1840s,[23] but was dissatisfied with his forays into what he essentially saw as the Hogarthian and Dickensian tradition, which he expressed in the following, rather snobbish way: 'Much as we admire their genius, we should not wish Hogarth to illustrate the Book of Job, or Dickens to translate Dante.'[24]

Frith's first move toward painting modern life was provided by Dickens through his novel *Barnaby Rudge* published in serial form between February and November 1841. Of course, the novel did not depict modern life, since it was set in the late eighteenth century, but as David Trotter has observed, '*Barnaby Rudge* enabled Frith to modernize himself because it was itself both an old lamp and a new one, at once historical and contemporary in reference.'[25] Frith chose to paint the character of Dolly Varden and the finished work was exhibited at the Society of British Artists in the spring of 1842. In November of the same year Dickens asked Frith to paint two companion paintings, one of Dolly Varden (later version: fig. 70) and the other of Kate Nickleby (untraced). On completion of the works Dickens was delighted and, rarely for him, wrote: 'All I can say is, they are exactly what I meant, and I am very much obliged to you for painting them for me.'[26] *Kate Nickleby* was what Frith later recorded as his first painting of modern life, both in its subdued colouring and in its intimacy: 'My first venture in modern-life subjects took the shape of a small picture of a mother and child . . . The grey-and-black dress of the mother and the white night-gown of the child made a sufficiently agreeable arrangement of negative colours.'[27] It had none of the gaudiness of the contemporary crowd, but it provided a further step towards giving the artist confidence to paint modern-life subjects, and engravings of the work proved popular (fig. 71).[28]

Throughout the 1840s Frith drew on earlier literary models from Shakespeare to Sterne as the basis for his paintings, which also led to narratives of his own invention depicted within period settings.[29] These were a great success but did not allow his art to fully flourish. Hogarth had faced a similar problem at the outset of his career when he turned from engraving to painting, beginning with miniature conversation pieces that the artist not only found a piece of 'drudgery' but also not profitable enough. 'I therefore turned my thoughts', he famously wrote, 'to a still more novel mode, viz., painting and engraving modern moral subjects.'[30]

Frith had begun to explore larger and more complex paintings in multiple groupings of figures with the variety of form needed to portray individual character and reveal plot and subplot. He was developing his art as far as he was able within its limitations yet was still fearful of turning to modern life. Thackeray, who championed the idea of a contemporary Hogarth who would depict his own age, criticized the setting of Frith's *Coming of Age in the Olden Time* (1849; private collection). 'Thackeray,' Frith wrote, 'advocating the more frequent illustration of modern life, asked, in a review of the exhibition, "Why, when a man comes of age, should it be thought desirable that he should come of the age of Elizabeth?" '[31] Despite this, Frith admitted: 'Fear of modern-life subjects still possessed me . . . I took refuge in bygone times.'[32] Yet he must have been encouraged by the words of such an eminent literary figure, and more importantly, he was supported by Dickens who had commissioned *Dolly Varden* and *Kate Nickleby* from him. Both paintings, however, were essentially portraits, 'too like portraits', as Frith recalled, and they lacked the ambition of scale, subject and variety to represent a whole-hearted depiction of contemporary Londoners.

In the end it was the seaside at Ramsgate that provided the inspiration for Frith to revolutionize painting of the 1850s. A family holiday in 1851 was the spark: 'The variety of character on Ramsgate Sands attracted me – all sorts and conditions of men and women were there.' If Tobias Smollett, Shakespeare and Laurence Sterne had allowed Frith to explore his own narratives in 'bygone times', it was Dickens who gave him the inspiration to attempt his own narrative of modern life. The writer, who was universally recognized by the 1850s, gave a legitimacy to such depictions even if there was some reticence on Frith's own part as well as from some of his artist friends. Like Dickens, he faced snobbery, one critic writing that *Ramsgate Sands (Life at the Seaside)* was 'a piece of vulgar Cockney business unworthy of being represented even in an illustrated paper'.[33] But, as with Dickens, 'high' art reservations did not hinder the popular reception that both men's work received. On three separate occasions a special picture rail was required to keep an eager public back and *Life at the Seaside* was bought by Queen Victoria.

In literature Dickens was at the forefront of this literary and visual tradition, which he had successfully reinvigorated. He had breathed new life into it and raised it to a higher, dynamic and relevant art form. Like Hogarth before him, he had shown that an art that was widely popular with the public could also be great. Visual art had struggled to develop this popular tradition, being limited to prints and illustrations in periodicals and books rather than oil on canvas. Frith and the modern-life movement in painting attempted to reverse this trend in the wake of Dickens. Inevitably, modern-life painters were the artists who most closely reflected the writings of Dickens, and it is worth exploring the parallel visual elements in text and image, often Hogarthian in spirit, that gave substance and direction to Dickens's painterly contemporaries.

The subject and settings of Dickens and Frith, like those of Hogarth, are essentially the same: London and Londoners. When Dickens wrote 'what inexhaustible food for speculation, do the streets of London afford',[34] he could also have been writing for Frith. Frederic Kitton noted of Dickens that 'as an artist *in* words, he is perhaps unrivalled' and that in 'many of his descriptive passages (in "Pictures from Italy," for example) suggesting subjects in which Rembrandt or Teniers would have revelled', he was referring primarily to the Old Masters and the places by which they had been inspired.[35] The more general point that the lucid and visual evocations of place in Dickens's work could be and were an inspiration to artists is most relevant here. Of course, it was not descriptions of mainland Europe but those of contemporary London, which abound in his writing, that provided inspiration to a new generation of artists. From his earliest writings Dickens described the great city around him as it appeared to him, real and imagined, the backdrop and even protagonist of the drama that unfolded within it. So, too, for the painters of modern life the streets and locations of Dickens are the settings for their works.

When Frith proposed a series entitled *The Streets of London* (1862; private collection) that was to consist of three large paintings, *Morning* (fig. 72), *Noon* (fig. 73) and *Night* (fig. 77), he looked both to the model of Hogarth's series *The Four Times of Day* (1736; Upton House [National Trust] and private collection), in which areas of London were illustrated in a visual perambulation around the metropolis, and to contemporary literary accounts. He found in Dickens's *Sketches by Boz* contemporary descriptions of the London streets, particularly in 'The Streets – Morning' and 'The Streets – Night', which offered a literary equivalent for the views that he set out to paint. 'I had read all that Dickens had written,' Frith later wrote, 'beginning with "Sketches by Boz" '.[36] Dickens had taken a journalistic genre and transformed it into a best-selling bound volume, which began to articulate his observations and vision of London, the genesis of 'Dickensian London'. As a visual

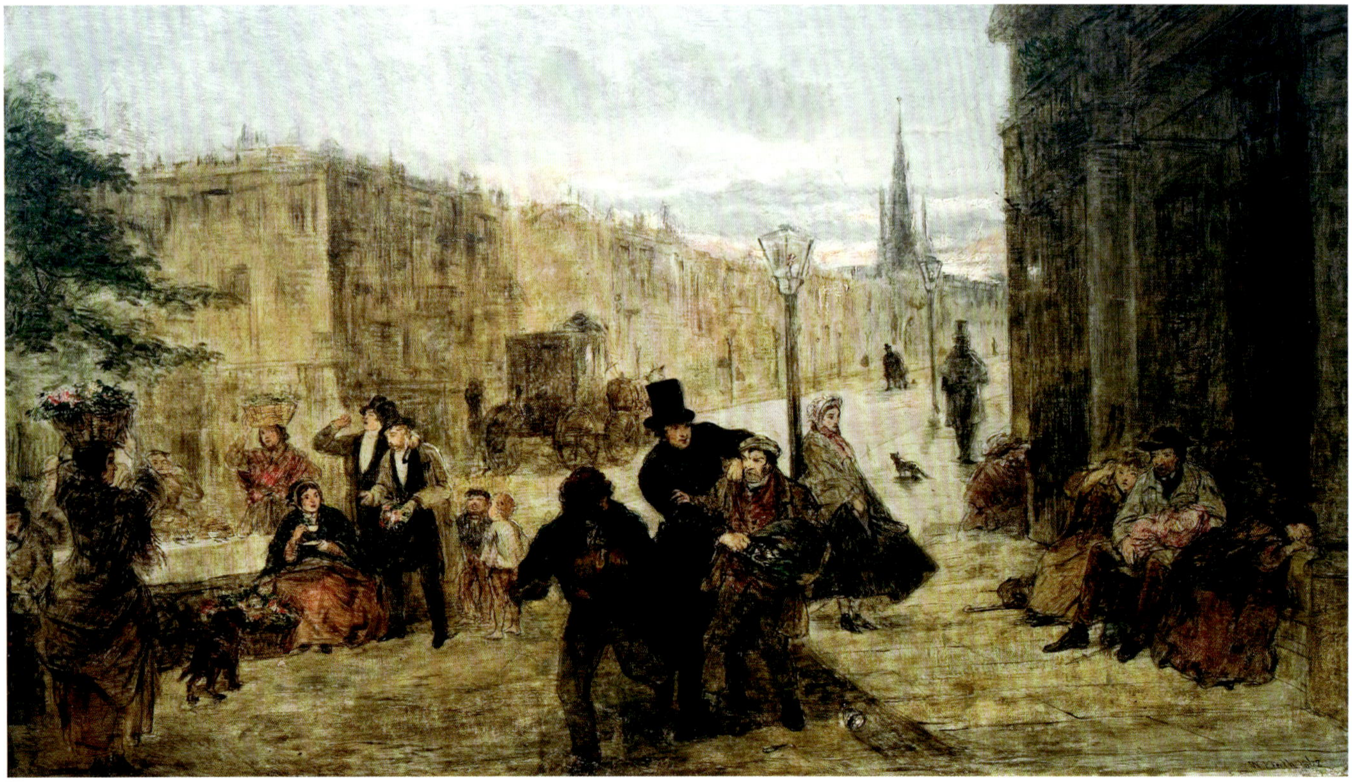

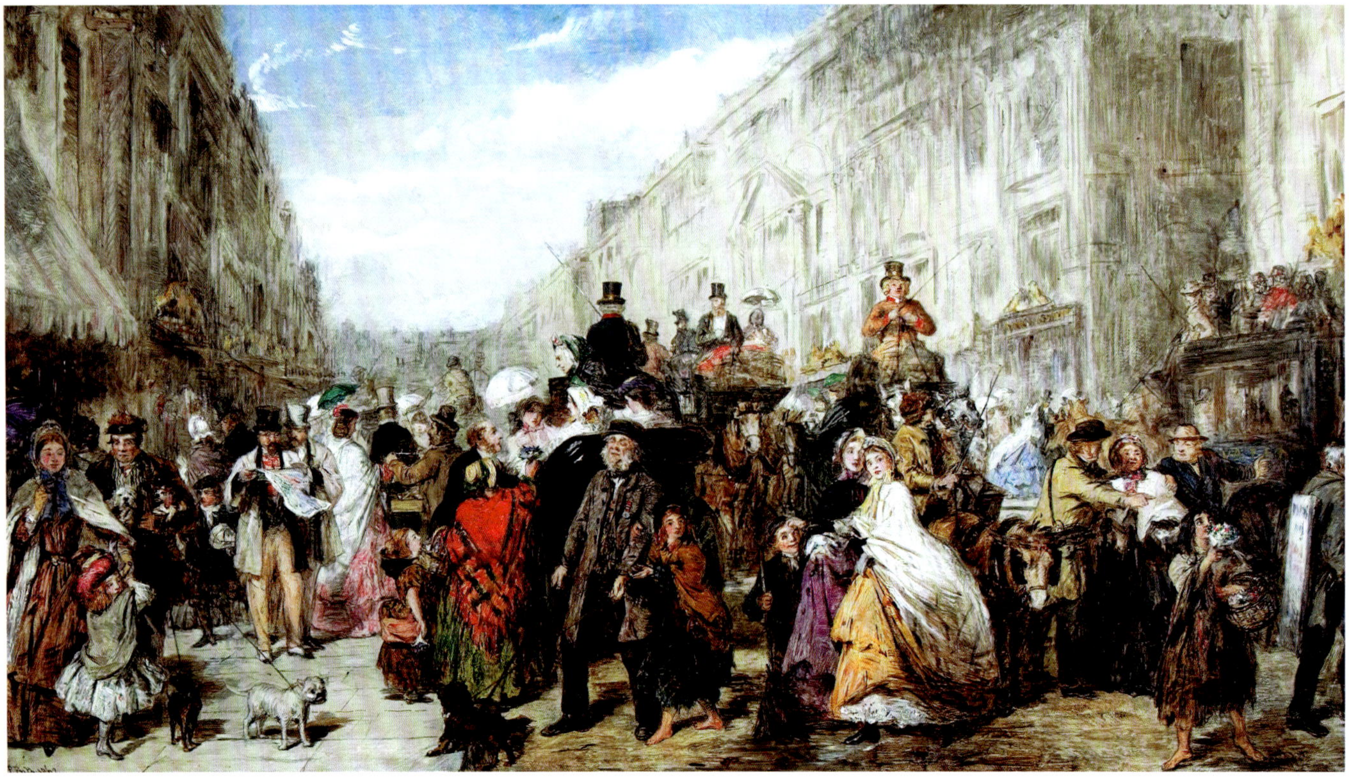

TOP LEFT
FIG. 72
William Powell Frith, *Morning – Covent Garden*, 1862, oil study. Private collection

BOTTOM LEFT
FIG. 73
William Powell Frith, *Noon – Regent Street*, 1862, oil study. Private collection

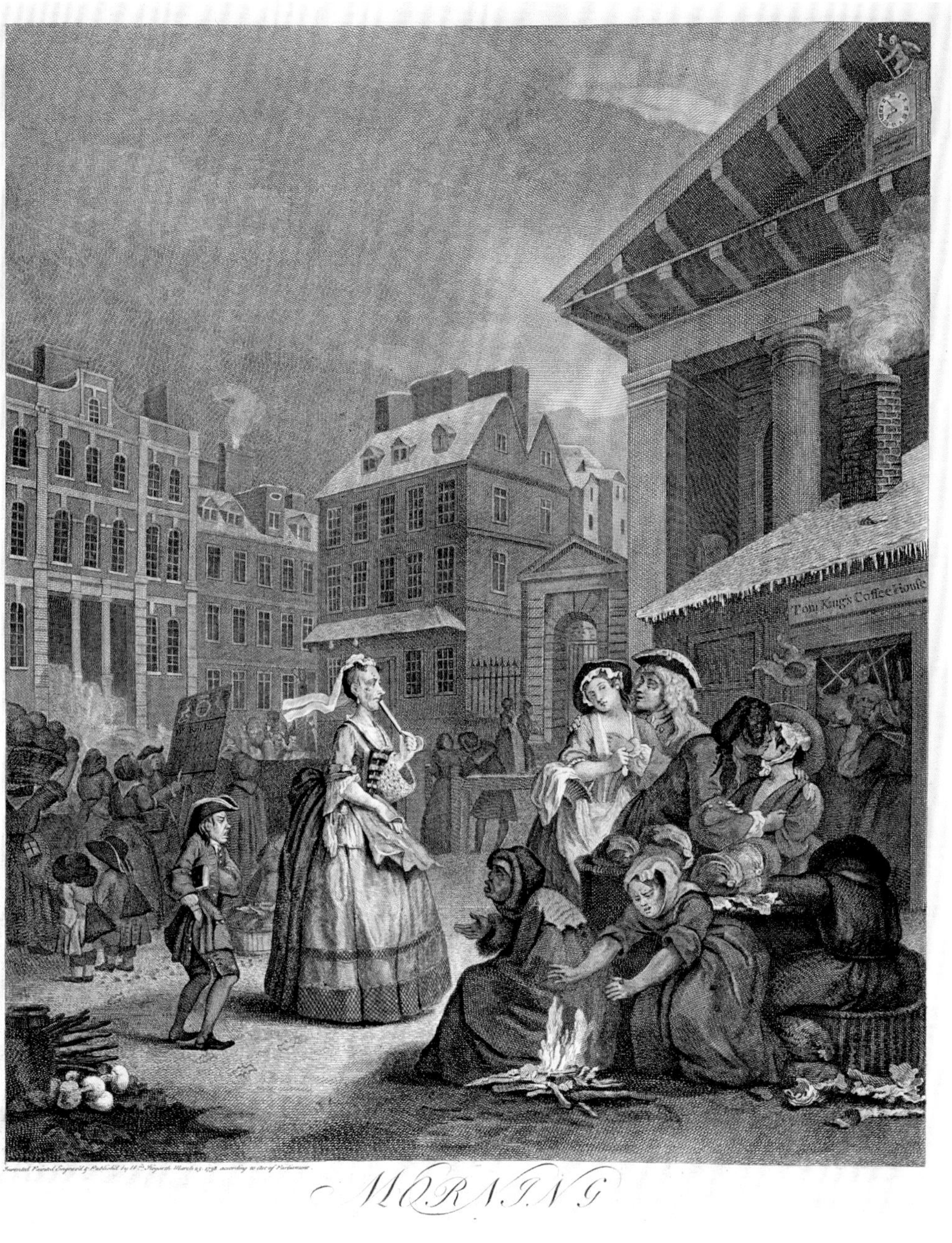

RIGHT
FIG. 74
William Hogarth, *Morning*, from *The Four Times of Day*, 1738, etching with engraving. Museum of London

model, Frith may have drawn on Hogarth, but in the specific depiction of the character of contemporary Londoners imbued with social conscience he turned to Dickens.

Frith's *Morning*, like Hogarth's *Morning* (fig. 74) in his *Times of Day*, was set in Covent Garden. Like Hogarth, both Frith and Dickens depict the flotsam from the night before: the drunken rakes central to Hogarth's image appear in the nineteenth-century text and image among the market stallholders setting up for the day. Frith later described them in his painting as 'belated young gentlemen whose condition

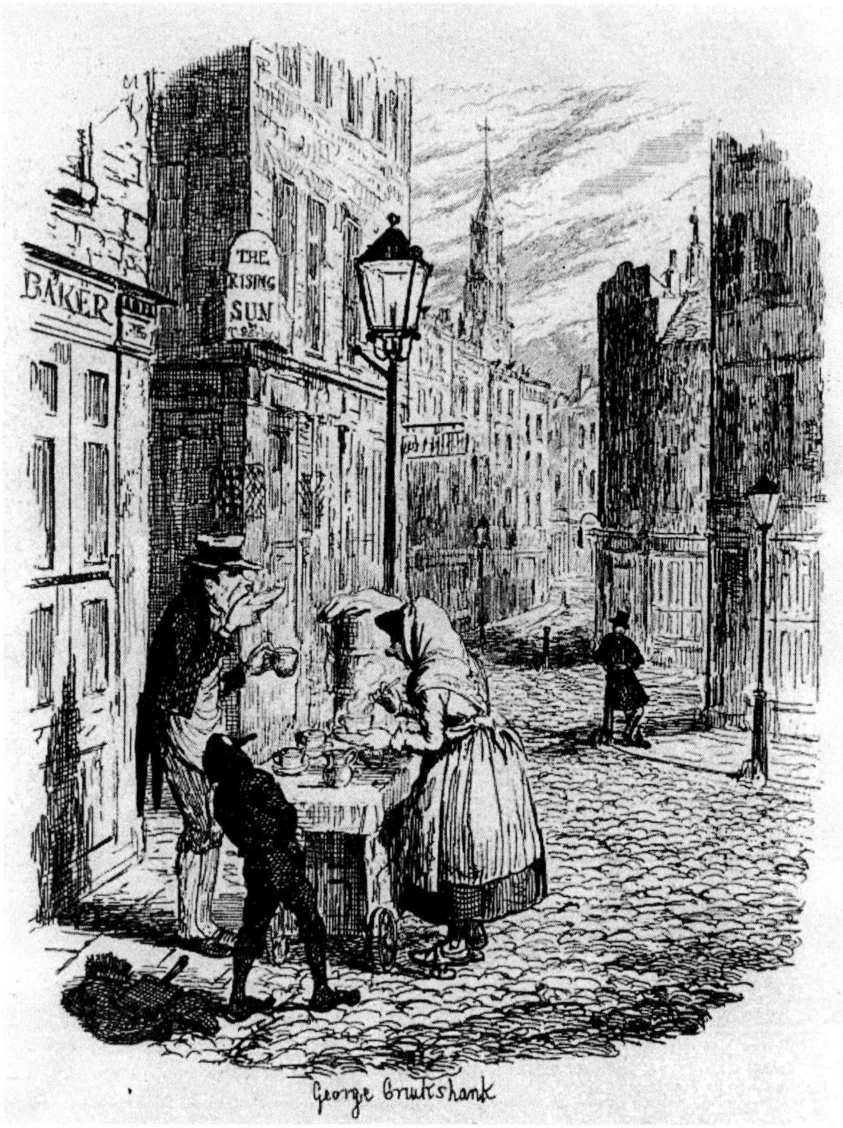

FIG. 75
George Cruikshank, *The Streets of London: Morning*, 1836, etching. Collection of the author

sufficiently proved that the evening's amusement would not bear the morning's reflection'.[37] Also present in Covent Garden's morning light among the traders are vagrants and criminals: 'homeless wanderers, asleep and sleepless; burglars stopped by police red-handed; flowergirls returning from Covent Garden with their early purchases.'[38]

A passage from *Sketches by Boz* shows how close Frith's painting was to Dickens's evocation:

> The last drunken man, who shall find his way home before sunlight, has just staggered heavily along, roaring out the burden of the drinking song of the previous night: the last houseless vagrant whom penury and police have left in the streets, has coiled up his chilly limbs in some paved corner, to dream of food and warmth.

FIG. 76
William Powell Frith,
Morning – Covent Garden
(detail of fig. 72)

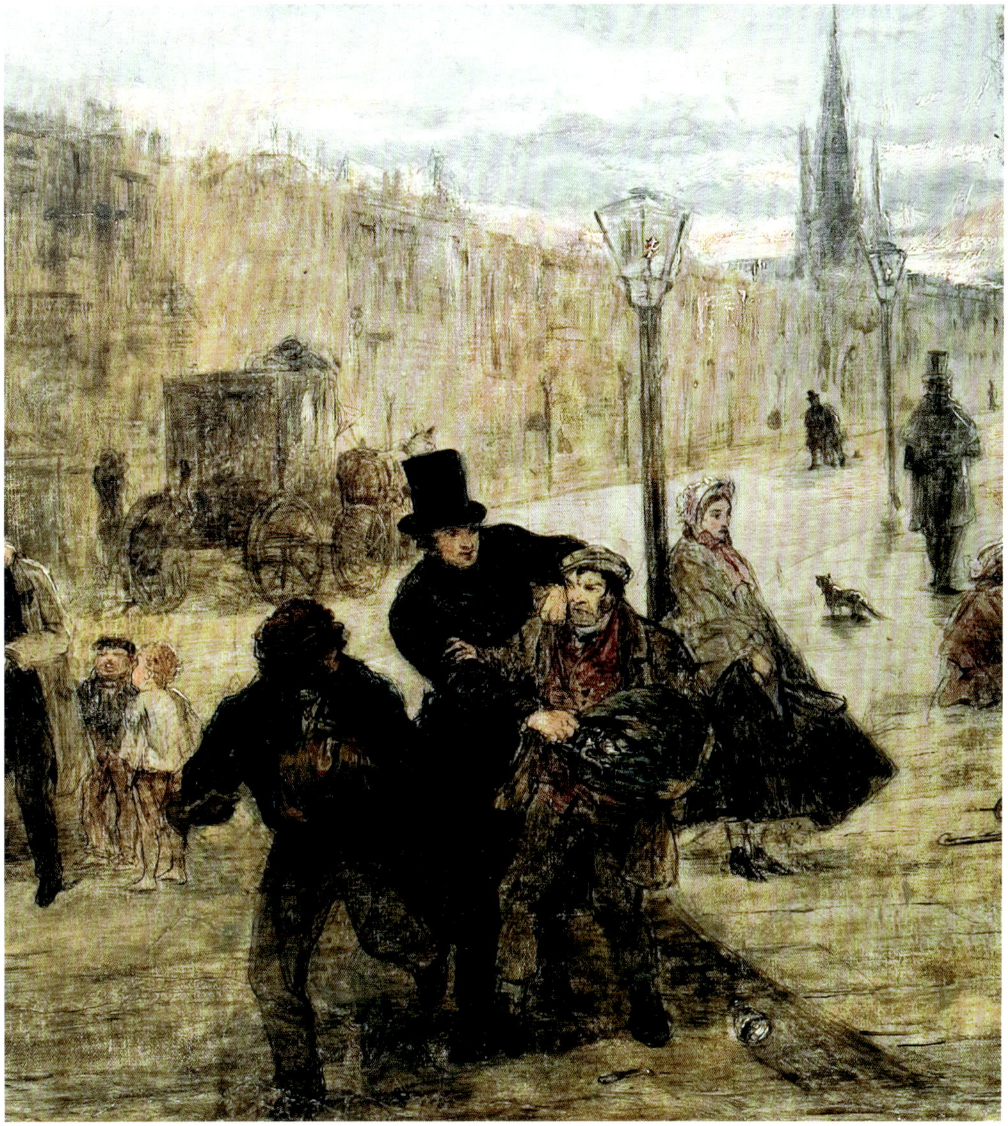

> Rough, sleepy-looking animals of strange appearance, something between ostlers and hackney-coachmen, begin to take down the shutters of early public-houses; and little deal tables, with the ordinary preparations for a street breakfast, make their appearance at the customary stations. Numbers of men and women (principally the latter), carrying upon their heads heavy baskets of fruit.[39]

The street breakfast described by Dickens can be seen in the left of Frith's composition, where a stallholder is drinking morning coffee with two rakes. Cruikshank's original illustration for Dickens's text depicts a coffee stall next to a lamppost with its counterpart in the distance supporting a policeman (fig. 75). The right-hand side of Frith's painting is in fact remarkably close to Cruikshank's etching with its two lampposts, a

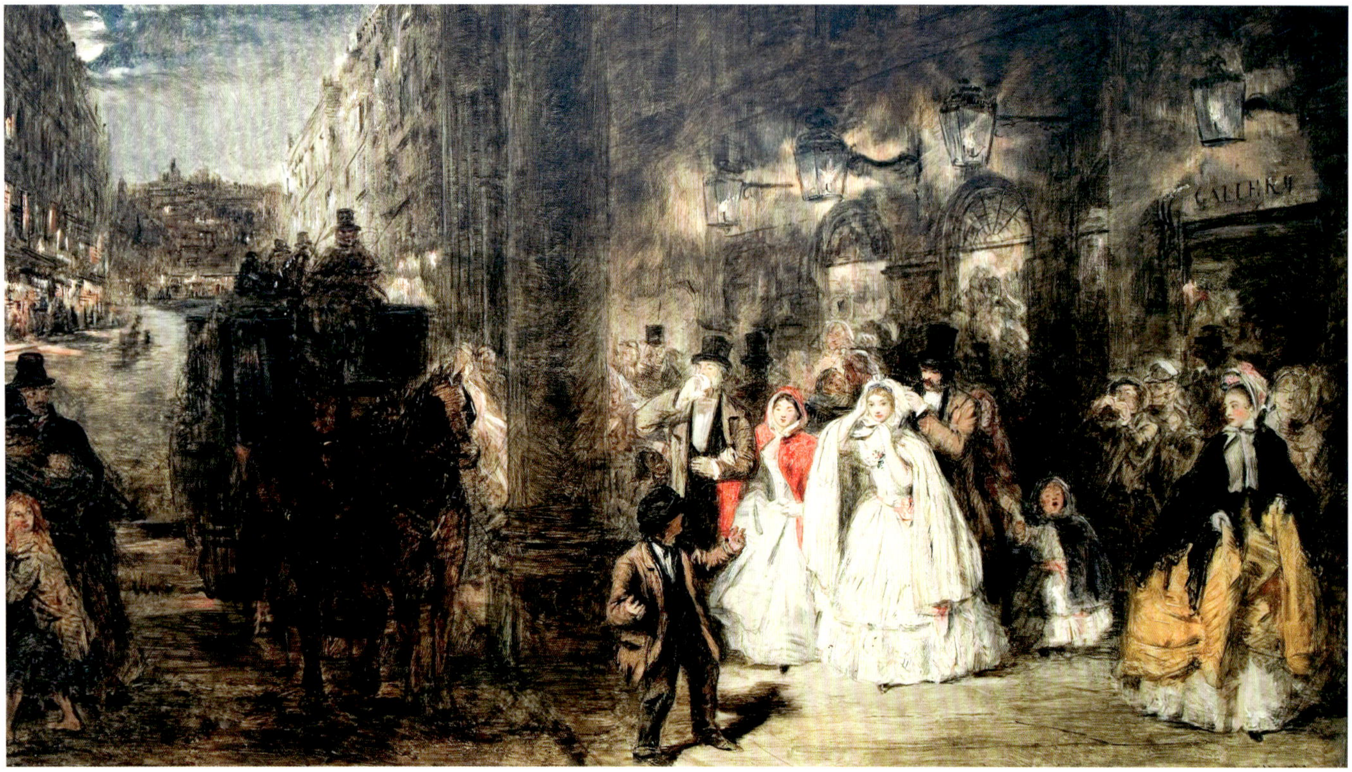

FIG. 77
William Powell Frith, *Night – Haymarket*, 1862, oil study. Private collection

church spire in between and the policeman in the distance (fig. 76). Both painting and print also appear to be illustrating the author's description: 'An occasional policeman may alone be seen at the street corners, listlessly gazing on the deserted prospect before him; and now and then a rakish-looking cat runs stealthily across the road and descends his own area with as much caution and slyness.'[40]

Although there is no 'Noon' in *Sketches by Boz*, Dickens suggests it at the end of his description of 'The Streets – Morning': 'The streets are thronged with a vast concourse of people, gay and shabby, rich and poor, idle and industrious; and we come to the heat, bustle, and activity of Noon.' This coming together of all aspects of society in a busy London thoroughfare appealed to Frith, whose own depiction of midday – a crowded Regent's Street – was teeming with life, character and variety.

Dickens does describe night and Frith takes the wonderfully atmospheric description of London streets at this time of day as his model. He uses light to create the emotional response to the cityscape that Dickens evokes:

> But the streets of London, to be beheld in the very height of their glory, should be seen on a dark, dull, murky winter's night, when there is just enough damp gently stealing down to make the pavement greasy, without cleansing it of any of its impurities; and when the heavy lazy mist, which hangs over every object,

> makes the gas-lamps look brighter, and the brilliantly-lighted shops more splendid, from the contrast they present to the darkness around.[41]

Frith's *Night* (fig. 77) is set in moonlight outside the Haymarket at the end of a performance when the audience are leaving the theatre. A third of the painting to the left shows the street illuminated by moonlight and the 'brilliantly lighted shops', while the remaining two-thirds depicts a scene within the portico of the Haymarket theatre illuminated by large gas-lit lanterns. The production has just finished and the audience descends the steps of the theatre out onto the street, the poorer from the gallery, the affluent through the main entrance. The characters in the central grouping are finely dressed, while in contrast, to the far right of the picture, a prostitute is looking towards them, a scene that Frith describes in some detail:

> A party is about to enter a carriage, and a gentleman is placing a young lady's cloak closely about her shoulders, in tender lover-like fashion. This is being observed by an overdressed and berouged woman, whose general aspect plainly proclaims her unhappy position; and by the expression of a faded though still handsome face, she feels a bitter pang at having lost forever all claim to manly care or pure affection.[42]

Frith's depiction of a pathetic 'fallen' woman is not that of Hogarth's harlots, although both artists express a moral tone. She is identified by her dress and make-up, 'overdressed and berouged', and his description echoes Dickens's observation of a prostitute in a pawnshop:

> In the next box, is a young female, whose attire, miserably poor, but extremely gaudy, wretchedly cold, but extravagantly fine, too plainly bespeaks her station. The rich satin gown with its faded trimmings, the worn-out thin shoes, and pink silk stockings, the summer bonnet in winter, and the sunken face, where a daub of rouge only serves as an index to the ravages of squandered health never to be regained, and lost happiness never to be restored, and where the practised smile is a wretched mockery of the misery of the heart, cannot be mistaken.[43]

Frith uses visual contrast to great effect in his sketch: tasteful finery with gaudiness, elegance with crudity, a distinction that, although less apparent to viewers of the painting today, was painfully obvious to a mid-Victorian audience. The contrast is not simply visual, however, and the young lady also acts as a catalyst of remorse, invoking both morality and pity in the scene. In the pawnshop Dickens uses the same contrast, one that awakens a deeper moral sense and tragedy played out to the observer, and describes the same 'bitter pang':

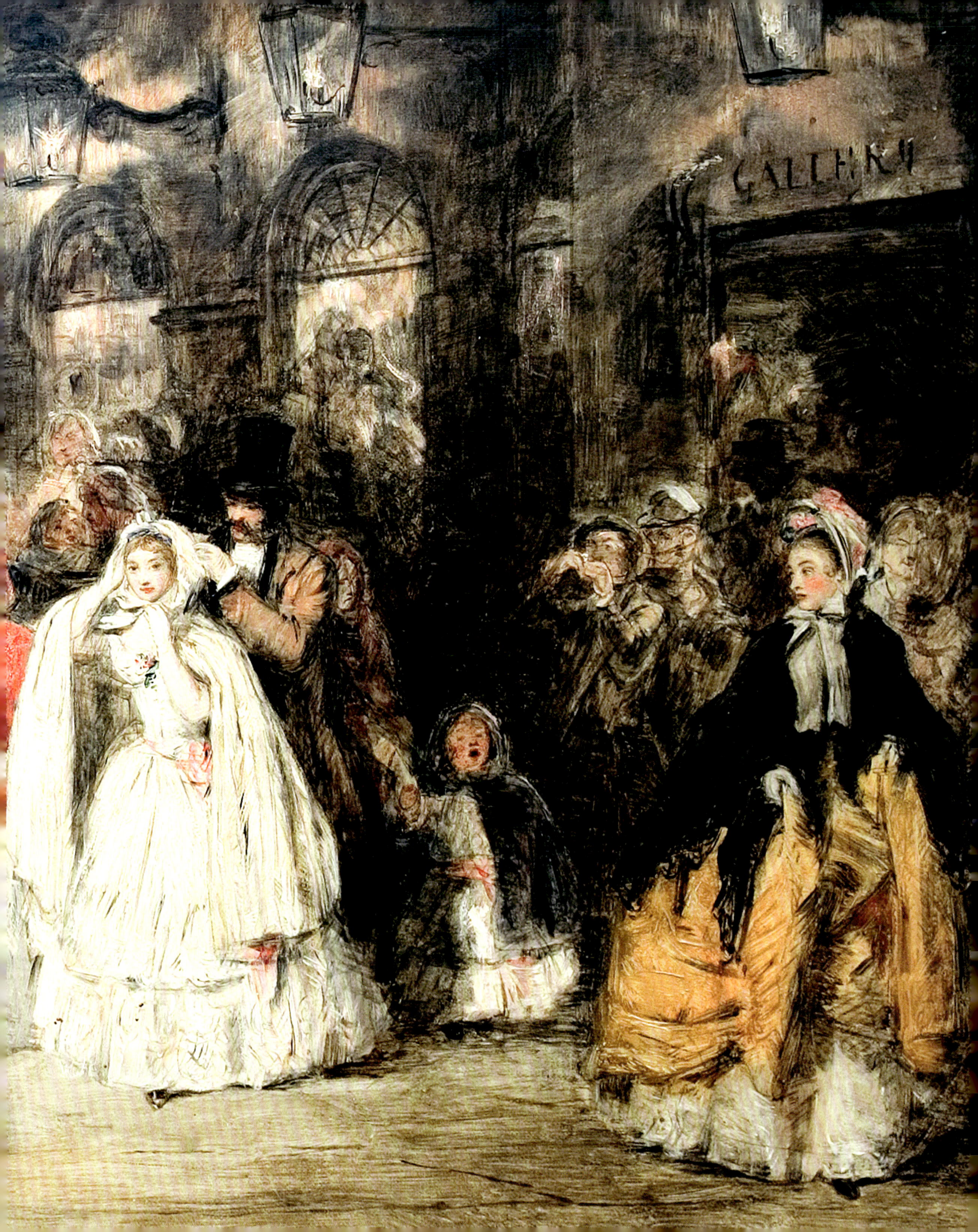
GALLERY

> There is something in the glimpse she has just caught of her young neighbour, and in the sight of the little trinkets she has offered in pawn, that seems to have awakened in this woman's mind some slumbering recollection, and to have changed, for an instant, her whole demeanour.
>
> Her first hasty impulse was to bend forward as if to scan more minutely the appearance of her half-concealed companions; her next, on seeing them involuntarily shrink from her, to retreat to the back of the box, cover her face with her hands, and burst into tears.[44]

In Hogarth, Frith and Dickens the prostitute is the victim. Unlike Hogarth, Dickens and Frith are far subtler in their depictions and rely on the subtext. They also rely on the device of contrasting womanhood underlining the prostitute's lost innocence and the bitterness of her position. The marked contrast of virtue and sin, and the awakening of remorse evoke the idea of redemption that Dickens allies to a universal and religious law explicitly expressed in his description of the pawnshop:

> There are strange chords in the human heart, which will lie dormant through years of depravity and wickedness, but which will vibrate at last to some slight circumstance apparently trivial in itself, but connected by some undefined and indistinct association, with past days that can never be recalled, and with bitter recollections from which the most degraded creature in existence cannot escape.[45]

Although Frith cannot directly expound such reflections in his painting, he could express the sentiment in visual terms through dress, facial expression and physiognomy. It is unfortunate that his depiction of *Night* remains only as a detailed sketch, rather than the planned large-scale finished version that, to Frith's regret, was never realized. 'How I should have delighted,' he wrote, 'in trying to realize all that these subjects were capable of, no tongue can tell.'[46] We can still clearly see the aped gentility of the prostitute lifting her skirts, as she appears to move quickly away from the object that has caused her pain, her face betraying her feelings.[47] In his depiction of a prostitute Frith, like Dickens, has elevated the figure beyond the archetype and given the woman an individual character that evokes empathy for a familiar sight on the London streets.

If *The Streets of London* was a conventional subject emerging from a long tradition of metropolitan rambles, it was brought up to date with consummate artistry in words and pictures by Dickens and Frith. But it was not just the traditional scenes, such as Covent Garden in the morning, that appealed to both artists: locations peculiar to their own time, reflecting the expansion of technology and empire, also attracted and repulsed. These places were the new palaces of the age where the great crowd with all its diversity congregated to carry out their everyday business. The railway station offered such a location and was artfully described in Dickens's *Dombey and Son*:

FIG. 78
William Powell Frith, *Night – Haymarket* (detail of fig. 77)

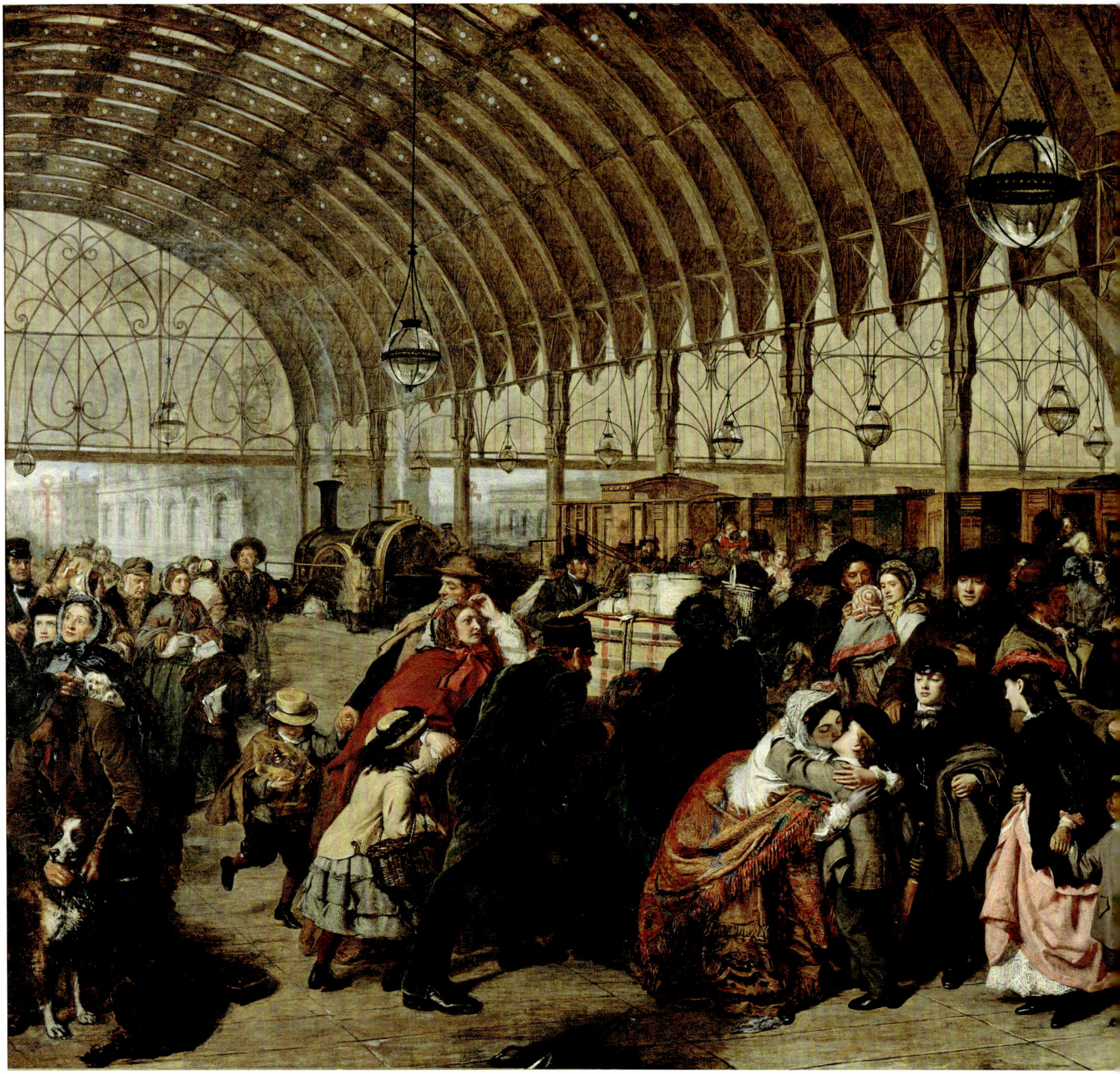

FIG. 79
William Powell Frith, *The Railway Station*, 1862, oil on canvas. Royal Holloway, University of London

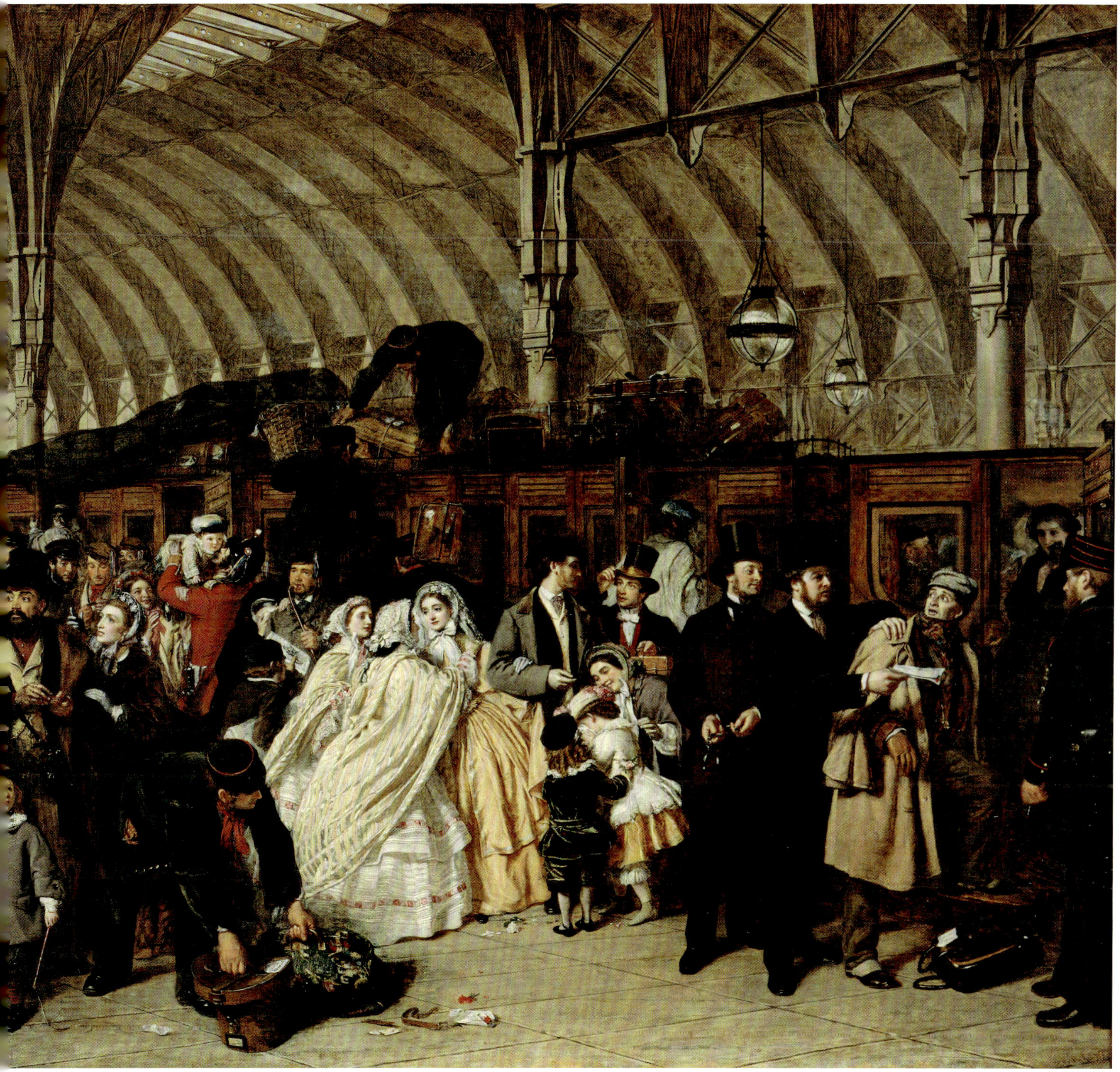

> To and from the heart of this great change, all day and night, throbbing currents rushed and returned incessantly like its life's blood. Crowds of people and mountains of goods, departing and arriving scores upon scores of times in every four-and-twenty hours, produced a fermentation in the place that was always in action. The very houses seemed disposed to pack up and take trips.[48]

The railway terminus at Paddington provided the backdrop for Frith's great painting, *The Railway Station* (fig. 79). Another of the great metropolitan temples of the age, the General Post Office in St Martin's-le-Grand, epitomized centralized communications from the heart of the empire to its far-flung outposts throughout the world. From here post, papers and journals were sent nationally and internationally. 'These were', as Dickens noted, 'from all parts of London to all parts of London and to the provinces and to the far-off quarters of the globe.'[49] The site was so famous that it even drew crowds of tourists to see not only the building with its great hub of activity but the activity at one minute to six when the Newspaper Fair or Shoot took place.[50] This was when the department opened its great window to allow huge numbers of newspapers to be literally thrown in. Dickens describes the scene in his opening edition of *Household Words*:

> It was then just drizzling newspapers. The great window of that department being thrown open, the first black fringe of a thunder-cloud of newspapers impending over the Post-Office . . . now in large drops . . . now in sudden plumps . . . By degrees it began to rain hard; by fast degrees the storm came on harder and harder, until it blew, rained, hailed, snowed newspapers. A fountain of newspapers broke from enormous sacks, and engulfed the men inside . . . Suddenly it struck six. Shut Sesame! Perfectly still weather. Nobody there. No token of the late storm.'[51]

A painting of this scene has become one of the most celebrated of the modern-life movement, *The General Post Office, One Minute to Six* by George Elgar Hicks (fig. 80). It received mixed reviews on its exhibition at the Royal Academy in 1860, but even then several critics understood its significance. W. Thornbury wrote that Hicks, who 'seems now resolutely bent on Hogarthian scenes of London life', renders them, 'if less powerfully than our great satirist, certainly more genteely . . . The last moment of posting time is a scene expressing the ardour and abundance of our national life, and well worth perpetuating.'[52]

If big metropolitan scenes, with their variety of crowds, provided a rich subject for modern-life painters, the task of depicting a crowd en masse was a particularly difficult and complex one. In terms of sheer artistry, Frith had the ability to do this, each character distinguished from the other, each different grouping held together in a fascinating whole. A photograph of a crowd merely reduced it to a flat mass, something at odds with the variety and interest in all parts of the canvas that Frith was able to produce.

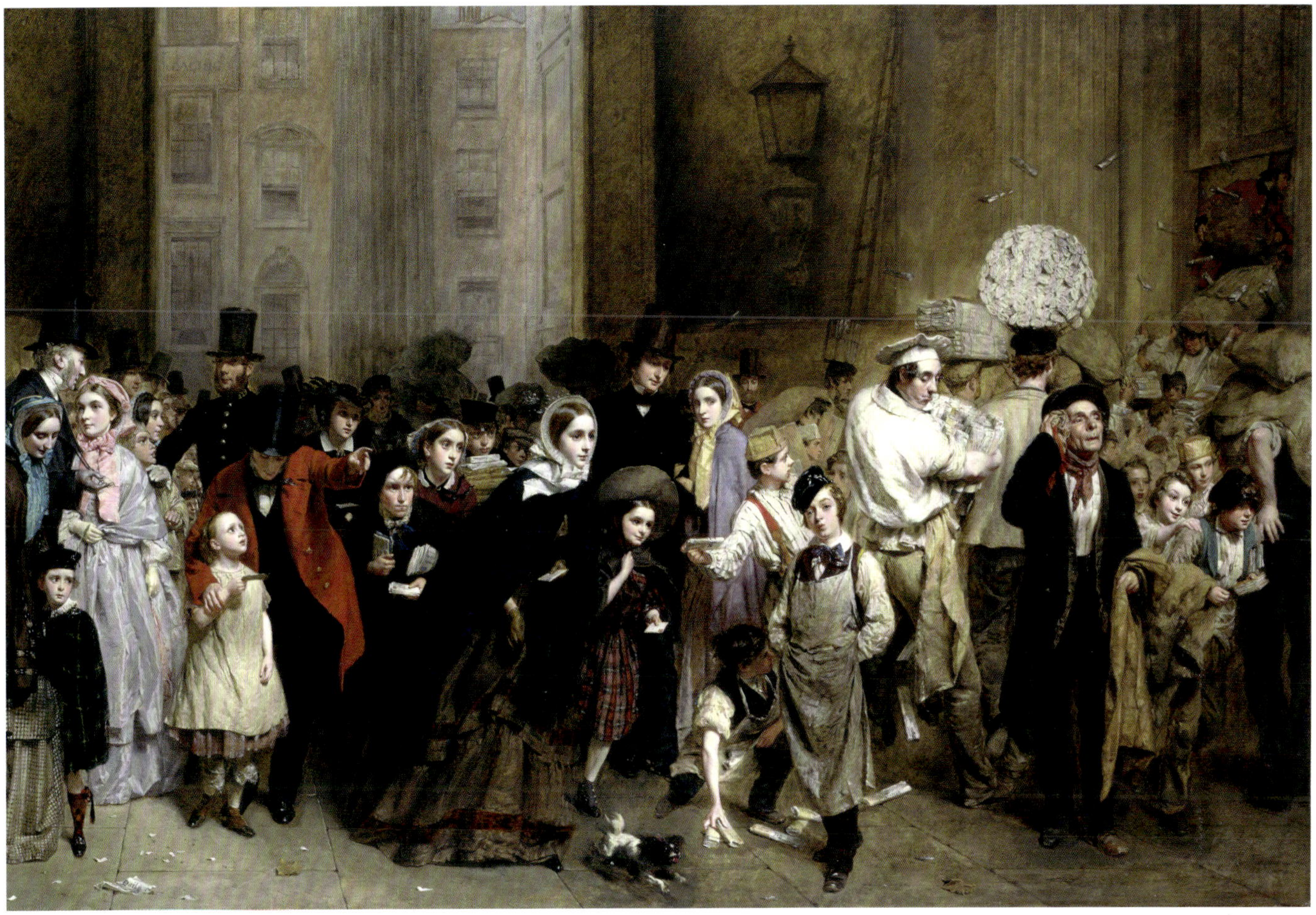

FIG. 80
George Elgar Hicks, *The General Post Office, One Minute to Six*, 1860, oil on canvas. Museum of London

Yet the delineation of character with all the diversity of the modern world was not simply a matter of painterly skill, and in order to convincingly depict type and narrative, the artist drew on references from illustration, journalism and literature, alongside the theory of physiognomy. Much has been written about the significant influence of physiognomy and phrenology on modern-life painting and most particularly Frith.[53] This is nowhere better illustrated than in the classificatory illustrations of Kenny Meadows in *Heads of the People: or, Portraits of the English* (1840), which depicts the trades or callings with pictures of generic types rather than specific portraits.[54] As Meadows himself expressed it, they 'have been intended as Popular Portraits; the aim, in each instance, being to concentrate in individual peculiarity the characteristics of a class. Their success must depend of course on the degree of fidelity with which this object has been accomplished.'[55]

What is less well known is that at around the same time that Meadows was engaged on his *Heads of the People* he was also creating an extra-illustrated volume, *Heads from Nicholas Nickleby: From Drawings by Miss La Creevy* (1839). Produced in six parts,

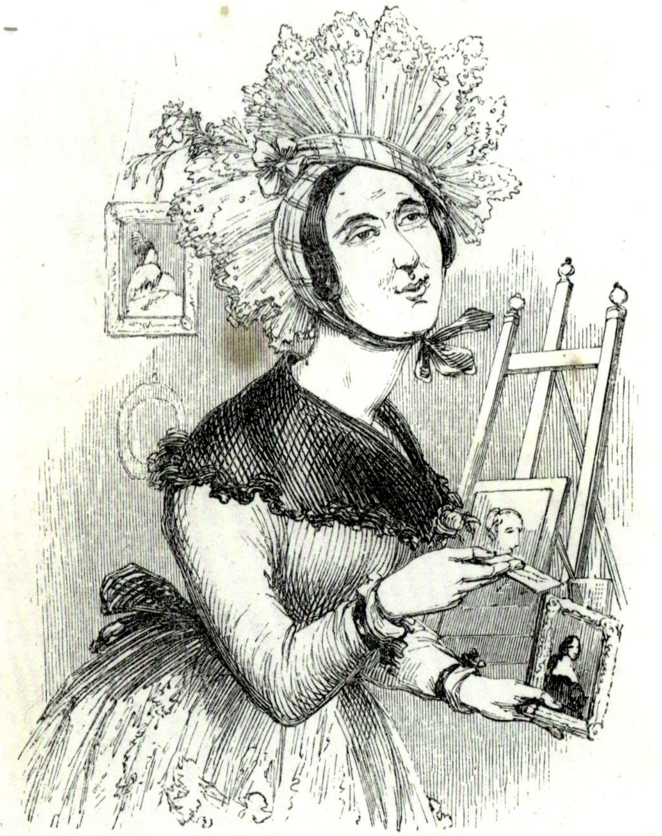

MINIATURE PAINTER.

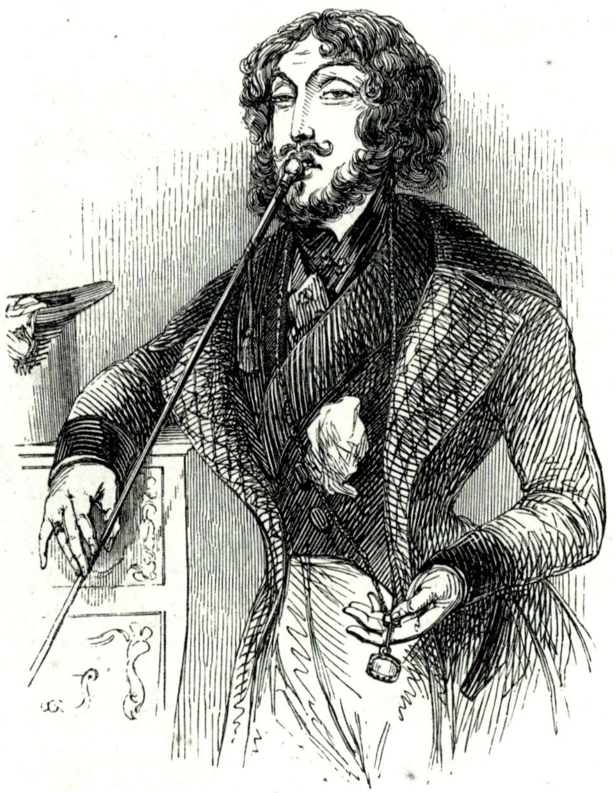

THE YOUNG LORD.

FIGS 81, 82
Joseph Kenny Meadows, 'Miniature Painter' (Miss La Creevy) and 'The Young Lord' (Verisopht), from *Heads from Nicholas Nickleby* reproduced in *The Scrap Book of Literary Varieties and Mirror of Instructive & Entertaining Information* (London, 1840), wood engravings

it contains twenty-four wood engravings that portray leading and subsidiary characters from Nicholas Nickleby, providing a physiognomic head of the character and suggesting through these illustrations an archetype that underlies Dickens's characters. Meadows declares his intention from the outset in the brief introduction:

> These 'Heads' will comprise Portraits of the most interesting individuals that appear in 'The Life and Adventures of Nicholas Nickleby,' selected at the period when their very actions define their true character, and exhibit the inward mind by its outward manifestations. Each Portrait will be a literal transcript from the accurate and vividly minute descriptions of this able and graphic author, and will present to the eye an equally faithful version of the maiden simplicity of Kate Nickleby – the depravity of Sir Mulberry Hawk – the imbecility of his dupe – the heartless villainy of the calculating Ralph – the generosity of the noble-minded Nicholas – the broken spirit of poor Smike

> – and the brutality of Squeers. These and many others furnish subjects for the display of the Artist's genius, and will form an interesting and most desirable addition to the work.[56]

Unlike the illustrations to *Nicholas Nickleby* by Hablot Browne that Dickens had so closely supervised, they are not etchings but wood engravings, portraits rather than detailed depictions, focusing on the head rather than the action of any scene described in the novel. Perhaps more interesting still is that the wood engravings were republished around 1840, this time in *The Scrap Book of Literary Varieties and Mirror of Instructive & Entertaining Information*, without any accompanying descriptions. Instead, each bears a generic title rather than the character's name, although the titles of some, such as the Yorkshire Schoolmaster who very obviously represents Wackford Squeers, are quite specific.[57] The level of caricature is more evident in characters outside the Nickleby family (Ralph excepted), and we can see in the depictions the use of the archetypes that were familiar to a London audience of 1840. The new generic titles reveal that each of Meadows's illustrations is almost equally readable for a generic type as for a specific portrait. They also indicate that Dickens used the same London 'types' that painters of modern life did, aware of their visual form and characteristics as popularly expressed in word and text, caricature and humorous story. What Dickens and Frith succeeded in doing, where Phiz and Meadows didn't, was to raise the archetype to the individual, moving from caricature to character.

Taking one of Meadows's wood engravings illustrates this point. The first of the heads that appears in *The Scrap Book of Literary Varieties* is 'The Young Lord', which started life as a depiction of Lord Frederick Verisopht (fig. 82). He first appears in *Nicholas Nickleby* when Ralph Nickleby introduces his niece to the young aristocrat:

> Seven or eight gentlemen were standing round the fire when they went in, and as they were talking very loud were not aware of their entrance until Mr. Ralph Nickleby, touching one on the coat-sleeve said in a harsh emphatic voice, as if to attract general attention –
>
> 'Lord Frederick Verisopht, my niece. Miss Nickleby.'
>
> The group dispersed as if in great surprise, and the gentleman addressed, turning round, exhibited a suit of clothes of the most superlative cut, a pair of whiskers of similar quality, a moustache, a head of hair, and a young face.
>
> 'Eh!' said the gentleman. 'What – the – deyvle!'
>
> With which broken ejaculations he fixed his glass in his eye, and stared at Miss Nickleby in great surprise.
>
> 'My niece, my lord,' said Ralph.
>
> 'Well, then my ears did not deceive me, and it's not wa-a-x work,' said his lordship. 'How de do? I'm very happy.' And then his lordship turned to another superlative gentleman, something older, something stouter, something redder

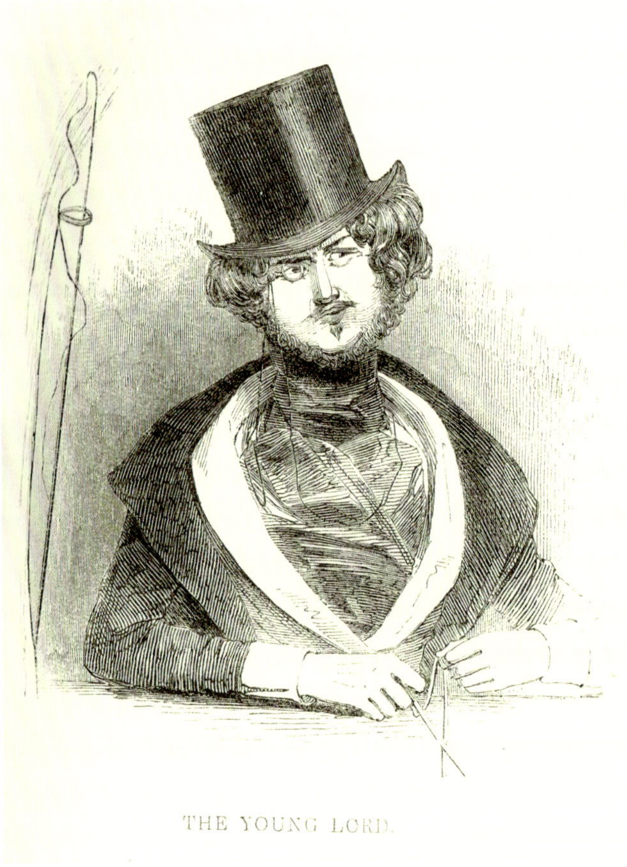

FIG. 83
Joseph Kenny Meadows, 'The Young Lord', from *Heads of the People: or, Portraits of the English* (London, 1840), wood engraving

> in the face, and something longer upon town, and said in a loud whisper that the girl was 'deyvlish pitty.'[58]

Here is a portrait of the young lord with all the affectations of manner, dress and speech. Verisopht is an archetypal character and Dickens is very visual in his characterization. In the accompanying illustration, 'Miss Nickleby introduced to her Uncle's friends', Hablot Browne follows, with fidelity, Dickens's description, but it is also clear that he is looking towards the visual archetype of a dissolute young lord (fig. 84).[59] This is the Victorian rake, his ancestors range from Hogarth's rake and the boisterous hell-raiser of Regency London to the lecherous and dissolute young lord of early Victorian London. Visually, he is showily and tightly dressed in fashionable mutton-chop whiskers and a monocle and, when outside, sports a top hat at a jaunty angle. In this, Browne is particularly influenced by Cruikshank and his depiction of the Regency dandy, although the lord's dissolute nature owes more to Hogarth as well as the growing moral censure of the Victorian age.

In *Heads of the People* Meadows depicts a wood engraving of the Young Lord with accompanying text by Douglas Jerrold (fig. 83). 'The Young Lord of the nineteenth century is a much less enviable person than the Young Lord of fifty years ago,' Jerrold

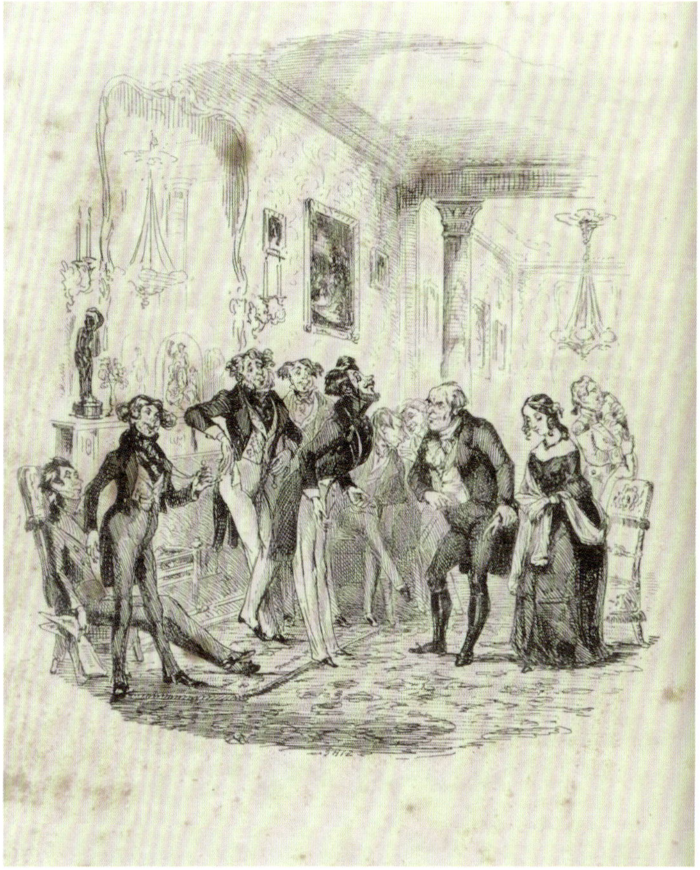

FIG. 84
Hablot Knight Browne, 'Miss Nickleby Introduced to her Uncle's Friends', original illustration from *Nicholas Nickleby*, 1838–9, etching

writes in acknowledgement of the eighteenth-century counterpart. Meadows's drawing of the lord with his dandyish moustache and mutton chops is archetypal, and the text emphasizes his dissolute nature:

> Westward, the Young Lord is a dangerous person, to be especially watched by prudent mothers . . . The Young Lord moves among fashionable heiresses to the liveliest distress of their disinterested natural guardians . . . His very look has in it an invitation to elope . . . his habits of play, his debts, his horrible *liaisons*, his wickedness in general.[60]

In *Heads from Nicholas Nickleby* Meadows endows the young Lord Verisopht with the same characteristics but makes him even more outlandishly foppish. His arrogance is shown by his posture, while the monocle in his hand and his cane to his lips further demonstrate his rakish and wicked behaviour.

In his *Derby Day* (figs 66, 85) Frith includes the figure of a dissolute young aristocrat who appears in the far right of the painting. He is leaning against a carriage, a cigar hanging from his lips, looking equally disdainfully and lecherously at a young flower seller, evoking Hablot Browne's illustration of Verisopht being introduced to Kate

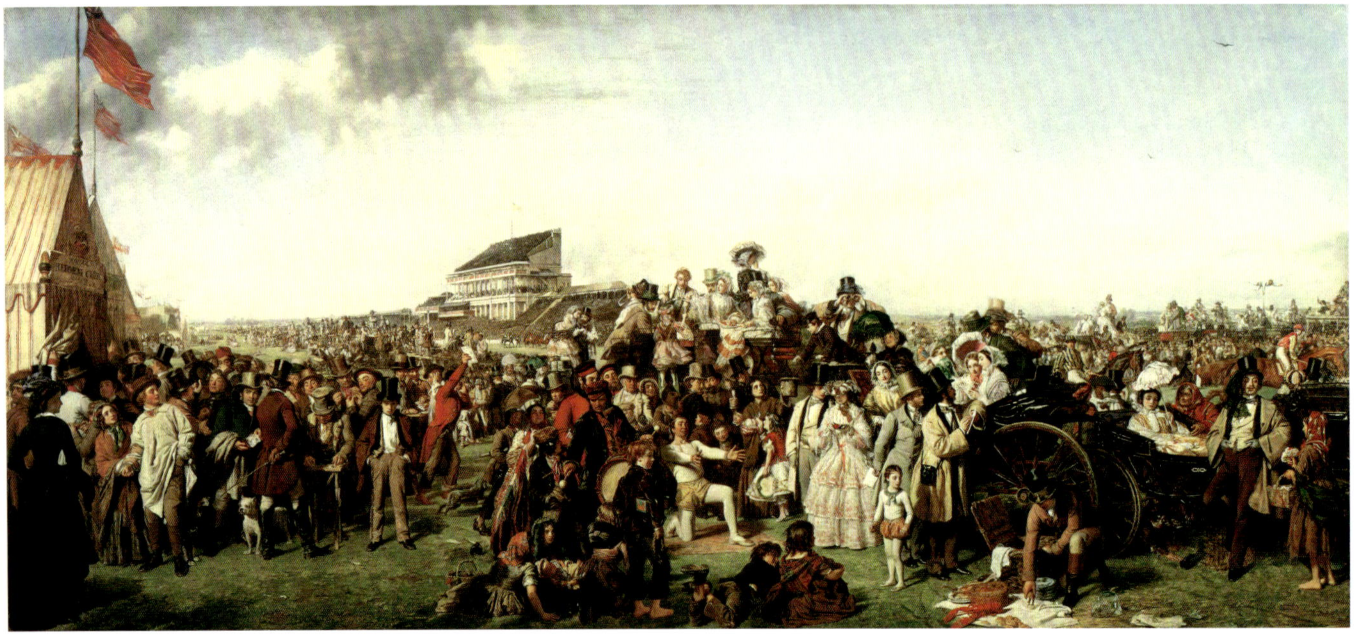

Nickleby. The heavy eyelids of half-closed eyes indicate both jadedness and lechery and are like those in Meadows's depiction of Verisopht. Although Frith avoids caricature in his depiction, there is clear acknowledgement of the archetype, and when the humour dissipates, a more real and repugnant figure is left than in the comedy of Browne or Meadows. This little vignette of the carriage is taken directly from chapter 19 of *The Old Curiosity Shop*, where the events are clearly described with a warning issued to the young girl at whom the young gentlemen had been staring:

> There was but one lady who seemed to understand the child, and she was one who sat alone in a handsome carriage . . . She motioned away a gipsy woman urgent to tell her fortune, saying that it was told already, and had been for some years, but called the child towards her, and, taking her flowers, put money into her trembling hand, and bade her go home and keep at home for God's sake.[61]

ABOVE
FIG. 85
William Powell Frith, *The Derby Day*, 1858, oil on canvas. Tate, London

On the whole Frith avoids painting specific characters from Dickens but instead uses the same kinds of characters that Dickens creates, evoking Dickens's characterization. A good example of this is a single figure painting, *The Crossing Sweeper* (fig. 86), painted as a 'stopgap' while working on *Derby Day*.[62] Crossing sweepers were a common sight on nineteenth-century London streets, where the large number of horse-drawn vehicles meant that crossing the road could be particularly hazardous and that sweepers provided a service to the more affluent. Even though it was only a small cabinet painting, it was hugely popular and Frith painted several versions; a print and even a Parian

RIGHT
FIG. 86
William Powell Frith, *The Crossing Sweeper*, 1893, oil on canvas. Museum of London

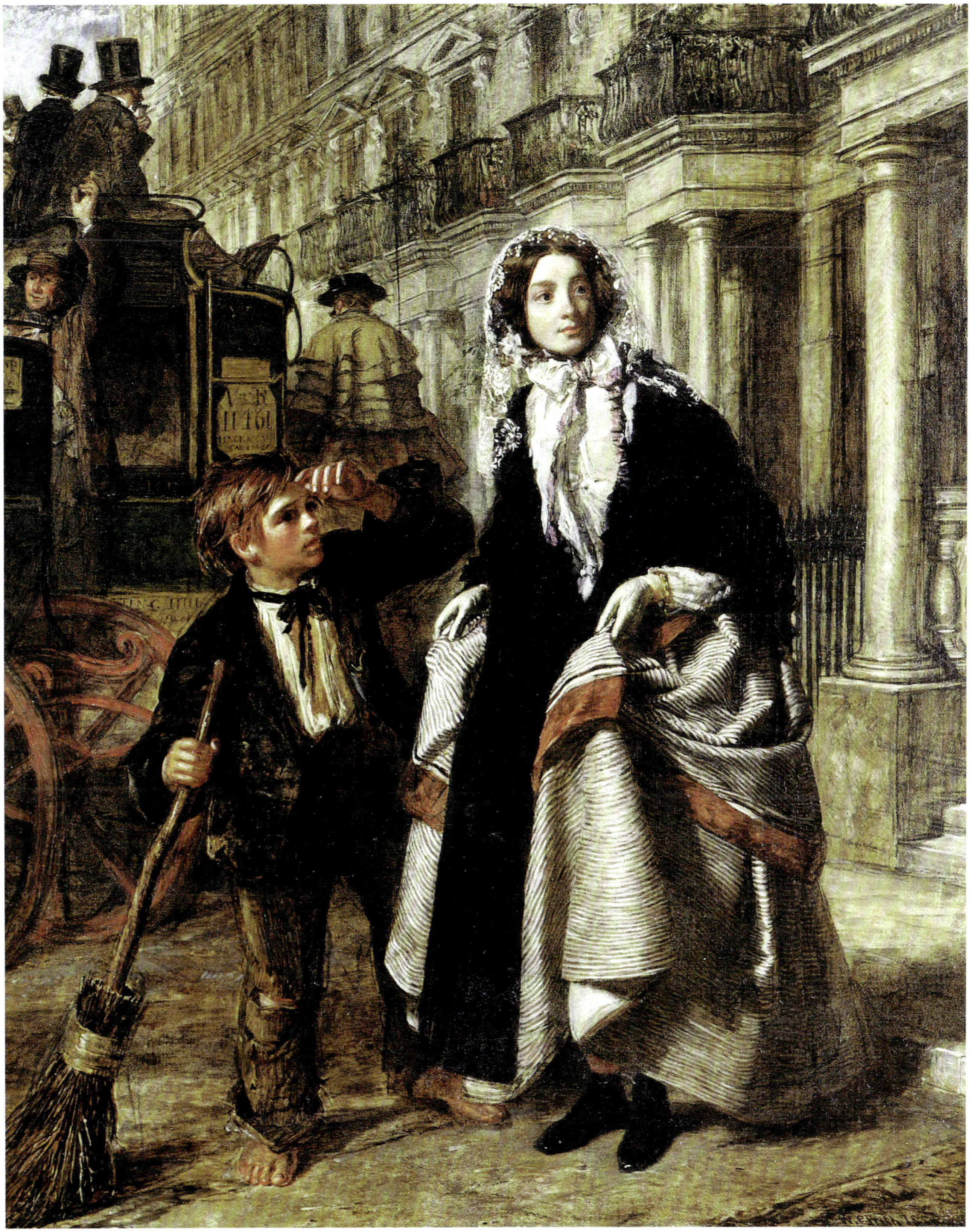

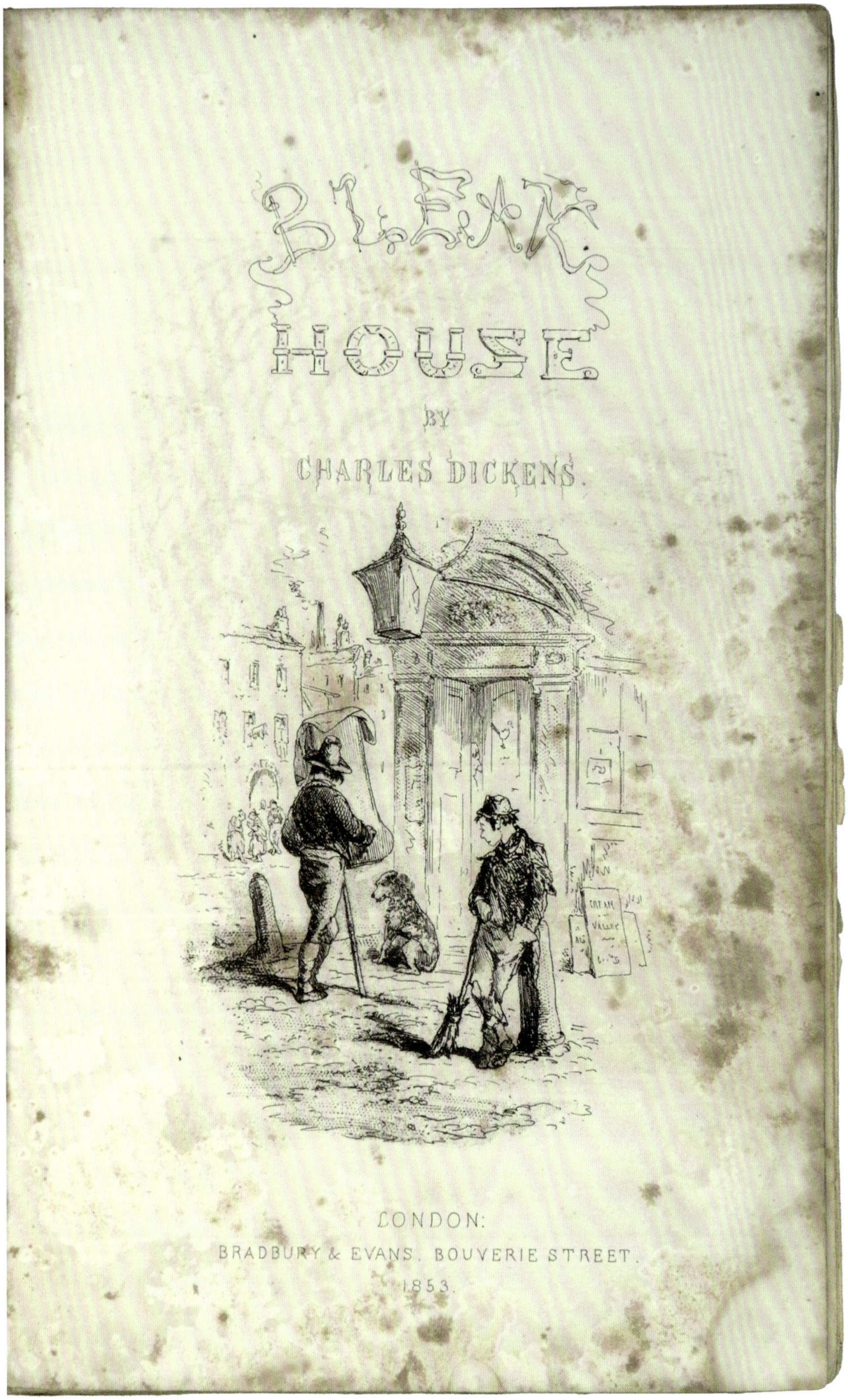

FIG. 87
Hablot Knight Browne,
'Jo' Frontispiece, original
illustration from *Bleak House*,
1853, etching. Collection of
the author

Ware figure were produced.[63] The crossing sweeper was a very familiar London 'type', but to fully account for the painting's popularity we have to acknowledge its Dickensian associations. The crossing sweeper became well known particularly through the characterization of Jo in Dickens's *Bleak House* (fig. 87), who as a crossing sweeper has his own 'broom-walk': 'He goes to his crossing, and begins to lay it out for the day . . . Jo fights it out, at his crossing, among the mud and wheels, the horses, whips, and umbrellas, and gets a scanty sum.' Like Jo, Frith's crossing sweeper is a boy, even though many grown men, particularly war veterans, were sweepers, and he is seen begging from a lady crossing the street. Often considered a street nuisance, the archetypal boy crossing sweeper can often be seen in *Punch* of the period. Frith knew *Bleak House* very well, and in the scene that he has created, the lady and the boy clearly evoke the passage where the disguised Lady Dedlock dresses as a servant and crosses at Jo's broom walk:

> She should be an upper servant by her attire, yet, in her air and step, though both are hurried and assumed – as far as she can assume in the muddy streets, which she treads with an unaccustomed foot – she is a lady . . . She never turns her head. Lady or servant, she has a purpose in her, and can follow it. She never turns her head, until she comes to the crossing where Jo plies with his broom. He crosses with her, and begs. Still, she does not turn her head until she has landed on the other side.[64]

On one level this is a charming genre scene, a familiar daily ritual represented in a modern-life painting at its observant best. In its choice of subject and its tenderness of depiction, however, it is clear that much more is implied than its immediate appearance indicates. The references to Jo in the painting suggest a particular reading to the viewer and evoke an empathy that is so different from the caricatures of *Punch*. A street archetype is at once transformed into a human being, deftly painted with all the irony and sentiment that Dickens had so poignantly described in *Bleak House*. If Frith had intended it to be a scene from *Bleak House* and called it such, he would have been forced to be more literal and reduce the painting to an illustration. Instead, he presents an idea of Dickens in everyday life, one that moved a critic of the *Art Journal* to write about the face of the boy as 'somewhat above the fraternity of St Giles (workhouse); it is bright and intelligent, showing material which would work well in the hands of the schoolmaster.'[65]

By depicting the crossing sweeper as the main figure, Frith takes a peripheral and background London street character and raises him to the centre of the action. As in *Bleak House*, he becomes a hero. In his great social panoramas, *Life at the Seaside*, *Derby Day* and *The Railway Station*, this is less easy, with the crowds and the peripheral street characters among the main protagonists, whom he also needed to endow with character and personality.

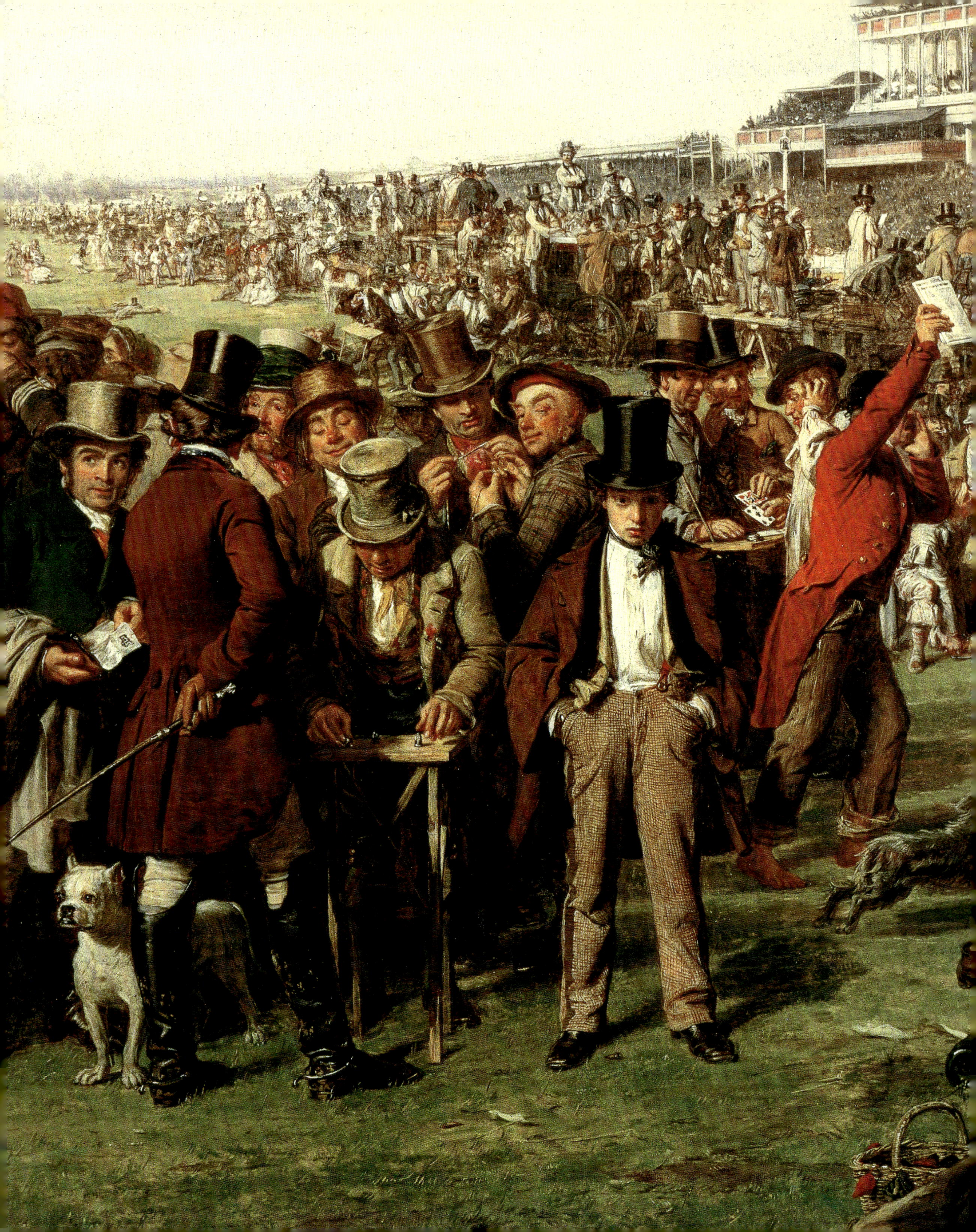

When Dickens describes Greenwich Fair in his *Sketches by Boz*, we encounter some familiar figures that are depicted by Frith in his *Derby Day*. How ironic that one unenlightened critic described one of Frith's great social landscapes as like 'Greenwich fair without the fun'.[66] Of the many characters whom Frith paints and Dickens describes, the thimble-rigger was a familiar figure on the streets and in the fairs that Londoners frequented. In *Derby Day* he can be seen to the left of the canvas plying his trade to the obvious detriment of the youth to the right of him, just as the farmer to the left of him is tempted by the game, although he is saved from a similar fate by his more sensible and pleading wife. Dickens describes the thimble-rigger and his victim at Greenwich Fair:

> Pedestrians linger in groups at the roadside, unable to resist the allurements of the stout proprietress of the 'Jack-in-the-box, three shies a penny,' or the more splendid offers of the man with three thimbles and a pea on a little round board, who astonishes the bewildered crowd with some such address as, 'Here's the sort o' game to make you laugh seven years arter you're dead, and turn ev'ry air on your ed gray vith delight! Three thimbles and vun little pea – with a vun, two, three, and a two, three, vun: catch him who can, look on, keep your eyes open, and niver say die! niver mind the change, and the expense: all fair and above board: them as don't play can't vin, and luck attend the ryal sportsman! Bet any gen'lm'n any sum of money, from harf-a-crown up to a suverin, as he doesn't name the thimble as kivers the pea!' Here some greenhorn whispers his friend that he distinctly saw the pea roll under the middle thimble – an impression which is immediately confirmed by a gentleman in top-boots, who is standing by, and who, in a low tone, regrets his own inability to bet, in consequence of having unfortunately left his purse at home, but strongly urges the stranger not to neglect such a golden opportunity. The 'plant' is successful, the bet is made, the stranger of course loses: and the gentleman with the thimbles consoles him, as he pockets the money, with an assurance that it's 'all the fortin of war! this time I vin, next time you vin: niver mind the loss of two bob and a bender! Do it up in a small parcel, and break out in a fresh place. Here's the sort o' game,' &c. – and the eloquent harangue, with such variations as the speaker's exuberant fancy suggests, is again repeated to the gaping crowd, reinforced by the accession of several new comers.[67]

The thimble-rigger might have been lost in the crowd, but Frith artfully allows him to exist beyond the impression of a general chorus, a diminutive and recognizable figure whose impact ripples through several characters in this pictorial narrative. We see Frith once more raising the type to the particular, the caricature to character. Within this great mêlée of humanity plot and subplot are also combined, reminiscent of a *tableau vivant*, where the canvas is a stage for a great, moral narrative. In *Household Words* W.H. Wills, with assistance from Dickens, contributed an article on 'Epsom' on 7 June 1851, which featured many of

FIG. 88
William Powell Frith, *The Derby Day* (detail of fig. 85: the thimble rigger)

the scenes and characters that can be seen in *Derby Day*. The thimble-rigger appears as 'a shabby man, with an overhanging forehead, and a slinking eye', who 'invites your attention to something novel and curious – three thimbles and one little pea'.[68] The central scene of *Derby Day*, where the young acrobat is distracted by the lobster and pie of a Fortnum and Mason hamper, is described in the article when it considers the wealthier visitors to Epsom: 'So many fine ladies in so many broughams, so many of Fortnum and Mason's hampers, so much ice and champagne! . . . And now Heavens! All the hampers are open, and the green Downs burst into a blossom of lobster salad!'[69]

The great social injustices of poverty and wealth are played out among the individual characters that centre on the acrobatic boy who loses concentration as he stares at a wealthy banquet. The good, the bad, the naive and the stupid rub shoulders in this great tapestry of mid-nineteenth-century life: 'equestrians, pedestrians, horse-dealers, gentlemen, nobilities, and swindlers, by tens of thousands', as *Household Words* put it.[70] Dickens's characterizations helped to give meaning to Frith's depictions. To the artist the picture was a stage for human life, an approach that owed a debt to Hogarth in its pictorial construction and to Dickens in its narratives and characters.

Hogarth's narratives were well known to Frith and Dickens, and when Hogarth famously wrote about his approach to painting, he offered a model to both artist and writer:

> I therefore wished to compose pictures on canvas similar to representations on the stage; and further hope that they will be tried by the same test, and criticised by the same criterion . . . In these compositions those subjects that will both entertain and improve the mind bid fair to be of the greatest public utility and must, therefore, be entitled to rank in the highest class.[71]

Hogarth created a human stage in which a moral tale unfolds through the visual image. A key point of the drama is depicted, the central actions of the actors made explicit by expression, posture and costume and echoed in the details and props of the scene. Visual symbols for the storytelling emphasize the main action in comic and tragic terms, drawing on nuances in the features with their physiognomic references or irony. When Dickens wrote so admiringly of Hogarth's *Gin Lane* (fig. 89), as well as describing the main tragedy depicted, he also noted how Hogarth included within the composition a church whose presence and passivity were core to the meaning:

> All are living and dying miserably. Nobody is interfering for prevention or for cure in the generation going out before us or the generation coming in. The beadle (the only sober man in the composition except the pawnbroker) is mightily indifferent to the orphan child crying beside its parents' coffin. The little charity-girls are not so well taught or looked after but that they can take to dramdrinking already. The church is very prominent and handsome, but

FIG. 89
William Hogarth, *Gin Lane*, 1751, etching with engraving. Museum of London

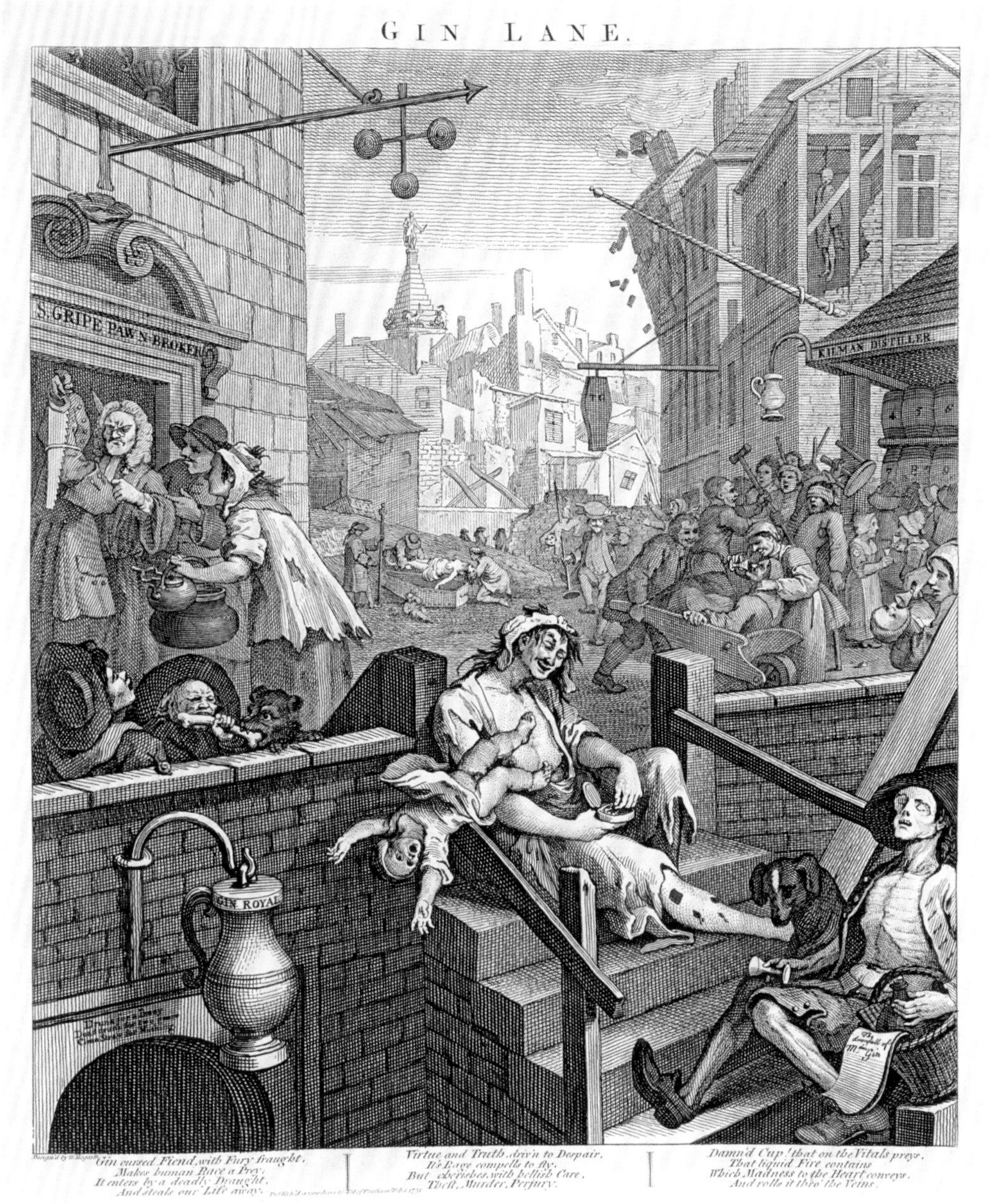

coldly surveys these things in progress underneath the shadow of its tower (it was in the year of grace eighteen hundred and forty-eight that a Bishop of London first came out respecting something wrong in poor men's social accommodations), and is passive in the picture. We take all this to have a meaning, and to the best of our knowledge it has not grown obsolete in a century.[72]

Dickens himself uses the presence of a church in a similar way in *Bleak House*, depicting the impressive St Paul's Cathedral as passive and ineffectual in the lives and

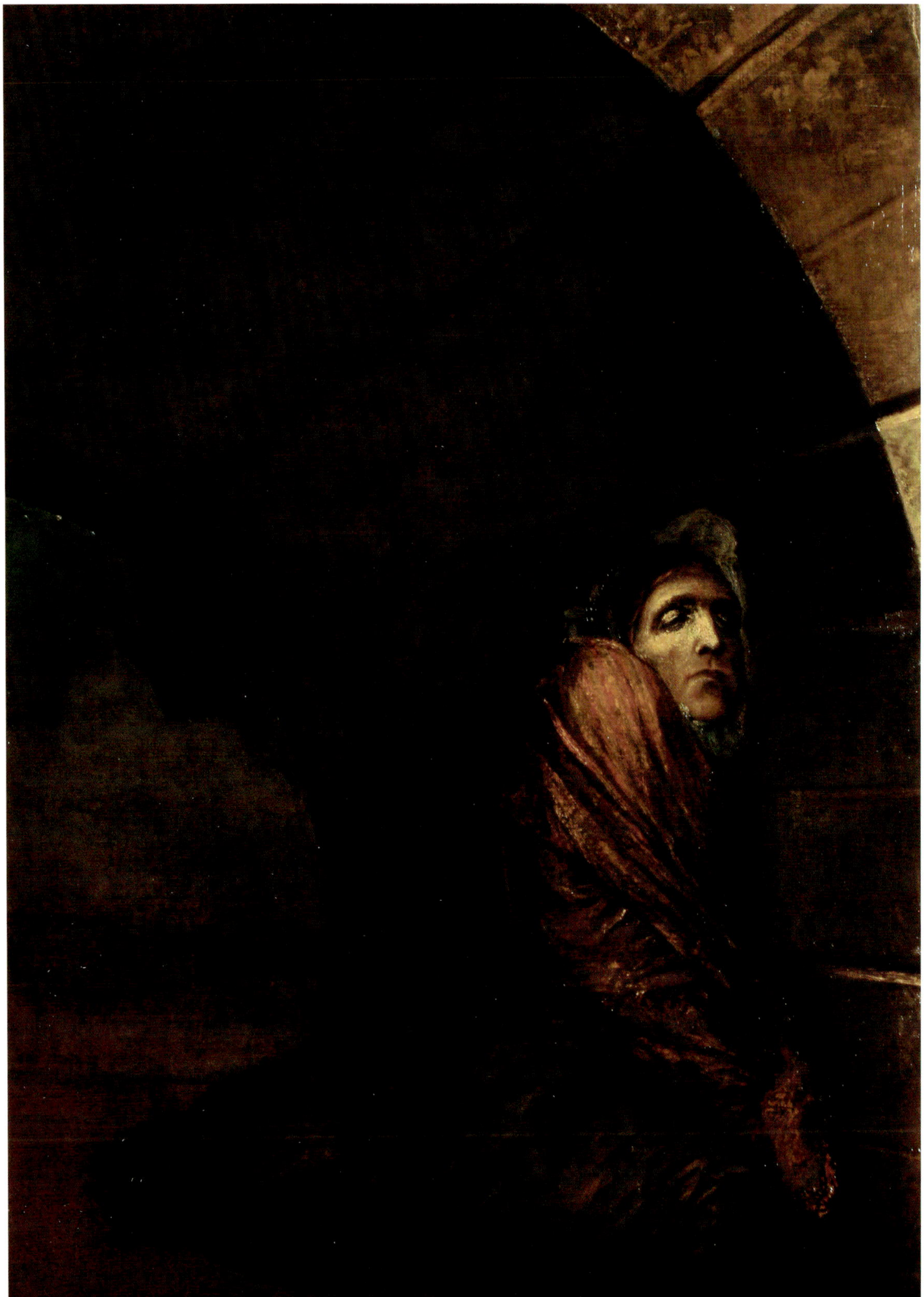

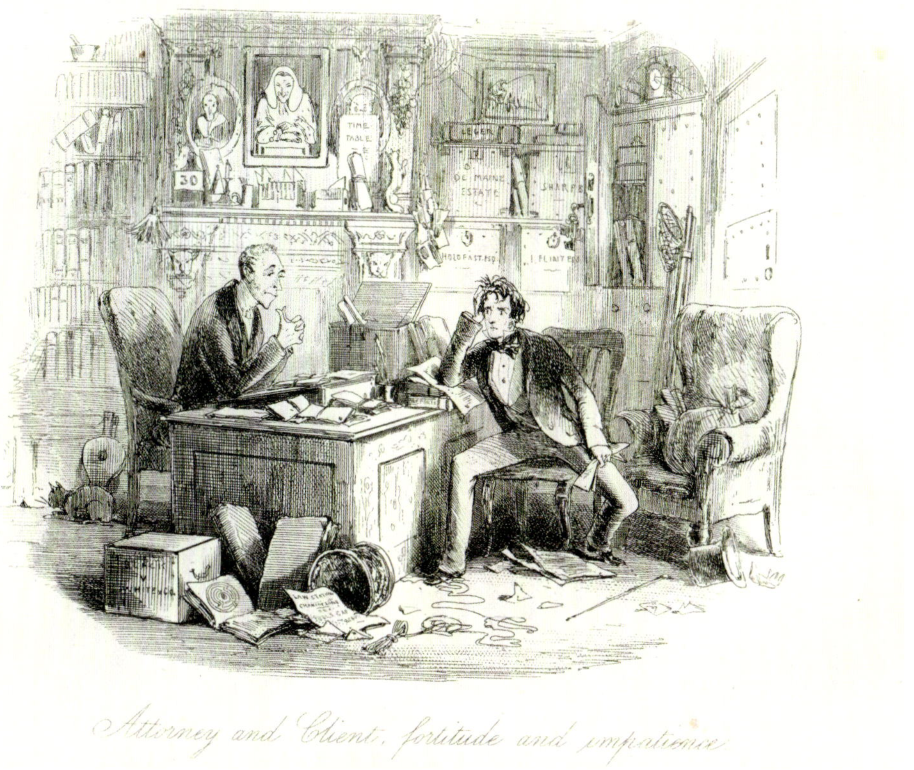

LEFT
FIG. 90
George Frederic Watts, *Under a Dry Arch*, *c.*1848–50, oil on canvas. Watts Gallery

RIGHT
FIG. 91
Hablot Knight Browne, 'Attorney and Client, fortitude and impatience', original illustration from *Bleak House*, 1852, etching. Collection of the author

affairs of the people who move around it. Jo, the crossing sweeper, has taken 'broken meats' from the table of the hypocritical preacher Mr Chadband and finds a quiet spot to eat his vittles on Blackfriars Bridge:

> And there he sits, munching and gnawing, and looking up at the great Cross on the summit of St. Paul's Cathedral, glittering above a red and violet-tinted cloud of smoke. From the boy's face one might suppose that sacred emblem to be, in his eyes, the crowning confusion of the great, confused city; so golden, so high up, so far out of his reach. There he sits, the sun going down, the river running fast, the crowd flowing by him in two streams – everything moving on to some purpose and to one end – until he is stirred up, and told to 'move on' too.[73]

For a short period G.F. Watts aspired to a Dickensian social realism, and in his painting *Under a Dry Arch* (fig. 90) the passive church is a strong symbol. A homeless woman is sheltering under a dry arch of Blackfriars Bridge, while in the background St Paul's Cathedral is a shadowy presence, ineffectual in the life of the poor whom it looks down on.

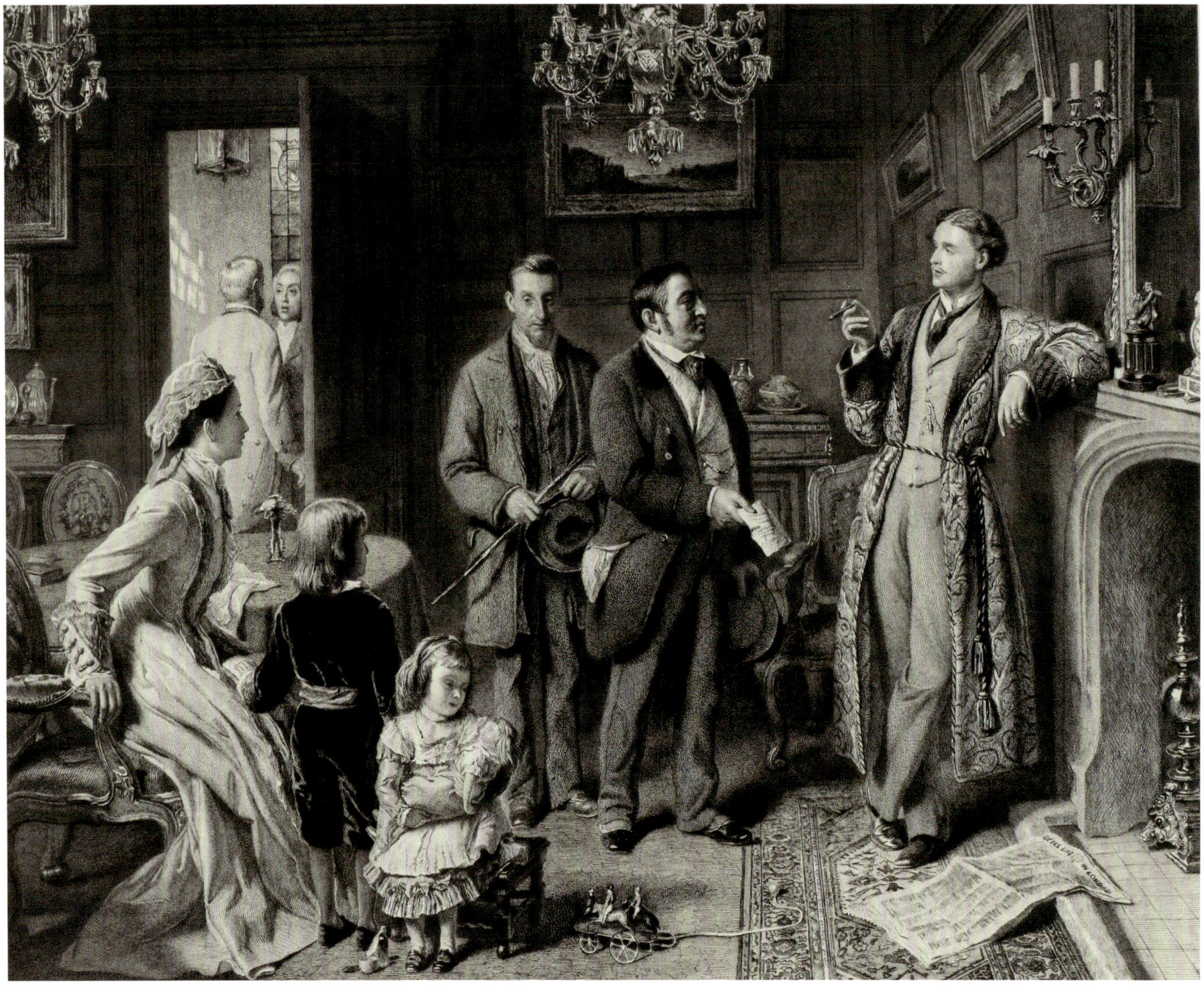

FIG. 92
Louis Flameng, after William Powell Frith, *Road To Ruin: Arrest*, 1847, etching. Collection of the author

In interior scenes Hogarth makes use of symbols, often comic, that reflect the main action and expose the undercurrents, a device that Dickens also employed. A good example of this, in chapter 39 of *Bleak House*, 'Attorney and Client', is the meeting of Richard Carstone (client) and Mr Vholes (attorney) in his office and its accompanying illustration by Hablot Browne, 'Attorney and Client, fortitude and impatience' (fig. 91). The scene is at once evocative and atmospheric, like a spider's lair, where the attorney Vholes plays on the confusion and delay that the judicial system offers him to extract a greater fee from the client:

> The atmosphere is otherwise stale and close. The place was last painted or whitewashed beyond the memory of man, and the two chimneys smoke, and there is a loose outer surface of soot everywhere, and the dull cracked windows

in their heavy frames have but one piece of character in them, which is a determination to be always dirty, and always shut, unless coerced.[74]

Having set the scene, Dickens uses a number of visual details and metaphors to emphasize the relationship of the two, particularly the very Hogarthian detail of the cat in the corner patiently awaiting his victim, the mouse:

> Mr. Vholes, after glancing at the official cat who is patiently watching a mouse's hole, fixes his charmed gaze again on his young client, and proceeds in his buttoned-up half-audible voice, as if there were an unclean spirit in him that will neither come out nor speak out.[75]

Hablot Browne's illustration seizes these symbolic visual details and adds more, the spiders' webs and the labyrinth seen in the open book, their meaning unambiguously clear.

Frith took the Hogarthian modern moral narrative from a single painting to a whole series in *The Road to Ruin* (fig. 92) and *The Race for Wealth* (1880; Baroda Museum, Gujarat), following the model of Hogarth's Rake's and Harlot's Progress. With a series Frith could develop his central narrative through different settings, demonstrating the changes wrought on the protagonists. The pivotal work in *The Road to Ruin* (number 3 of 5) shows the bailiffs arriving; the arrogance of the gambler, the main protagonist, incredulous about what is happening; his alarmed wife raising herself from her chair; one child aware of something; and the other blissfully unaware. Most telling is the scene in a back room, which we can just glimpse into, where two servants discuss the arrival of the bailiffs and consider their next position.

For all their artifice in telling a story through depicting a scene both Dickens and Frith felt that there must be an overwhelming dedication to the truth, truth in the depiction, in the main action and in the details. As Frith expressed it:

> My desire to discover materials for my work in modern life never leaves me, and will continue its influence as long as my own life lasts; and, though I have occasionally been betrayed by my love into themes somewhat trifling and commonplace, the conviction that possessed me that I was speaking – or, rather, painting – the truth, the whole truth, and nothing but the truth, rendered the production of real-life pictures an unmixed delight.[76]

Dickens judged the success of a work of art by the reality of the face or scene that it depicted. When he criticized works, it was with this criterion in mind. In famously deriding Millais it was because, in the author's opinion, he had veered too much away from the truth. Hugely criticized for his lack of judgement in this criticism, even his daughter Kate Perugini sought to excuse his harsh words. Conversely, taking the same viewpoint of art needing to mirror the truth of the moment, Dickens was able to praise

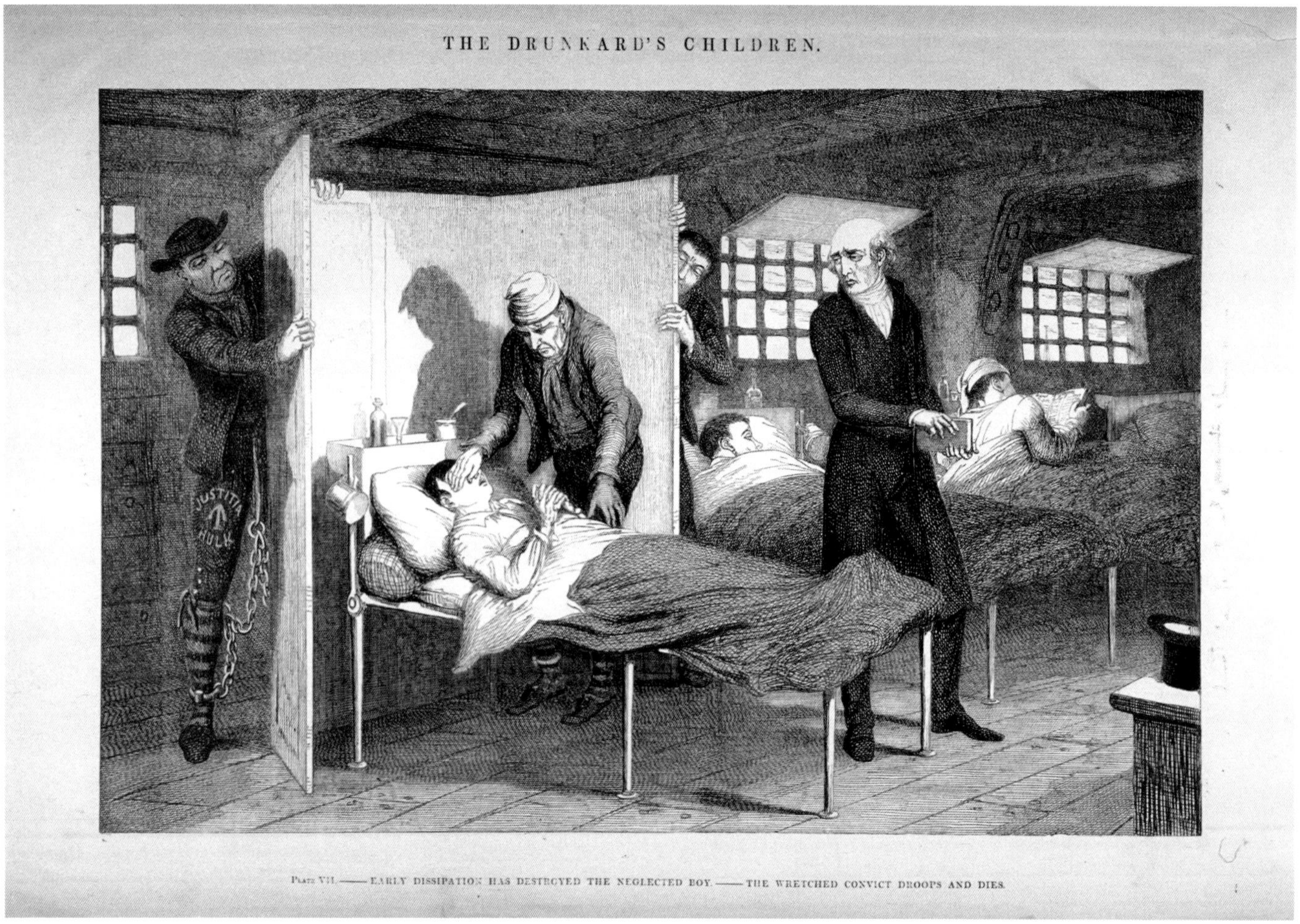

a Cruikshank scene that he particularly felt captured the reality, as opposed to the Millais work, which he felt was so unlike the scene he had imagined. In writing of George Cruikshank's *The Drunkard's Children* (fig. 93), he felt the depiction had so much fidelity to the truth that he claimed it as great art:

> The death-bed scene on board the hulks the convict who is composing the face and the other who is drawing the screen round the bed's head are masterpieces, worthy of the greatest painter. The reality of the place, and the fidelity with which every minute object illustrative of it is presented, are quite surprising. But the same feature is remarkable throughout. In the final scene at the Old Bailey the eye may wander round the court, and observe everything that is a part of the place. The very light and atmosphere of the reality are reproduced with astonishing truth. So in the gin-shop and the beer-shop; no fragment of the fact is indicated and slurred over, but every shred of it is honestly made out.[77]

FIG. 93
George Cruikshank,
The Drunkard's Children,
Plate VII: 'Early dissipation has destroyed the neglected boy – the wretched convict droops and dies', 1847, wood engraving. London Metropolitan Archives

As an art critic, Dickens is perhaps flawed even though ultimately he is able to make some poignant and idiosyncratic observations. His view of his own art has many parallels with the painters of modern life: an art form that aspires to depict the truth of the surrounding world, highlighting the social issues and essentially moral in its choice of depiction.

Modern-life painting in general and Frith in particular succeeded in raising its art from illustration to create its own internal narratives, a feat that could not have been achieved without Dickens. When critics assessed the contribution of Frith to painting, as one reviewer did when considering his *Railway Station*, they saw a contemporary Hogarth: 'Hogarth's works show the value of that art which records with insight the manners and dress, occupations and amusements, the domesticities and out-door doings of the painter's age. Mr. Frith is helping to do for our time what Hogarth did for his.'[78] The critic was quite right but it would have been much more accurate to add that the contemporary Hogarthian vision was essentially Dickensian.

In his illustrators Dickens found artists who reflected and enhanced his own very particular and brilliant vision. The painters of modern life created works of art independent of specific illustration but reflecting a wider Dickensian vision. Both writer and painters exploited to the full the sophistication of their own particular medium, and because of the genius of Dickens, it is not a criticism of the modern-life movement to see their art as Dickens in paint.

NOTES

1. Frith 1887, vol. 1, p. 121
2. The famous portrait is now in the V&A. Dickens commissioned Frith to paint two of his characters, Dolly Varden and Kate Nickleby.
3. Frith 1887, vol. 1, p. 101.
4. Brian Sewell, 'A Dickens of a Painter', *Evening Standard*, 15 Dec. 2006, and Richard Dorment, 'Dickens, with a Paintbrush,' *Daily Telegraph*, 5 Dec. 2006.
5. Frith referred to Dickens as 'one of the greatest geniuses that ever lived' (Frith 1887, vol. 1, p. 103).
6. John Ruskin, 'Introduction', in Chesneau 1887, p. xiii.
7. Chesneau 1887, pp. 5–6.
8. William Powell Frith, *John Leech: His Life and Work*, 2 vols (London, 1891), vol. 2, p. 96.
9. Thackeray 1911, p. 160.
10. Thackeray 1911, p. 22:
   [London] March 23, 1855.
   My dear Thackeray, I have read in the 'Times' to-day an account of your last night's lecture, and cannot refrain from assuring you, in all truth and earnestness, that I am profoundly touched by your generous reference to me. I do not know how to tell you what a glow it spread over my heart. Out of its fulness I do entreat you to believe that I shall never forget your words of commendation. If you could wholly know at once how you have moved me and how you have animated me, you would be the happier, I am certain.
   Faithfully yours ever,
   CHARLES DICKENS.
11. James Thomas Fields, *In and Out of Doors with Charles Dickens* (Boston, 1876), pp. 114–15.
12. Dickens 1911, p. 115.
13. Thackeray 1911, pp. 159–60.
14. Thackeray 1911, p. 218. 'The care and method', Thackeray (1911, p. 161) further writes, 'with which the moral grounds of these pictures are laid is as remarkable as the wit and skill of the observing and dextrous artist.'
15. Thackeray 1911, p. 166.
16. Frith 1887, vol. 3, p. 315.
17. Frith 1887, vol. 1, p. 102.
18. Dickens quoted in Kitton 1902, vol. 2, p. 473.
19. Frith 1887, vol. 2, p. 17.
20. See Mark Bills, '"The line which separates character from caricature . . .": Frith and the influence of Hogarth', in Bills & Knight 2006, pp. 40–55.
21. Frith 1887, vol. 1, p. 243.
22. G.F. Watts in Watts 1912, vol. 3, pp. 88–9.
23. Watts painted four social-realist paintings in the late 1840s: *Found Drowned*; *Song of the Shirt*; *Under a Dry Arch*; and *Irish Famine* (all Watts Gallery).
24. G.F. Watts in Watts 1912, vol. 3, p. 178.
25. David Trotter, 'Dickens and Frith', in Bills & Knight 2006, p. 32.
26. Frith 1887, vol. 1, p. 104.
27. Frith 1887, vol. 1, p. 243.
28. The work left Dickens for two to three years, frustrating the author, who jokingly advertised the picture as missing and asked it to 'return to disconsolate friends . . . Think of your dear sister [Frith's *Dolly Varden*]' (Frith 1887, vol. 1, pp. 105–6).
29. These include works such as *An English Merry Making a Hundred Years Ago* (1847; private collection) and *Coming of Age in the Olden Time* (1849; private collection).
30. William Hogarth quoted in Goldwater & Treves 1976, p. 179.
31. Frith 1887, vol. 1, p. 192.
32. Frith 1887, vol. 1, p. 185.
33. Frith 1887, vol. 1, p. 246.
34. Dickens 1836, vol. 1, 'Scenes', ch. 3.
35. Kitton 1902, vol. 2, p. 472.
36. Frith 1887, vol. 1, p. 102.
37. Frith 1887, vol. 1, p. 336.
38. Ibid.
39. Dickens 1836, vol. 1, 'Scenes', ch. 1.
40. Ibid.
41. Dickens 1836, vol. 1, 'Scenes', ch. 2.
42. Frith 1887, vol. 1, p. 326–7.
43. Dickens 1836, vol. 2, 'Scenes', ch. 21.
44. Ibid.
45. Ibid.
46. Frith 1887, vol. 1, p. 337.
47. Presumably, too, if the paintings of the London streets had been completed, they would have had an accompanying catalogue describing the scene.
48. *Dombey and Son*, ch. 15.
49. Dickens & Wills 1850, p. 7.
50. See Mark Bills, '"The General Post Office – One Minute to Six" by George Elgar Hicks', *Burlington Magazine*, Sept. 2002, p. 550–56.
51. Dickens & Wills 1850, p. 9.
52. W. Thornbury, *The May Exhibition: A Guide to the Pictures at the Royal Academy*, (London, 1860), pp. 40–41.
53. Mary Cowling, *The Artist as Anthropologist* (Cambridge, 1989).
54. See Caroline Arscott, 'William Powell Frith's *Railway Station:* Classification and the Crowd', in Bills & Knight 2006, pp. 78–93.
55. Meadows 1840, preface, unnumbered.
56. Joseph Kenny Meadows, *Heads from Nicholas Nickleby: From Drawings by Miss La Creevy* (London, 1839).
57. Joseph Kenny Meadows, *The Scrap Book of Literary Varieties and Mirror of Instructive & Entertaining Information* (London, 1840). Characters depicted include the following: 'The Young Lord – Lord Frederick Verisopht; Miniature Painter – Miss La Creevy; Philanthropists – Charles and Ned Cheeryble; The Accountant – Mr Linkinwater; The Young Heir – Nicholas Nickleby; Country theatrical manager – Mr Vincent Crummles; The man of fashion – Mr Mantolini; The belle – Mrs Mantolini; The scandal-monger – Fanny Squeers.'
58. *Nicholas Nickleby*, ch. 10.
59. Other illustrations are 'Nicholas attracted by the mention of his Sister's name in the Coffee-room' and 'The last brawl between Sir Mulberry and his pupil'.
60. Douglas Jerrold, 'The Young Lord', in Meadows 1840, p. 284.
61. *The Old Curiosity Shop*, ch. 19.
62. Frith 1887, vol. 1, p. 296.
63. See Mark Bills, 'William Powell Frith's "The crossing sweeper": an archetypal image of mid-nineteenth century London', *Burlington Magazine*, May 2004, pp. 300–307.
64. *Bleak House*, ch. 16.
65. *Art Journal*, March 1864, p. 64.
66. Frith 1887, vol. 1, p. 246.
67. Dickens 1836, vol. 1, 'Scenes', ch. 12.
68. Wills 1851, p. 246.

69. Wills 1851, p. 245.
70. Wills 1851, p. 244.
71. William Hogarth quoted in Goldwater & Treves 1976, p. 179.
72. Dickens 1911, p. 115.
73. *Bleak House*, ch. 19.
74. *Bleak House*, ch. 39.
75. Ibid.
76. Frith 1887, vol. 2, p. 34.
77. Dickens 1911, p. 116.
78. *The Times*, 19 April 1862, p. 5, review of *The Railway Station*.

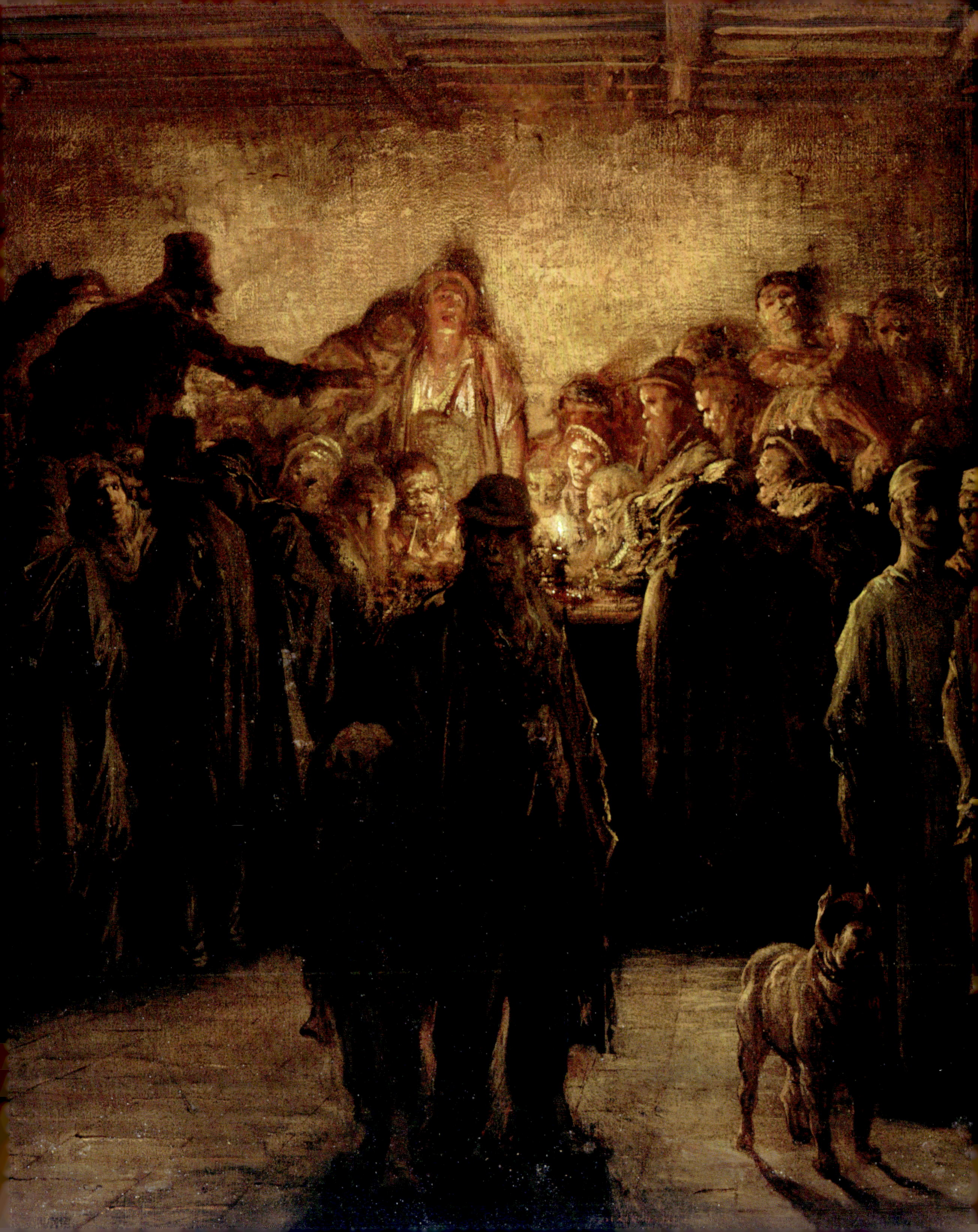

Dickens AND THE SOCIAL REALISTS

PAT HARDY

Dickens's biographer John Forster wrote that *Bleak House* was 'too real to be pleasant', and critics made similar points about a group of British artists, known as social realists, who came to prominence with the launch in 1869 of a new illustrated journal called *The Graphic*.[1] Luke Fildes, Hubert Herkomer and Frank Holl specialized in depicting contemporary scenes of poverty, deprivation and homelessness and all emphasized the factual and authentic nature of the scenes they painted. Commissioned by *The Graphic* to draw subjects of contemporary urban concern, Frank Holl produced *Deserted – The Foundling*, 26 April 1873 (fig. 95), with an oil of the same title at the Royal Academy in 1874; Hubert Herkomer created *Old Age: A Study at the Westminster Union*, 7 April 1877 (fig. 100), translating it to *Eventide: A Scene in the Westminster Union* (1877–8; fig. 99); and Luke Fildes's 'Houseless and Hungry', 4 December 1869 (fig. 104), became *Applicants for Admission to a Casual Ward* (1874; fig. 103).

The works of this group represent a more assertive and coordinated response, in subject matter, form, composition and reception, to the social issues of the late 1860s and 1870s than had been the case for earlier painterly representations of poverty and social injustice, and can be credited with absorbing much from Dickens's descriptive accounts of social problems in his novels. Dickens's campaigning interest and interpretation of subjects like the operation of the Poor Laws, the fate of the fallen woman, the role of the police and the administration of justice were all issues that these artists sought to visualize in a new and distinctive way, blending claims to realism with an overlay of aestheticized atmospheric intangibility.

As images of urban social deprivation had been produced since at least the 1840s, these social-realist artists have not been readily categorized as marking an artistic departure in the analysis of the changing patterns of treatment of the urban poor. But where earlier paintings, for instance by Richard Redgrave and Thomas Faed, have been closely allied to literary sources, the social-realist artists referenced events that they claimed to have witnessed with their own eyes on the streets of London in the 1870s. They were all at the very beginning of their careers and eager to make their names.

FIG. 94
Gustave Doré, *A Poor-House*
(detail of fig. 102)

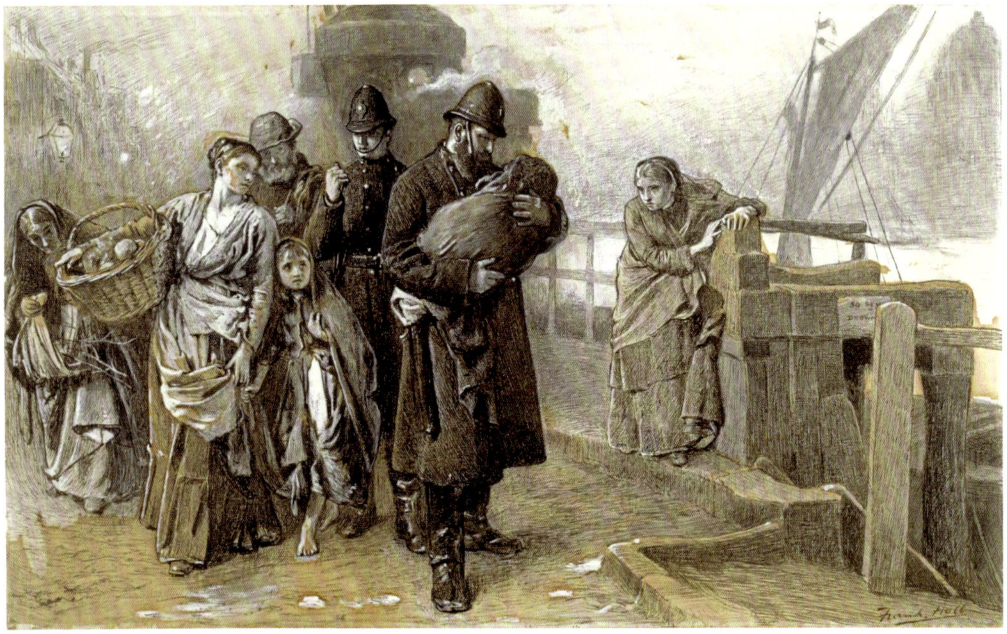

FIG. 95
Frank Holl, *Deserted – The Foundling*, 1874, pen, ink, watercolour drawing. Art Gallery of New South Wales, Sydney

Fildes finished his training at the Royal Academy Schools in 1863 (and was elected Royal Academician in 1887), Herkomer finished his studies at the Department of Science and Art, South Kensington, in 1867 and Holl, accepted aged fifteen at the Royal Academy Schools, began exhibiting at the Royal Academy in 1864. Their viewpoint was necessarily of the later rather than the early nineteenth century and they used the platform of *The Graphic* to focus attention on their new treatment of this urban landscape. One way they did this was to insist in subsequent autobiographies, letters and interviews that the paintings were derived from recollections of their own eyewitness explorations and findings (in the same way as Dickens's investigatory reporting had been championed), and other methods involved the adaptation of current artistic conventions to convey the sense of social deprivation rife in London in the 1870s and the introduction of new, modern motifs, compositional devices, light and tone, characters and description.

Writers, not only Dickens, had frequently published accounts from the mid-century of visits to the poorer areas of London, such as Augustus Mayhew's *Paved with Gold or the Romance and Reality of the London Streets* (1858) and James Underwood's exploratory trips to the East End published in *The Pall Mall Gazette*, particularly his night spent in the Lambeth workhouse in January 1866. All were informed by Henry Mayhew's monumental *London Labour and the London Poor* (first published in periodical form in 1851). The editor of *The Graphic*, William Luson Thomas, was undoubtedly aware of the interest that such works generated and, eager to capitalize on the market and audience that these explicit accounts as well as the sale of Dickens's novels had

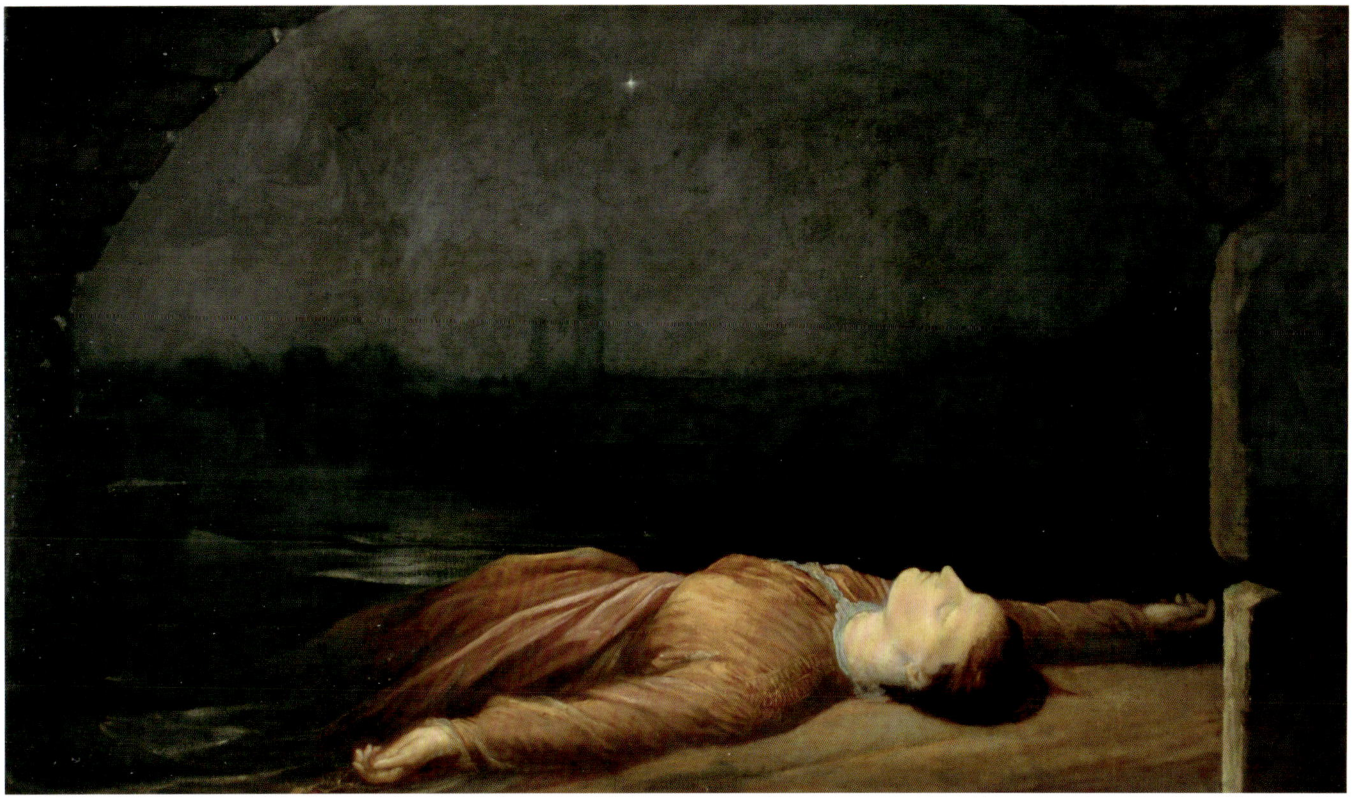

FIG. 96
George Frederic Watts, *Found Drowned*, *c.*1848–50, oil on canvas. Watts Gallery

created, sought articles and sketches of such scenes. Thomas wanted to focus on the portrayal of contemporary social deprivation in London life in order to provide a different kind of newspaper from the older *Illustrated London News*. He also wanted to use a different method in *The Graphic*, namely wood engravings rather than steel etching and engraving, to produce linear compositions conveying greater contrasts of light and shade, accompanied by lengthy textual descriptions explaining the context of the illustration and the fact that such a scene had been witnessed and drawn contemporaneously. With the help of such techniques, Fildes, Herkomer and Holl became known for creating works that were unsettling in their accounts of the proliferation of the deprived and poor in Victorian society, with dark pictures of workhouses and prisons and poignant narratives of the fallen woman.

Deserted – The Foundling (fig. 95), published as an engraving on 26 April 1873 as part of a 'London Sketches' series, was worked into an oil painting and exhibited in 1874 (now untraced but identifiable by a watercolour study). It demonstrates the development in the treatment of social issues from the earlier paintings of fallen women by artists, such as G.F. Watts's *Found Drowned* (fig. 96), showing a young woman lying dead on the shore having been washed up from the Thames, and Augustus Egg's *Past and Present* triptych (fig. 97). The latter presents a sequence of images telling the story of

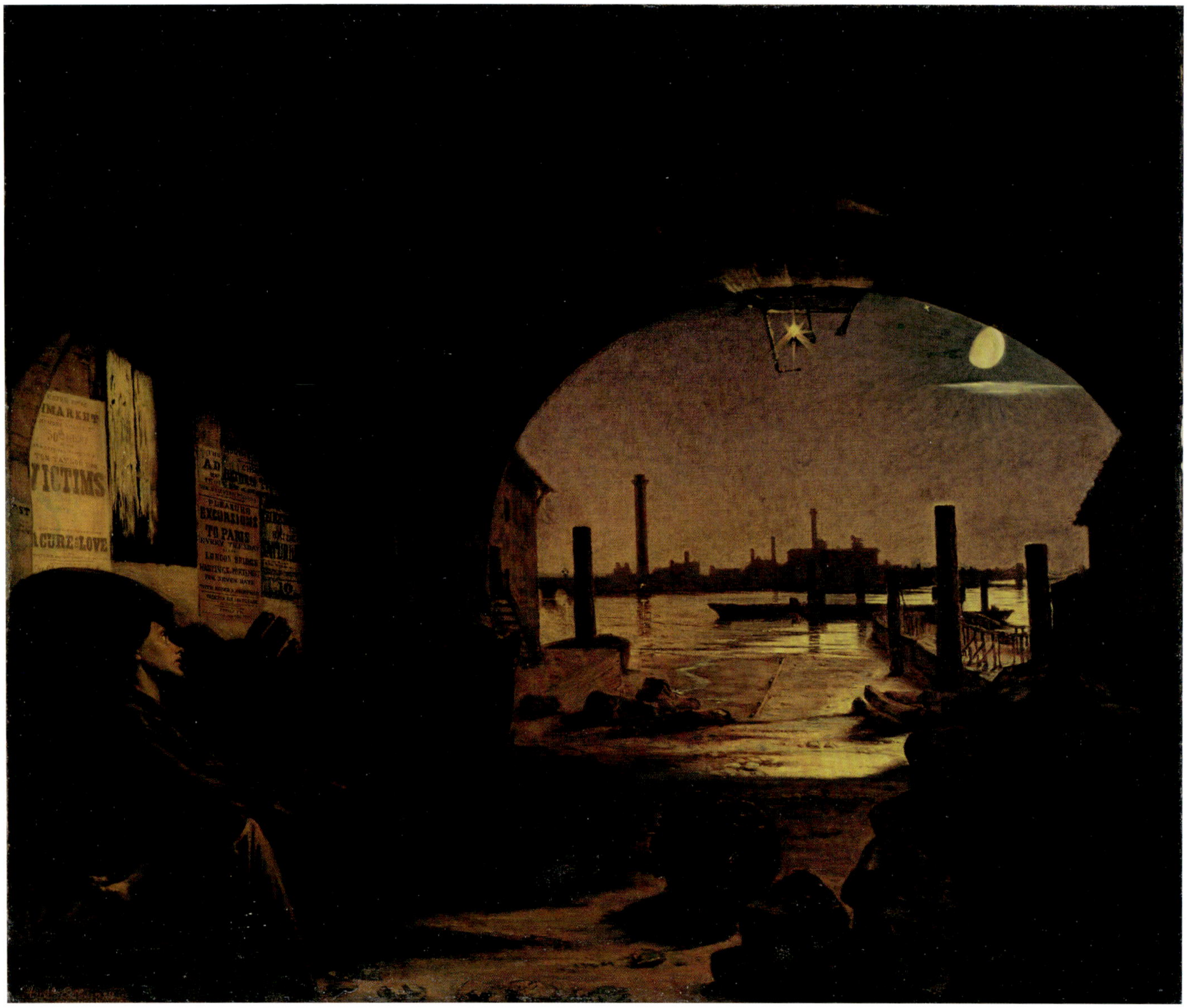

FIG. 97
Augustus Leopold Egg, *Past and Present, No. 3*, 1858, oil on canvas. Tate, London

the fallen woman, the first showing the discovery of the woman's adultery, the second her sad fate as a single woman in London, and the third depicting her just before her demise under an archway at the Adelphi Terrace.

The focus of *Deserted – The Foundling* is the policeman who has just picked up an abandoned baby and is seemingly oblivious to the crouching mother nearby who seems to be on the point of drowning herself. The scene is set, as in the earlier works, beside the Thames at a spot identified in the accompanying *Graphic* commentary as Bankside between Blackfriars and Southwark. The earlier paintings focused very much on the figure of the fallen woman, Watts in a scene marked by an absence of narrative, and

Egg with a degree of theatricality in the composition. The title of Watts's *Found Drowned* was taken from the daily column in *The Times* that published the lists of those found drowned in London and gives the main narrative clue for the work. Dickens also used the notice as a plot device in several novels: in *David Copperfield* David and Mr Peggotty note 'the rags of last years' handbills offering rewards for drowned men'.[2] Esther Summerson in *Bleak House* glimpses a bill while driving through the streets with Mr Bucket,[3] and Arthur Clennam in *Little Dorrit* passes 'a wretched little bill, FOUND DROWNED . . . weeping on the wet wall'.[4] But *Found Drowned* did not reference contemporary news stories and scandals or propose a reason for the incidence of drowning. It is essentially without narrative, likely to have been influenced by Thomas Hood's poem, 'The Bridge of Sighs' (1844). Egg's work, exhibited with no title in 1858 at the Royal Academy, seeks to provide a degree of contemporaneous authenticity by the addition of the exhibition text, 'August 4th – Have just heard that B– has been dead more than a fortnight, so his poor children have now lost both parents. I hear she was seen on Friday last near the Strand, evidently without a place to lay her head. What a fall hers has been,' and by the insertion on the arches of playbills for current performances at the Haymarket Theatre of *A Cure for Love* and *Victims*. However, the sequential nature of the triptych's stage-set tableaux and the dramatic lighting and colouring locate the work less in the world of reportage than in the theatre.

Holl, by contrast, like Fildes and Herkomer, was eager to prove that he had actually witnessed the incident depicted in *Deserted – The Foundling*. A.M. Reynolds, Holl's biographer, wrote:

> It was scarcely a morbid attraction for the seamy side of life which led him forth upon these unsavoury peregrinations but rather I take it a latent idea that by depicting them forcibly and poignantly in his own work he might bring home to the indifferent eyes and hearts of the public the wretched and iniquitous state of affairs which lies close to our own doors.[5]

Holl is highly likely to have been aware of the popular interest in the contemporary scandal of Margaret Waters, a professional baby farmer executed for conspiracy to obtain money by fraud and the murder of a baby in 1870. The term 'baby farming' first appeared in the *Times* in the late 1860s and, according to one medical practitioner, was used 'to indicate the occupation of those who receive infants to nurse or rear by hand for a payment in money, either made periodically (as weekly or monthly) in one sum'.[6] It had been mentioned in *Oliver Twist*, but with the increased publicity later in the century acquired a greater resonance to which Holl, eager to produce a popular subject, would have been alert.[7]

By focusing attention on the policeman Holl moves the dynamic of the work towards the fate of the foundling baby and away from the mother. The policeman adopts a protective paternal posture and *The Times* wrote that he looked at the baby

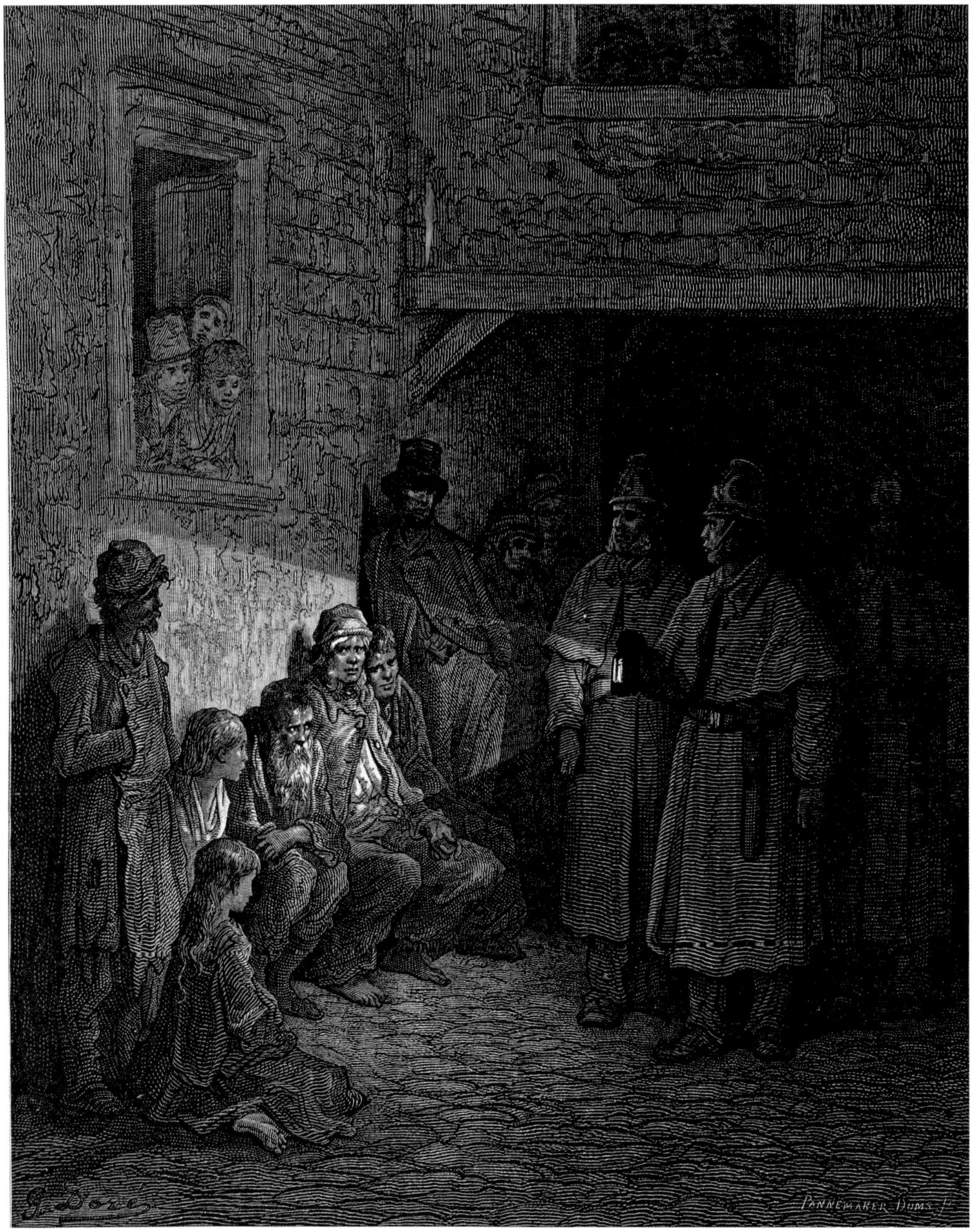

FIG. 98
Gustave Doré, *The Bulls-Eye*, 1872, wood engraving. Museum of London

'with the eye of a man who has babies of his own'.[8] A second policeman in *Deserted – The Foundling* acts as a further barrier against the growing crowd to provide additional protection for the baby. Both policemen work as reassuring presences against the assumption of anonymous, dispassionate officialdom found in, for example, Gustave Doré's *The Bulls-Eye* (fig. 98), in which the policemen illuminate the bundles of rags by shining a light directly into the faces of the huddled mass of poor, enabling visitors to observe them.

Dickens used the figure of the fallen woman in several of his works, from Nancy in *Oliver Twist* to Martha and Emily in *David Copperfield* and Lady Dedlock in *Bleak House*, but he also demonstrated an acute awareness of the narrative usefulness of the police, expressed, for instance, in the figure of Mr Bucket in *Bleak House*, in the police in *Our Mutual Friend*, and in articles in *Household Words* on 'The Detective Police', 'Three Detective Anecdotes', 'On Duty with Inspector Field' and 'Down with the Tide', collected in *Reprinted Pieces* (1858). In *Our Mutual Friend* the police feature prominently in the discovery of the drowned bodies in the Thames, which the inspector seeks to investigate, roaming the East End with Mortimer Lightwood and Eugene Wrayburn and shining his bulls-eye lantern into dark corners but not quite succeeding in uncovering all the secrets. The police link characters and places, connect storylines and act as a means of deciphering mystery and understanding the urban world.

Holl appreciated this in his central foregrounding of the police in their waterproof capes, dividing the composition between the attractive street seller on the left and the wretched mother on the right, the latter merging into the fog and vapour around the Thames. Although in the final oil the mother was moved further to the right than in the engraving, some critics continued to believe that the mother was far too close to the police not to be recognized as the one who had just abandoned the child. *The Times*, for instance, wrote: 'The real mother is apparent enough to the spectator in the poor creature sobbing.'[9] But if the focus is on the presence of the policemen and the articulation of the city in the solid fences, planks and beams of the embankment against the foggy blurring of the sail on the Thames and the distant skyline, then the narrative becomes less inconsistent, marking a break with previous treatments of the fallen woman and focusing attention on the urgency of the discovery and protection of the child, a theme recognizably more 'modern' than the dramatic stage sets of the mid-century.

Holl's other main adaptation of the fallen woman theme lies in the depiction of the river, which is practically obliterated from the canvas in contrast to the inky blackness of the Thames in *Found Drowned* and in Egg's painting, *Past and Present*. The river becomes a source of atmosphere, infinitely changeable, a means of gauging mood and storyline, and adaptable to the main narrative. For Dickens, too, the Thames was used in a multitude of ways, not just as a means of disposing various disreputable characters (for instance Quilp in *The Old Curiosity Shop* and Bradley Headstone and Rogue Riderhood in *Our Mutual Friend*) and of linking various geographies and characters around the city, but also more generally to signpost forthcoming action and to create and reflect suspense and tension.

It could be viewed in a positive light – 'the great serene mirror of a river seemed as if it might have reproduced all it had ever reflected between those placid banks and brought nothing to light save what was peaceful, pastoral and blooming'.[10] It was also playful on occasion – 'the young river, dimpled like a young child, playfully gliding away among the trees, unpolluted by the defilements that lie in wait for it'.[11] Always

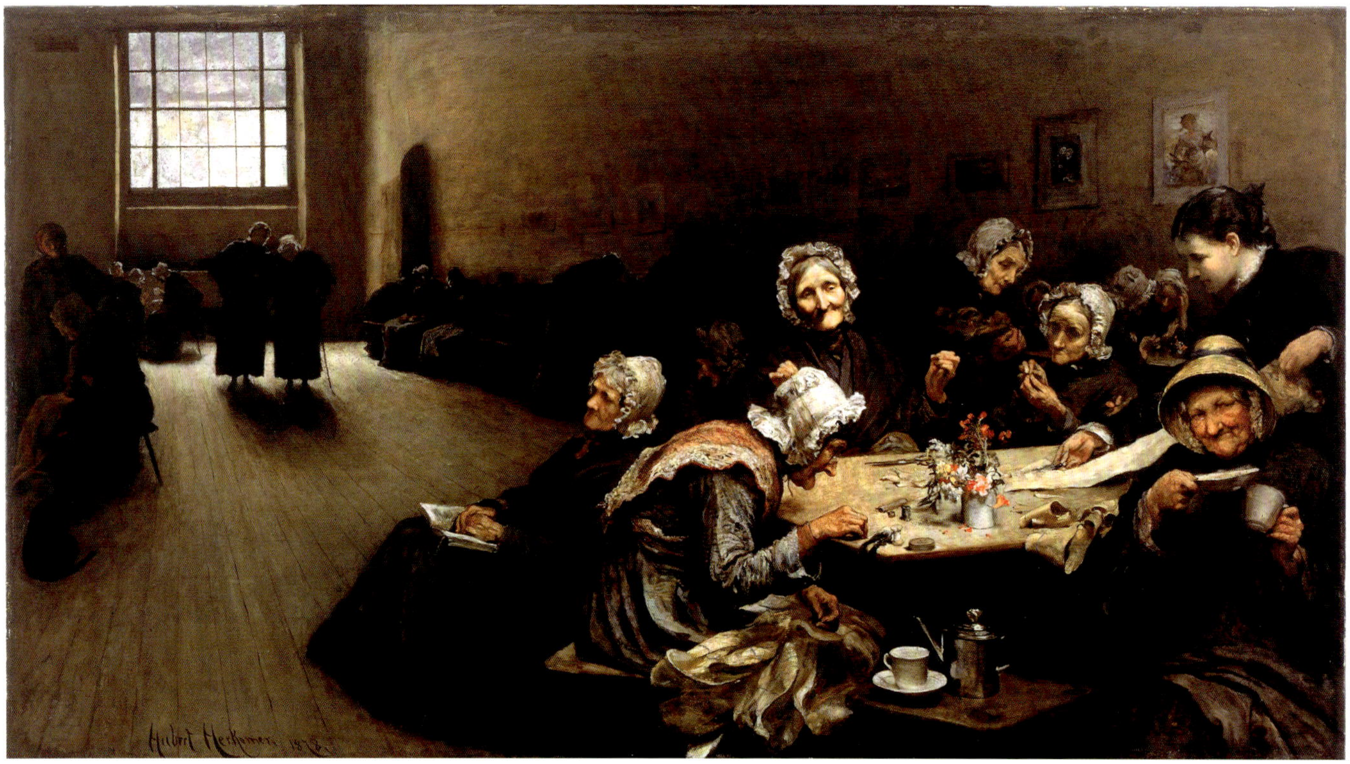

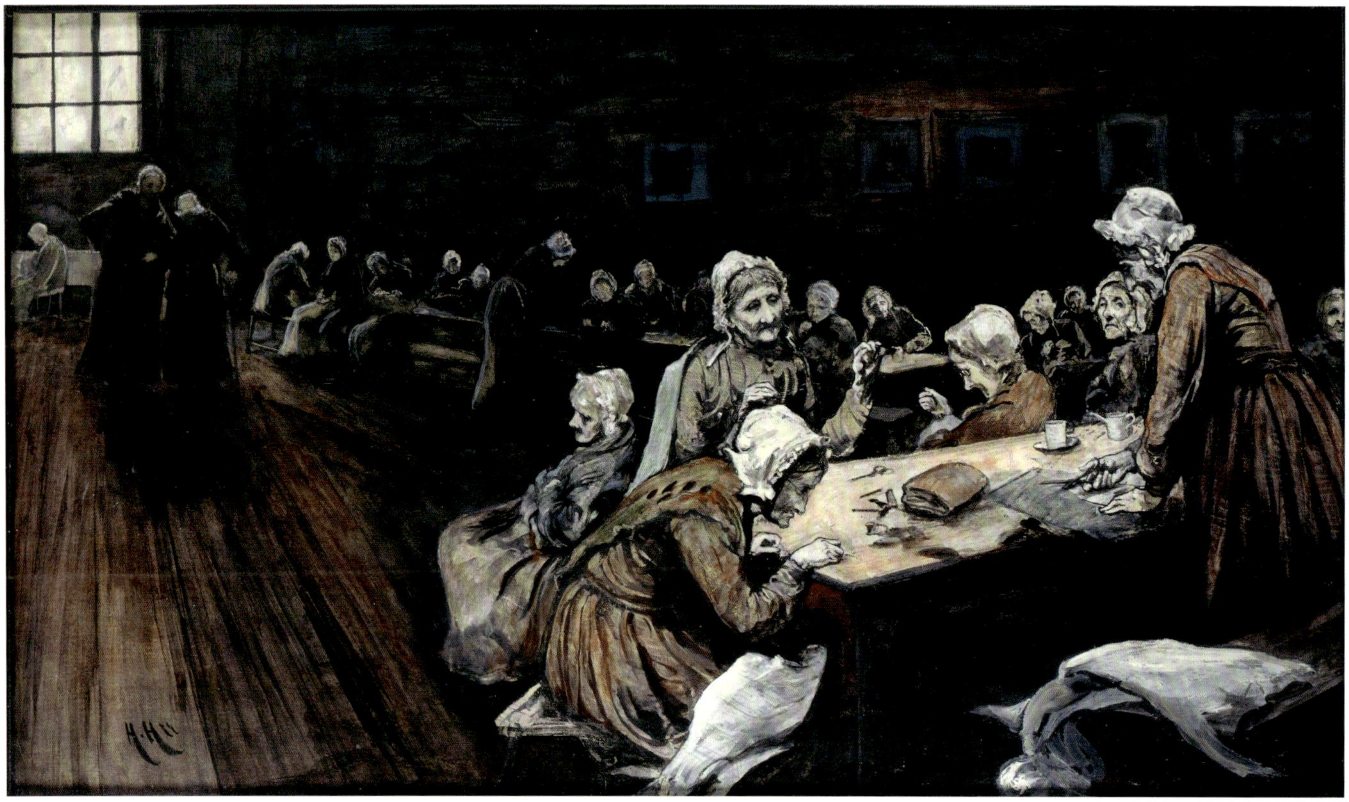

busy with industrial traffic in the east, particularly around Wapping and Rotherhithe, it was full of barges, sailing colliers, coasting-traders and scullers:

> colliers by the score and score, with coal whippers plunging off stages on deck as counterweights to measures of coal swinging up which were then rattled over the side into barges . . . tiers of shipping, rusty chains, frayed hempen hawsers, bobbing buoys, scattering floating chips of wood and shaving, cleaving floating scum of coal in and out of hammers in shipbuilders' yards.[12]

But more usually the Thames is seen as a place of dread and dirt, sometimes exuding horror and death, and described, for example, as having 'a fearful look, so overcast and secret, creeping away so fast between the low flat lines of shore: so heavy with indistinct and awful shapes, both of substances and shadow so death-like and mysterious'.[13] The last description is captured in *Deserted – The Foundling* with its momentary suspension of time, leaving the viewer to contemplate whether the fallen woman will throw herself from the embankment into the abstract indistinctness of the Thames.

Social-realist artists were also daringly modern in depicting such dismal interiors as prisons and workhouses, not places that traditionally formed the subject matter of Royal Academy paintings. Glimpses of the workhouse had been given in graphic material such as George Cruikshank's etching 'Oliver asking for more' (1838), which closely followed the text and focused more on the large vat of gruel than the surrounding room, the 'large stone hall, with a copper at one end, out of which the master dressed in apron for the purpose, and assisted by one or two women, ladled the gruel at meal-times'.[14] But one social-realist artist, Herkomer, produced several compelling scenes, including *Eventide: A Scene in the Westminster Union* (fig. 99) exhibited in 1878.[15] Derived from a wood engraving that appeared in *The Graphic*, *Old Age: A Study at the Westminster Union* (fig. 100), Herkomer, like Fildes and Holl, claimed to have witnessed the scene as he roamed around London.[16] It depicts the interior of a female workhouse, identified as the day room of the St James workhouse on Poland Street in Soho, in which the elderly inmates are shown at teatime dressed in regulation blue uniform and white caps with numbers on them.

Herkomer's vision included the use of exaggerated plunging perspective, forcefully applied paint and long symbolically laden shadows, all of which dominate the picture's cavernous space to the extent that Comyns Carr wrote that *Eventide* 'overpowers the elements of purely human interest by laying stress upon the cheerless spaces of bare wall and the expanse of boarded floor'.[17] The *Illustrated London News* considered this modelling technique to emanate from 'muscular and petulant ardour' due to Herkomer's German training, and critics were generally divided on its reception.[18]

Herkomer's scene conveys an atmosphere of darkness and despair reminiscent of the poignant account of Betty Higden in *Our Mutual Friend*. She is depicted in 'The

FIG. 99
Hubert von Herkomer, *Eventide: A Scene in the Westminster Union*, 1877–8, oil on canvas. National Museums Liverpool

FIG. 100
Hubert von Herkomer, *Old Age: A Study at the Westminster Union*, 1877, watercolour. Private collection

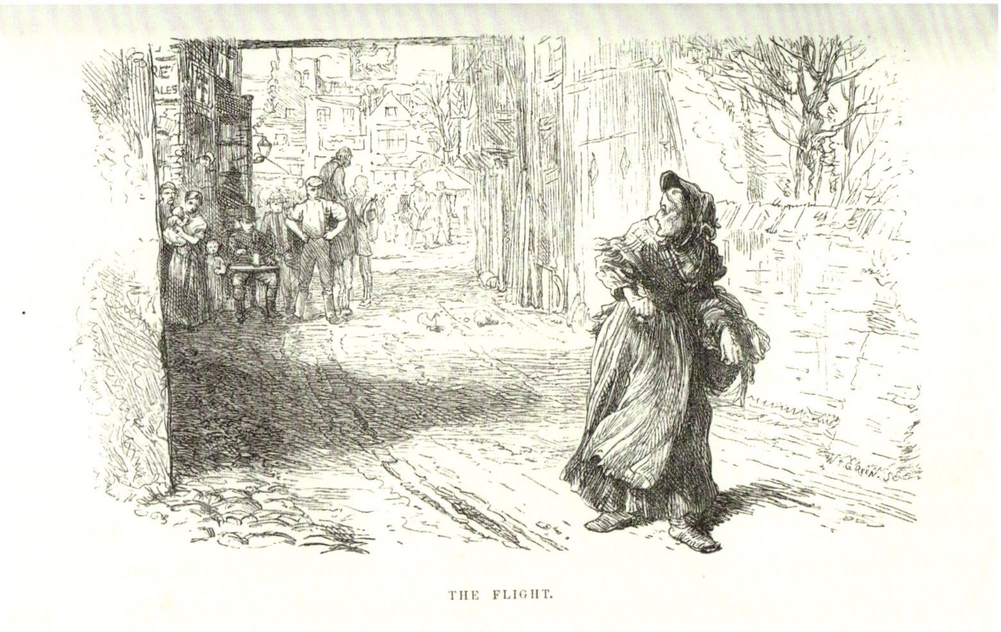

FIG. 101
Marcus Stone, 'The Flight', original illustration from *Our Mutual Friend*, 1865, wood engraving

Flight' (fig. 101) drawn by Marcus Stone to accompany the book, and Dickens describes her as terrified of being placed in the workhouse as she trudges along the country roads. She meets others who spur her on by their hopelessness, 'wretched ragged groups . . . with children among them, huddled together like the smaller vermin for a little warmth – lingering and lingering on a doorstep where the appointed evader of the public trust did his dirty office of trying to weary them out and so get rid of them'.[19] On her journey Betty Higden is plagued by the pursuing fury of the Good Samaritan who threatens to place her in the workhouse as a Casual if she does not hand over her money and move on:

> Old Betty Higden however tired, however footsore would start up and be driven away by her awakened horror of falling into the hands of Charity . . . faring on and hiding, hiding and faring on, the poor harmless creature, as though she were a murderess and the whole country were up after her.[20]

Here the themes of homelessness and dread of the workhouse are matched against the official state desire to place and retain the poor in segregated areas where they were visible and accountable. *Eventide: A Scene in the Westminster Union* conveys in the sharply delineated faces of the elderly women and the shadowy figures silhouetted against the large window what would happen to Betty Higden if she entered the workhouse. Despite the aestheticization of the scene in its translation to oil, with softened lines detailing the caps of the elderly inmates and colour in the form of the flowers on the table, the image remains poignant, heightening the emotional intensity while retaining the claim to verisimilitude and reportage.

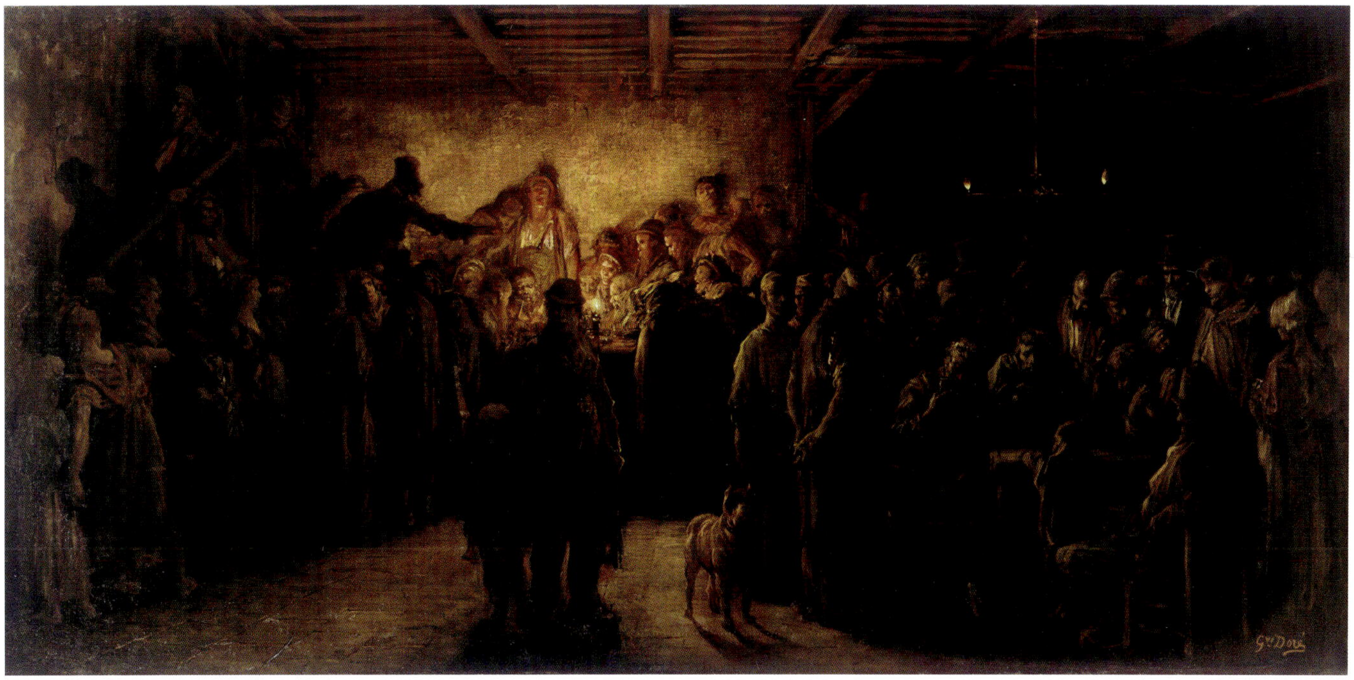

FIG. 102
Gustave Doré, *A Poor-House*, *c.*1869, oil on canvas. Museum of London

Eventide: A Scene in the Westminster Union can be contrasted with another oil painting, *A Poor-House* (fig. 102), painted by another artist with claims to produce realist art, the French-born Gustave Doré, who has been bracketed with both the British social-realist artists and with Dickens. He patrolled London with Douglas Jerrold to produce the heavily illustrated *London: A Pilgrimage* (1872), which included engravings like *The Bulls-Eye* (fig. 98), and could claim to be the same type of urban explorer as Dickens. However, although Doré produced sketches on his travels, he worked from visual memory rather than life models and authentic props, so his works resemble apocalyptic dark visions of seething, crowded London rather than claiming to be actual accounts.

It is clear that Doré did not produce works directly from life, as *London: A Pilgrimage* had a lengthy gestation period. Doré made brief sketches during his exploratory journeys, working up an album of drawings between 1869 and 1870 in London, then returned to France, before coming back to London in July 1871 to carry on with the book. Doré probably painted *A Poor-House* in Paris, as he did not have a studio in London, and it presents a clear distinction from the studied efforts of the social realists to authenticate their work by reference to actual places and incidents. *A Poor-House* derived from a drawing, 'Gray's Inn Lane – Robber's Kitchen' (published in *London: A Pilgrimage* as *Thieves Gambling*), and shows a rough (unidentified) lodging house in London populated by about seventy men, women and children in a gas-lit basement.

A Poor-House is shown as an episodic interlude rather than a narrative, an imaginative effort that is based on visual memory and captures the silent, ranked masses of the poor, hidden in shadows.[21] Differentiated figures stare out of the canvas as the crowd

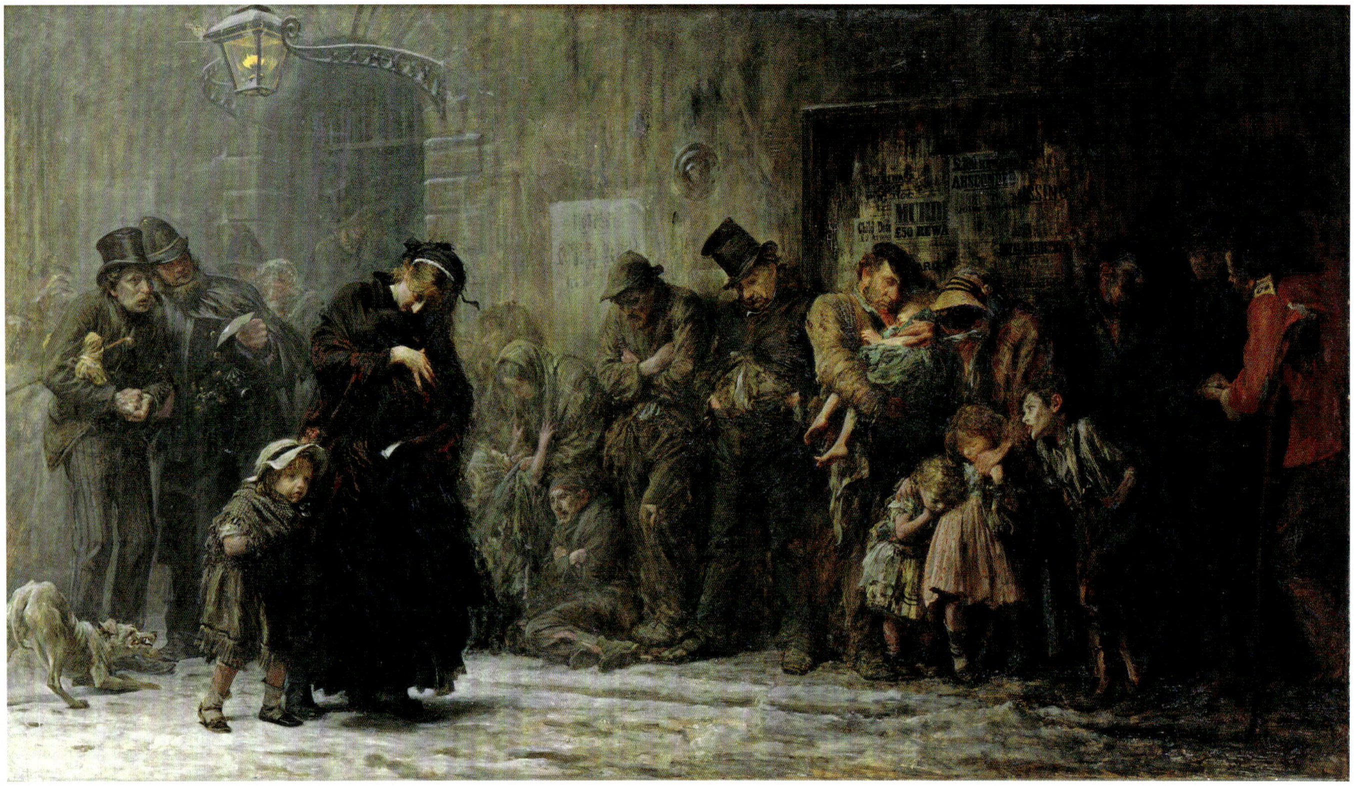

appears to part to provide an entrance for a visitor to the lodging house, thus immersing the viewer in this urban exploration. However, there is no stark compositional delineation, no experimental lighting illuminating this work as in *Eventide: A Scene in the Westminster Union* and little sense of the kind of observational exactitude that marked both Herkomer's and Dickens's works.

FIG. 103
Sir Samuel Luke Fildes, *Applicants for Admission to a Casual Ward*, 1874, oil on canvas. Royal Holloway, University of London

One of the most celebrated paintings produced by the social realists, in which modern elements and motifs are combined, is Fildes's *Applicants for Admission to a Casual Ward* (fig. 103), exhibited at the Royal Academy in 1874. Fildes is the social realist most closely associated with Dickens, as he produced the illustrations for *Edwin Drood*. He came to the attention of Dickens through his engraving, 'Houseless and Hungry' (fig. 104), in the first issue of *The Graphic* on 4 December 1869. Dickens saw it and promptly commissioned him to draw the engravings for his final novel. A detailed, chatty and colloquial text accompanied the 'Houseless and Hungry' engraving, stressing the realism of the incident and setting out the storylines for each figure.

In *Applicants for Admission to a Casual Ward* a huddled, ragged queue of the destitute and homeless are shown lining up to obtain a ticket from a police station on a winter's evening with snow on the ground. The ticket provided entry for a night in the casual ward of a local workhouse, a procedure refined in the Homeless Poor Act, 1863, by which the poor who were on the move between towns, transients or casuals,

FIG. 104
Sir Samuel Luke Fildes, 'Houseless and Hungry', 1869, wood engraving. Museum of London

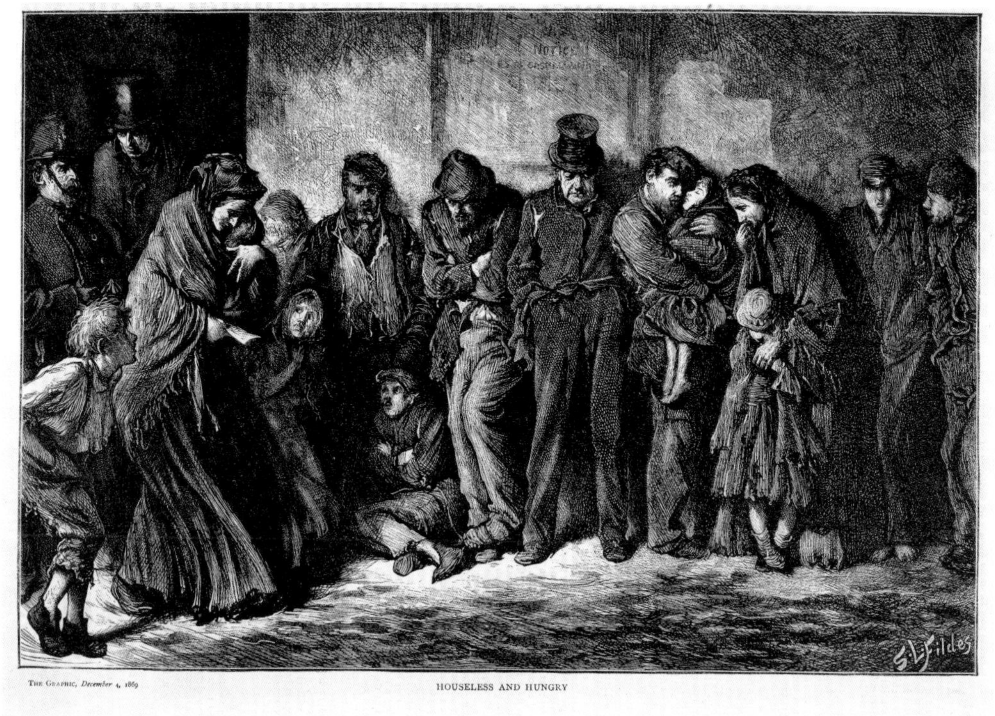

could seek a bed for one night in a workhouse. The building in *Applicants for Admission to a Casual Ward* is therefore not the workhouse itself but a police station, one step removed from the workhouse, with policemen employed to sift through those who were entitled to a bed in a workhouse and those who were not, separating the deserving from the undeserving poor. This procedure extended the 1834 Poor Law Act, which introduced workhouses as places of penal correction, whereby everybody seeking poor relief had to obtain it in the workhouse. These institutions were made as uncongenial as possible, with strict discipline, poor food, repetitive tasks, separation of families, loss of dignity and ultimately loss of hope.

All this was funded by the Union Chargeability Act of 1865 and the Metropolitan Poor Act of 1867, which transferred a considerable portion of the expenses of local poor administration to the common Metropolitan Poor Fund, to which each Poor Law Union was to contribute according to the rate or value of the property in the area. The Act was intended to equalize the levying of Poor Law rates to prevent the poorest districts paying the highest rates. Before this time each union was responsible for the relief of its own poor. A further piece of legislative tinkering showed that the system was not as responsive to alleviating the problem of social poverty as the legislators had hoped. The Metropolitan Poor Amendment Act was passed in 1870 and centralized the finances for poor relief. Indoor relief, namely that expended on workhouse inmates, was restricted to 5 pence per pauper per day, administered by the Metropolitan Poor Fund.

Dickens frequently railed against the workhouse, but in the form of Mr Podsnap in *Our Mutual Friend* he specifically targeted these funding changes to the Poor Laws. Podsnap is an admirer of the harsh Poor Law Amendment Act of 1834, where the poor were to be taught they were responsible for their own plight, and he is hostile to the plans in the 1860s to alleviate some of the iniquities in the system, especially in the big cities, where rate payers were required to fund the relief for the residents of their own parish with inevitable hardship to the poorer districts. Regular cases of starvation in the streets fuelled the debate about the centralization of the poor relief, as at a dinner party in *Our Mutual Friend*, where

> a stray personage of a meek demeanour . . . [made] a highly unpolite remark; no less than a reference to the circumstance that some half a dozen people had lately died in the streets, of starvation . . .
>
> 'I don't believe it,' said Mr. Podsnap . . .
>
> The meek man was afraid that we must take it as proved because there were the Inquests and the Registrar's returns.
>
> 'Then it was their own fault,' said Mr. Podsnap . . .
>
> The man of meek demeanour intimated that truly it would seem from the facts as if starvation had been forced upon the culprits in question . . . – as if they would rather not have been starved upon the whole, if perfectly agreeable to all parties.
>
> 'There is not,' said Mr. Podsnap flushing angrily, 'there is not a country in the world, sir, where so noble a provision is made for the poor as in this country.'
>
> The meek man was quite willing to concede that, but . . . there must be something appallingly wrong somewhere.
>
> 'Where?' said Mr. Podsnap.
>
> The meek man hinted Wouldn't it be well to try, very seriously, to find out where?
>
> 'Ah!' said Mr Podsnap. 'Easy to say somewhere, not so easy to say where! But I see what you are driving at . . . Centralization. No. Never with my consent. Not English . . . '
>
> Might he ask, was dying of destitution and neglect necessarily English? . . .
>
> 'And you know; at least I hope you know,' said Mr Podsnap with severity, 'that Providence has declared that you shall have the poor always with you? . . . I have also said that if they do occur (not that I admit it), the fault lies with the sufferers themselves.'[22]

By 1871 the Pauper Inmates Discharge Act was enacted to punish those casuals who returned to the same area twice in one month, in order to allay concerns that an increasingly indigent section of society was taking up free accommodation in the

FIG. 105
Sir Samuel Luke Fildes, *Applicants for Admission to a Casual Ward* (detail of fig. 103)

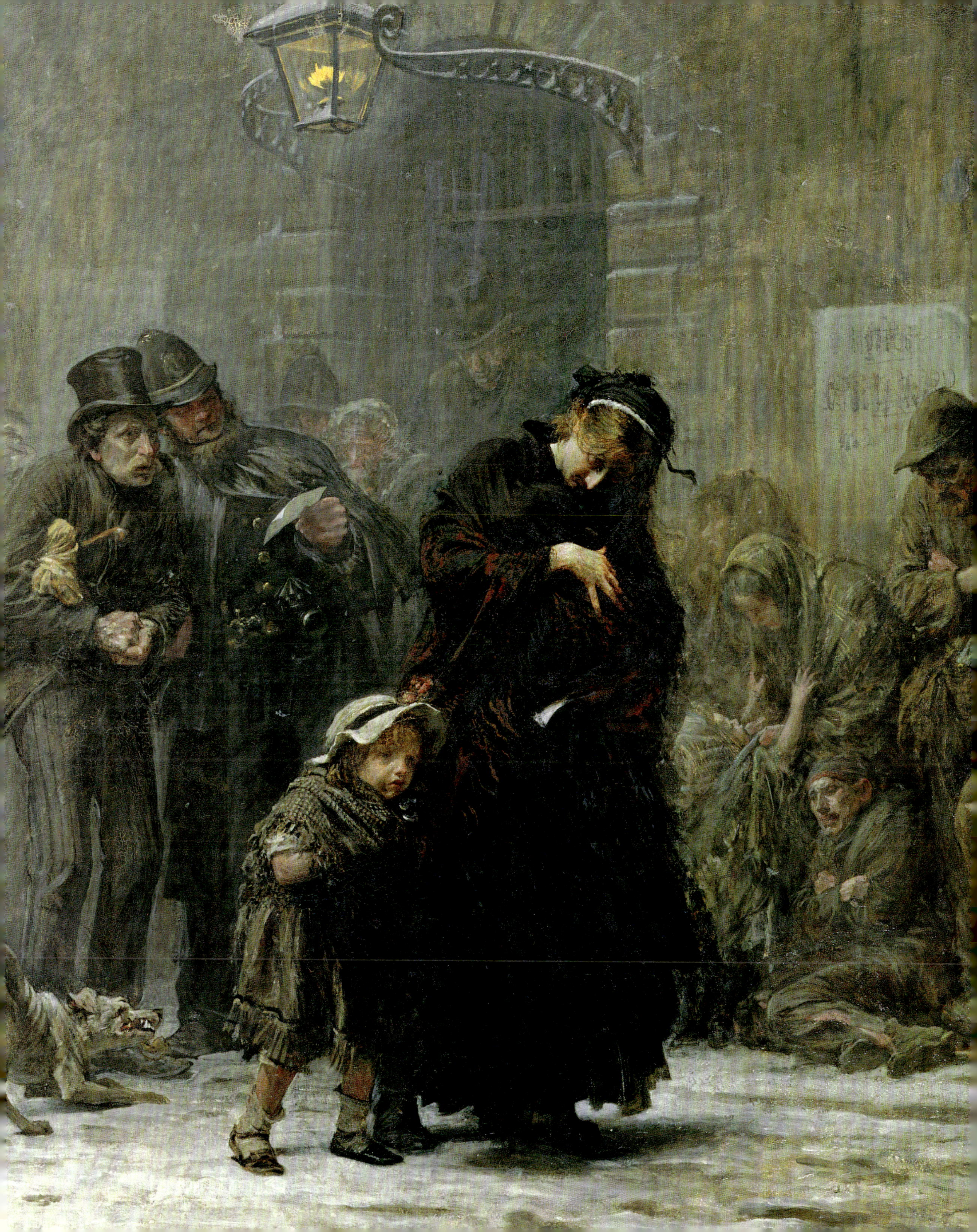

workhouse, creating a financial burden on the state. The policemen on duty assumed a more invigilatory role in granting tickets to the casual ward, assessing those who applied for entrance tickets in order to determine whether they had been before and whether they had been working in the meantime. Casuals had to provide a history and a reason for requiring board for the night. *Applicants for Admission to a Casual Ward* was therefore displayed at a time when the financing of poor relief and the visible and transparent treatment of the metropolitan poor had become a matter for political consciousness and public comment and scrutiny, as well as a long-standing cause for social concern. The state in the guise of the policeman at the station was now authorized to judge the need and worthiness of an individual in an unprecedented legislative procedure that favoured those who appeared to be deserving, which meant temporarily impoverished and not staying long term in the particular area.

Signs that the poor relief is being administered in an orderly way are conveyed by certain compositional devices in *Applicants for Admission to a Casual Ward.* Strong vertical lines structure and control the composition as in *Eventide: A Scene in the Westminster Union*, namely the outline from police station entrance to the junction of the policeman and the widow with children, the sides of the posters advertising 'Lost and Found' and the downward thrust of the crutch supporting the wounded soldier. Corresponding horizontals such as the long kerb dividing street and pavement, and between the exiting widow and the queue of applicants, balance and frame the work. But other factors contrive to unsettle the composition. One is the fragmented positioning of the figures. The traditional structure, employed by history painters in the past, of a circle of figures arranged around a central focal event is abandoned, but neither is a processional structure wholly adopted in which the figures are shown moving towards a specified objective without interruption.

The radical nature of Fildes's creation can be contrasted with an earlier painting of the treatment of the poor and transient, in which the narrative was much more legible, David Wilkie's *The Parish Beadle* (fig. 106). The parish official (on whom the later fictional Mr Bumble in *Oliver Twist* could have been based) is shown in this painting arresting a family of northern Italian street entertainers, parents, two children and a menagerie of monkey, dog and bear dancing to the music of the fair glimpsed in the distance, giving a burlesque air to the picture. The beadle looks resplendent in his robes and with wooden staff points to the law on vagrants pasted on the wall outside the prison door, passed in 1822, which justifies his action. The Vagrancy Act of 1822 was consolidated and amended in 1824 enabling parish officials to imprison vagrants who were classed, for example, as persons of a disreputable mode of life, committing offences such as begging, trading as a pedlar without a licence, telling fortunes, or sleeping in outhouses and unoccupied buildings without visible means of subsistence; or offences against the poor law, such as returning and becoming chargeable to a parish after being removed or refusing or neglecting to perform the task of work in a workhouse.

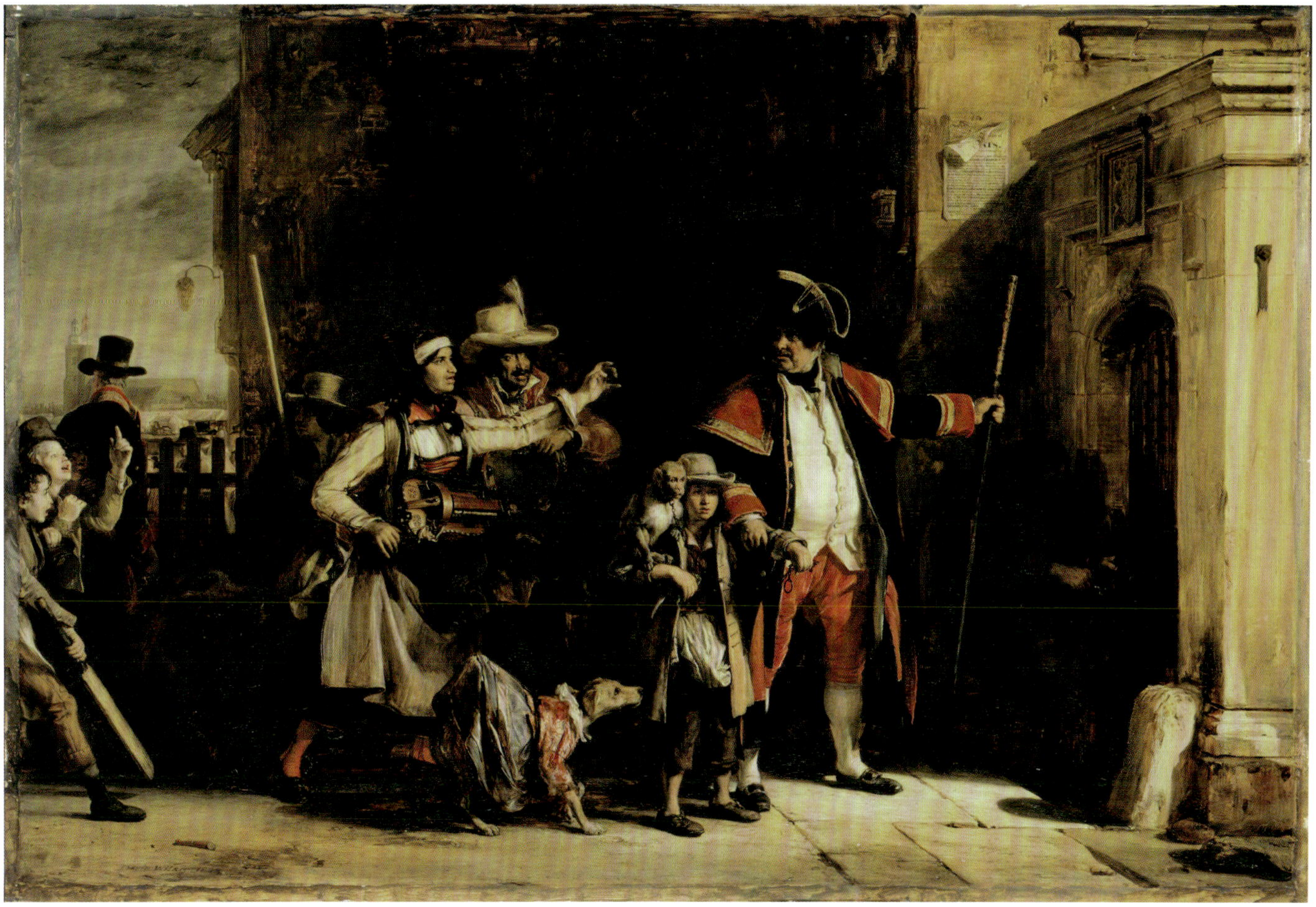

FIG. 106
David Wilkie, *The Parish Beadle*, 1820–3, oil on panel. Tate, London

The painting was exhibited with the following quotation from a standard legal authority: 'And an officer giveth sufficient notice what he is when he saith to the party, I arrest you in the King's name and in such case the party at their peril ought to obey him.'[23] Vagrancy and the fear of public disorder are the subjects of this work, but here the dating suggests that the insularity embedded in the national consciousness by the Napoleonic Wars had not dissipated and that the Italian entertainers are being harried for their different mode of life not only by local officialdom but by local youths, one of whom carries a bat. Despite patches of colour in the beadle's robes and the dress of the female entertainer, dark shadows engulf the group, for future incarceration is imminent, and society, in the form of the figure looking away into the distance with his back to the arrests, is uncaring. There is no doubt in the narrative as to what has happened and what will happen next, and the characters are all well differentiated and explained.

In *Applicants for Admission to a Casual Ward*, despite the claims to realism there is an absence of such legibility. Instead, within the queue of figures there are internal circular clusters of two particular families, those of the labourer and the widow (following the sympathetic identification given by the contemporary reviews), both of whom puncture the narrative by turning their backs on the groups ahead in the queue and avoid the official gaze of the policeman in a prominent place at the head of the queue on the left of the painting. Nor is a unitary narrative held together by interaction among other figures, the majority of whom are wrapped in self-absorption and look down or away, not engaging with the viewer and some even dissolving into a mass of blurred forms against the wall of the police station.

Without a detailed textual accompaniment (unlike the engraving) the viewer of the painting has to work out the narratives of these figures, while differing messages are transmitted as to their worthiness and deserving nature. For example, the black velvet dress of the widow, the decorative dress of her child and her ticket of admission (with the safety of a night's accommodation) contrast with her pale countenance, her claw-like hands, her distance and lack of communication with the small child beside her and with the main group, the lack of a father figure and the close positioning of the ravenous dog knawing at a bone. In pose she is linked to the fallen woman detailed in Frederick Walker's *The Lost Path* (1863; The Makins Collection) and Richard Redgrave's *The Outcast* (1851; RA). In Fildes's painting she is allied through the action of cradling a child to the labourer figure, but the exact role she plays is confusing, as it is not clear whether she is a mourning widow, fallen woman, respectable or not, or indeed whether she is deserving of poor relief at all. Her nebulous status is accentuated by the use of light in the painting. Harshly lit directly under the police light, she turns away from it towards the shadows, her profile unattractive, eyes appearing closed, her wispy hair escaping her black cap, under surveillance from the policeman whose lantern points towards her.

The police lamp hanging above, by contrast, suffuses the labourer's family with a warm light, highlighting the attractive colours of pink and blue, and also falls on the deserving red-jacketed soldier at the end of the queue, suggesting (through the crutch) that he has been invalided out of the army and cannot avoid the workhouse. But the very nature of the lighting, picking out some figures, throwing others into shadow, paradoxically serves to increase the undeserving poor's lack of visibility, as the viewer struggles to make out the form and features of this amorphous crowd blurring into a muddy mass of browns and greys and dissolving into the wall behind them. This is not a bustling street, bank, railway station or post office, as in a Frith or Hicks painting in which the anecdotal life moves easily from storyline to storyline; there is little movement and communication between the figures as they block each other's progress, compressed in space and suspended in time. Close to the picture surface many of them remain unreadable, separated into two sections, deserving and undeserving poor with the narrative of homelessness and deprivation underscored by several references such as the poster setting out the word 'MURDER' in bold letters above the labourer's head and the rewards of £2 for a missing child and £20 for a missing dog.

This sort of difficulty in reading character was not assisted by the exhibition catalogue entry that accompanied the painting: 'Dumb, wet, silent horrors! Sphinxes set up against that dead wall and none likely to be at the pains of solving them until the general overthrow.' The quotation was an extract from an account by Dickens of a night walk in which he passed the Whitechapel workhouse on 8 November 1855, cited by his biographer John Forster. Dickens gave some money to one of the women outside the workhouse and the group then melted away.[24] A fuller (and slightly different) account of Dickens's alleged encounter appeared in 'A Nightly Scene in London' in *Household Words* on 26 January 1856 (pp. 25, 26):

> Crouched against the wall of the Workhouse, in the dark street, on the muddy pavement-stones, with the rain falling upon them, were five bundles of rags. They were motionless, and had no resemblance to the human form. Five great beehives, covered with rags – five dead bodies taken out of the graves, tied neck and heels, and covered with rags would have looked like those five bundles upon which the rain rained down in the public street . . . Five awful Sphinxes by the wayside, crying to every passer-by, 'Stop and guess! What is to be the end of a state of society that leaves us here!' . . .
>
> We went to the ragged bundle nearest to the Workhouse-door, and I touched it. No movement replying, I gently shook it. The rags began to be slowly stirred within, and by little and little a head was unshrouded. The head of a young woman of three or four and twenty, as I should judge; gaunt with want, and foul dirt; but not unnaturally ugly.
>
> 'Tell us,' said I, stooping down. 'Why are you lying here?'
>
> 'Because I can't get into the Workhouse.'

The idea that the shapes seen on the street who have descended to the lowest levels of poverty are inanimate and depersonalized is conveyed in *Applicants for Admission to a Casual Ward*, but there is also the sense that the figures who are superficially recognizable as 'worthy members of society', such as the widow, may not be all that they seem, due to the unsettling nature of their appearance and the puzzling placing in the narrative. Dickens makes frequent use of such twists in the plot, in which characters are meticulously classified and physiognomically detailed but do not remain transparent; they can stay hidden and slide up or down the social scale in the fluid society in which inheritances and family fortunes are lost and found and social status can be wrongly confused with moral worth.

One example in which this slippage is vividly described by Dickens is the unravelling of Lady Dedlock, the fallen woman in *Bleak House* who lives a life of deception. She evades even the persistent bloodhound Mr Bucket, the police officer based on the real life detective, Inspector Charles Frederick Field of the Metropolitan Police. Even he is defeated by her diversionary tactics, as she changes her clothes to avoid detection

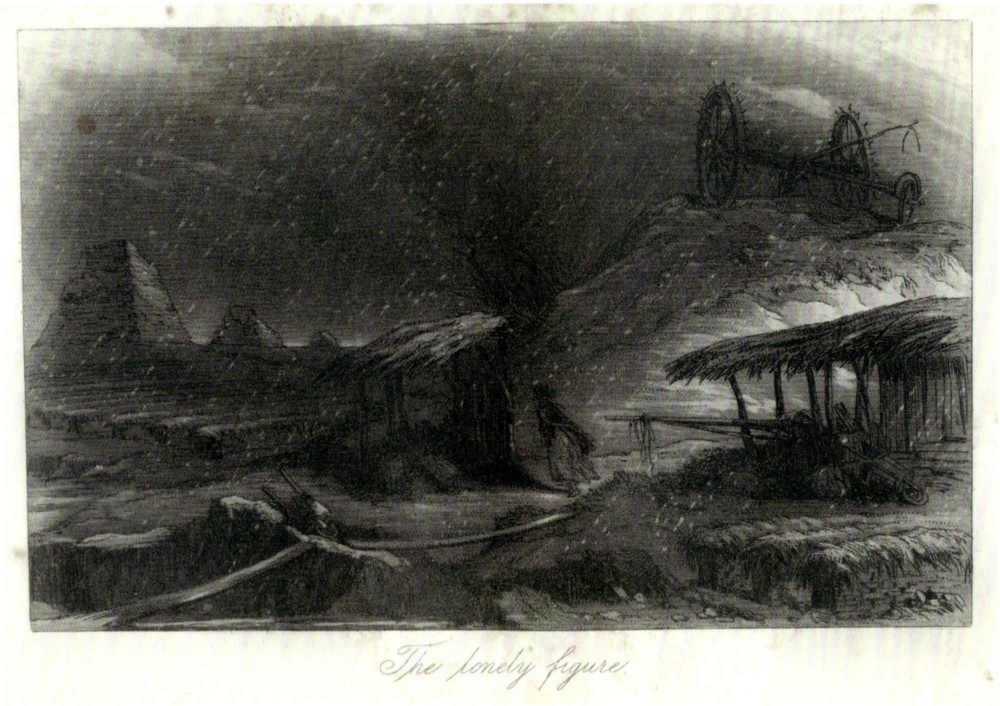

FIG. 107
Hablot Knight Browne, 'The lonely figure', original illustration from *Bleak House*, 1853, etching

and slips through the net. Although Bucket's exceptional powers of deduction can locate, in the high tower of his mind, where Lady Dedlock may be, he doesn't recognize her in her disguise and, outwitted, cannot apprehend her until it is too late.

> On the waste where the brick kilns are burning with a pale blue flare, where the straw roof of the wretched huts in which the bricks are made, are being scattered by the wind, where the clay and water are hard frozen and the mill in which the gaunt blind horse goes round all day looks like an instrument of human torture – traversing this deserted blighted spot there is a lonely figure with the sad world to itself pelted by the snow and driven by the wind and cast out, it would seem, from all companionship. It is the figure of a woman but it is miserably dressed and no such clothes ever came through the hall and out at the great door of the Dedlock mansion.[25]

One of Dickens's most prolific illustrators, Hablot Knight Browne ('Phiz'), illustrated this scene in 'The lonely figure' (fig. 107), in which the figure of Lady Dedlock is almost submerged in the landscape, overcome by the elements, hinting at the likely outcome. The winter landscape, the suffering of the innocent, homelessness, friendlessness and the horror of a sudden fall in society, wrapped up in a theme of the fallen woman, were all subsequently picked up by Fildes and appear in *Applicants for Admission to a Casual Ward*.

Fildes evidently thought the quotation, 'Dumb, wet, silent . . . sphinxes', highly appropriate in conveying the lack of communication of the poor and their ultimate

FIG. 108
Sir Samuel Luke Fildes, 'Study for "The Casuals"' (drawing of drunkard), 1869, pencil. Reproduced in *Strand Magazine*, Vol. VI, 1893, p. 124. Private collection

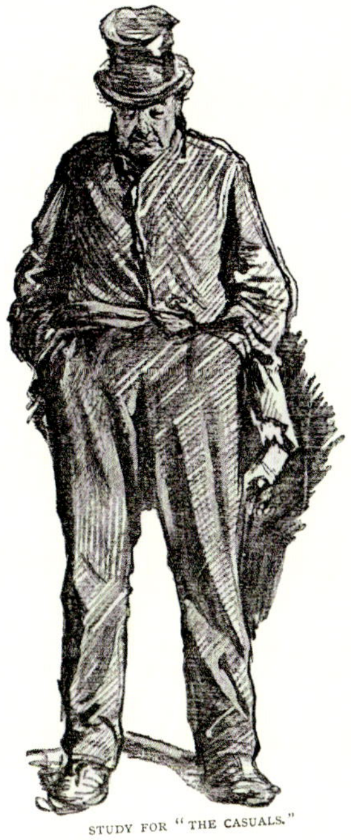

elusiveness, and later documented how he, like Dickens, roamed the streets at night to look for subjects. The history of the engraving ('Houseless and Hungry') and then the painting thus became embedded as one of the investigative journeys undertaken by nineteenth-century urban explorers who dared to visit the poorest areas in London to report on the poor. There was an increasing sense that voluntary organizations could not deal with the escalation in the numbers of the poor in the industrializing cities, necessitating the expansion of state and legislation into these areas, with all the attendant bureaucracies and the development of monitoring by visitors to the poor areas of London. *Applicants for Admission to a Casual Ward* therefore became mythologized, like the other social-realist paintings, as a work that was conceived and drawn through the perceptive insight and persistence of Fildes.

It is, however, likely that Fildes, determined to make his reputation and, when invited to contribute to the opening issue of *The Graphic*, realizing the significance of the newspaper, found inspiration from the poor groups waiting outside the Holborn police station next to his flat at 53 Hunter Street.[26] He spent much of 1869 drawing detailed sketches of professional models, on the back of which are their names and addresses, to arrange into his composition for 'Houseless and Hungry'.[27]

Seeing the impact of the engraving and keen to present a successful picture at the Royal Academy in 1874, Fildes took the subject up again and worked on it, writing to his grandmother on 30 September 1873, 'I am anxious about its success. I want it to be one, very much, as so much depends on it. It is a very important work and like all things that are pretentious if they are not very successful they have a corresponding

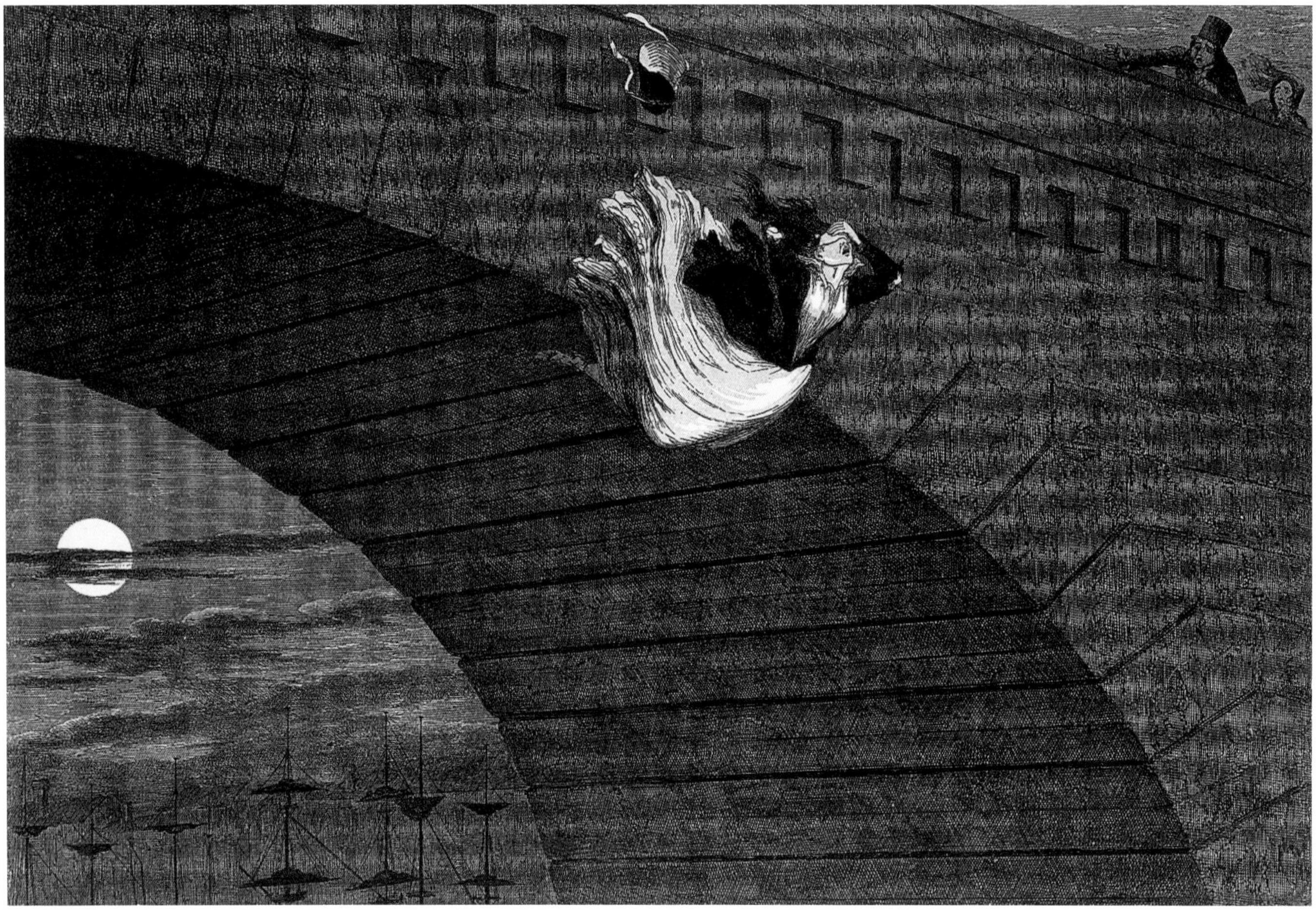

failure.'[28] The major talking point in 1874, guaranteed in part by the unprecedented size (137.1 × 243.7 cm), *Applicants for Admission to a Casual Ward* was exceptionally popular and did make Fildes's reputation.[29] The painting was not, therefore, the product of a direct copying by Fildes of an incident from life but an aestheticized vision of something he may have witnessed. Key changes were made to the engraving in form, composition and arrangement as well as colour (as was to happen in *Eventide: A Scene in the Westminster Union*), so the whole became a painterly representation of the original scene. And just as the source of the work has been shown not to be rooted in a scene copied from life, so the composition became one that, while highly legible when read with the chatty accompanying article in *The Graphic*, was less readable when transferred to paint.

The contemporary art critics were divided in their responses but all focused on the extent to which the subject matter was consistent with a prevailing artistic aesthetic. The *Art Journal* wrote that a 'picture cannot be shut up and put away like a book and therefore a subject in painting which cannot always make an impression of satisfying

FIG. 109
George Cruikshank, *The Drunkard's Children*, Plate VIII: 'The poor girl, homeless, friendless, deserted, and gin mad, commits self-murder', 1848, engraving. Wellcome Library, London

beauty is so far unfitted for the purposes of artistic expression'.[30] The *Saturday Review* described the subject as 'too revolting for an art which should be to please, refine and elevate'.[31] The *Manchester Courier* found in realist art 'the sort of Dickensian exaggeration which led to the production of Le Sphinx and kindred horrors on stage'.[32] Although most of the reviews sought to impose their own storylines on the painting, ultimately the subject matter and composition did not enable such a close reading and the dissonant note was reiterated. In *Applicants for Admission to a Casual Ward*, as in Dickens's description of his encounter at Whitechapel workhouse, the poor remain in the shadows, dissolving into the night despite the attempts at illumination through the night rambles and explorations of artists and writers.[33]

Figures here are obscured by the wintry darkness; in other paintings and engravings lighting effects such as fog and smoke are employed, both of which were vividly and memorably described by Dickens. On the fog that encircled and penetrated London in *Bleak House* he wrote:

> Fog everywhere. Fog up the river where it flows among green cuts and meadows; fog down the river where it rolls defiled among the tiers of shipping and the waterside pollutions of a great (and dirty) city . . . Fog in the eyes and throats of Greenwich pensioners, wheezing by the firesides of their wards . . . most of the shops lighted two hours before their time – as the gas seemed to know, for it has a haggard and unwilling look.[34]

And artists took up the challenge of portraying a foggy, smoke-ridden London in pictures ranging from documentary-style engravings in *The Graphic* to the coloured abstractions of Whistler.

Artist William Small captured the disorientating consequences of walking in the foggy streets of London in an engraving called *London Sketches: A November Fog*, published in *The Graphic* on 9 November 1872. This is ostensibly a reportage-style work with carefully differentiated characters and action – for example in the bottom right-hand corner a young pickpocket is shown stealing a woman's purse – and the blindness elicited by the fog is underscored by the ineffective spectacles of the victim, the blinkered horses and the smoke from the burning torches. The sightlessness, self-absorption and lack of communication, shrouded in an encompassing cold, foreshadow Fildes's *Applicants for Admission to a Casual Ward* and convey the new urban landscape.

Dickens wrote in *Household Words* that he wanted 'to show that in all familiar things, even in those which are repellent on the surface, there is Romance'.[35] His ability to control narrative, acute characterization, and passionate campaigns for solutions to social problems provided artists with a complicated and compelling analysis for the exploration of modern life. In novels from *Oliver Twist* (1838), *Bleak House* (1852–3) and *Great Expectations* (1860–61) to *Our Mutual Friend* (1864–5), as well as countless newspaper articles and journal reports, Dickens campaigned against the social ills of the day,

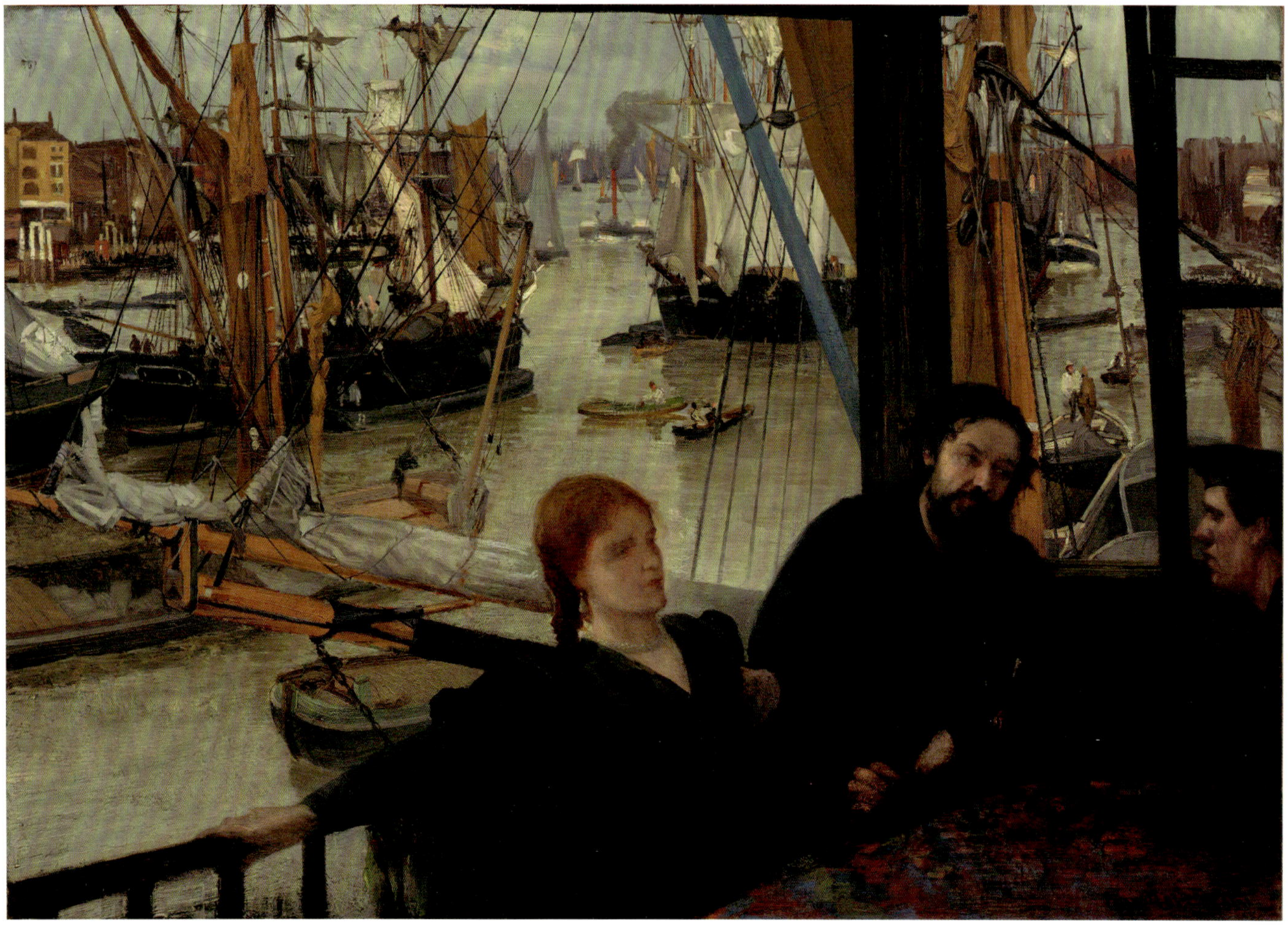

including the scandals of the workhouses, the Ragged Schools, the law courts, prisons, slum clearances and sanitary reform, and the ill-judged private philanthropic efforts of well-meaning individuals.

Artists could see that issues such as homelessness, the condition of the workhouse and the plight of fallen women had been given a huge amount of publicity by such campaigns, which habituated a reading public to these concerns. The intensely worked descriptions of London's landscapes by Dickens also facilitated the popular reception of such raw contemporary topics, while the evocative descriptions of light and shade, moonlight, fog and smoke advertised the visual possibilities of such phenomena. Many of the critics disliked certain novels (as they were divided over the social-realist paintings) – *Bleak House*, for example, was ignored in the chief critical journals, the *Edinburgh Review*, the *Quarterly Review* and the *Saturday Review* – but the public took no notice and monthly sales of *Bleak House* were between 34,000 and 43,000.

The fact that Dickens's works can be allied to the social-realist paintings despite these times of great social change shows that Dickens's constructs, while rooted in fact

FIG. 110
James McNeill Whistler, *Wapping*, 1860–4, oil on canvas. National Gallery of Art, Washington

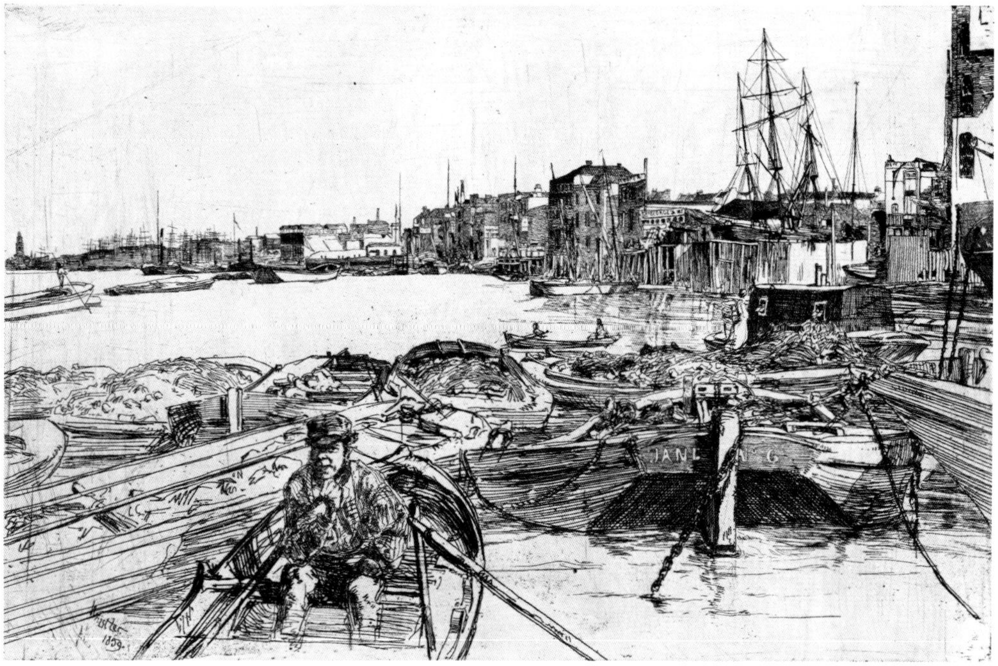

FIG. 111
James McNeill Whistler, *The Pool* from 'The Thames Set', 1859, etching. Museum of London

and observation, were founded on accurate perceptions, which conveyed universal truths. The subjects that he discussed still dominated the popular consciousness in the 1870s in the same way that they had done in the 1840s. But the artistic treatment of such subjects in the blending of graphic and fine art, drama and documentary record, artifice and recorded memory, and clarity of gaze and blurred vision meant that the social-realist paintings represented a distinctive shift away from the earlier imagery in the visualization of social issues and in the development of modern narrative artworks.

Like Dickens, the artists used models from life, but drawing from the individual, they went beyond identity and recognition to create a construct of type and topicality in their manipulation of narrative, composition, colour, mode, structure, character and atmosphere. Like many of Dickens's plots (Ruskin wrote in relation to Little Nell's death in *The Old Curiosity Shop* that 'she was simply killed for the market as a butcher kills a lamb'), the artists' occasional staginess was offset by accuracy of vision and intense observation. While they were not creating reportage, their insistence on the truth of their vision grounded them in a view of contemporary modern society and enabled them to experiment with their compositions.

They could explore the discrepancy between detailed physiognomical description and the increasing unreadability of the urban characters inhabiting the expanding cities, alluded to in Dickens's works in the frequent use of misidentification, disguise and masking, despite classification and assessment of characters through facial type and expression (figs 110, 111). For they shared a key characteristic of the urban city with Dickens, namely the realization that however much investigatory work on the subject was carried out, London and its inhabitants remained a complex construction with a multiplicity of representations and an increasingly inscrutable and unknowable set of urban characters. Despite the growing state control of aspects of Victorian life combined with a new institutional regulatory framework, the works of both the social realists and Dickens convey a sense that appearances can be deceptive in an industrializing Britain in which social boundaries are fluid.

The lack of orientation, the unsettling anxieties and uncertainties of urban life and the difficulties of precise identification and characterization led to the fragmentation of narrative in the social-realist paintings and became identified with a modern view of nineteenth-century society. The social realists pointed the way to future artistic developments epitomized by Whistler and Tissot, who dispensed with clear narrative structures and created figures who were increasingly interchangeable and unreadable unlike the transparency and surface realism of the mid-century works. Dickens was a master storyteller; it is not surprising that the intricate plots he weaved were taken up by artists; what is surprising is the ease with which such literal descriptions were adapted by this new artistic movement.

NOTES

1. *The Examiner*, 8 October 1853, cited in Claire Tomalin, *Charles Dickens: A Life* (London, 2011), p. 456 n.12.
2. *David Copperfield*, ch. 47, para 5.
3. *Bleak House*, ch. 57, para 15.
4. *Little Dorrit*, Book the First, ch. 3, para 14.
5. A.M. Reynolds, *The Life and Work of Frank Holl* (London, 1912), p. 109.
6. J.B. Curgenven, 'On Baby-farming and the Registration of Nurses, read at a meeting of the Health Department of the National Association for the Promotion of Social Science', 15 March 1869 (National Association for the Promotion of Social Science), p. 3. See also James Greenwood, *The Seven Curses of London* (London, 1869), pp. 29–57.
7. *Oliver Twist,* ch. 2, para 1.
8. *The Times*, 26 May 1874, p. 6.
9. *The Times*, 26 May 1874.
10. *Our Mutual Friend*, Book the Third, ch. 9, para 97.
11. *Our Mutual Friend*, Book the Third, ch. 8, para 8.
12. *Great Expectations*, ch. 54, paras 6 and 13 (vol. III, ch. 15).
13. *Bleak House*, ch. 57, para 19.
14. *Oliver Twist*, ch. 2, para 61.
15. An oil study (private collection) and watercolour (Walker Art Gallery) were also produced.
16. See Herkomer's letter to the editor quoted in 'Aged women in a London Workhouse', *The Graphic*, vol. 15, 7 April 1877, p. 326.
17. J.W. Carr, 'Hubert Herkomer, ARA', in *Modern Artists*, ed. F.G. Dumas (London, 1882–4), p. 69.
18. *Illustrated London News*, 11 May 1878, p. 435.
19. *Our Mutual Friend*, Book the Third, ch. 8, para 10.
20. *Our Mutual Friend*, Book the Third, ch. 8, para 11.
21. J. Treuherz, ed., *Hard Times: Social Realism in Victorian Art* (London, 1987), p. 65.
22. *Our Mutual Friend*, Book the First, ch. 11, paras 113–33.
23. Richard Burn, *Justice of the Peace and Parish Officer*, 3rd edn (London, 1756), p. 49.
24. J. Forster, *The Life of Charles Dickens*, 3 vols (first pub. 1872–4; London, 1969), vol. 3, pp. 54–5.
25. *Bleak House*, ch. 56, final para.
26. Graves 1905, p. 107.
27. Bernard Myers, 'Studies for Houseless and Hungry and the Casual Ward by Luke Fildes RA', *Apollo*, July 1982, pp. 36–43.
28. Letter from Luke Fildes to Mary Fildes, 30 September 1873, National Art Library, V&A 86 PP Box, 1(x), 3.
29. L.V. Fildes, *Luke Fildes, ARA: Victorian Painter* (London, 1968)
30. *Art Journal*, XIII, 1874, p. 201.
31. *Saturday Review*, 2 May 1874, p. 562.
32. *Manchester Courier*, 6 May 1874, p. 6e.
33. Sheila M. Smith, ' "Savages and Martyrs", Images of the Urban Poor in Victorian Literature and Art', in I.B. Nadel and F.S. Schwarzbach, *Victorian Artists and the City* (Oxford and New York, 1980), pp. 14–29.
34. *Bleak House*, ch. 1, para 2.
35. *Household Words*, 30 March 1850, Preface, p. 1.

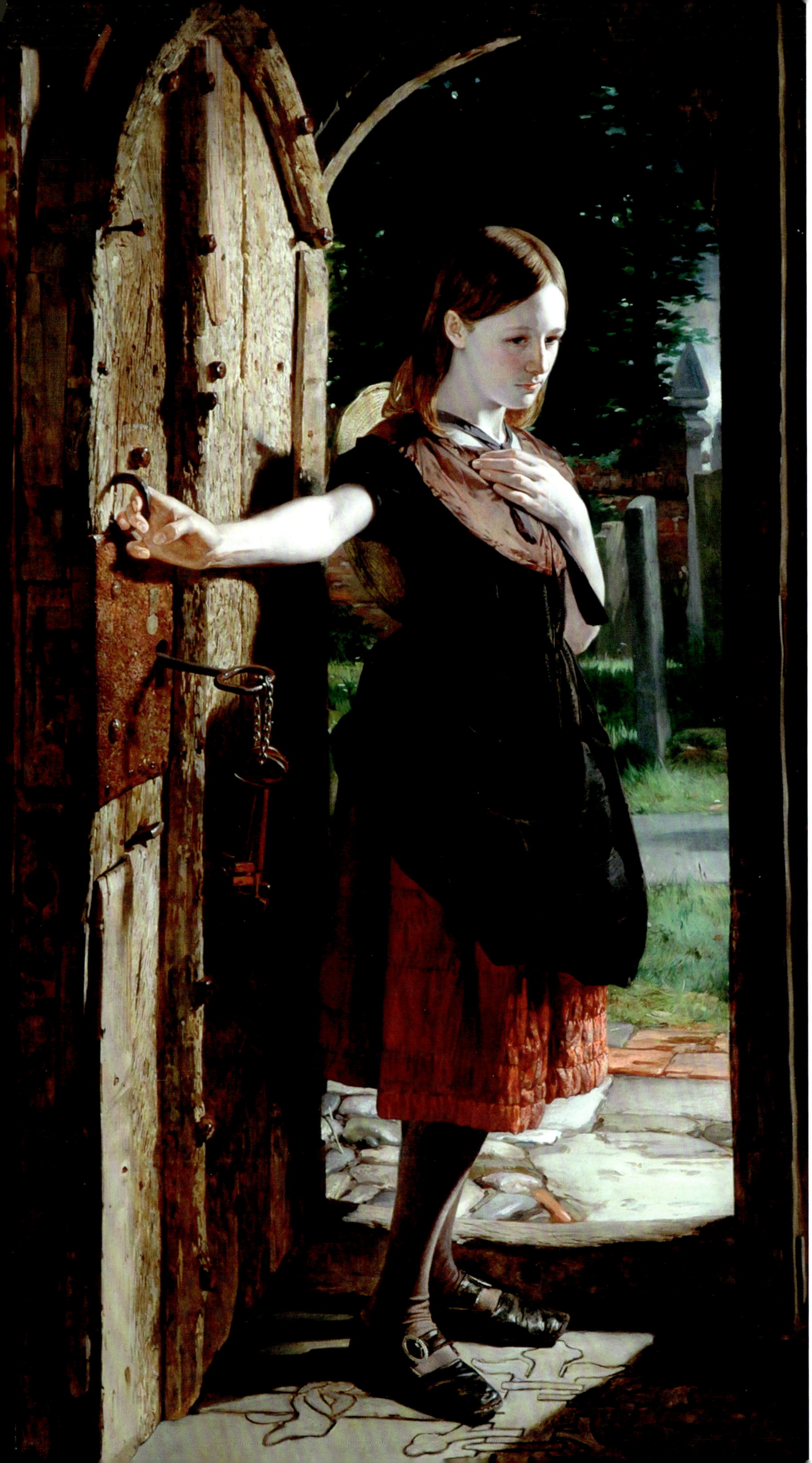

James Lobley,
Little Nell Leaving the Church
(The Old Curiosity Shop)
(detail of fig. 61)

SELECT BIBLIOGRAPHY

ALLWOOD 1982 Rosamond Allwood, *George Elgar Hicks: Painter of Victorian Life* (exh. cat., Geffrye Museum, London, 1982)

BILLS & KNIGHT 2006 Mark Bills and Vivien Knight, eds, *William Powell Frith: Painting the Victorian Age* (New Haven and London, 2006)

CHESNEAU 1887 Ernest Chesneau, *The English School of Painting*, 3rd edn (London, 1887)

COLLINS 1981 Philip Collins, ed., *Dickens: Interviews and Recollections*, 2 vols (London, 1981)

COWLING 2000 Mary Cowling, *Victorian Figurative Painting: Domestic Life and the Contemporary Social Scene* (London, 2000)

DICKENS 1836 Charles Dickens, *Sketches by 'Boz,' Illustrative of Every-Day Life, and Every-Day People*, 2 vols (London, 1836)

DICKENS 1846 Charles Dickens, *Pictures from Italy* (London, 1846)

DICKENS 1911 Charles Dickens, *Miscellaneous Papers*, 2 vols (London, 1911), vol. 1, 'Cruikshank's "The Drunkard's Children"' (first published 8 July 1848), pp. 113–17, and 'Leech's "The Rising Generation"' (first published 30 December 1848), pp. 147–50

DICKENS & WILLS 1850 C. Dickens and W. H. Wills, 'Valentine's Day at the Post-Office', *Household Words: A Weekly Journal, Conducted by Charles Dickens*, vol. 1, no. 1, 30 March 1850

FRITH 1887 William Powell Frith, *My Autobiography and Reminiscences*, 3 vols (London, 1887)

GOLDWATER & TREVES 1976 Robert Goldwater and Marco Treves, eds, *Artists on Art*, 2nd edn (London, 1976)

GORDON 1971 Catherine Gordon, 'The Illustration of Sir Walter Scott: Nineteenth-Century Enthusiasm and Adaptation', *Journal of the Warburg and Courtauld Institutes*, vol. 34 (1971), pp. 297–317

GRAVES 1905 Algernon Graves, *The Royal Academy of Arts: a complete dictionary of contributors and their works from its foundation in 1769 to 1904*, 8 vols (London, 1905–6), vol. 3 (1905)

HUNT 1905 William Holman Hunt, *Pre-Raphaelitism and the Pre-Raphaelite Brotherhood*, 2 vols (London, 1905)

Journalism *Dickens' Journalism*, ed. Michael Slater and John Drew, 4 vols (London, 1994–2000)

KITTON 1899 F.G. Kitton, *Dickens and his Illustrators* (London, 1899)

KITTON 1902 F.G. Kitton, *Charles Dickens: His Life, Writings, and Personality*, 2 vols (London, 1902)

Letters *Letters of Charles Dickens* (Pilgrim Edition), ed. Angus Easson, Madeline House, Graham Storey & Kathleen Tillotson, 12 vols (Oxford, 1965–2002)

MEADOWS 1840 Joseph Kenny Meadows, *Heads of the People: Or, Portraits of the English* (London, 1840)

MERWE 1979 Pieter van der Merwe, *The Spectacular Career of Clarkson Stanfield: 1793–1867* (Gateshead, 1979)

MULVEY 1989 L. Mulvey, *Visual and Other Pleasures* (London, 1989)

ORMOND 1984 Leonee Ormond, 'Dickens and Painting: Contemporary Art', *Dickensian*, Spring 1984, vol. 80, part 1, no. 402, pp. 2–25

PARKINSON 1990 Ronald Parkinson, *Victoria and Albert Museum: Catalogue of British Oil Paintings, 1820–60* (London, 1990)

PERUGINI 1903 Kate Perugini, 'Charles Dickens as a Lover of Art and Artists', *Magazine of Art* (1903), pp. 125–30 and 164–9

PICKVANCE 1974 Ronald Pickvance, *English Influences on Van Gogh* (exh. cat., Arts Council/ Nottingham University Art Gallery, 1974)

ROOS 1977 David A. Roos, 'Dickens at the Royal Academy of Arts: A New Speech and Two Eulogies', *Dickensian*, May 1977, vol. 73, part 2, no. 382, pp. 100–107

SCHWARZBACH & ORMOND 1977 F.S. Schwarzbach and Leonee Ormond, *American Notes and Pictures from Italy* (London, 1977)

SLATER 2009 Michael Slater, *Charles Dickens* (New Haven and London, 2009)

SLATER 2011 Michael Slater, 'Dickens, Charles John Huffam (1812–1870)', *Oxford Dictionary of National Biography* (Oxford, 2004), online edn, May 2011 (http://www.oxforddnb.com/view/article/7599, accessed 17 Nov. 2011)

Speeches *The Speeches of Charles Dickens*, ed. K.J. Fielding (Oxford, 1960)

STRONG 1978 Roy Strong, *And When Did you Last See your Father?: The Victorian Painter and British History* (London, 1978)

THACKERAY 1911 William M. Thackeray, *Thackeray's English Humorists of the Eighteenth Century*, ed. and annot. J.W. Cunliffe and H.A. Watt (Chicago and New York, 1911)

WATTS 1912 Mary Seton Watts, *George Frederic Watts: The Annals of an Artist's Life*, 3 vols (London 1912)

WILLS 1851 W.H. Wills with assistance from Charles Dickens, 'Epsom', *Household Words: A Weekly Journal, Conducted by Charles Dickens*, vol. 3, no. 63, 7 June 1851

WOOD 1995 Christopher Wood, *Victorian Painters*, 3rd edn, 2 vols: vol. 1, The Text; vol. 2, Historical Survey and Plates (Woodbridge, 1995)

WRIGHT 2008 Thomas Wright, *Oscar's Books* (London, 2008)

INDEX

Note: Works by Dickens appear as main entries in italics (novels) or inverted commas (articles).
Major characters in Dickens's novels appear as main entries in italics. The abbreviation CD is used for Charles Dickens.

aestheticism, and decline of Dickens paintings 103–4
Ainsworth, Harrison 41, 61
All the Year Round 22, 40
American Notes 39–40
archetypes 135–44
art, 'high' and 'low' 118–21
Art Journal 86, 141, 174–5
Atkinson, W.A., *Little Nell and the Two Gravediggers* 98, 107
authority, and taste 21–2, 27

Babb, Charlotte E. 109 n.66
baby farming 159–60
Barnaby Rudge 51
  and literary painting 73, 82, 102, 119–20
Barnard, Frederick 92
Barnes, E.C., *The Seducer* 101
Barthes, Roland 86
Baynes, F.T., *Kate Nickleby* 73, 106
beadles 144, 170–1
Bell, Quentin 102
Bellini, Giovanni (workshop), *The Virgin and Child* *20*, 21
Bills, Mark 82–3
Birmingham Daily Post 6
Bleak House 28–31, 49, 51, 55, 62–3, 141, 145–7
  illustrations *140*, 147–9, *147*, 174, *174*
  and literary painting 73, 74
  and social realism 147–9, 155, 159, 161, 173–4, 177–8
Boxall, William 60
British Impressionism 104
British Institution, and Dickens subjects 73, 78, 82, 100
Broadstairs, Dickens House Museum 38
Brooks, Maria 109 n.69
Brough, Robert, 'Calmuck' 56
Brown, Fred 104
Browne, Hablot Knight (Phiz) 135–6
  'Attorney and Client' 147–9, *147*
  'Grinder's Lot' showing the 'exhibitors of the freaks of Punch' 90, *90*, 92
  'Great excitement of Miss Kenwigs at the hair dresser's shop' *2*, 3
  'Jo' *142*
  'The lonely figure' 174, *174*
  'Miss Nickleby Introduced to her Uncle's Friends' *137*, 138
Browning, Robert 46
Bulwer-Lytton, Edward, *Not so Bad as We Seem* 38, 40
Burne-Jones, Edward 61
Burnett, J.P., *Jo, or, Bleak House* 74

Calderon, Philip Hermogenes:
  Hide and Seek 64
  The Letter 64
Callow, William 62
  Old House, High Street, Tewkesbury 52
capital punishment 59
Carr, Comyns 163
Carter, William, *Sketch on the Spot of Jacob's Island, Southwark, Mentioned by Boz in 'Oliver Twist'* 72, 106
Cattermole, George:
  The Grave of Little Nell 62, 90, *91*, 98
  The Old Curiosity Shop/The Home of Little Nell 62, 90, *93*, 94
Cawse, Clara 98, 109 n.66
  Poor Nell 100–1, 107
Chabanne, Laure 57
Chapman and Hall (CD's publisher) 43
Chapman, John Watkins 108 n.27
  The Old Curiosity Shop 80, *80*, *81*, 91, 106
characters:
  in literary paintings 73
  as types 73, 135–44
Charles Dickens Museum (Holborn) 43
Chesneau, Ernest 112
children:
  in literary subject paintings 95, 98
  see also Little Nell
Christmas books:
  The Battle of Life 39
  The Chimes 39, 41, 105
  The Cricket on the Hearth 39, 41
  The Haunted Man 39
  A Christmas Carol 73–4, 104
Clay, Alfred Barron, *Finishing Bleak House* 73, 106
Collins, Charles Allston 22–4, 56–7
Collins, Wilkie 1, 21–2, 55, 62, 76
  The Frozen Deep 39
  The Lighthouse 38–9
  The Woman in White 22
Collins, William 21, 51–2
  Ischia Bay of Naples 52
Collinson, James, *The Writing Lesson* 84–6, *85*, 106
Compton, Charles, *A Sketch of Nell – Vide 'Old Curiosity Shop'* 108 n.27
Coningham, William 21
Cooper, Henry (collector) 80
Cope, Charles West 57
  A Life Well Spent 88, 106
Copping, Harold 96
Correggio, Antonio Allegri:
  Assumption of the Virgin 12, *14*, 54
  Madonna of the Basket 15, *16*
  The Vision of St John on Patmos 12, *15*
Cowling, Mary 86
criticism, new 104
crowds, depicting 132–3
Cruikshank, George 136
  The Drunkard's Children 115–16, 149–50, *150*, *176*
  and Hogarth 4, 74, 115–16
  'Oliver Asking for More' 163
  The Streets of London: Morning *124*, 125–6
'Cruikshank's The Drunkard's Children' 144–5, 150

David Copperfield 37, 159
  and fallen women 161
  in literary paintings 73, 101, 104
Dedlock, Lady (Bleak House) 141, 161, 173–4
Delaroche, Paul 25
  Hemicycle 61
Dennis, W.T., *Captain Cuttle and Uncle Sol Examining Charts* 100
Devéria, Eugène, Avignon cathedral frescoes 61
1 Devonshire Terrace (CD's London home) 52, 61–2, 64
Dickens, Catherine (wife of CD) 35, 43–4, *44*, 63–4
Dickens, Charles (1812–1870):
  and amateur theatricals 38–9, 40, 46, 51
  art collection *4*, 40, 61–2, 64, 76
  as art critic 3, 12–28, 53–60, 149–51
  children 43, *43*
  and contemporary art 35–64
  editions, cheap 29, 39, 76; *see also* Household Edition; Library Edition
  friendships with artists 36–49, 55–7, 61–3, 112
  grave 72, *72*
  Parian Ware busts 71
  and Philistinism 11–32
  portraits *facing p. 1*, 11, *40*, 41, 61, 70–1, *71*
  readings from works 74
  sale of paintings 6, *6*
  as social campaigner 155, 177–8
  and social realism 55, 91, 177–80
  subjects in Victorian art 69–107
  verbal style 90–4
  as visual writer 1, 3, 10, 32, 55, 112, 121, 136
  see also characters
Dickensianism 104
Dicksee, Herbert, *The Grandfather at the Grave of Little Nell* 98, 107
Disraeli, Benjamin, *Coningsby* 12
Dombey, Florence (Dombey and Son) 73, 82, *83*, 98, 101, 102–3, *103*
Dombey and Son 25–7, 129–32
  in literary paintings 73, 74, 82, 100, 101, 102–3, *103*, 111
Doré, Gustave:
  The Bull's-Eye 160, *160*, 165
  'Gray's Inn Lane – Robbers' Kitchen' 165
  London: A Pilgrimage 165
  A Poor-House *155*, 165–6, *165*
Douglas Jerrold's Shilling Magazine 46

Eastlake, Charles 17, 25
  A Contadina Family *17*

Edinburgh Review 178
Edwin Drood, illustrations 166
Egg, Augustus Leopold 3, 59, 62, 82–3
Past and Present triptych 157–9, *158*, 161
Peter the Great Sees Catherine, his Future Empress, for the First Time 59, *59*
Used Up 62, *63*
Egley, William Maw, *Florence Dombey in Captain Cuttle's Parlour* 82, *83*, 101, 102–3
Eliot, George, and literary paintings 82
Elwell, Frederick (d. 1958):
Still Life: The Pickwick Club (1956) 104, 107
Still Life: The Pickwick Club (1958) 104, 107
Etty, William 27, 57
Everett, Ethel F., *Tiny Tim* 104, 107

Faed, Thomas 155
Kate Nickleby *77*, 78, 101, 102, 106
Fairholt, Frederick William 102
Farmer, Mrs Alexander, *An Anxious Hour* 109 n.61
Felton, C.C. 44
Fields, J.F. 113
Fildes, Sir Samuel Luke (1843–1927) 5
Applicants for Admission to a Casual Ward 166–7, *166*, *169*, 170–7
The Doctor 109 n.61
'Study for "The Casuals"' (drawing of drunkard) *175*
'The Empty Chair, Gad's Hill – Ninth of June, 1870' *5*
The Grave of Charles Dickens, Poets' Corner, Westminster Abbey 72, *72*
'Houseless and Hungry' 5, 155, 166, *167*, 175
and social realism 155–7
Flameng, Louis (after Frith), *Road to Ruin: Arrest* *148*
Forster, John 35, *39*, 40, 46, 57–60, 71, 80, 155, 173
Forster, Selina, *Reading the 'Household Words'* 73, 106
Frampton, George James, *Martin Harvey as Sidney Carton* 74, 106
frescoes 61
'The Friend of the Lions' 60
Frith, William Powell (1819–1909) 3, 4, 51, 62–3, 70, 111
Bailiff Scene from Road to Ruin *148*, 149
Charles Dickens in his Study 71, *71*, 106, *113*
Coming of Age in the Olden Time 120, 152 n.29
The Crossing Sweeper 138–41, *139*
The Derby Day 4, *110*, 137–8, *138*, 141–4, *142*
Dolly Varden 6, *50*, 51, 76, *76*, 78–80, 94, 106, *119*
An English Merry Making a Hundred Years Ago 152 n.29
and Hogarth 116, 120, 121–3, 144, 151
and invention 82–3
Kate Nickleby 76, 119–20, *119*
Kate Nickleby at Madame Mantalini's 51
and modern-life movement 111–12, 116–23, 131–3, 137–44, 151
Morning – Covent Garden *122*, 123–6, *125*
Mr Honeywood Introduces the Bailiffs to Miss Richland as his Friends *34*, *58*, 59
Night – Haymarket 126–9, *126*, *129*
Noon – Regent Street *122*, 126
and Paris Exhibition of 1855 57, 59
The Race for Wealth series 149
The Railway Station *130–1*, 132, 141, 151
Ramsgate Sands (Life at the Seaside) 111, 120–1, 141
The Road to Ruin series 149
The Salon d'Or, Homburg 118
The Streets of London 121–9, *122*

Gaddi, Taddeo 19
Gad's Hill, art collection *4*, 40, 62, 64, *115*
Gale, William, *Mr F.'s Aunt* 76
Gamp, Sarah (Martin Chuzzlewit) 73
genre painting:
and book illustration 84–94
by women 78
Christmas 73–4
Dutch 37
English 57, 80–3
of readers 72–3
rustic 51–2
see also modern-life movement
Gérome, Jean-Léon 25
'The Ghost of Art' 1–3, 49–51
Gill, R.A., *Bleak House Broadstairs* 72, 106
Goldsmith, Oliver:
The Good-Natured Man 59
Vicar of Wakefield 51, 58
Gordon, Catherine 84, 101
Gowan, Henry (Little Dorrit) 1, 61
The Graphic 155–8, 163, 166, 175–7
Great Expectations 31, 163, 177
Green, Charles 78, 90, 92
Little Dorrit's Visit to her Sister at the Theatre *102*, 103, 107
Little Nell Mending the Puppet's Dress 92, *92*
Greenham, Robert D., *Edna May Oliver as 'Aunt Betsy Trotwood'* 104, 107
Grosvenor Gallery (London) 103–4
Guildhall Art Gallery (London) 112

Haghe, Louis 41
Hannah, Robert:
The Novel 62, 73, 106
The Play 62
Hart, Solomon Alexander, *Reading Dickens* 73, 106
Harvey, Sir John Martin 74, *75*, 104, 106
Hawker, Charles (dealer) 80
Hawksley, Lucinda 64
Haydon, James Bouverie, *Nell Asleep: Curiosity Shop* 98, 107
Herkomer, Hubert (1849–1914):
Eventide: A Scene in the Westminster Union 155, *162*, 163–6, 170, 176
Old Age: A Study at the Westminster Union *162*, 163
and social realism 5, 155–7
Hicks, George Elgar (1824–1914):
A Cloud with a Silver Lining 109 n.61
The General Post Office, One Minute to Six 132, *133*
and modern-life movement 111
Woman's Mission 86
history paintings 57–9, 102
Hogarth, Georgina 44, *44*
Hogarth, William:
and Cruikshank 4, 74, 115–16
and Dickens 115–18, *115*, 121
The Four Times of Day 121, 123, *123*
Gin Lane 116, 144–5, *145*
and invention 108 n.38
and modern-life movement 112–23, 136, 144, 147–9, 151
and pre-Raphaelites 89
and prostitution 129
Self-Portrait *112*
and Thackeray 112–14, 116–17, 120

Holl, Frank (1845–1888):
Deserted – The Foundling 155, *156*, 157–63
and social realism 5, 155–7
Holl, William Jr (after Frith), *Kate Nickleby* *119*
Holmes, James, *The Streets of London: A Female Dombey* 73, 106
Hood, Thomas, 'The Bridge of Sighs' 159
Household Edition of Dickens 78, 91, 103
Household Words 1–3, 18–21, 49–51, 53–6, 60, 132, 143–4, 161, 173, 177
Humphris, W.H., *At a Dickens Character Ball* 104, 107
Hunt, Charles, *A Coffee Stall* 101
Hunt, G. Sidney, *Charles Dickens Memorial Stamp* 104, 107
Hunt, William Henry 62
Moss Roses/Roses in a Blue and White Jug 52
Hunt, William Holman 54, 55–7, 70
The Awakening Conscience 83, 106
The Finding of the Saviour in the Temple 57
The Lady of Shalott 86
The Light of the World 88
and literary subject painting 86–8
Little Nell and her Grandfather *68*, 78, *79*, 82, 91, 95, 103, 106
and Martineau 88–9
Our English Coasts, 1852 (Strayed Sheep) 60
Hurley, Ninian, *A Visit to Pegotty's* 104, 107
Hutchinson, Sir William, *Presenting Jimmy Snodgrass* 104, 107

I. P., *'Cross-readings at Charing-Cross'* *12*
The Illustrated London News 118, 157, 163
illustration 3–4
and genre painting 84–94
'Insularities' 60
insularity, British 60
invention, and art 82–3
Irving, Washington, 'The Voyage' 40

Jerrold, Douglas 136–7, 165
Jo the crossing sweeper (Bleak House) 55, 63, 74, *140*, 141, 145–7
Jonson, Ben, *Every Man in his Humour* 38, 46, 51
Journal l'Union 57–8

keepsake painting 78, 100
Kennington, Thomas Benjamin, *Recalled to Life* 74, 106
Kitton, F.G. 70, 121

La Creevy, Miss (Nicholas Nickleby) 1, 11, 35, 61, 133–4, *134*
landscapes 51–3, 59, 61
associated with Dickens subjects 72–3
Landseer, Edwin, *The Sanctuary* 59–60
Lawrence, Sir Thomas 27
Portrait of George IV *48*, 49
Lee, Jenny (actress) 74
Leech, John 4
Leighton, Frederic 62–3
Cimabue's Madonna Carried in Triumph Through the Streets of Florence 62
Leonardo da Vinci:
and invention 108 n.38
Last Supper 22
Leslie, Charles Robert 28–9, 51, 57–8, 60
and invention and art 108 n.38
Mr Pickwick and Mrs Bardell 76
Sancho Panza in the Apartment of the Duchess 51
Library Edition of Dickens 76
literacy, working-class 85–6

literary painting:
book illustration and genre painting 84–94
decline 101–4
and Dickens's novels 69–107, 111
patterns of production 73–83
and verbal and visual styles 90–4, 112
and Victorian values 84–6, 95–101
Little Dombey 74
Little Dorrit 57, 159
illustrations 63
in literary paintings 76
and painters 1, 49, 61
Little Em'ly (David Copperfield) 101
Little Nell (The Old Curiosity Shop):
appearance 90, 91
and childhood innocence 95
death 96–8, 105, 179
and piety 95–6, *97*
and Victorian female ideal 86–9
vulnerability 98–101, *99*
Lobley, James 91
Little Nell Leaving the Church 96, *97*, 107
London:
fogs 177, 178
General Post Office 132, *133*
and modern-life painting 116–17, 121–43, *122–5*
Paddington Station 132
River Thames 161–3
and social-realist painting 155–80
looking, in art 98–100

Macbeth-Raeburn, Henry, *Miss Jenny Lee as 'Jo'* 74, 106
MacColl, D.S. 104
McIan, Fanny:
Little Nell Reading the Inscription on the Tombstone 78
Little Sick Scholar 98, 107
Nell and the Widow 62
McIan, Robert Ronald 62
Macirone, Emily 109 n.69
Nelly in the Churchyard 98, 107
Macleod, Jessie, *The Employment of Oliver Twist in the Jew's House* 74, 106
Maclise, Daniel 3, *39*, 40, 41–9, 60–1, 62
Catherine Dickens 43
Charles Dickens 11, *13*, *42*, 43
Charles Dickens, his wife, nee Catherine Thomson Hogarth, and his wife's sister Miss Georgina Hogarth 44, *44*
Dickens's Four Elder Children 43–4, *43*
Girl with Parrot 27
Othello and Desdemona 28, *29*
The Play Scene from Hamlet 46
and Royal Academy 35
The Serenade 46
The Spirit of Chivalry 18–19, *18*, 24, 46, *47*
Waterfall at St Nighton's Kieve, near Tintagel in Cornwall 44, *45*
Macready, William 35
Maes, Nicholas, *A Woman Scraping Parsnips, with a Child Standing by her 10*, 24, *24*
Maguire, Thomas Herbert 109 n.66
Manchester Courier 177
Martin Chuzzlewit, in literary paintings 73
Martineau, Robert Braithwaite (1826–1869) 70
Kit's Writing Lesson 84–7, *84*, *87*, 91, 95, 106, 109 n.47

Mayhew, Augustus, *Paved with Gold or the Romance and Reality of the London Streets* 156
Mayhew, Henry, *London Labour and the London Poor* 156
Meadows, Joseph Kenny:
Heads from Nicholas Nickleby: From Drawings by Miss La Creevy 133–5, *134*, 137
Heads of the People: or, Portraits of the English 133, 136–7, *136*
Meissonier, Ernest 64
Merwe, Pieter, van der 37
Metropolitan Poor Act 1867 167
Michelangelo, *Last Judgment* 21–2
Millais, John Everett 19, 149
Charles Dickens on his Deathbed 56
Christ in the House of His Parents 3, 53–6, *53*
Ophelia 60
The Rescue 55
milliners 101
miniature painters, in Dickens 1
models, artists 1, 17, 28, 44, 49–51, 91, 175, 179
modern-life movement 78, 82–3, 111–51
and characters as types 135–44, 151
and Frith 111–12, 116–23, 131–3, 137–44
and 'high' and 'low' art 118–21
and Hogarth 112–23, 136, 141, 144, 147–9
and London 116–17, 121–43, *122–5*
and morality 116–17, 120, 127–9, 136, 144, 149–51
and truth-telling 149–51, 179
Monaco, Lorenzo, *The Coronation of the Virgin* 19, *19*, 21
Moore, George 104
Morse, Belinda 62
Mulready, William 57–8
The Whistonian Controversy 58
The Wolf and the Lamb 58
Mulvey, Laura 100

narrative:
in art 4, 78, 86, 100, 103–4
in Dickens 29–30, 89, 95, 100, 112, 116–17, 161, 177
in modern-life movement 112, 116–17, 133, 144–5, 149, 151
in social realism 157–9, 161, 165–6, 170–3, 179–80
National Gallery, London:
construction 11, *12*
and Old Master paintings 13–24
popular appeal 22–5
naturalism, and decline of Dickens paintings 103–4
Nazarenes 19
New English Art Club 104
newspapers 132
Nicholas Nickleby:
illustrations *2*, 3, 11, 62
in literary paintings 73, 76, 82, 98, 102
and miniature painter 1, 11, 35, 61
and modern-life movement 133–6, *134*, *136*
publication 11, 43
Nickleby, Kate (Nicholas Nickleby), in literary paintings 51, 73, 76–8, *77*, 101, 119–20
'A Nightly Scene in London' 173

The Old Curiosity Shop 138, 161, 179
illustrations 62, *63*
in literary paintings 62, 73, 82, 84–9, *84*, *85*, 90–2, 95–101, 106
'Old Lamps for New Ones' 3
Old Masters 3, 11–32, 121

Old Water Colour Society, exhibition 1849 52
Oliver Twist 41, 170, 177
and baby farming 159
and fallen women 161
illustrations 163
in literary paintings 74
O'Neill, George Bernard, *Public Opinion 70*
Orchardson, William Quiller, *Little Nell and her Grandfather in the Wood* 98–100, *99*, 107
'Our Eye Witness' *see* Collins, Charles Allston
Our Mutual Friend 26, 31–2, 168, 177
illustrations 63
and literary paintings 73
and social-realist painting 161, 163–4

Pall Mall Gazette 156
Papworth, Edgar George, *Poor Little Nell* 98
Parian Ware figures 71, 95, *96*, 141
Paris International Exhibition (1855) 51, 57–61, 62
Parker, John, *Little Nell's Garden* 98, 107
Pater, Walter 103
Pauper Inmates Discharge Act 1871 168–70
Penny, Nicholas 117
Perugini, Kate (daughter of CD) 1, 3, 22, 36, 52–3, 55, 57, 60–4, 149
paintings 82, 108 n.35
Philistinism 11–32, 117
Phiz *see* Browne, Hablot Knight
physiognomy 133, 144, 173, 179
Pickett, Mary, *Little Nell in the church* 96, 107
Pickwick Papers 69
illustrations 29, 76
in literary paintings 73, 76, 104
Pictures from Italy 3, 12, 24–5, 40, 54, 61, 121
piety, in Victorian illustrations 95–6
police:
in art 124–6, 155, 158–61, 166–7, 170, 172, 175
in Dickens 161
Pollaiuolo, Antonio and Piero del, *Martyrdom of St Sebastian* 22, *23*
Poor Laws 155, 167–8, 170
portraiture:
contemporary 35, 49, 61
fancy 78, 100–1
theatrical 74, 104
Pre-Raphaelites 18–19, 53–7, 60, 78, 83
and lighting effects 88
Prig, Betsy (Martin Chuzzlewit) 73
prisons, in social-realist painting 157, 163
prostitutes 127–9, 155, 157–8, 161–3, 172–4, 178
Prout, Samuel, *Beauvais Cathedral* 52, *52*
Punch 118, 141
Purismo 19

Quarterly Review 178

railway stations 129–32, *130–1*
Raphael, Dickens's admiration for 54
realism:
artistic 74, 78, 91–4, 95, 104
of Dickens 3, 55, 91, 177–80
and modern-life movement 117–19
in religious painting 55, 57
social 4, 5–6, 117–19, 147–51, 155–80
Redgrave, Richard 155
The Outcast 172
religious painting 53–7

Reprinted Pieces 161
Reynolds, A.M. 159
Reynolds, Sir Joshua 21–2, 108 n.38
Richter, H., *Mr Pickwick and the Spinster Aunt* 73, 106
Ritchie, John:
Little Nell and her Grandfather Leaving London 91, *94*, 95, 106, 108 n.27
and modern-life movement 111
Roberts, David 40–1, 52
A Recollection of the Desert on the Approach of the Simoon 40, *41*, 57
Roberts, Edward, *The Sick Boy* 98, 107
Romano, Giulio 54
romanticism 57, 95
Rooke, T.M. 61
Roos, David 64
Rose, William, *An Artful Dodger* 73, 106
Rossetti, Dante Gabriel, *Found* 83
Royal Academy:
and Dickens's subjects 70, 73–4, 78–80, 104, 111
dinners 35, 40, 49, 64
and exclusion of illustrators 4
exhibitions 35, 40, 53, 62, 64, 100, 132
and Maclise 46
and modern-life paintings 111
and National Gallery 11, 21–2, 35
and social-realist painting 166, 175
Ruff, George Sr, *Broadstairs, 'Our Watering-place of Charles Dickens'* 72, 106
Ruskin, John 4, 89, 112, 179
Russell, John 31

satire 116–18
Saturday Review 177, 178
Saville, Josephine 109 n.66
Scharf, Sir George 64
Scheffer, Ary, portrait of Dickens 61, 71
Scott, Sir Walter, in literary subject paintings 70, 82, 109 nn.44,65
The Scrap Book of Literary Varieties and Mirror of Instructive & Entertaining Information 135, *136*
sculpture, and Little Nell 95, *96*, 98
Shakespeare, William, in literary subject paintings 104, 109 n.44, 120
Shannon, James Jebusa, *Sir John Martin Harvey as Sydney Carton* 74, 75, 104, 106
Sharp, Eliza, *Little Nell in the Church* 96, 107
Sheepshanks collection 82
Sheridan, Richard Brinsley, *The Rivals* 62
Shilling Magazine 18
Sikes/Sykes, Bill (Oliver Twist) 41, 74
Sketches by Boz 35
'Gin-Shops' 116
'Greenwich Fair' 143
'The Pawnbroker's Shop' 127–9
'The Streets – Morning' 121, 124–6
'The Streets – Night' 121, 126–7
Slater, Michael 69
Small, William, *London Sketches: A November Fog* 177
Smith, Edward (engraver), *A Contadina Family … Prisoners with Banditti* *17*
Society of British Artists, and Dickens subjects 73, 78, 80, 105, 119
'The Spirit of Chivalry in Westminster Hall' 46
Stanfield, Clarkson 3, 37–41, 44, 58, 62
The Abandoned 40
Avignon on the Rhone 40
The Battle of Roveredo 59
A Dutch Dogger Carrying Away her Sprit 59
Eddystone Lighthouse against a Stormy Sea *38*
HMS Victory Towed into Gibraltar 40
The Land's End 40
Logan Rock with Dickens, Stanfield, Maclise and Forster *39*, 40
The SS Britannia at Liverpool Embarking Charles Dickens 39–40
Steer, Henry Reynolds, *Little Paul and Florence Dombey* *103*, 107
Stewart, James Lawson 98, 107
Stone, Frank 3, 63
Kate Nickleby 76
Madeline Bray 76
Tilda Price 62, 76
Stone, Marcus 3, 32, 52, 61–2, 63–4
'The Flight' 163–4, *164*
Rest 63
Strong, Roy 84
Strutt, Alfred W., *Oliver Twist* 74, 106
Stubbs, George 31
subject paintings 49–51, 57–9, 61, 64
and Dickens's novels 69–107
Swiveller, Dick (The Old Curiosity Shop) 95
Sykes, Sir Francis 41

A Tale of Two Cities, in literary paintings 74, 75, 102, 104
taste, and authority 21–2, 27
Tavistock House (CD's London home) 38, 64
Taylor, Leonard Campbell 103
Tennyson, Alfred Lord, and literary subject painting 86–8
Thackeray, William Makepeace 1, 35, 46, 51, 63
'Codlingsby' 12
and Hogarth 112–14, 116–17, 120
in literary paintings 82
and satire 116–18
theatre
amateur 38–9, 40, 46, 51
and Dickens subjects 74
thimbleriggers *142*, 143–4
Thomas, Flora Elizabeth, *Rosa* 74, 106
Thomas, William Luson 156–7
Thornbury, W. 132
The Times 6, 20, 64, 159–61
Tintoretto:
Paradiso 12
St George and the Dragon 15
Tissot, J.J. 180
Titian:
Assunta 12
Bacchus and Ariadne 13
Tonks, Henry 104
Topham, Francis, *Little Nell* 62, *63*
Trotter, David 119
Turner, J.M.W. 52–3

Underwood, James 156
Union Chargeability Act 1865 167
Uwin, Thomas, *Vintage in Medoc* 58

vagrancy 170–1
values, Victorian 69, 84–6, 95–101
Van Eyck, Jan, *The Arnolfini Portrait* 19, *19*
Van Gogh, Vincent 1, 5–6
Varden, Dolly (Barnaby Rudge) 6, *50*, 51, 73, 76, *76*, 78–80, 82, 94, 106, 119–20, *119*
Veck, Trotty (The Chimes) 105
Vernon collection 82
Vernon, Robert 25
voyeurism 100

Waagen, Gustav 21, 25
Walker, Frederick, *The Lost Path* 172
Ward, E.M. 59
The Royal Family of France in the Prison of the Temple in 1792 59
watercolours:
CD's admiration for 52–3
and Dickens subjects 72–3, 78
Waters, Margaret (baby farmer) 159
Watkins, Charles, *Charles Dickens xii*
Watts Gallery (Compton, Surrey) 6
Watts, G.F.:
Death Crowning Innocence 76
Found Drowned 152 n.23, 157–8, *157*, 161
and high art 118–19
Irish Famine 152 n.23
Song of the Shirt 152 n.23
Under a Dry Arch *146*, 147, 152 n.23
Webster, Thomas 57
Dotheboys Hall (Squeers's School) 62
Sickness and Health 109 n.61
Westmacott, James Shewood, *Statue of Little Nell* *96*
Westminster Abbey, grave of CD 72, *72*
Weston, Nancy 46
Whistler, James Abbott McNeill 103, 177, 180
Nocturne: Grey and Gold – Chelsea Snow 105, *105*
The Pool *179*
'The Red Rag' 105
Wapping *178*
Whiston, William 58
Wilde, Oscar 104–5
Wilkie, David 4, 36–7, 57, 62
The Cotter's Saturday Night *36*, 37
The Parish Beadle 170–1, *171*
The Reading of a Will 37
The Rent Day 37
Wilkins, William 11
Williams, Frank, *Captain Cuttle Watching the Slumbers of Florence* 100–1
Williams, Samuel, 'The child in her gentle slumber' *93*, 94
Wills, W.H. 143–4
women:
fallen *see* prostitutes
as objects of gaze 100–1
as painters 78, 100–1
as readers 100
in Victorian ideology 86, 100–1
Woolmer, Alfred Joseph:
Dolly Varden 82, 106
Five Sisters of York 82, 106
workhouses 156–7, 163–78
working class, in literary paintings 85–9
Wren, Jenny (Our Mutual Friend) 73

Young England movement 18

Zamaçois, Eduardo, *Le Garde Champêtre* 64

PHOTO CREDITS

Art Gallery of New South Wales, Sydney: 95
Bradford Museums and Galleries: 61
Charles Dickens Museum, London: 5, 23, 27, 35, 38, 58
Collection of the author: 68, 69, 75, 87, 91, 92
© Culture and Sport Glasgow (Museums): 22
Duomo of Parma, Italy / Alinari / The Bridgeman Art Library: 10
Fogg Art Museum, Harvard University Art Museums, USA / Bequest of Grenville L. Winthrop / The Bridgeman Art Library: 65
Image courtesy of Henry Sotheran Limited, London: 13
Leeds Museums and Galleries (City Art Gallery) UK / The Bridgeman Art Library: 41
London Metropolitan Archives, © City of London: 8, 93
Museum of London: front cover, 4, 74, 80, 86, 89, 94, 102, 98, 104, 111
© The National Gallery, London: 7, 12, 15, 16, 17, 18, 19
Image courtesy of the National Gallery of Art, Washington: 110
Courtesy of National Museums Liverpool: 99
National Art Union for Ireland, © National Portrait Gallery, London: 71
Private collection: 46, 60, 72, 73, 76, 77, 78, 100, 108
© Private collection c/o Christie's Images 2012: 20
Private collection / Photo © Christie's Images / The Bridgeman Art Library: 48, 49
Private collection / Photo © The Fine Art Society, London, UK: 25
Private collection from Roy Miles Fine Paintings / The Bridgeman Art Library: 44
Rob Dickins Collection, Watts Gallery Archive: 1
Royal Academy, courtesy of Sotheby's Picture Library, London: 52
Reproduced by kind permission of Royal Holloway, University of London: frontispiece, 79, 103, 105
Photograph reproduced with the kind permission of the Royal Pavilion and Museums (Brighton & Hove): 59
San Giovanni Evangelista, Parma, Italy / The Bridgeman Art Library: 11
Sheffield Museums: 14, 30, 40, 47, 62
© Tate, London, 2012: 9, 26, 34, 51, 53, 66, 85, 88, 97, 106
By kind permission of the Trustees of the Wallace Collection, London: 31
© Victoria and Albert Museum, London: back cover, 24, 28, 29, 32, 21, 36, 42, 43, 45, 50, 55, 56, 67, 70
Watts Gallery: 90, 96
Watts Gallery Archive: 3, 6, 33, 37, 39, 63, 64
Wellcome Library, London: 109